The Moon in Your Life

The Moon in Your Life

BEING A LUNAR TYPE IN A SOLAR WORLD

Donna Cunningham

SAMUEL WEISER, INC.

York Beach, Maine

First published in 1996 by
Samuel Weiser, Inc.
P.O. Box 612
York Beach, ME 03910-0612

This is a revised and expanded edition based on *Being a Lunar Type in a Solar World*, copyright © 1982 Donna Cunningham.

Library of Congress Cataloging-in-Publication Data

Cunningham, Donna.
    The moon in your life : being a lunar type in a solar world / Donna Cunningham.
       p. cm.
    Includes bibliographical references and index.
    1. Astrology. 2. Moon—Miscellanea. I. Title.
BF1723.C84   1996
133.5'3—dc20   95–52002
                                       CIP

ISBN 0-87728-837-2

TS

Cover art is a painting titled *Kosmische Malerei* by von Gabriele Berndt. Copyright © 1996 von Gabriele Berndt. Courtesy Walter Holl Agency, Germany.

Typeset in 10 point Garamond.

Charts reproduced in this book have been calculated using a Solar Fire program, distributed in the United States of America by Astrolabe, P.O. Box 1750, Brewster MA, 02631.

Printed in the United States of America.

04   03   02   01   00   99   98
10 9 8 7 6 5 4 3 2

The paper used in this publication meets the minimum requirements of the American National Standard for Permanence of Paper for Printed Library Materials Z39.48-1984.

The information on flower remedies and other healing tools in this book is for reference only and is not intended to treat, diagnose, or prescribe. This information is not a substitute for a consultation with a qualified health care professional or psychotherapist.

This book is dedicated, as any book on the Moon should be, to the Dianas of today. In particular, I'd like to acclaim Diana Couper, who loved me as a teen even when I didn't know how to love myself, and my sister Diana Hill, a mother in the face of great hardship.

—Donna Cunningham

TABLE OF CONTENTS

Chapter 1: Mythical, Magical, and Modern Views of the Moon 1

Moon myths and magic; the Moon and modern science; everything under the Moon—astrological correspondences; are you a lunar type; crossing the lunar thresholds; women as daughters of Diana; reclaiming the strengths of the Moon and the feminine side.

Chapter 2: Moonchild in the Promised Land 17

So many of them—and such a pain in the neck; the psychology of the Sign Cancer; Cancer and the good old days; the Cancer child—and how she grew; a Cancer in remission; the Cancer rising wheel as a symbolic tool; the greatest crab of them all—the United States; a cheat sheet of places for Cancers to live; why are they so crabby?

Chapter 3: Since Earthlings Landed on the Moon, the Neighborhood Just Isn't the Same 35

The outer planet transits to the sign Cancer; other transits with an impact on the sign Cancer; the splits between Cancer and Aquarius; Uranus, the Age of Aquarius, and individual freedom; you can't go home again.

Chapter 4: Moon Madness and Mood Swings 55

The Moon and public mood swings; the outer planet transits and loony tunes; women as lunatics; what kind of lunatic are you; the effect of the house placement of your Moon; do you use emotions to get nurturing; learning to cope without dope.

LIST OF CHARTS

List of Tables

List of Figures

ACKNOWLEDGMENTS

To Donald Weiser and Betty Lundsted for believing in this book all along, for encouraging me to write it, keeping the first edition in print, and for suggesting and supporting this new edition.

To those friends whose input on the various topics in this new edition was invaluable: Bill Baeckler, Zylpha Elliott, Brendan Feeley, Gretchen Lawlor, Joyce Mason, Andrew Ramer, Lois Rodden, Linda Stone, and Matthew Wood. To my most recent brother-in-law, Jim Hill, for cruising the Information Superhighway on my behalf; and to Madge, whom you'll meet in Chapter 16.

To my unseen helpers, among them Richard and Izzie, whose middle of the night dictations account for some of the more inspired writing in this and other books. And, to my computer, one of the solar world's greatest gifts to me.

To Cheryl Woodruff, for patiently editing draft after draft of the first edition of this book with me, even when I didn't care for the idea of another rewrite. And, for her many contributions to my life since then, both personal and professional.

To the women who assisted me with the first edition by typing, reading drafts, and giving me feedback and encouragement: Amy Fleetman, Heidi Ruthchild, Janice Murray, Jeannie Granata, and Reseda Mickey.

To Ideal Publishing for permission to reprint "How Astrology Can Help You Understand Your Weight Problem," from the May, 1980 issue of *Astrology Plus* and "Messages from Mom," from the January, 1981 issue of the same magazine.

To Sterling Magazines for permission to reprint portions of the following: 1) "The Astrology Bookshelf: New Evidence on Moon Mysteries," from the September, 1979 issue of *Astrology Guide*; 2) "Mothers and Daughters," from the September, 1980 issue of *Astrology Guide*; and 3) "What's Ahead for the Man of Steel?" from the October, 1980 issue of *Your Personal Astrology*.

To Can-Am Publishing for permission to reprint parts of "What Gets Into Men?" from the 1981 *Starcraft Horoscope Yearbook* and "Let the Moon Guide You through 1982" from the 1982 *Starcraft Horoscope Yearbook*.

To CBS Publishing for permission to reprint "Go With the Flow of Life," from *Astrology: Your Daily Horoscope*.

FOREWORD TO THE REVISED EDITION

Being an author is a funny thing. On one hand, your words may stay in print long enough to be an embarassment to you, as parts of *Being a Lunar Type in a Solar World* had become over the years. On the other hand, you might just get the chance to go back and rewrite them. I was delighted when Weiser's approached me about revising this book. So much about the world and about my own view of things has changed from when it was written in the late 70s. That was at the height of both the women's movement and the human potential movement. It was back when we were all convinced we could be, do, or have anything we wanted, so long as we just thought properly.

I was 35 then and had all the answers, especially to women's issues. Now I'm over 50 and don't have so many answers—but you'd probably like me better. Most especially, I hadn't a clue about the menopause. It was something that happened to other people's mothers, but I was far too psychologically sophisticated for it to ever happen to me. Read chapter 14 to discover just how wrong I was, and how much we all can learn about and from this phase of life. When I wrote the original, I had lost a great deal of weight. I was maintaining it well and knew all the answers about that, too—now I'm not, and I don't. Still, chapters 11 and 12 should prove enlightening about our collective struggles with food and weight.

So, what is the world like now as opposed to what it looked like in the late 1970s? Things are changing so fast as this is written that it would be premature to draw conclusions—just as it was unfortunately premature then to hail the progress in women's roles. There were family secrets we didn't know about then that we do know now: the word incest would have been a shocker, the dysfunctional family hadn't been invented yet, and we were blissfully unaware of codependency. Buzz words come and buzz words go, but one thing remains constant—the less attention we pay to our lunar side, the more we suffer. And, of course, 15 years ago AIDS had just begun its silent invasion. Now it is a nightmare that has stolen many of our finest lunar men. It increasingly threatens women, infants, and youth. It can't help but alter our love relationships, whoever we are, when unprotected sex is so potentially deadly.

Women aren't doing that well in 1995. Certainly, we have made progress, but for every freedom won, there has been a loss. Many more women are struggling to head up single parent families. Men are more free to leave their families and not pay support. Women who marry or remarry may confront the stresses involved in the growing number of stepfamilies. Our income hasn't changed all that much compared to men's, and our new careers don't excuse us from bearing the caretaker responsibility for our homes and families. We are expected not only to bring home the bacon but to cook it. Almost as the price of our progress, we labor under a vastly increased pressure to be perfect—and especially to look perfect. Men now routinely dump their girlfriends if they gain weight. And, yes, men are also living more and more stressful lives as competition in the workplace intensifies and as support for their lunar needs also erodes. Read chapter 13 for more about men.

This new edition also provides an opportunity to include some of the healing tools that have become so important in my work in the last fifteen years. The flower remedies, introduced in the new chapter 5, are particularly helpful with lunar issues. Being able to include them was almost enough of a reward for doing the revision. Throughout the book, there are tools and techniques to help you work with your lunar side to keep it balanced. Some will be right for you, others won't appeal, but enough tools are presented that there should be something for every reader. If you are suffering from serious lunar dysfunction (a new buzz word!), you will need more than this book and a bottle of flower remedies to resolve it. However, these tools can support your work with your health care provider, therapist, or self-help group.

The original version of this book was more self-help than astrology. This new edition generally contains more astrological material, such as chapter 15, on transits to the natal Moon and what to do with them. Many chapters contain descriptions of the twelve Moon signs. You will be getting the benefit of what I have continued to learn about astrology and lunar issues in the intervening years. Newcomers to the field can still read much of this book comfortably. However, they will need a computer printout of their birth charts or use the tables in my book *Moon Signs*, which is meant as an introduction for the general public.

At the end of the *Consulting Astrologer's Guidebook*, I wrote that it was my last astrology book and said that you could have a good laugh at my expense if I was wrong. A scant two months after it was published, Weiser's enticed me into doing this revision of *Being A Lunar Type*. It was just a rewrite, they said, but it became a whole new book. So maybe I was wrong—maybe there will be more. What I won't be writing is another book on Pluto, nosiree, so those of you out there who delight in calling me "Our Lady of Pluto" can relax. (Don't relax too much. I KNOW who you are!)

This rewrite reminded me how endlessly fruitful astrology is as a tool for understanding life. It serves as a lens for examining the world, and it serves as a looking glass for examining ourselves. The always-enigmatic ephemeris has proven to be a guidebook for me. This book, based on my observations and experiences with clients, students, and friends over the years is meant to be a lunar survival manual. It is meant to help you avoid the potholes and pitfalls of living in the solar world. Every chapter contains unsettling material about the difficulties of integrating the Moon and its corresponding psychological urges and needs. Every chapter also contains techniques for regaining balance. I hope you will find it helpful.

Donna Cunningham
Port Townsend, Washington
February, 1996

INTRODUCTION

Moonscapes

It has a ring to it, doesn't it? *Being a Lunar Type in a Solar World.* But who are the lunar types? All women are lunar, for one thing. The Moon represents women in traditional astrology, so this book has a great deal to say about the role of women in modern life. The Moon is connected with the sign Cancer, so all people born under the sign Cancer, or with other planets in that sign, are lunar. Therefore, all Americans are lunar—we are a Cancerian nation with four planets in that sign—and we will discover that astrology gives us valuable insight into the changes in American life in this century.

We are all lunar types to some degree because the Moon is a major force in everyone's horoscope. The Moon symbolizes our emotional side, dependency and security, our need for home and roots, and our ties to our mothers. These are normal human needs but the world teaches us that these things are bad, that we must be independent, non-emotional, and accomplishment-oriented. This book will explore conflicts in these lunar areas along with the consequences of suppressing our lunar needs. Suggestions will be offered on how to reconnect with the Moon.

My method was to dig deeply into each of the meanings of the Moon in traditional astrology—the sign Cancer, the emotions, food, mothering, the menstrual cycle, the breast, and the stomach. We will discover how deeply connected the meanings of the Moon are in real life, through research by such disciplines as medicine, science, and psychology. The connections are so pervasive that it was often difficult to separate the material into chapters. You can't write about weight problems without talking about emotions or mothers or even the menstrual cycle. You can't write about premenstrual tension without considering emotions, or food, or mothers. Every chapter goes around and around this way, like the Moon's own endless cycles.

My background is in both astrology and social work, and this dual perspective is reflected in my approach. It was uncertain for some time whether this book was about astrology, self-help, or women's issues. Hopefully, it is a combination of the three, one which will deepen the astrology student's knowledge while giving the general reader a new perspective and suggesting ways to combat the stress. The insights and tools for growth are astrological, yet you need not be an astrologer to grasp or use them. If you are new to astrology, just skip over the parts you don't understand. I only put them there to make the astrologers happy. The important ideas are in plain English. (Or Swedish or Portuguese or whatever language you may using.)

What working on this book made real is that things are NOT right with women today—nor with men—due to society's rigid beliefs about what men and women should be. We will examine these beliefs by exploring astrology's designation of the Moon as women and Mars as men. Briefly, the Moon symbolizes the nurturing and caretaking roles assigned to women, as well as the supposedly feminine preoccupation with emotions, dependency, intuition, and security needs. Mars, on the other hand, represents supposedly male preoccupations such as aggressiveness, competitiveness, winning, physical mastery, anger, and sexuality. We all have both the Moon and Mars in our charts, and we all have to integrate the human needs and urges both planets represent or suffer from a lack of wholeness. It was never easy to live out these one-sided sex roles, and today's conditions are such that it is impossible to do so without a great deal of stress. Men suffer as much as women from these rigid definitions, as well as from the growing pressure to suppress the lunar side.

Each chapter, each area of life ruled by the Moon, was a revelation. At times I felt like a lady astronaut on my own solitary spaceship to the Moon, exploring the craters and crevices of my own being. For instance, my period always seemed like an inconvenience to be worked around, certainly not anything that could be useful. My attitude toward the chapter on menstruation was similar. I didn't want to tackle it, but the structure of the book dictated that everything connected with the Moon had to be covered. "Very well," I thought, "I'll treat that chapter just like my period—something to be gotten over with as quickly as possible without focusing any attention on it." As I delved into the menstrual cycle, however, the rewards were very rich. I found that the connecting link between many of the Moon's astrological meanings is the hormone estrogen. It also became clear that this cycle could be a key for women in blancing their bodies and emotions.

We will cover every lunar phase, every significant part of women's life cycles. We'll especially concentrate on what we will be calling the lunar thresholds—the shifts from one mode of lunar functioning to another. These include going from girlhood to womanhood at puberty when the menses begin, going from young adult to mother at childbirth, as well as the menopause, when the menstrual cycle ends. Not all of those phases will apply to you right now, so there may be chapters that you skip over.

Maybe you're not planning to be a parent or the kids are grown, so you might skip chapter 9, on the passage to parenthood. Or, maybe you're 35 and menopause seems like only a distant and rather ludicrous possibility. In a few years, when odd things start happening to your body and emotions, you may want to look that chapter squarely in the eye. This may be a reference that you come back to over time. Or, you may have friends or family members who go through those phases later, and you'd find the relevant sections helpful in understanding them. For now, skip the parts that don't apply to you, and go forward. The last two chapters, on transits to the birth Moon and on balancing the lunar side of our nature, will apply to everyone.

As far as my orientation toward women's problems is concerned, I would have to describe myself as a feminist with burnout—liberated but tired. I no longer see women as a race of noble savages who'd be saints if freed, nor men as vile oppressors. There are still times when I am a fire-breathing feminist, like when I uncovered the material in chapter 9 on synthetic estrogen, but those times are neatly balanced by the moments in my private life when I am the total woman. I am a welter of contradictions which may show up despite all guidance from my editors. *La donna é mobile.*

The most difficult part of writing this book wasn't the research, organizing the concepts, or putting the words on paper. It was coping with the feelings that were dredged up by every single topic. If I was stirred up by many of the issues covered here, no doubt many of you will be also. Consciousness is the prerequisite to change, so hopefully the new light this work sheds on the Moon's dark side will help you integrate your lunar and solar halves to form a balanced whole.

CHAPTER 1

Mythical, Magical, and Modern Views of the Moon

Throughout this book, we will explore how various matters associated with the Moon in traditional astrology are actually associated in our lives. The Moon traditionally rules women, emotions, mothering, security, food, the stomach, the breasts, and the menstrual cycle. Exciting confirmations of these ancient links will be found through modern research. This chapter presents an overview of the Moon and the spiritual practices pertaining to it to see if they help us connect with our lunar side. Women will be revealed as lunar creatures, and the problems inherent in suppressing their lunar nature will be explored.

Moon Myths and Magic

From our simplest beginnings well into the time we had developed complex cities, we considered the universe essentially feminine, born of God herself. The Great Mother was a complex deity . . . and she could appear in any form, but we cherished her most as the Moon.[1]

Goddess worship was once the dominant religion throughout the world. The Moon Goddess had a thousand names: Diana, Artemis, and Hecate

---

[1]Geraldine Thorsten, *God Herself* (New York: Doubleday, 1980), p. xiii.

being the most familiar. She was an object of worship, ritual, and sacrifice. As a special patroness of women, women made offerings to her to ensure fertility and safe childbirth. Traits associated with women were attributed to the Moon, so she was considered changeable, moody, sometimes open and sometimes secretive. Sometimes the Moon symbolized the Great Mother, sometimes the Destroyer. According to some feminist theorists, the Moon religion in which there were female priests and oracles apparently went along with a matriarchy. About 1500 B.C., we apparently began converting to a patriarchy, a Sun god, and a male priesthood. The witch burnings in Medieval Europe and the Salem era were the last major destructions of the Moon goddess cult.

Throughout history, the Moon and its ever-changing shape have been a source of mystery to religious leaders, poets, and the rest of us. Those close to nature used it to time important activities. Cultures ranging from Native American to orthodox Jew to Mohammedans measured the year by lunar months, beginning with the New Moon and including one complete lunar cycle. Activities were recommended for each phase of the Moon and each lunar month. Even today, the New Moon in Taurus is called the Planter's Moon, and farmers regard it as the most fruitful time to sow crops. Astrology students who try lunar timing still find the technique useful. (Ways to use the Moon for timing will be given later.)

Psychiatrist Dr. Arnold Lieber, who is not a believer in astrology, explored the Moon's impact in his book, *The Lunar Effect*.[2] Lieber says there are two modes of thought: 1) the rational, logical, linear mode associated with left half of the brain, which he labels *solar*, and 2) the intuitive, emotional, creative mode associated with the right half of the brain, which he labels *lunar*. The two halves of the brain have been the subject of much study in recent decades. Researchers generally agree that men function more from the left (solar) brain, while women are far more active than men in the right (lunar) brain.

Lieber says that in the course of history, the solar mode of thought won out and the lunar side got suppressed. He feels this suppression made us more susceptible to psychiatric illness and sudden outbursts of violence. As his research shows, these outbursts can be triggered by the full or new Moon. He feels that the rituals of Moon religions provided an outlet for the emotional and intuitive side of our nature, an outlet lost when persecution suppressed those rituals. Moon rituals and meditations help integrate the lunar half of consciousness and increase awareness of the lunar parts of our-

---

[2]Arnold Lieber and Jerome Agel, *The Lunar Effect* (New York: Anchor Press, 1978).

selves so that we are balanced. Part of what it means for both men and women to be lunar in today's world is the strain of suppressing the lunar hemisphere. A major remedy we will explore is the reintegration of that half of the brain.

Even today, remnants of the Old Religion based on Moon worship survive through the witches of various traditions, who prefer to call their practice *Wicca*. These groups are not to be confused with Satanic, devil worshiping, or Black Magic cults. At the full Moon, they hold a *sabbat*, a ceremony to worship Diana and to do healing work. Many covens have ancient and often matriarchal lineage, for families pass down the knowledge. Nontraditional pagan groups, some springing from feminist roots, worship the goddess as part of their rejection of the patriarchy. They reclaim their full spiritual power through joining with other women in meditation and rituals of their own devising. Books, workshops, and ritual groups honoring the feminine aspect of the divine have proliferated over the last two decades.[3]

Esoteric students in the 20th century disagree among themselves about the Moon and its power. Many teach that all planetary bodies are living beings on a level of consciousness we can scarcely imagine. Thus, some believe the Moon is a powerful female being whom we can tune into at certain times via fasting, celibacy, and ritual. Others, like Alice Bailey, believed the Moon was once a vehicle for such being, but is now a dead thought form that will crumble in the distant future.[4] Gurdjieff disagreed, feeling the Moon is a planet waiting to be born, and it is coming to life by devouring human souls at the moment of death. He believed that only those rare beings who arise from automaton-like behavior into full consciousness are able to survive past physical death.[5] These are two extremes—the Moon having absolute destructive power on one hand and none beyond the considerable power of gravity on the other.

Various teachings agree on the usefulness of group meditation at the full Moon. Hundreds of occult and spiritual organizations throughout the world hold meditations at that time. Bailey's followers teach that the practice is not for individual growth but for the good of the planet, to expand human consciousness and align us with higher spiritual energies. Fasting, special prayers and rituals are often part of the preparation for this practice,

---

[3]The wholesale catalog published by Samuel Weiser has four pages of books about the goddess and women's spirituality, and Weiser is carefully neutral about spiritual preferences!

[4]Alice Bailey, *Esoteric Astrology*, Vol. III (New York: Lucis Publishing, 1971), p. 13.

[5]P. D. Ouspensky, *In Search of the Miraculous* (New York: Harcourt Brace, 1949), pp. 81–85.

which they see as service. The full Moon moment, itself, is especially powerful, a time when a strong flow of energy opens between the spiritual and earthly realms. This full Moon moment is not safe for individual meditation, as sometimes more force is brought in than the student can handle alone. Meditating in the safety of a group is more constructive and produces a better flow of energy.

Three full Moons are considered especially powerful. The first is near the Christian festival of Easter, when the Sun is in Aries and the Moon is in Libra. The second is the Buddhic full Moon, called Wesak, with the Sun in Taurus and Moon in Scorpio. The third, not currently celebrated by any world religion, is the full Moon of Goodwill, when the Sun is in Gemini and the Moon in Sagittarius. These are times of special power to esoteric and spiritual groups all over the world. Any group tuning into these full Moons, when so many people unite their energies, should experience a particularly strong meditation.

The Moon and Modern Science

Though science ridicules Moon lore and astrology as superstition, recent research proves that the Moon as a planetary body influences those areas of life traditional astrology assigns to it. Intelligent skeptics can sometimes be the astrologer's best friend. They work so hard to debunk astrology that they wind up uncovering evidence for the very thing they set out to disprove. A case in point is Francoise and Michel Gauquelin, the French psychologists who became astrology's foremost researchers.[6]

Dr. Arnold Lieber certainly qualifies as a skeptic. He calls astrology "cosmic pseudoknowledge" and says its popularity is due to society's failure to come to terms with the intuitive side of human nature. Yet *The Lunar Effect* is one of the most valuable and exciting proofs of astrology in years. It reports his own research (and many others') into the Moon's effects on behavior. The research reports different effects at different phases of the Moon and different distances from the ocean. Despite astrological ignorance, these researchers demonstrate links between the Moon's various astrological meanings.

For example, the Moon in astrology shows our emotions and how we express them. Lieber cites dozens of studies showing increased emotional

---

[6]You can read more about their work in Michel's *Cosmic Influences on Human Behavior* (Santa Fe: Aurora Press, 1979).

stress at the full and new Moon. A state mental hospital in Texas found significantly more admissions at the full Moon and last quarter. Another psychiatrist, M. H. Stone, charted increases in manic episodes at the full and new Moon. Lieber's research also showed that crime follows Moon phases. In Cincinnati, the full and new Moons brought increases in assault, drunk and disorderly conduct, and rape. Lieber studied homicides and found that Florida cases showed a marked peak at the full Moon and a lower peak at the new Moon. Ohio's pattern was different but still consistent, with homicides peaking about three days after the full and new Moon. In New York City, Philadelphia, Los Angeles, and Miami, arson rises at the full Moon.

In astrology, the Moon is connected with women and the menstrual cycle. Without knowledge of astrology, Lieber cites studies which show that women are more prone to emotional crises like mental hospital admissions or suicide attempts while premenstrual. (We will explore reasons for this in the chapter on the menstrual cycle.)

The Moon rules the stomach, food, and feeding habits. The shrimpers in Miami are out *en masse* at the full Moon because that is when shrimp rise to the surface to feed. Lieber believes fish have increased metabolic activity at certain phases of the Moon, so they burn more energy which in turn makes them hungry. (I notice that my cat is frantically hungry at the full Moon and so are some people.) Many fishermen use calendars showing the best days to fish. These calendars are based on Moon phases and the lunar day, for the lunar day gives more accurate timing for Moon-related events. The lunar day of 24 hours, 50 minutes goes from Moonrise to Moonrise, marked by the moment when the Moon's center crosses over the Ascendant. The Moon affects human metabolism, too, so the Ananda Yoga Society recommends fasting the fourth day before the full and new Moon. Gravitational stresses begin to accumulate on those days and create imbalance in the system. Fasting and meditating on these days restores the balance.

Another area connected with the Moon and the sign Cancer is old age. Lieber finds that his geriatric patients do not do well at the full and new Moon, often going into emotional crises. After reading this, I wondered why older people might be so susceptible to the Moon's influence. It struck me that old age is a lunar phase of life, when we are often more dependent and under less pressure to be rational. Those freed of rigid work structures might be more in touch with the rhythm of the Moon. In consequence, they may be more affected by changes that occur at peaks of the Moon cycle.

You'll hear the term *solar world* often in this book. It's my shorthand for all the ways modern urban life demands that we suppress our lunar side. It

TABLE 1. MODERN MIRACLES FOR MOON MATTERS.

WOMEN: No argument—we do have more career opportunities than ever before.

HOME: Central heat and air conditioning.

FAMILY: You CAN go home again, thanks to the airlines. Genealogical records are being computerized so we don't lose them.

FOOD: Fabulous foods from all over the world, any season of the year. Microwave ovens. (Your *yes buts* don't count here!)

CHILDBIRTH: Infertility techniques help many people who want children but haven't been able to have them. Maternal and infant mortality rates are way down.

BREASTS: Mammograms and mass-produced brassieres.

MENSTRUATION: Mass-produced sanitary napkins first appeared in the 1920s.

THE PAST: Carbon dating, genotyping and other technology help us recover the distant past.

has to do with the way society values success, achievement, and progress above emotions, instincts, and personal needs. It is about technology that runs rampant over human physiology and the natural world in order to fix or improve things. It never stops to think that perhaps nature established its balance for good reasons. For instance, menopause is not a disease but a part of the life cycle, yet medicine tries to obliterate it by giving women synthetic estrogen. Synthetic estrogen then creates a host of problems all its own, like an increased risk of breast cancer—but medicine has answers for that, too.

Technology and modern medicine have also had amazing and benign achievements. Just so you won't think I'm a complete curmudgeon, I set myself the challenge of listing ways each of the lunar areas of life has been enhanced by science and commerce. The rules of the challenge said they had to be ones I couldn't counter with, "Yes, but." Thus all the solar goodies and panaceas with undesirable lunar side effects had to be eliminated. My nominations appear in Table 1.

Despite all the advances, the lunar parts of our physiology and emotions cannot be legislated out of existence without creating a deep disturbance in the force. For example, breast-feeding has existed as long as we have, and yet in this century, it virtually disappeared. Women's careers may make breast-feeding impractical, but this change is bound to alter the relationship between mother and infant in far-reaching ways. We will find many more examples of changes in the lunar areas of life and will examine their consequences. The solar world has won—and no doubt that's part of the divine plan—but the lunar side and the needs related to it are not going to disappear. We must find ways of consciously balancing the lunar and solar sides of our nature. That balance is the focus and the purpose of this book.

Everything Under the Moon— Astrological Correspondences

In the birth chart, the Moon sign is as influential as the Sun sign. The Moon shows such important segments of life as your emotional makeup, the effects of your early home environment, your subconscious motivations, and your instinctual response to challenging situations. It shows your degree of security and your trust or lack of trust in the world. Physically, it rules the breasts, ovaries, the menstrual cycle, and the stomach. It also rules women, food, habit, memory, and the effect of the past and family. The Moon's sign and aspects describe how you operate in these crucial areas of life. Various chapters contain readings for all twelve Moon signs. The Moon also rules women and the sign Cancer in traditional astrology. These two categories are important to the theme of the book, so long sections will be devoted to them. We need to understand why women and Cancerians are considered lunar, and why they experience special stress under conditions of modern life.

The link between many of these lunar matters is the mother, whose influence was powerfully imprinted on us long before we could reason. She taught us whether the world was a safe place, and what emotions were okay to express. She taught us about food and shaped our eating habits. The Moon also shows how we deal with dependency in ourselves and others—our personal capacity to cherish and nourish others. We tend to respond to the needs of others—and to our own needs—in the same way our mothers did. As the first and most influential female in our lives, our mothers taught us what it means to be a woman and what we can expect of women. The

Moon in your own chart shows what kind of mother you had. See chapters 7 and 8 for further discussions of how your mother affected you.

The Moon rules intuition, yet not all intuition is psychic in nature. Some of it has to do with the mirror-like reflectiveness of the Moon. Just as the Moon reflects back the Sun's light, we pick up and respond on a subconscious level to messages, such as body language and tone of voice. When we cannot verbalize the reasons for our response, it gets labeled intuition or irrationality. When we ignore these responses, we lose touch with them and often get into trouble. In your own chart, the Moon shows how you deal with intuitive perceptions.

The Moon rules habits—both good and bad ones. We learned these patterns of behavior so early or so long ago that we no longer recall when or why they began. Mother or family members transmitted most of them. Midsummer Night's Dream (June 23rd) is traditionally considered an excellent time to break a bad habit forever. That happens to be the beginning date of the sign Cancer, which the Moon rules. If you can muster the determination to stop an unwanted habit under the sign Cancer, you can more quickly form a desirable one.

Astrologer Bob Mulligan says the Moon rules not only habit, but the cravings you have for habit-forming substances. You can be imprisoned by habit and by your desire nature. Moon rituals and meditations can help in getting free of the cravings. This idea will have special relevance in our chapter on food addictions, but not all cravings are for physical substances. You may crave excitement, attention, or sex, for instance, or you may be in thrall to your credit cards. The Moon in your chart would give clues to your own habit-traps. Bob also feels the Moon rules the astral body and the astral plane, the plane most closely connected with our emotional nature. To function safely on the astral we have to be firm in our emotional and desire natures, not easily swayed by them. In chapter 5, we will explore a significant habit pattern—our emotional habits—and find some tools to transform undesirable ones.

The Moon is also associated with memory. Our responses are not just based on the present, but also on emotionally-laden memories of similar situations, so we cannot always respond clearly and logically. Without memory, we could not learn from our past. Astrologer Marcia Moore said the Moon rules the akashic records, which are imprinted with memories of all our lifetimes. The strongly lunar person may be influenced by past life memories and also more able to tap into them so as to be freed of karmic influence.

Every area connected to the Moon has been harmed by our culture's tendency to deny our lunar side. Parts of the personality governed by the lunar hemisphere—the unconscious, the emotions, the intuition, the feminine side—can be badly thrown out of balance when ignored. These neglected facets of ourselves become threatening, mysterious, and increasingly subject to suppression.

Are You a Lunar Type?

Throughout this book, you will encounter the term *lunar type*, and you may be wondering if it applies to you. On an emotional level, a lunar type is someone whose energies are bound up in the matters associated with the Moon. You're lunar if your home, mother, family, food, and other matters discussed in this chapter are the stuff of life for you. If you're new to astrology, suspect that you're lunar if the subtitle, "being a lunar type in a solar world" reverberated strongly within, even if you couldn't explain it in so many words. (It could be worse. No doubt there are inhabited planets in our galaxy that have three or four Moons, so our lives, our psyches, and our horoscopes must be simple by comparison.)

For readers who are astrologically sophisticated, I regard a lunar type as someone with the Moon or the sign Cancer prominent in the birth chart. Perhaps the Sun, Moon, Ascendant, or several planets are in Cancer, the sign the Moon rules. The term applies if the Moon falls in the Gauquelin sectors ten degrees either side of the four angles—the Ascendant, Midheaven, IC, or Descendant. (The Gauquelins found that planets in these positions were powerful in determining how the person was seen.) Or, maybe the Moon is one of the most aspected planets in the chart, especially in a major configuration like a t-square or grand trine. A strong 4th house containing several planets, or the Sun or Moon, can also make you lunar. These 4th house folks are among my favorite lunar types, for, depending on the sign involved, they can be nurturing home-lovers, yet aren't excessively emotional.

While there are many ways in which the lunar and solar domains are at odds at this point in history, how well do you personally integrate the two? If your Sun and Moon signs are in harmony, you probably integrate them well and thus find modern life less stressful than those who can't. If your Sun and Moon signs are at odds, the demands of modern life probably create both inner tension and external conflict. The Sun/Moon connection also shows how well you balance the male and female energies within yourself—and often how well you can integrate them into your love life. (I won't go into the

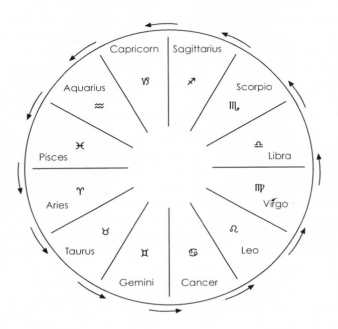

STEP ONE: Start with your Moon sign and count around the zodiac to your Sun sign to determine the number of signs they are apart.

STEP TWO: Look in the table below under the number you arrived at in Step One to see how compatible your Sun and Moon are.

NUMBERS	TYPE OF ASPECT	HOW COMPATIBLE ARE THEY?
Same sign	Conjunction	Powerfully reinforcing.
1 (or 11)	Semisextile	Somewhat supportive.
2 (or 10)	Sextile	Supportive, easy connection.
3 (or 9)	Square	Clashing, at odds.
4 (or 8)	Trine	Harmonious, natural.
5 (or 7)	Quincunx	Extremely different.
6	Opposition	Conflicting but can be balanced.

Figure 1. The relationships between Sun and Moon signs.

subject of relationship compatibility based on Moon signs here, but devoted a chapter to it in my book, *Moon Signs,* published by Ballantine in 1988.)

If you know both your Sun and Moon, use figure 1 to determine whether the signs are compatible. If you don't know your Moon sign, you will need it not only here, but in many of the chapters. Refer to the tables in *Moon Signs* or get a computer chart from one of the many available chart services. For the novice, the zodiac wheel starts with Aries and continues counterclockwise through Pisces, as the arrows show. To determine the correct direction, find Aries in your own chart. (It is probably not at the same place as it is in the wheel below.)

Then start with your Moon sign and count around the wheel in zodiac order to find out how many signs it is from the Sun. Look under that number in the table to see how the two signs relate. If they are at odds, you will need to work more consciously to see that the needs of both signs are met and that you don't neglect one in favor of the other. From the various techniques given in this book, you will find some that help resolve the tensions between the two signs.

Crossing the Lunar Thresholds

A theme we will return to frequently is that of the lunar thresholds. These are times in our lives when we pass from one state of functioning related to the Moon to another. The first of these is teething, when we become less passively dependent on the breast or bottle, and progressively move toward feeding ourselves. In other thresholds, the girl child becomes a young woman and the young woman becomes a mother. An older woman must find a new focus for her energies as her offspring leave home or she retires. Men cross similar thresholds in their lives as well, although not all of their transitions are lunar.

In the individual horoscope, transits to the birth Moon, which will be considered in chapter 15, mark many of these passages. When we reach major thresholds, all of the functions of the Moon may come to the fore and need realignment. Even such a taken-for-granted lunar shift as a major geographic move may require a lunar year—a full cycle of new and full Moons—for us to adjust. The solar world gets impatient if we take as much as a lunar month to get back to normal, much less a lunar year.

The demands of the solar world have eroded more and more of our lunar support systems. While adjusting to threshold crossings, we need to nurture ourselves with the tools given in this book—and then some. In earlier societies there were rites of passage—culturally-sanctioned rituals—to mark the lunar thesholds. The collective gave special support and instruction to those undergoing them. Marcia Starck, a noted medical astrologer, has written an excellent book detailing feminine rites of passage in many cultures. Called *Women's Medicine Ways*, it also helps today's women (and women's groups) design rituals of personal relevance.[7] Ritual can help us get in touch with our womanhood and with femininity as a source of power and fulfillment.

Women as Daughters of Diana

Many Moons ago, when astrology and the women's movement intersected on my life map, traditional astrology's designation of women as the Moon and men as Mars or the Sun seemed sexist. Both men and women have the Moon, Mars, and the Sun in their charts and have to integrate all three to be whole. Investigation led me, however, to the inescapable conclusion that women are more lunar than men to begin with. Women are also pressured to live out the Moon more than other planets.

Women's bodies are lunar—the Moon rules breasts, ovaries, and menstruation. In several chapters, we will see links between the female hormone estrogen and the Moon's meanings. It makes us prone to physical and emotional cycles resembling the Moon's. As we'll see in chapter 7, our breasts and our capacity for motherhood profoundly affect our self-image and our relationship to the world. The Moon rules feeding. We'll explore, in chapters 10 and 11, how women's hormonal balance and their position as perpetual feeders make them especially prone to eating disorders.

Profound emotional and mental processes accompany changes in women's bodies. We will talk about several of these transitions in depth— puberty, the birth of the first child, and menopause. These are major lunar thresholds, and at times like these, many lunar issues come to the fore and need adapting. We tend to feel vulnerable, insecure and unsettled. We will discover many tools that can help in these adjustments.

The first of these tools, however, is knowledge, because in the solar world we may have few role models and little validation for the stress we are experiencing. For instance, the 45-year-old career woman, living far from

---

[7]Marcia Starck, *Women's Medicine Ways* (Freedom, CA: Crossing Press, 1993).

family and under tremendous pressure to produce, may not know the signs of menopause or recognize that it is beginning. Instead, she may conclude that she is going crazy. She may not discuss it or address the symptoms because she fears her job is at stake. In today's business world, she may be right!

The Moon rules the emotions. Women are more emotional not only because of their physiology, but because of the pressure of being confined to lunar roles while being denied the proper lunar outlets. In chapter 4, we'll see why women are far more prone to depression and other emotional upsets, and why they are also more prone to seek psychotherapy. The Moon rules mothers, and as discussed in chapter 7, women are far more influenced by their mothers than most men.

Part of the difference between men and women is *nature*, and part is *nurture*. Female hormones and physiology do have a profound effect on our emotions and behavior. However, society conditions women to take on the lunar qualities—to be caring, compassionate, maternal, protective, responsive, and submissive—and to make the lunar roles of mother, homemaker, and wife the main focus of energy. If we don't want to be "Moon" and instead want to be "Mars," we may be labeled as dykes or castrating females. Carried to an extreme, liberated women may suffer social and economic reprisals. Some have been abandoned by their men or by women friends, some have been sexually harassed, and some have even been put in the "loony bin."

At some level, no matter what else she may achieve, society considers a woman without a husband *and* children a failure. Yet, women who *do* confine themselves to those roles are also regarded as failures because society places such a low value on women and women's roles. The solar world values achievement, things that can be written on a resume. Women lose either way, and our self-esteem suffers. Our society decries the fact that women are becoming too much like men. It is not prestigious to be a woman, so of course we try to be more like men. There are serious consequences to this devaluation of feminine qualities, because then we try to close off our lunar hemisphere.

Many career women look down on their mothers because they were "just housewives," and disconnect from this important tie. In the U.S. today, many of us are so anti-Mom that anyone who says she loves her mother and claims to have a good relationship with her is considered seriously codependent. We say she is out of touch with her true feelings and denying the anger she "must" feel. We not only cut the connection with our mothers, but we may also dislike, devalue, and distrust other women. We

take on the predominant attitude that women are not worthwhile companions. In so doing, we lose an important source of support women are able to
give each other. In the past, we shared mutual aid, emotional comfort, and
intuitive and spiritual strength.

We learn to distrust or ignore other lunar areas of our lives as well. To
function in a man's world, we suppress needs we have during menstruation,
at costs to be explored in more detail in chapter 10. Both men and women
are taught that it is a weakness to be emotional or to cry. We try to shut off
our feelings and be rational and logical. In a society that worships scientific
thought and discounts anything you can't measure, feminine intuition is
considered silly or crazy. We learn to ignore the promptings of intuition and
instinct, qualities that are part of our feminine strength. (Men have intuitions, too, but we're supposed to call them "hunches.")

When we cut ourselves off from our innards—running from feelings
and ignoring intuition—they become unfamiliar and threatening. We are
afraid to look within, because we think there is madness there. Because
we've neglected this area, when we do look within, it does look like madness
at first. We haven't cultivated the inner self, haven't sorted it out, just shoved
in more and more material haphazardly. Our dreams make no sense, psychic
material comes up helter-skelter with our own personal mishugas. The unconscious becomes a jumbled-up, overstuffed closet, and we wind up confused and more leery of self-examination than ever. Only by systematically
cleaning and organizing the inner closet do we restore balance to our emotional and spiritual lives.

Meditation, especially in a group at the full and new Moon, is one crucial way of balancing and reintegrating the lunar hemisphere. We often
"fail" at meditation because we approach it from the mental, solar, male
model. We need to open the lunar or feeling side of the brain, not the solar
or mental side. Don't try to *analyze* how to do it—just direct your subconscious to connect with the Moon and to open the right side of your brain for
brief periods. Your constructive, loving, lunar, higher self already knows
how, and is waiting for you to reopen the contact. (Chapter 16 contains
some techniques to help in this process.)

Society scorns us for not being solar, then persuades us that it is not
good to be lunar, so women often wind up emotionally, socially, and spiritually disenfranchised. This decline of women's power began thousands of
years ago. Chapter 3 shows that the astrological conditions in this century
represent a crisis, intensifying women's struggles to a critical degree. The cost
of suppressing the lunar hemisphere is that it gets fretful, distorted, and even
neurotic. The one solution I find to these problems is a conscious return to

the feminine, to the Moon within. This surprises me, as I am not an active feminist or a goddess worshipper.

As explained in chapter 13, we expect men to fit the stereotype of the planet Mars, to be aggressive, competitive, sexually conquering, tough, and active. They are often taught to ignore their lunar side altogether, relegating it to the women in their lives. Nonconforming men suffer social and economic consequences just as severe as those nonconforming women experience, and they also suffer physical and emotional consequences if they do conform.

Reclaiming the Strengths of the Moon and the Feminine Side

Our goal is to reclaim the constructive strengths of the Moon. If we can reconnect with the strengths of our lunar side, we can be blessed with intuitive knowing and an instinctive capacity to care for ourselves and others. We will have compassion for ourselves and others, emotional sensitivity and responsiveness. These qualities will enable us to nurture, cherish, and preserve those things we care for—be they children, creative work, lovers, or careers. To do this, we must nurture ourselves first, or else we will feel depleted, deprived, and angry. Each chapter contains information that will further your awareness of both the problems and the solutions connected with areas ruled by the Moon.

CHAPTER 2

MOONCHILD IN THE PROMISED LAND

Have you noticed that Cancer isn't a terribly popular sign? People aren't paranoid about them, as they are about Scorpios. Still, there's a kind of eye-rolling, head-shaking smugness—"At least I'm not a CANCER!" Granted, it's hard to get inspired over a sign that has a crab for its symbol. More than that, the areas of life governed by the Moon are primary motivations of the typical Cancerian. The solar world despises people who are too emotional, too hung up in the past, too attached to Mom, too fond of food, and too openly insecure. Cancerians who have those qualities stir up unwanted feelings others are trying hard to contain in order to survive.

Many of us have difficulty dealing with lunar issues, so we scapegoat Cancerians and others who are outwardly lunar. If we close off our feelings, we call those who are openly emotional weak. The truth is, it takes far more strength to feel than it does to drug ourselves with any of our society's many addictions. If we hide from the pain of lost family ties, we scorn those who are attached to family and are sentimental about the past. Many people are depressed around the holidays—traditional family times—and we mourn lost ties. The suicide rate skyrockets, and the rest of us numb ourselves with food and alcohol. Many of us struggle desperately against our bonds to our mothers, so we put down those who remain close to Mom as "codependent." Sometimes a loving attachment between parent and child can be one of the major satisfactions of life.

Due to the social changes we will be discussing, we have suffered great losses in the lunar areas of life, so we detach from them. We pretend they aren't important and decide that people who are trying to reclaim them are losers. If you label Cancerian traits as bad or neurotic, the neurosis may have less to do with the sign's problems than with your own. If it weren't for our families, we Cancers would get no respect at all!

The Moon rules the sign Cancer. You are Cancerian if your Sun, Moon, Ascendant, or several inner planets, are in that sign. These are true lunar types. Perhaps the most lunar of all is Moon in Cancer, since it is in its own sign. (I'm a Cancer Sun with the Moon on the Midheaven, in case you were wondering.) Lest you think segments of this chapter or book don't pertain to you, remember that we all have Cancer somewhere in our charts and we all have a Moon, so we must all learn to balance and integrate the lunar hemisphere.

In the personality portrait that follows, I'm talking about "pure" Cancers. The traits would be modified by aspects to the Sun, if you're a Sun sign Cancer. For example, if you were born between 1948–1956, while Uranus was in Cancer, you may be a wild admixture of lunar and Uranian qualities. In any event, Cancer Suns are especially affected by the Moon's sign and aspects. A Cancer with an Aries Moon wouldn't have much patience with either kids or cooking. A Cancer with a Capricorn Ascendant will not readily show the world his tender or sentimental side. Still, if you have Sun, Moon, or Ascendant in Cancer, you will probably find yourself agreeing privately with many of the qualities we'll discuss, even if you don't let others see them. Publicly, you can disavow the more unpopular traits and say that it's because your Moon or rising sign offset them—or that you've evolved beyond them.

So Many of Them—And Such a Pain in the Neck!

Did you know that there are more Cancerians than almost any other sign? Census figures over the past century consistently show seasonal fluctuations in the birth rate. There is a yearly peak of births that begins with Taurus and lasts through Virgo, but the high point is in Cancer. There is a corresponding low that starts with Sagittarius and continues to slide downward, with the low point in Aries.[1] So, if you feel like you know loads of Cancers and rarely meet an Aries, it's not just your imagination. These figures are for the

[1]The seasonality of birth rates was discussed in "Birth, Marriages, Divorces and Deaths for 1989," in the National Center for Health Statistics' journal, *Monthly Vital Statistics Report*, v.38:12, 4/4/90. I read a census publication in the 1970s with the same pattern, so it is consistent over time.

U.S.A., but should hold true of other northern hemisphere countries. Birth patterns may be different in the southern hemisphere, where the seasons are reversed. (The last Sunday in June is also the date each year when by far the most couples get married. Thus, their wedding charts would have Sun in Cancer.)

Additionally, more people are born with Cancer rising on any given day. Due to astronomical factors, there are signs of long ascension (meaning they are on the Ascendant longer) and of short ascension (meaning they are on the Ascendant a shorter time). According to Nicholas deVore's invaluable classic, *Encyclopedia of Astrology*,[2] Aquarius, Pisces, and Aries are the signs of shortest ascension. Aquarius is only rising for an hour and 26 minutes at New York's latitude, while Cancer is rising for two hours and 23 minutes. (This varies slightly with distance from the equator. At the latitude of San Diego, it is an hour and 33 minutes for Aquarius and two hours and 10 minutes for Cancer.)[3]

These variations should be considered in any astrological research—or in the less formal conclusions you draw. You can't do a project on wife-beating or new-home-buying and conclude that Cancers and Cancer Risings are more prone to either of these than any other sign. Or, suppose you decide to do a study to validate Cancer's fabled longevity and Aquarians' reputed tendency to live fast and die young. You go to your local senior center and nursing homes, gather birth dates, and, sure enough, there are way more Cancers over 70 than there are Aquarians. Before you call the tabloids with your findings, adjust for these seasonal fluctuations. There were more Cancers born in the first place! On a more psychological level, these figures mean that there are a great many lunar types trying to cope with the solar world.

The Psychology of the Sign Cancer

Cancer and the Good Old Days: Cancer is noted for its nostalgia for the past, and we will find that there are good reasons for this yearning. It is misleading to talk about the sign Cancer out of context, for massive social changes have taken place in this century. (The astrological reasons for these trends will be analyzed in chapter 3.) Briefly, however, there has been constant pressure on the sign Cancer from the outer planets for the past ninety years.

[2]Nicholas deVore, *Encyclopedia of Astrology* (New York: Littlefield, Adams, & Co., 1977).
[3]Nicholas deVore, *Encyclopedia of Astrology*, p. 353.

This pressure correlates with radical alterations in areas of life necessary to Cancerians' well-being. The changes rob them of many satisfactions that made their lives fulfilling. Cancer may have been a fine, mellow sign a hundred years ago. We only know it as the insecure, emotionally-turbulent sign it has become.

Cancer's love of family was once a pleasure of life fairly simple to maintain. With disruptions due to divorce and geographic moves, the modern-day Cancerian frequently loses crucial ties and may mourn them consciously or unconsciously for long periods. She tries to create and maintain a family atmosphere wherever she goes—on the job, among friends, and with her own husband and children. For those of us who have also suffered great losses in our family ties, she can be a great comfort.

Cancer has a fine capacity to form and preserve ties. Because our ties are constantly being broken—we move, they move—the Cancerian can become obsessive about them and latch on as if she were drowning. Alternatively, she may become very self-protective and reluctant to form ties lest they be severed. Cancer wants to be secure and to make others feel secure also. It is only because modern life is so wrought with insecurity that the Cancerian must continually reestablish it.

Cancer was once attuned to natural rhythms. Due to city life and scientific advances, we are now far removed from our natural rhythms and are taught to override our instincts. We don't pay attention to the Moon as a timing mechanism like we used to, for instance. Our elders knew when to undertake various tasks for the best results, from gardening to self-care. Today the Cancerian is often ignorant of mechanisms that once kept him balanced and in touch with his world. (Llewelyn's annual *Moon Sign Book and Gardening Guide* still gives these best days and a vast amount of lunar lore.)

Cancer loves food and once got pleasure from growing, preparing, and preserving it. Now our only contact with food may be nuking the frozen veggies or adding water to the mix. The same amount of energy gets fastened onto the act of eating, and Cancerians can have weight problems. Also, Cancer's fine natural instincts for food have been subverted by the changes in our diet we will discuss in chapter 11.

Cancerians have a keen sensitivity that was once part of a capacity not only to survive but to enjoy life and the world of the senses. When those keen senses are barraged by noise, unpleasant smells, crowds, and other strong stimuli, an overload is created. They become hypersensitive, irritable and have to withdraw or numb out. Cancer craves a protective shell and periodically retreats to become reattuned to instincts, needs, and emotions.

Our culture no longer provides such retreats, and urban life is so over-crowded that we lack privacy. Under these conditions, the protective shell can become an obsession. The Cancerian nostalgia for the good old days is not unfounded, because these social developments have affected everyone who struggles along without family unity.

The Cancer Child: Let me give you a natural history of the Cancer child. There is often either *too much* or *too little* in the way of lunar supports like mother-ing, home life, or food in early childhood. The result is that the energy gets fixated there. Some Cancerians have been over-nurtured with a kind of smother love, while others have suffered an intense and painful deprivation of nurturing. Even worse are instances where smother love was followed by deprivation when family circumstances changed. Cancer placements are also common in dysfunctional families where the child wound up caretaking the mother or father. In any of these cases, the result is the same—a compulsive need to be nurtured.

The over-nurtured Cancerian is often the first or last born, or at least a gap in ages exists between the Cancerian and the next child. Due to the birth order, the child receives an unusual amount of attention, particularly from the mother, but often from grandparents, older siblings or other rela-tives as well. With the first-born, the mother may be insecure, especially if she hasn't had much experience with children. She self-consciously monitors her own mothering abilities. If it's the first grandchild, the grandparents may also be watchful and critical. The child's well-being becomes an indi-cator of the mother's worth as a person. Feeding can be a particular source of anxiety, as the first-time mother may not be familiar with the ups and downs of infant digestion.

The Cancerian who is the last-born, especially if the other children are much older, becomes "the baby of the family." Often such children are overindulged and receive a great deal of attention. Possibly the mother may have been tired of bottles and diapers and didn't much want the child, but overcompensated out of guilt. Or, if it had been some time since the mother had a baby, perhaps she really wanted one. Knowing it might be the last, she indulged herself and the child in a prolonged infancy. If mothering has been her main fulfillment, she may cling to the child as justification for her exis-tence.

Either the first-born or the last-born can come to feel the world is safe only so long as mother is there. Smother love is not only their due, but also makes life comfortable. The child becomes dependent and isn't encouraged to venture forth alone. As with all of us, there comes a fall from paradise.

Another sibling is born and mother has to be shared, mother goes to work, or the child goes to school. The mother's ambivalence or guilt may reinforce the child's fear of being without her. Fear makes the loss of maternal attention all the more difficult.

And How She Grew: Regardless of which pattern was true—too much or too little mothering—dependency needs remain strong. They may be quieted by oral addictions like food, alcohol, gum, or cigarettes. Overly-dependent Cancerians may seek help from others compulsively, reacting angrily when the world doesn't coddle them. This is more common with the Cancer who got smother-love, while those who were severely deprived often turn it around and become Mother to the world.

This second type appears extremely independent in a fiercely-protested self-sufficiency called *counter-dependence.* It's not real, and the needs are stronger and more painful for being forced underground. She seeks to fulfill herself by taking care of others. She literally acts out the Golden Rule—"Do unto others as you would have them do unto you." However, one-way relationships based on parenting leave her empty. Her needs threaten to spill over, and she can become angry at having to mother people without getting anything back. This counterdependent stance rarely succeeds over the long haul. It frequently has to be bolstered by excessive eating, drinking, or smoking because it is so draining. Yet, she nurtures compulsively, unaware that she really wants someone to take care of her. We'll see counter-dependency in various lunar types as we go along; for instance in food addicts or macho men.

Either type of Cancer can have a "baby-faced" look, since the inner self molds their bodies. Cancerians often act childlike, yearning almost palpably for someone to take care of them. Part of the bait is a "good little boy" facade. It is fostered by the belief that if they work hard, obey the rules, and placate enough, they will finally win love—and a good Mommy or Daddy. When they find a person with a parental streak, they may latch on with great intensity. When I taught astrology at the alcohol treatment center, one of my students was a black street guy with a great sense of humor who was a Cancer. In our class on this sign, he warned, "When the crab grabs, watch out!"

If your mate is Cancerian, family ties may be very strong, and you may have in-law problems. The bond is not always one of love. Somewhere in my astrological meanderings, it occurred to me to look up Lizzie Borden's chart. If you remember, she was accused of the axe murder of her mother and father. ("Lizzie Borden took an axe and gave her mother forty whacks.")

Born July 19, 1860, she had Sun and Venus conjunct in Cancer. Despite a reputation for loving the family, Cancerians may spend their lives hating their parents for what they did or didn't do. A tie of hate is in some ways more binding than a tie of love. The grudges aren't limited to parents—no one can carry on a family feud like a wounded Cancerian! It is crucial that Cancers work through unhealthy family ties so their adult relationships can be constructive. Energy bound up in the past is a power drain on the present. Those who are too grounded in the past may need help in getting free. (The tools in chapter 8 may be useful.)

The Moon rules emotions, and a Cancerian trait that deserves our attention is emotionality. In other chapters, we will consider the charts of some famous but troubled Cancers like O. J. Simpson. Cancers don't have to be troubled, but they must work to integrate their emotions. Many Cancers fasten onto feelings with great tenacity, being almost addicted to them and getting a charge out of living intensely. We Cancerians are hypersensitive, taking everything personally. We constantly imagine slights or emotional brutality when often people are simply wrapped up in their own lives and (horrors!) not really thinking of us at all.

Whether emoting all over the place or suffering in clamorous silence, we Cancerians make our moods felt. Many people are uncomfortable with emotional displays, so this trait can create distance. We Cancers are well aware of this reaction and sometimes use it defensively to keep from getting too close or too dependent. At other times, unpleasant emotions, such as anger or jealousy may be threatening. We may turn to overeating, drinking, or smoking to keep the feelings down. We need to strive for balance, neither denying these responses nor being swallowed up in them. We must be able to feel and then digest our feelings to grow from them. We need to admit that emotions are valid without allowing them to control our lives.

Another Cancerian characteristic is reflection. Just as the Moon shines with reflected light, we Cancerians tend to reflect whatever is going on around us like a mirror. We automatically respond to, and reflect back, the emotional mood of anyone we are talking to, calling that feeling out of our facile repertoire. We also respond automatically to cries for help, becoming whatever others need us to be at the moment. We are reactive, depending on others to set the tone. Thus, we experience ourselves—and are experienced by others—as ever-changing, not in conscious control of our moods or behavior.

The positive potential is that conscious use of this reflective capacity can help us light others' way for them, just as moonlight brightens a dark night. When we reflect what another is going through, it becomes clearer.

They see it from outside, as in a mirror, so it is easier to gain a new perspective. By feeling with you, we help you know exactly what it is that you do feel. We Cancers unconsciously shape ourselves to those around us. We present healing or teaching in a form which fits the other's frame of reference.

Cancerians are seen as moody and unpredictable because of our cyclical nature. Like the Moon that rules us, Cancerians go through constant changes. Yet, upon observation, our moods have phases, just as there are phases to the Moon. We have internal rhythms that are not nearly as erratic and unpredictable as they seem. The Cancerian attuned to internal rhythms is not nearly so prone to emotional imbalance as the Cancerian who is locked into a rigid schedule. Cancerians are extremely responsive to the Moon itself, especially the full and new phases. Following its monthly orbit around the natal chart (as explained in chapter 6) will help make sense of these patterns.

One thing to know about the care and feeding of Cancers is that we really need our sleep. Maybe we just need more time immersed in the healing bath of the lunar hemisphere. Otherwise, we get crabby and, frankly, childish. (I don't know if this is true of other lunar types.) The sleep cycle—and thus the emotional balance—can be thrown off by abusing stimulants like caffeine or nicotine to face the solar world's demands for productivity. Jet lag on business trips can put us at a disadvantage, so don't fly red eye.

Extra sleep does wonders to restore us to normalcy. The need for an occasional nap isn't limited to the children—adults of our sign also benefit. A late Sunday afternoon nap can help the working Crab face the week in better form. (My Cancerian friend, the Reverend Michael Carter, informs me that adults don't take naps, they *rest*. Got it!)

We need to sleep longer when we are under stress. Was it Shakespeare who said that sleep knits up the raveled sleeve of care? Part of what makes crossing a lunar theshold so hard on Cancers is the sleep loss that often accompanies it. Think of the middle of the night feedings of the new parent, the often lengthy biorhythm shift to a new time zone after a cross-country move or trip, the drenched sheets of the menopausal, or the 4:00 A.M. sobbing of the bereaved. Crossing the theshold from dream time to the waking world is tough for some Cancers. If so, find slower and gentler ways to wake up—alarms may be too jarring.

If you're ever house hunting with a Crab, look for one with plenty of closet, basement, garage, and attic storage space. Cancers accumulate possessions and have a hard time letting go of them. They are notorious for their collections. Mementos, souvenirs, keepsakes, and family heirlooms are all dear to their hearts, as they bring the past alive again. An object that looks like junk to you has a whole history attached to it, so ask before you toss it out. If you're saddled with clearing out your dear old Cancerian auntie's home when she dies, bring along a dumpster (and a savvy antique dealer)!

Cancers want more than anything to feel secure. This may stem from an insecure childhood—possibly involving frequent moves, economic hardship, parental separations, or other traumas. In adulthood, a home and financial security may assume great importance. To maintain the status quo, we cling to past patterns no matter how unsuited they are to the present because they are *familiar*. Trying something new brings insecurity, so the Cancerian sticks by old habits and old habitats. Many become politically and socially conservative, especially at midlife and beyond.

The crab is Cancer's symbol, and the crab must shed its shell periodically as it grows or it will die. If Cancerians are not willing to shed the shell of the past from time to time, growth stops and they can't deal effectively with new demands. Cancers assume a protective shell to avoid feeling vulnerable. The shell may take the forms of acting tough, excess weight, being a home-bound recluse, or isolating themselves from outsiders. If the crab's shell hardens too much it cripples, so it is important for Cancers to retain some willingness to be open.

In various chapters, we will speak of times when that shell is normally shed—the typical lunar thresholds like puberty, the birth of the first child, and menopause. Simply because they are so lunar, Cancerians can find these transitions unsettling. The shell is off, and they are vulnerable until a new one grows. Moving, particularly far from home, is stressful. Even minor transitions may be hard for the slow-moving Crab. Cancer kids can find transitions from home to school or camp traumatic—like the first day of kindergarten or the first day back after a vacation. In transitions, Cancers may find the various tools and perspectives in this book helpful.

A Cancer in Remission: Once while waxing optimistic about the benefits of the therapy I had undergone, I called myself "a Cancer in remission." (The word for the sign Cancer and the disease *cancer* is the same in many languages.) Therapy certainly helped sort out suppressed emotions and resolve negative ties to my past and parents. Yet the way to insight and healing through therapy was far too long, inefficient, and torturous. Other experiences, particularly astrology, spiritual pursuits, and healing tools like the flower essences, contributed as much to my growth. Much of what was wrong with me was due to being a Cancer in this society—the stress of being a lunar type in a solar world.

If you are a Cancer and are troubled with the difficulties described here, what can you do to feel better? First, accept your lunar needs as real and even valuable, and be responsible for fulfilling them. Find out what makes you feel secure and do it consistently. Learn to let your emotions surface and deal with them. Keep up the family ties, or make a new family of your friends. Pay attention to your love of food by feeding yourself lovingly in healthful ways. Give yourself that periodic retreat, and be protective of yourself and your privacy when you need it. Meditate regularly, especially in groups at the full and new Moon, to integrate your lunar hemisphere. By doing these things for yourself, you will reclaim the strengths of the sign Cancer. They are the same as the strengths of women and of all lunar types detailed in earlier sections. Many chapters will address how to accomplish these ends.

Cancerians who are handling lunar issues well can be a solace to all of us who are buffeted by the solar winds. They make you feel right at home when you visit, and they create a family feeling, even when you've just met them. They keep the home fires burning by feeding you good and healthy foods and by honoring the more pleasant traditions. Their loony sense of humor can make you laugh and conclude that life isn't so bad after all. They nurture, often without being asked, but they are also sensitive enough to know when it is better to leave you alone. They know just how you feel, even when you, yourself, hardly know what's troubling you. They are repositories of home remedies and wise but homespun advice. What's not to like?

From time to time, we will celebrate some lunar luminaries, men and women who are lunar types and who have contributed to our world's lunar needs in memorable ways. My first nomination, my all-time lunar heroine, is Dr. Elisabeth Kübler-Ross, the advocate for the dying. She was born at the dark of the Moon just before an eclipse, with Sun and Moon in Cancer, Sun conjunct Pluto. According to Lois Rodden's *Profiles of Women*, her birth data is July 8, 1926 at 10:45 P.M. MET, Zurich, Switzerland. (The information comes from a letter from Ross to Robert Chandler of London.)

Running a close second in lunar excellence in our time is John Bradshaw, whose seminars on the dysfunctional family have helped hundreds of thousands of people. If you think about it, what else could he be but a Cancer? The father of all Cancers! In *Homecoming*[4], Bradshaw gives the birth information of one of his "elves." That data is June 29, 1933 at 3:05 A.M. CST, in Houston, TX. When I checked with Bradshaw's office, his sister, Barbara Bradshaw, told me on the phone that the data given was John's actual birth

---

[4]John Bradshaw, *Homecoming: Reclaiming & Championing Your Inner Child* (New York: Bantam, 1990), p. 52.

date and place. She wasn't certain of the time, but assumes he got it from his birth certificate.

The Cancer Rising Wheel as a Symbolic Tool

In trying to understand Moon-related problems, such as obesity and PMS, intuition led me to draw a chart wheel with Cancer on the ascendant. (See figure 2 on page 28.) That put Leo on the 2nd house, Virgo on the 3rd and so on around the zodiac. The areas described by the twelve houses are shown on the inside of the wheel. This is a symbolic chart rather than an actual one.

For instance, not all overweight people are born with Cancer rising, and not all Cancer rising people have food problems. Yet, the psychology of eating disorders is described by this wheel. That is, Leo on the 2nd house should show the values involved, Virgo on the 3rd should match the thinking processes, Libra on the 4th should describe the role of the family, and so on. In chapter 12, you will see that the Cancer rising wheel describes food addictions amazingly well. For instance, Aries on the 10th house shows that many overweight people eat out of anger toward authority figures or about their status in the world. The structure of the zodiac contains profound keys for understanding life and human behavior.

The wheel makes it possible to explore many lunar dysfunctions. It explains such diverse phenomena as PMS, why the macho man needs to love 'em and leave 'em, and why obese people ignore the health hazards they are courting. Relevant chapters will discuss the wheel and its applications in detail. Many uses of the wheel relate to the stresses of crossing lunar thesholds like childbirth and menopause. It may also be applied to thresholds that are not covered in this book, such as moving out on your own for the first time or mourning your mother.

Many astrologers, Isabel Hickey in particular, have pointed out that the characteristics of any sign show up most clearly when that sign is rising. The Cancer rising wheel correlates with traits we covered in defining the sign Cancer. For example, Libra's house placement shows what you're really married to. With Libra on the 4th house, the Cancerian's strongest ties are often with the 4th house concerns of home, past, and mother. The house where Scorpio is found indicates where you are most possessive, as well as what matters you consider life and death. With Scorpio ruling the house of children—the 5th house—Cancerians are often possessively attached to their offspring. We won't follow the whole sequence, since we'll do that in

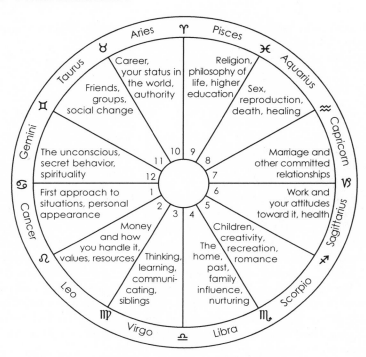

Figure 2. The Cancer Rising Wheel. The inner circle lists the basic house meanings. The outer circle shows the signs that symbolically apply to the twelve houses when the sign Cancer is on the first.

several chapters. The student will find new insights into the sign Cancer by going through the complete wheel as an exercise. (Those who have Cancer rising in the birth chart will get a bonus, for each tour of the wheel is also a tour of their own horoscope.)

If this device were simply descriptive and not prescriptive, that would be depressing. Awareness is only useful if it points to action. My approach to astrology is a homeopathic one. Among other things, this means that the problem always contains the seeds of the solution. Each sign has several related ways of expressing the same basic urge, both constructive and destructive. At its most destructive, Libra on the 4th house is married to the past and unable to cope with the present. One constructive use of Libra on the 4th would be to balance the scale by making amends to people you've harmed. This frees you of guilt that binds you to the past. Healing comes from uplifting a sign's energies to a healthier expression. Whenever the wheel is used, we will consider how each sign/house combination can be expressed well, drawing on strengths rather than weaknesses. The wheel is one of our more useful tools in learning how to be a lunar type in a solar world. It can teach us how to nurture and cherish ourselves.

The Greatest Crab of Them All—The United States

First, we have to choose a chart for the United States, since books, articles, and astrology conferences by the score have debated one version or another. There is even debate as to the birth date, itself. I've been amused to notice that a number of astrologers who laboriously rectified the U.S. chart somehow came up with their own ascendants. A Scorpio rising person I knew rectified it to Scorpio; Rudhyar, who had Sagittarius rising, gave it Sagittarius rising; and there are other examples.

The traditional U.S. chart makes a great deal of sense. When Uranus, the planet of revolution, is placed on the Gemini ascendant, that puts four planets in the 2nd house (money), and we are one of the richest nations in the world. What many astrologers experience as strongly Sagittarian traits can be explained by the Sun-Jupiter conjunction, Jupiter being the ruler of Sagittarius. The time must have been recorded because many of our founding fathers were involved in occult disciplines. They certainly would have noted the time of something as earth-shaking as the decision to become an independent nation.

The late Charles Emerson felt the traditional chart was the true one, perhaps the time of a late-night vote to secede, even though the actual document may not have been signed until the next day. (See chart 1 on page 30.) He rectified the traditional chart and found it essentially correct, the time being just a few minutes off. (No, he didn't have Gemini Rising, nor do I!) His work was impressive. Many aspects worked out exactly to the minute, by transit or progression. For example, the Civil War broke out when progressed Mars, the planet of aggression, made an exact opposition to the Midheaven.

We have the Sun and three other planets in Cancer and the Moon on the Midheaven, which makes our country extremely lunar. As Charles pointed out, we call it the Motherland and speak of patriotism as Motherhood and Apple Pie. With a chart like this, we are prone to being a rather conservative, family-centered people. To have four personal planets in that sign means that all lunar concerns—home, family, mother, security, feeding,

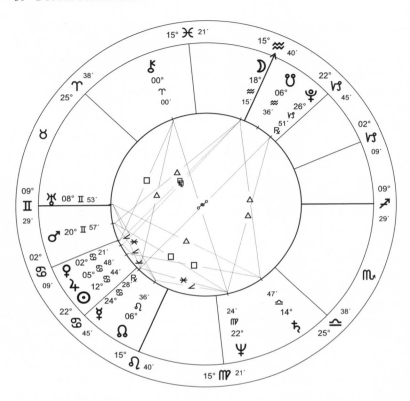

Chart 1. The horoscope of the United States. The traditional chart is calculated for July 4, 1776 at 2:13:32 A.M. in Philadelphia. This version was rectified by A. Charles Emerson to 2:21:05 A.M., based on information gleaned from solar arc directions, planetary pictures (in the Uranian system) and eclipses for all major events in U. S. History. Mr. Emerson's rectification changed the U.S. ascendant from 7 Gemini 14 to 9 Gemini 29. Placidus houses are used here. (Chart courtesy of A. Charles Emerson.)

and emotions—are crucial to our well-being. They cannot be neglected or altered without throwing us badly off-base. Yet, as we shall see in the next chapter, transits to our Cancer planets in this century have symbolized profound changes in these areas.

The four planets the U.S. has in Cancer are: 1) *The Sun*—the core character, the center of being; 2) *Jupiter*—the desire for growth and expansion, the belief system; 3) *Mercury*—the mode and focus of thought; and 4) *Venus*—the criteria for female attractiveness, the mode of relating, and conditions to be met for love. For women to be considered good Americans, they would have to play the traditional roles of wife and mother. With Venus—an indicator of our feminine ideal—in Cancer, it is no wonder U.S. women have such strong ties to their mothers and struggle to become separate individuals.

The Moon is important in any chart, due to its crucial functions. In the chart of a Cancerian, it is doubly important. It shows how the native goes about expressing and meeting the lunar needs so crucial to a Cancer's peace of mind. The fact that there are four Cancer planets in our national chart further emphasizes the Moon. The U.S. Moon is in the sign Aquarius, a very difficult Moon sign for a Cancer. We'll see manifestations of the tensions between these two signs as we consider various issues.

Since the Moon rules women, the U.S. Moon in Aquarius shows attitudes toward women and the role of women in our society. With that U.S. Moon in Aquarius, we've always had free-thinking, progressive women among us, from Susan B. Anthony and Margaret Sanger all the way down to Hillary Clinton. Despite oppressive conditions and intimidation, our women kept pushing until they won the rights to education, the vote, reproductive freedom, and equal opportunity employment.

For a nation with four planets in Cancer to have an Aquarian Moon produces many contradictions. The Cancer planets suggest a nation that is heavily emotional, while the Aquarian Moon wants to cut off feelings by intellectualizing. The aspect between Cancer and Aquarius is a quincunx, a 150 degree angle that produces strange juxtapositions. The U.S. is a country where Green Peace demonstrators shackle themselves to nuclear reactors while Right-to-Life demonstrators gun down abortion doctors, and both get equal time on the Oprah Winfrey show.

The Aquarius/Cancer duo partially explains why it is so difficult for Americans to be lunar types in a solar world. Aquarius is idealistic, but sometimes deals more in rhetoric than reality. Thus, there is often a split between our high-minded ideals and what we do. Aquarius is capable of a kind of doublethink where a nation based on liberty and justice for all almost dissolved rather than free its slaves—and took 144 years to give women the vote! Aquarius is elitist. It is an elitist approach that maintains we are all equal, but in practice makes some so much more equal than others that we need Equal Opportunity laws. We pride ourselves on being the defenders of freedom and democracy throughout the world, and yet the Republicans are usually in the majority.

What do you get when you cross an Aquarian with a Cancer? You get a computer that only runs when it's in the mood. That's not a joke, it's a metaphor for the contradictions in our national character. Naturally, the combination doesn't cause any of the problems we are experiencing, it only describes national traits that make it hard to deal with lunar matters like dependency and emotions. What positive result might you get by crossing an Aquarian with a Cancer? You could get a space ship captain who is also a fine Shakespearian actor. That would be Patrick Stewart of "Star Trek—The Next Generation," born 7/13/49 with a Cancer Sun and an Aquarius Moon.

Another Cancer/Aquarius combination was Mary Baker Eddy, the founder of Christian Science, and arguably of the entire metaphysical movement, where the mind is applied to human woes. According to Lois Rodden's *Profiles of Women*, she was born July 16, 1821, at 5:38 P.M. LMT, in Bow, NH. (Rodden says the data comes from the Church of Light files from Keifer; Craswell writes 5:30 Local Time.) This gives her a Cancer Sun and Aquarian Moon.

Could we dish Aquarians for a moment? It only seems fair, considering how often they look down their uppity noses at Cancers. A few little slams from my old astrological standup routine, that's all. How many Aquarians does it take to change a light bulb? It takes eleven: nine to get onto the Internet to research state of the art methods, one to fax for a replacement, and one to execute the maneuver. (An Aquarius is just a Leo with brains.) What's the meanest thing you can say to an Aquarian? You Aquarians are all alike.

Some Cancers and other lunar types might find solace in moving to the more lunar areas of our land. Table 2 (page 33) lists some cities and states you might consider, based on Carolyn Dodson's *Horoscopes of the U.S. States and Cities.*[5] However, never make a major move without consulting your Astro*Carto*Graphy map and transits, as explained in chapter 15. It would also be prudent to compare your chart with the chart of the city or state involved, and to read about the city in *Places Rated Almanac.* Scanning Dodson's book, it was striking to see how few of our cities or states are Cancerian, as opposed to the numbers with Aquarian Suns, Moons, or both. Still, cities are inherently more Uranian than lunar. The other interesting finding was how many were founded the day of a new Moon—exactly when astrological wisdom says to start something new. It makes you wonder how many of their founders had studied astrology!

[5]Carolyn R. Dodson, *Horoscopes of the U.S. States and Cities* (San Diego: ACS Publishing, 1975).

TABLE 2. CHEAT SHEET OF PLACES FOR LUNAR TYPES TO LIVE.
(AND FOR URANIANS TO AVOID!)

CANCERIAN STATES

Idaho, New Hampshire, Virginia, and Wyoming have Sun in Cancer. Arkansas has Moon in Cancer.

U.S. CITIES WITH SUN IN CANCER

(The starred cities had both Sun and Moon in Cancer.)

Stockton, CA	Santa Fe, NM
Orlando, FL	Niagara Falls, NY
Gary, IN	Oklahoma City, OK*
Baton Rouge, LA	Norman, OK
Portland, ME	Watertown, SD
Muskegon, MI*	Richmond, VA
Greenville, MS	Casper, WY
Concord, NH	Sheridan, WY

U.S. CITIES WITH MOON IN CANCER:

Montgomery, AL	Portsmouth, NH
Fayetteville, AR	Albuquerque, NM
Newark, DE	Columbus, OH
Chicago, IL	Medford, OR
Detroit, MI	Nashville, TN
St. Joseph, MO	Houston, TX
Sparks, NV	San Angelo, TX
Manchester, NH	La Crosse, WI

CANCER/AQUARIUS COMBINATIONS

Two wild and woolly places with Sun in Aquarius and Moon in Cancer are the state of Oregon and the city of San Francisco. (This is according to the chart most commonly used by S.F. astrologers, dated 1/30/1847, rather than the one in Dodson's book.) They share some of the contradictions and tensions shown in the U.S. chart.

What about the rest of the world? The United Kingdom, with Moon in Cancer, is also very lunar. Other countries with Moon in Cancer are France (oo la la, the food!), Mexico, Monaco, Nepal, and Tunisia, according to Moon Moore's invaluable classic, *The Book of World Horoscopes*.[6] Cancer Sun countries include Afghanistan, Algeria, the Bahamas, Iraq, the Philippines, Somalia, Thailand, Viet Nam, and Zaire. These have not been among the most serene of places in recent times, and the transits we will be talking about in the next chapter will tell you why.

Why Are They So Crabby?

We've begun to see why Cancerians and women are having a hard time. Both groups are often insecure and emotionally unsettled, due to the strain of dealing with lunar needs and the lunar hemisphere in a world that does not provide support. The security blanket that once comforted them is now a tattered rag, and they must let go of it. Some who are experiencing greater stress, deprivation, or losses, wind up with emotional difficulties, parenting problems, or eating disorders. For clues to sources of the stress, read the next chapter.

[6]Moon Moore, *The Book of World Horoscopes* (Birmingham, MI: Seek-It Publications, 1980).

CHAPTER 3

SINCE EARTHLINGS LANDED ON THE MOON, THE NEIGHBORHOOD JUST ISN'T THE SAME

History is not generally a subject that captures my attention. However, when I noticed that between 1902 and 1956 the outer planets (Uranus, Neptune, and Pluto) had all moved through the sign Cancer, I became curious about how that combination affected Moon-ruled concerns. This era was unique. Uranus moves through the sign Cancer once every 84 years. Neptune only moves through Cancer once in 164 years and Pluto's orbit takes 248 years. The last time both Pluto and Neptune were in Cancer must have been eons ago. They are only in the same sign once in 493 years, and there are twelve signs in a cycle.

Curious, I delved into census reports, statistics, and history texts. To my excitement, they showed that in this century the lunar areas of life have changed dramatically. Basic patterns such as women's roles, home, family, and even food habits altered during these heavy transits. These changes are a striking demonstration of the validity of astrology. They also clarify why it has become so hard to be a lunar type in a solar world.

The Outer Planet Transits to the Sign Cancer

Let's examine the transits through Cancer to see what happened. First, however, it is important to counteract the impression that we are being besieged by big bad planetary forces out in space. The planets are not causing the problems we are having; they only reflect the stage our culture is going through. If you look in the mirror and see that you've gained weight, do you blame the mirror? It is not responsible for your weight gain, any more than the planets are responsible for the rising crime rate or the epidemic of teenage pregnancies. The planets' movements correlate with—but do not create—the broad social changes we are about to explore.

The importance of these trends may become clearer if we examine the meanings of Uranus, Neptune, and Pluto to see how their energies mix with the sign Cancer. Because these planets move so slowly, they are said to be *generational*. That is, during the years one of them is transiting a particular sign, a whole generation is born. Important characteristics of that age group are described by the outer planet and its sign. Psychoanalysis aside, we are affected by more than our parents. We are affected by social conditions, major world events, and the climate of the time—the background music we heard as we grew up. Over the years, I have come to appreciate how profound these placements are and how different from one another astrological generations can be. For instance, World War I and the Great Depression deeply affected Pluto in Cancer natives. As a result, many of them became obsessed with family and security. The Pluto in Leo peple had more leisure time and became self-obsessed.

Neptune in Cancer (1902–1916): Neptune is associated with illusion and deception, showing what your generation idealizes to almost mythical status. It shows social conditions that are dissolving because they are no longer functional. For each Neptune sign, the concerns of that sign become the fading dream, the elusive hope, the Santa Claus that never came. The thing we lost—or the thing we never really had—hooks us, so we keep seeking it for the rest of our lives. It becomes our slave master, our jailer, and our great disappointment, as nothing could live up to such inflated ideals.

For the Neptune in Cancer generation, and the generations to which they gave birth, this binding illusion was the Perfect Mother, the fantasy female typified by the phrase Motherhood and Apple Pie. Women were beginning to go out to work, and the industrial revolution was already changing family life. As a result, that group idealized the all-giving, totally loving, self-sacrificing mother. Yet, Neptune shows our illusions, so our dream Mom never really existed in the first place, and she became a nightmare. (Our most sentimental tribute, Mother's Day, was first celebrated in the U.S. on May 10, 1914, with Neptune in Cancer.) Since that era, women have slaved to live up to these ideals of motherhood, yet because the expectations are so inflated, they fail. Women who buy the dream suffer from tremendous feelings of inadequacy and guilt.

What's interesting is that Motherhood and Apple Pie are recent inventions. By that I mean the romanticized version typified by television programs—Mom, Pop, and the kids living far from relatives, Dad going out to work, and Mom at home alone with the kids. Life wasn't that way before the late 19th or early 20th century—before the transits we are discussing. The whole family, from children to grandparents, lived and worked in the home. Men, women, and children cooperated to produce food, clothing, and other necessities. Everyone shared the long, exhausting labor, and all were valued for their contribution. With several generations at hand, women helped each other through times of stress or illness. They taught each other about caring for babies, about cooking and other homemaking skills.

The idea of childhood as a separate stage of life is also recent. According to Signe Hammer, the division of masculine and feminine roles, with women submerging their identities to their husbands and children, rose out of social changes due to the industrial revolution. Only as these changes came about did femininity mean the sacrifice of selfhood and living through others.[1] (Neptune rules sacrifice and martyrdom.)

Pluto in Cancer (1914–1938): Pluto represents death, rebirth, and profound transformation. It has a strong association with power and our ambivalence about it. It can show overt oppression as well as covert, manipulative and controlling psychological warfare. It has to do with sexuality and the power struggles between the sexes. Pluto in Cancer was the most powerful and longest lasting of the processes represented by the three transits. It brought profound changes to women's roles and family life like synthetic formulas for infants, the fight for acceptance of birth control, a precipitous decline in the birth rate, and women's growing participation in the work force. With Pluto transiting Cancer, we dealt the death blow to many lunar institutions. Yet, the Myth of the Perfect Mother and Housewife, arising while Neptune was in Cancer, became a tool to control women and keep them dependent.

Neptune and Pluto have been traveling 60 degrees apart almost continuously since 1943, so it is difficult to separate the trends they represent. For instance, Neptune transits often correlate with inflation and Pluto with debt. Inflation has been continuous throughout the century, with the worth of the dollar falling slowly but inevitably. Impacting the 2nd house of the U.S. chart, the Cancer transits during the Depression and World War II laid

---

[1]Signe Hammer, *Daughters and Mothers/Mothers and Daughters* (New York: Signet, 1976), p. 70 ff.

the foundation for our crippling national debt. Debt financing, both national and personal, is part of what creates the illusion of affluence in the U.S. If everyone paid cash and if we stopped exploiting Third World countries and Earth, herself, we'd be nearly as poor as the rest of the world.

Uranus in Cancer (1948–1956): Uranus is associated with revolution, breaking down traditions and institutions, and breaking away from the past. It rules Aquarius and is connected with liberation movements, social change, and an urge for freedom. As Uranus moved through Cancer, women mobilized to change their social status. That trend was true of a transit of Uranus through Cancer in 1865–1873, which coincided with the peak of the first women's suffrage movement. The Uranus transit to Cancer from 1948–1956 represented the seeds of revolt (*The Second Sex* being published, the pill bringing liberation from childbearing, and the highest peak of divorce ever).

The "real" Women's Liberation movement took off while Uranus was in Libra (1968–1975), when women born with Uranus in Cancer were old enough to be a moving force. Uranus in Cancer showed us breaking the physiological bonds of parenthood, and Uranus in Libra showed people more free to leave relationships in which they were unhappy. The climate of the times shapes the thinking of the generation born then. The children born with Uranus in Libra absorbed the ideas we tried out so self-consciously and vehemently during the peak of Women's Liberation. As adults, they are likely to carry the process even further.

Other Transits with an Impact on the Sign Cancer

Although we've discussed periods when the outer planets were in Cancer, the actual picture was more complicated. There were also transits through the sign Libra during parts of this century, forming a stressful 90-degree angle (square) to the sign Cancer. In addition, planets have been moving through the sign Capricorn, which forms a stressful 180-degree angle (opposition) to Cancer. Table 3 shows that the sign Cancer has been under continuous pressure throughout the 20th century. As we'll see, each lunar area has undergone vast changes during this period.

Neptune, Uranus, and Pluto in Libra: The outer planet transits through Libra coincided with deep changes in relationships between men and women.

TABLE 3. A TIME-LINE OF ASTROLOGICAL TRANSITS DURING THE 20TH CENTURY.

CANCER		LIBRA		CAPRICORN	
Neptune:	1902–16				
Pluto:	1914–38				
Saturn:	1915–17*				
Saturn:	1944–46	Neptune:	1943–57		
Uranus:	1948–56	Saturn:	1951–53*		
		Uranus:	1968–75		
		Saturn:	1980–83		
		Pluto:	1971–84		
				Neptune:	1984–98
				Saturn:	1988–90*
				Uranus:	1988–95

* Note: There were other Saturn transits to these signs during this century, but these provided additional stress in the periods in question.

Those planets also squared the sign Cancer, so the changed relationships had to have a profound effect on family life, as well as our outlook on women's roles.

As discussed more fully in my book *Astrology and Spiritual Development*, the Neptune in Libra (1943–1957) years were an era when men and women struggled to reestablish their relationships after World War II. Men went off to war and returned deeply changed, while many women went to work for the first time in war industries, earned their own living and governed their own lives. After the war, there was the great Baby Boom, followed by the highest peak of divorces seen up to that time. To preserve security and the family, women hastily retreated from their wartime freedom and tried to emulate Donna Reed. This was the era of the great Hollywood romance—an antidote to the pain and disappointment about these relationship changes. The Neptune in Libra generation, who grew up with this process as background music, still watches old movies and hopes to someday find that perfect romance.

Uranus in Libra—I remember it well! Much of the original edition of this book was written under its influence. The Uranus years (1968–1975) were the peak of the most recent women's liberation movement. Those heady times brought advanced ideas about women's roles, new careers and opportunities for women, and a new freedom to be ourselves. Alas, it didn't last, didn't go as far as we hoped, and has been followed by some retrenchment and even backlash. Pluto in Libra (1971–1984) overlapped the Uranus transit and continued the alteration of relationships between the sexes. In many ways, it was the death knell of the traditional marriage, as divorce rates soared to fifty percent in many areas.

Pluto next moved through Scorpio. Power struggles between the sexes became even more intense, with sexual harassment becoming an important legal issue and with aberrations like stalking and Right-To-Life fanatics shooting abortion doctors. The Right-to-Life movement is less pro-life than it is anti-woman. If the preservation of life were the true goal and not the control of women, these same people would be demonstrating against capital punishment and animal experimentation. They would have been agitating against the Gulf War, rather than flying yellow ribbons on their car antennas. They'd be lobbying congress for money to find a cure for AIDS or a vaccine to prevent it. They'd even—although this is far-fetched—be campaigning for more day care, health, and welfare benefits for children born because of their efforts. Overpopulation will arguably prove to be the greatest world problem of our time and increasingly of the decades to come. It causes death due to starvation and contributes to deaths due to disease, overcrowding, pollution, and violent crimes. In 1994, the Right-to-Life movement brought about the collapse of the World Population Congress.

Uranus and Neptune in Capricorn: During the overlapping transits through Capricorn of Uranus (1988–1995) and Neptune (1984–1998), the world altered drastically. Major, but decaying, political and social institutions crumbled and fell. On the world level, the breakdown of the former Soviet Union into ever smaller and more belligerent factions is an example. Two expressions of how deeply the lunar areas of life have been impacted during these transits are the tragic growth of homelessness and world hunger.

Mainstream Americans breathed a sign of relief when, by 1994, the threat of a depression seemed to have receded. Like so much that Neptune touches, the recovery was illusion. We had tightened our belts and cut back. Those who were working were fewer, those without jobs more invisible. The rates of joblessness and bankruptcies rose. There was a new layer at the poverty level, not all of them uneducated. Corporations "downsized," meaning fewer jobs. In many companies, those with gray hair were offered early retirement, like it or not. Age discrimination increased even as it was denied, so it wasn't easy for those over 50 to find new jobs.

Many of those whose charts were personally affected went through breakdowns of crucial structures as well. (Important transits would be those to the Sun, Moon, Ascendant, Midheaven, or to a t-square or stellium—or to several of these positions.) Because Capricorn is a universal sign, these personal passages were often connected with what was happening on a world level. The global village is now a reality—for better or worse—and an action taken in one place now directly and rapidly impacts people living on the other side of the world.

Cancer and Capricorn are opposite signs. Opposites can share similar goals, concerns, and ways of operating. They can act to balance one another. Both Cancer and Capricorn seek security and can be traditional or even conservative. The passage of Uranus and Neptune through Capricorn was accompanied by a collective yearning to return to the safe lunar structures—especially to the family and home. Yet, those besieged structures no longer exist in their old forms, and to think we can go back is an illusion. Part of the work of this book is to help you figure out how to replace them.

During the series of transits just outlined, the pressures on the sign Cancer and the lunar areas of life have been relentless and have produced vast changes. These alterations will be discussed in greater detail in relevant chapters, but Table 4 (page 42) presents an overview. With the background of how these transits correlated with broad changes in lunar areas, we will look at more specific signposts as we go along. In many of these areas, the planet Uranus and the sign Aquarius are especially relevant.

As one example of a statistic that has great meaning in individual lives, the transits to the sign Cancer corresponded with the virtual disappearance of breast-feeding in the United States. Although it is again on the rise, especially among educated urban white women, several generations were raised on condensed milk or infant formulas. We've seen how deeply interrelated the lunar functions are on the unconscious level, so one function cannot stop abruptly without producing disturbances in others. The end of breast-feeding eliminated a certain kind of loving intimacy that gave joy to both mother and infant. It may be one reason for our culture's current alienation from our mothers.

We will be considering many statistics about lunar losses, here and in other chapters, and statistics can be boring. Lest you think these numbers are irrelevant to your life, consider their effect on our relationships. The more loved ones we lose, the more our hearts are wounded. The earlier and more central the loss, the greater the impact. Little by little, we grow afraid to become involved or unable to love others. We harden our hearts in order not to feel the pain, we lose compassion, and we fear to love again. Since men are pressured not to feel and especially not to grieve, many of them close down after a major loss and become emotionally inaccessible. Sugar and alcohol warm the physical heart, which we easily confuse with the heart center in the energy body, the part of us all those love songs are about. After a serious heart wound, many turn to sugar and alcohol for consolation and risk addiction. Translated to the mass level, what all those statistics mean is that we are a society of the heart center wounded, and it affects all our relationships, from the most casual to the most committed.

The Splits between Cancer and Aquarius

The U.S. Moon in Aquarius is significant, especially in a nation with four Cancer planets. Uranus, the ruler of Aquarius, is on the U.S. Ascendant, further emphasizing the Cancer/Aquarius tension. The changes in lunar areas are the birth pangs of the Aquarian Age. To alleviate stress, we must develop new ways of meeting lunar needs, since they cannot simply be dismissed.

The Cancer/Aquarius Split: Planets combine more readily with some signs than with others, depending on how natural it is for them to express their preoccupations in that sign. The Cancer-Aquarius quincunx in the U.S. chart represents deep conflicts within our national character. By its very nature, Aquarius is at odds with concerns dear to Cancerians—not always antagonistic, but simply beyond them. Aquarius is detached and logical, focusing on intellect rather than feelings. It rebels against authority and traditional values. It rejects the past, embraces the future, pushes for change, and perpetually seeks what is new and different. Aquarius places a high value on independence, freedom, and individualism—often at the expense of family ties or personal relationships.

Aquarians are fascinated with science and technology. They worship reason, scorning intuition in favor of facts and numbers. Cancer is subjective, bordering on anti-intellectual. The Aquarian Moon in the U.S. chart shows how dependent we as a people are on science. We try to ignore our needs, emotions, and bodily rhythms in favor of a scientific approach that only leads to further insecurity and alienation. Science has become the parent we expect to provide all the answers, the ultimate authority which we obey unquestioningly. A Moon keyword is *gratification*, and an Aquarian one is *instant*. We are losing our ability to wait, insisting on instant gratification. We expect science and industry to provide us with instant answers to our problems, and we jump at these quick fixes without taking time to test them thoroughly. As a result, we have fast foods, fast cars, and fast friends, but no hard and fast rules.

TABLE 4. WAYS OUTER PLANET TRANSITS AFFECT LUNAR CONCERNS.

WOMEN'S ROLES: In 1890, fewer than one in five women worked outside the home, but by 1970 it was 41%.

THE HOME: We now move thirteen times in a lifetime, or once in five years. If we aren't moving, family members and friends are doing it, so we suffer frequent losses of loved ones.

THE BREAST: Breast-feeding was practically universal in the first part of the century, but by 1946 only two-thirds of women breast-fed, and by 1970, fewer than one in ten did so.

CHILDBIRTH: The birth rate has declined by almost half since 1900. Midwifery all but disappeared and now 95% of those delivering babies are men.

THE MENSTRUAL CYCLE: Even the average age of the first menstrual period has changed—in 1900 it was 14, and now it is 12-1/2.

THE STOMACH: The ulcer rate among women has skyrocketed in the past thirty years. It used to be twenty men for every woman who had ulcers, but now it's only a 2:1 ratio, apparently related to the entry of women into the work force.

FOOD: More than half of all Americans now eat over half their meals away from home. Our national diet has changed for the worse and we are getting fatter.

Uranian traits are not bad in themselves. Aquarians can be visionary and humanitarian, with a goal of freedom and equality for all. We need some detachment to avoid being run by emotion. Certainly there is a place for logic; certainly there are things about our social structure that need changing; certainly many scientific discoveries have been wonderful; and certainly it is counterproductive to be mired in the past. We cannot grow if we remain codependantly attached to our parents. However, when we carry these traits to extremes and attempt to force all lunar needs into a rigid Aquarian mold, we ask for trouble. Aquarians can reach a high degree of consciousness, however, and in this difficult transitional era we have to consciously identify and meet our lunar needs. We must nurture ourselves, find out what we are feeling, do what we need to feel secure, and tap into our lunar hemisphere in order to be whole and integrated.

The Boob Tube: Uranus symbolizes mass media, and the media have transformed modern life, television in particular. Both radio and television began during the outer planet transits to Cancer. (The first U.S. transcontinental TV broadcast occurred while Uranus was in Cancer.) Today 96 percent of U.S. homes own at least one television set. When we call it the boob tube, we don't just mean idiot box, for TV acts as an electronic nursemaid for our kids—for all of us. Many of us are TV junkies and would go into withdrawal if it were taken away. Especially for isolated people—single adults, women at home alone during the day, the elderly—TV replaces family, friends, groups, and activities. Supper used to be a time when the family gathered and talked. Now many of us eat on trays in front of the set, shushing our children when they want to talk to us. Then we wonder why they don't stay home, why they'd rather run with their friends.

Uranus rules consciousness, and television is shaping our consciousness. Programs and commercials affect our values, morals, and beliefs, where once these were instilled by our families. Uranians—people with a strong natal Uranus—can be addicted to excitement. Television provides continuous excitement, adventure, and glamor. Yet the picture of life we get from TV is unrealistic, full of adventure and happy endings. Young people expect that kind of excitement and chase glamour or find stimulation in drugs. Constant exposure to media stars also creates unrealistic expectations of ourselves and others. We make comparisons, and our self-esteem suffers when we are not as beautiful or talented as the stars.

Uranus detaches from feelings. Many of us watch TV hour after hour, in order not to feel anything or deal with our problems. Family conflict gets suppressed by having the box on constantly. Due to the lack of communication, these feelings build up to sudden explosions in a typical Uranian way. At its worst, Uranus also rules violence, and TV teaches us to deal with emotions and conflict through explosions of violence. The very popular video games, which a large percentage of boys play for hours each day, are also usually violent. Parents have begun pressuring the television industry to decrease the violent content. Programs now advise parental discretion for certain kinds of material.

On the positive side, TV also brings educational and cultural exposure we would never find locally. Even talk shows, for all their sensationalism, make us aware of individual and family problems and some solutions. By front line coverage of world events and trends, TV contributes to the sense of a global village. There are plenty of excellent programs, and the point is to make informed choices. Be alert to the implied values and speak out about the ones you don't accept.

The Aquarian Moon and U.S. Women: We spoke in the last chapter about some of the splits in consciousness between the U.S.'s four planets in Cancer and our Aquarian Moon. The splits between what we say about women, and what we actually do, create some strains of modern living. Women are brought up to believe that motherhood is woman's highest purpose, but when they devote themselves to mothering, they are, "just a housewife." When women work outside the home, as they increasingly must, they are still expected to remain the perfect wife, homemaker, and mother. Many women are raised to be dependent and submissive, then thrust into situations such as divorce and single parenthood where they must function independently. There is an enormous split between these high expectations and the lack of support to enable women to fulfill them. The support systems we once enjoyed have been eroded during the heavy transits. One remedy is to create our own support systems independent of any our society is prepared to provide.

One related statistic is that women are twice as likely as men to suffer from high blood pressure. Uranus rules the circulatory system. Metaphysically, high blood pressure and other circulatory problems are associated with a feeling of having your freedom constricted. Hypertension is typical of the powerless in society—black people also have a high incidence of this disease. We shall see, as we go along, that societal pressures are doing other physical and emotional damage. For instance, women make up two-thirds of those in outpatient psychiatric treatment.

Our supposed equality notwithstanding, women have played an important role in the economy of the United States with their free or cheap labor. (Those Cancer planets fall into the 2nd house of the U.S. chart.) Women make up over 40 percent of the work force, yet earn 20 percent less than men in the same positions. We earn only $.59 for every $1 earned by a man.[2] Women are also commercially exploited with a barrage of advertising that plays on our emotions, to get us to look and smell better than nature made us. Cosmetics are a billion dollar industry, and women buy 90 percent of weight reduction products.

Aquarius and Family Disruption: The Aquarian Age so far is marked by broken homes, single parents, and other family disruptions. The slow-moving transits through Cancer and Libra correlated with a stunning increase in divorces. It was nearly unheard of at the beginning of the century and is now

---

[2]Statistics released by the President's Council of Economic Advisers in 1973, quoted in *Woman's Almanac* (New York: Lippincott, 1976), p. 535.

up to 50 percent in many parts of the U.S. These are not just young married. The divorce rate among couples married more than twenty years has increased 40 percent in the last decade.

Another disruption is our increasing geographic mobility, which separates us from home town, parents, relatives, and friends. We have become a nation of nomads—we used to be born, live, and die in our home town; now we move thirteen times in a lifetime, or once every five years. Each major move requires a great adjustment, creating emotional strain and the loss of important relationships. In a new environment, we feel isolated and lack the help that extended families once provided. The burden of this isolation falls heavily on the woman. She is more than ever responsible for the children without the support of grandparents, aunts, sisters, and other family members.

The Moon in the U.S. Chart is in the 10th house, showing that many women wind up being in charge of families by default—husbands gone to work, gone to war, or just plain gone. The life of the divorced woman is not an easy one, as she is most often responsible for the care and support of the children. In the first year after a divorce, a woman's standard of living drops by 73 percent, while a man's improves by 42 percent.[3] Only 14 percent of divorcees are awarded alimony and only half of that group collect it regularly. The number of female heads of households rose by 40 percent between 1980 and 1990, and one in three had incomes below the poverty level.[4] Thus many divorced mothers have to choose between going on welfare and going to work, and many have no training or recent work experience. Women's wages are far lower than men's, and yet a third of the women who work are the sole support of their family.

There are other reasons for the growing number of households headed by women. As we will see elsewhere, the death rate at all ages is far higher for men than women. Throughout this century, wars have done their share toward unbalancing the male-female ratio. Furthermore, as sexual mores change and pregnancy is no longer a binding cause for marriage, the rate of illegitimate births is rising drastically.

Especially when living far from family, the strain on women who are single parents is enormous. They have to work as well as take sole responsibility for raising children. The highest rate of suicide for women is during the period of separation from their husbands. Among widows, five are suc-

---

[3] *Information Please Almanac, Atlas, and Yearbook*, 48th edition (Boston & New York: Houghton Mifflin, 1995), p. 433.
[4] Ibid., p. 435.

cessful at suicide for every one who tries and fails. (For most people the number of successful suicide attempts is many times lower than failures.) Female heads of households have a far higher rate of psychiatric admissions than their male counterparts. Divorced and separated women are far more likely to drink heavily alone. The loss of a spouse is hard on both men and women. The admission rate to psychiatric outpatient services is five times higher for the separated or divorced than for married people.

The loss of a spouse is a major emotional crisis. Since these losses are no longer rare, we need to develop support systems. Women need special nurturing in this kind of crisis. Uranus rules divorce, but it also rules independence, freedom, and greater degrees of consciousness. Particularly for a woman who has never been on her own, a divorce can be shattering. Yet, it is often a turning point where she becomes her own person, able to think for herself. Today's divorcees are also developing new life styles and new forms of loosely-knit families with friends, which enhances the individuality and freedom of all.

Uranus and the Disease of Non-Attachment: The Moon rules mothering, security, and our sense of basic trust. During the Uranus transits to Cancer, Libra, and Capricorn, more and more children have suffered disruptions to family continuity that lead them to be insecure and mistrustful of adults. Not only is divorce becoming a way of life, but also more and more mothers have to work while their children are young. Child care arrangements can be erratic, with constantly changing babysitters and day care centers. More and more homes are headed by working women who have to do double duty—mother and father, parent and employee—and who don't have much energy left over to fill their children's needs, much less their own!

Selma Fraiberg, an expert in child development, believes disruptions like these can lead to "diseases of non-attachment."

> "The distinguishing characteristic is the incapacity of the person to form human bonds. There is an almost imperceptible feeling of intervening space, of remoteness, of no connection. . . . The other striking characteristic is their impoverished emotional range. There is no joy, no grief, no guilt, no remorse, and no humor.[5]

She finds these people have a high potential for mental illness, violence, crime, and illegitimate children who turn out the same way.

---

[5]Selma Fraiberg, *Every Child's Birthright* (New York: Basic Books, 1977), p. 79.

Fraiberg says that emotional impoverishment creates an appetite for powerful sensation. She equates the disease with explosions of violence or cold-blooded brutality, done simply to feel alive. The deadness creates an intolerable tension in which the person experiences terror of non-being. Drugs and violence jolt the deadness. Even when the results are not so drastic as this, Fraiberg considers the person afflicted with this disease a hollow man. He drifts through life, forming no close or long-lasting relationships, lacking the capacity for self-awareness, and indifferent to society.

While what she describes is an extreme, increasing numbers of children and youth suffer family disruption and can have the potential for milder forms of the disease of non-attachment. Sometimes life circumstances make family disruptions unavoidable. Thus, if you are divorced or separated, it is important to think in terms of prevention. Conscious effort to meet the emotional needs of all involved can lessen the blow. Invest energy to maintain family ties, to keep both parents involved when there is divorce, and to develop surrogate families when blood ties must be broken. Don't neglect the non-custodial grandparents, no matter how bitter the separation, for they have much love to give the children and can be part of your support system.

Uranus and Youth: A growing number of teens are suffering from family disruptions. Not only is divorce common, but the Census Bureau reports that the average 20-year old will have moved more than three times with his family. Ties to relatives and peers are frequently broken when we move or they do.

Uranus rules adolescence and groups, and young people of many nations are increasingly reacting to family and societal disruption by running with their peers. The more kids are thrown back on the group without strong family influence, the more social pressure can dictate their behavior. Today's alienated teens face powerful group pressures to drink, smoke, use drugs, and have sex. There is a corresponding increase in teenage alcoholism, drug addiction, and pregnancies.

Teenage crime and violence is also skyrocketing—guns in schools are an increasing worry. The success of gangs and cults is largely due to young people's need for a family and a sense of belonging. Both hold out the promise of a family atmosphere and a strong father figure. Gang members call each other *home boy* or *homie* to evoke feelings of loyalty and belonging. Cults achieve brainwashing by such Uranian tactics as breaking ties with the past and family and depriving the convert of food.

If the condition of today's youth alarms us, it helps to take the long view. Uranus rules both adolescence and individuation, so adolescence is a developmental stage when the person becomes a separate individual, not so dependent on family. We are more rebellious as teens than as adults. The hippies and radicals of the 60s are now the Establishment they scorned, yet with greater social awareness than past generations. Today's teen may grow up to become a special kind of adult—more free-thinking and independent than any preceding generation. Given the social conditions that are developing, the capacity for existing without strong family ties may be crucial in the future. Today's teens think differently than we do, because they are not so rooted in the past and because they are more group-oriented. With these qualities, they may be better able than we are to develop solutions to problems they are sure to face in the 21st century.

Uranus and the Older Population: Cancer also rules old age. The transits by Uranus reflect both the economic decline of our older population and the increased prejudice against the aging in our youth-oriented culture. Older people no longer enjoy the respect they once had. They are patronized, isolated, and alienated. Together with those heavy transits, conditions of life for older Americans have changed vastly. In 1900, the life expectancy was only 47, where now it is 71. The elderly may spend many of those added years in poor health, living on a fixed income in an era of double-digit inflation. Given our national mobility, they no longer have family to surround and support them. Instead they are often segregated into retirement communities or group living situations.

Uranus, the Age of Aquarius, and Individual Freedom

It is said that we are in a post-feminist era. The phrase smacks of doublespeak, of the type of euphemism that glosses over the loss of our dreams. It is a sociological term related to mass change and directs our attention away from our own individual stresses and deprivations. We are also possibly in a post-Civil Rights era, and, with anti-gay propositions on the ballots in several states, we are definitely in a post-Gay Rights phase. Jupiter and Sagittarius have to do with the law, while Pluto has to do with power. With Pluto's ingress into Sagittarius in 1995–1996, it is possible that many of the hard-won rights of the 1960s will be lost and then some, unless we remain awake, aware, and active. I do not buy this transit as the dawn of an enlightened and kindly new era of legal reform. I hope to be proven wrong.

What comfort can we draw in 1995, as Uranus also changes signs and moves into Aquarius for the first time in 84 years, and as we, arguably, move

into the Aquarian age? Uranus signifies liberty and equality and rules freedom-loving Aquarius. The glyph for the sign Aquarius is ♒. If Aquarius
rules equality, we might wonder why the glyph isn't =. This led me to the
conclusion that the glyph looks like waves. The progressive liberation of victims of inequality seems to happen in waves, with high tides of active protest
followed by lower tides.

This is possibly the only safe route to liberation. Were it to happen
overnight, with no time to adjust, the stress would be unbearable. We do
not readily accept change, and we are already pushed to our limit by rapid
alterations in the lunar areas and the status of women. A greater degree of
freedom and independence means we must function at a higher level than
when we were dependent. If the tide is lower just now, it gives us time to adjust to the freedom already won.

Uranus also rules consciousness, and that is another reason for the low
tide periods. Our consciousness needs time to rise to a new level before we
can move forward. Metaphysics teaches that our thought patterns shape our
reality, determining what experiences we allow into our lives. If we cannot
conceive of more equality for women and other groups, if our gut level conviction is that we are unequal, then equality cannot happen.

The purpose of demonstrations like those of the Suffragettes, Civil
Rights, or Women's Liberationists is to demonstrate a new idea. The more
our culture as a whole is unable to conceive of an idea, the more vigorous
the demonstration must be. (The higher the wave rides on the ocean, the
deeper the underlying disturbance.) The vigorous protests of the 1960s and
1970s were to bring home a new concept of women's potential and the po-
tentials of minorities. After the bigger waves break on the shore, the idea settles in with smaller and smaller waves—it is no longer so shocking, because
we are assimilating the idea.

If you once have a idea, even if you don't act on it immediately, you never
think the same way again, because your consciousness has changed. Maybe we
can't all move toward equality just now, but the EXAMPLE is there for those
who can do it, and the IDEA is there for others to absorb and act on during
later waves. Ideas have impact, like waves breaking on the shore, and if people
hear the ideas of equality long enough, the tide will come back in.

The truth is, we have come a long way in this century. At the beginning
of the century, it was almost inconceivable for a woman to show her ankle,
much less run a business of her own. This century has produced a whole new
understanding of women and their capabilities. Many women and men are
now living life styles that would have been inconceivable fifteen years ago.
In the longer view, universal education of women began only moments ago,

the vote only an eye blink away. Until 1879, it wasn't illegal for a man to beat his wife to death in this country. We are also leaders in the world in liberation—women in the Mideast are still forced to have their clitorises removed so they won't stray from their husbands. In India, female infants are generally considered a burden, and large numbers are abandoned, aborted, or killed. Maybe we aren't where we should be, but we certainly aren't where we were, and we're still moving forward. Our consciousness IS rising, although slowly. The Aquarian Age holds promise that we will continue to move forward, although we experience growing pains in this transitional era.

A time like ours only makes sense when you take the long view. To understand why we are going through a time of intense trauma and loss, let's take a deeper look at Uranus and Aquarius. As Donald Bradley observed, Uranus is akin to the birth process, and its glyph (⛢) in stylized form shows the infant passing through the birth canal. Birth is a violent process in which the individual is forcibly expelled from a safe, but confining, environment to one that is insecure and unknown, but one that offers greater freedom.

Throughout life, particularly under Uranus transits, we go through many births, where we leave security and safety behind and become more separate individuals. Psychologist Erich Fromm called this process individuation. When we go to school, we leave the family womb for a few hours a day. When we go out on our own, we leave that womb behind for good. Uranus rules divorce, and the divorced woman may be completely on her own for the first time. For many divorcees, after they make the adjustment, it is the beginning of a true sense of self. Even geographic mobility has its positive side. Travel broadens us, and more individual development is possible when we separate from our roots than if we were all stuck back home on the farm.

We experience insecurity at each of these separations. Yet, once we master the new situation, we function more independently than ever. Birth is a trauma; yet, if the baby remains too long in the womb, it will die. If we stay too long in a secure but stagnant environment, we stop growing. The thing that once nurtured us we wind up throwing away—the umbilical cord is useless ten minutes after birth.

You Can't Go Home Again

Maybe you haven't been much affected by the changes we've been discussing and so you feel content in the lunar areas of life. Or, maybe by hard work and diligent attention you've found your own ways of keeping the lunar hemisphere balanced. Maybe you have a good marriage and a family that is healthy and happy. Maybe you are close to your parents and brothers and sisters, not only emotionally but geographically. Maybe you feel fulfilled as a woman or man and in your work. If so, consider yourself blessed, for you live in a kinder, gentler, world. Never take your bounty for granted.

The difficulties are more pronounced in overcrowded, high-pressure urban areas than in slow, sleepy small towns. They are more obvious among the poor than the affluent, more pronounced with women than with men. People with painful lunar dysfunctions like psychiatric problems, obesity, or severe PMS may be the canaries in our collective mineshaft. Their cries for help may alert all of us that something is wrong down there in the dark.

From the statistics presented here and in coming chapters, it becomes obvious that many old lunar institutions are on the way out. Much as we might feel nostalgic and want to hold the changes back, we can't recreate the old ways. The goal is to live as comfortably as we can through this transitional era, so we don't break down and become statistics ourselves.

We do have needs—we aren't machines you can plug in and expect to keep on performing regardless. If anything, our lunar needs are greater in such anxious and uncertain times. Given the abrasiveness of urban life, we may have an even greater need to be sheltered and nourished. Our needs are human needs and there is nothing wrong with them. We have to devise ways to nurture ourselves and learn the skills we need for greater independence.

Often dependency is only a function of consciousness. We are programmed to believe we can't do certain things and that we need others to do them for us. Most women could readily learn to change a lock, fix a leaky faucet, or manage a stock portfolio. Most men could learn to change a diaper, sort the laundry, or cook a pleasant meal. Our consciousness says we can't do them, and, thus, entraps us in dependent relationships. Most of the time, we don't really need others to do things for us. We need people for emotional support and for learning skills we don't have yet. As our consciousness changes, we will be less dependent and will relate more equally. In order to be equal, we must first be separate, and that is what this often anguishing period of history is about.

The pressure of all these social changes, I believe, will ultimately create an independent new breed. It is useful to speculate on the ultimate result of a currently difficult situation. Because many women live far from family and spend many years without a man to rely on, they will come to a far higher level of functioning than if society stayed the same. Simply because there is no longer anyone to tell us what to do, we will learn to think for ourselves and to do what is best for us, and we will be freer than any women in history. Men, freed from our dependency and forced to meet their own lunar needs, will also have the opportunity to come to terms with their lunar side. To the extent that we integrate solar and lunar functions, we can evolve into a higher order of being.

CHAPTER 4

MOON MADNESS AND MOOD SWINGS

Each topic in this book is so interconnected with emotions that a separate discussion of the subject hardly seemed necessary. Here, however, we will see how the Moon as a heavenly body affects our emotions and how the transiting Moon affects the public. We will discover why women statistically have come to have more psychiatric problems than men. Finally, we will look at your own Moon sign and house to see what we can learn about you as an emotional being.

The Moon and Public Mood Swings

You've probably noticed that there are times when all the people around you seem to be in a certain mood—maybe outgoing and jovial. A few hours later, the mood shifts, and people on the street seem to bristle. The Moon rules the public, so the current Moon sign and aspects reflect the emotional overtones of the masses at the moment. Tracking the transiting Moon signs (as we'll learn to do in chapter 6) is one way of making sense of the mood swings of the public. If the world were more aware of how deeply the Moon affects us, the media would carry an emotional weather forecast based on the Moon's daily course. The Moon is in each sign about 2-1/2 days and goes through the zodiac (and around your chart) in about 29 days. The position of the current or transiting Moon in its orbit has much to do with your personal mood swings as well.

The public has long associated the full Moon with emotions, and has been uneasy about its appearance in the sky. The mentally ill were called *lunatics*. Until 1808, patients in English mental institutions were flogged routinely at the full Moon to prevent outbreaks of violence. (This form of violence perpetrated by the staff on patients at the full Moon was apparently considered perfectly sane.) In traditional astrology, the Moon hours of the day and Monday (MOONday) were associated with emotionality—and don't we call it Blue Monday?

Science ridicules old beliefs about the Moon as superstition, but modern research is proving that the Moon affects our emotions powerfully. The full and new Moon periods signal emotional unrest, with higher crime rates and greater numbers of people requiring emergency psychiatric care. The Moon exerts a powerful gravitational pull on Earth's electromagnetic field and on the tides. Since our bodies are about 80 percent water, the Moon can have as strong an effect on the human body as it does on Earth. In *The Lunar Effect*, Lieber talks about *biological tides*, which are highest at the full and new Moon. He doesn't believe these tides cause emotional explosions, but they can trigger them in individuals predisposed to such behavior. Those who are repressing their Moon's functions or not dealing with their lunar hemisphere would be especially susceptible.

> It is not accurate to declare that the Moon causes madness and crime, but it is precisely accurate to say that it is the repression of the Moon's influence and what the Moon stands for that brings about social tension, disharmony, and lamentable, often bizarre results.[1]

The connections between the Moon, water, and emotions are interesting. The water signs—Cancer, Pisces, and Scorpio—are highly emotional. From what Lieber discovered, the metaphysical teaching that water symbolizes the emotions is literally true, due to the way water in our bodies acts on our emotions. Crying is an emotional reaction, often due to loss, and colds are well recognized as unshed tears. Tears are seen as female because men don't cry except under the most extreme circumstances. Men are often overwhelmed by women's tears, for they imagine that women must be in as much pain as they would be if they cried.

Water retention seems greatly related to emotions. Women's greater emotionality has been associated with the fact that certain phases of our

---

[1]Arnold Lieber and Jerome Agel, *The Lunar Effect* (New York: Anchor Press, 1978), p. 107.

monthly cycle make us more prone to water retention. Water retention is also one physical correlate of serious depression. Interestingly, we all weigh more in the summer (during the sign Cancer) due to a seasonal increase in body fluids, so we all tend to be more emotional during that time.[2] (Whenever water retention is a problem, cutting down on sodium intake can be helpful, as can foods and herbs like asparagus, celery, corn silk, dandelion leaves, and parlsey.)

The Moon's gravitational pull also affects Earth's electromagnetic field, with peaks or drops occurring unpredictably at the full and new Moon. Changes in these fields apparently greatly affect emotions. Psychiatrist Dr. Leonard Ravitz found that disturbances in the electromagnetic field correspond with mental illness, while return to a normal state heralded a return to mental balance.[3] The Moon may not disturb the electromagnetic field of the average person so strongly, but it can produce subtle changes that alter our moods.

Few of us are affected by the full or new Moon to the point of suicide or assault. Most of us are somewhat affected, if only by having to cope with the lunatics around us. Lieber says that if we suppress and neglect the vital lunar hemisphere, we reach a delicate balance that can be toppled by the Moon's phases. Full Moon meditations and the techniques presented in various chapters help us explore buried parts of ourselves to restore balance.

Often, what comes up at the full and new Moon are our REAL feelings, possibly exaggerated because we've suppressed them. If we happen to be premenstrual at the same time, we must confront what is bothering us, unless we overeat or otherwise narcotize ourselves. Neither the full Moon nor the menstrual cycle is responsible for our distress. Both the full and the new Moon give us a chance to confront our true reactions. A painful confrontation is a stimulus to work on emotional awareness.

The Moon may also affect our moods indirectly by its effect on the weather, which has been scientifically documented. (Have you ever noticed how, if it rains on a particular day of the week, it will often rain on that day for three more weeks? This correlates with the pull of the Moon's quarters.) The weather affects all our moods to some extent; e.g., a gloomy day produces a gloominess in the public at large. Some of us are more weather sensitive, particularly the lunar types.

Recently given a psychiatric classification, Seasonal Affective Disorder, or SAD, affects many in the winter when there is less sunlight—but more

---

[2]Edmund Van Deusen, *Astrogenetics* (New York: Pocket Books, 1977), p. 114.
[3]Reported in Arnold Lieber and Jerome Agel, *The Lunar Effect* (New York: Anchor Press, 1978), p. 58.

moonlight! Such people are depressed and lethargic during winter, sleeping long hours. They do not respond much to psychotropic drugs, but they do improve as the days lengthen in spring and summer. The groups who are most affected are arguably lunar. Depending on the study, anywhere from three to five times as many women as men are seriously affected, particularly at the premenstrual phase. This is still another reason women are more prone to mood swings. People are also more likely to suffer from SAD if there is a family history of serious depression. (This hereditary type of depression frequently shows up in the birth chart with Saturn aspects to the Moon.) Another group more likely to be affected are the night owls, who are habitually up late and who find it hard to get up the next day.[4]

You will be learning about the flower remedies in the next chapter. For future reference, several remedies from the Alaskan Flower Essence Project can help the winter blues—**Solstice Sun, Sunflower**, and **Orange Calcite**. One of the Flower Essence Project directors, Jane Bell, finds that people do better with the long winter nights if they allow their bodies to establish their own rhythms. Sleep longer, eat a bit more, and let the right brain (lunar hemisphere) take the lead, giving yourself more time to moon around, meditate, and do creative work. Those who force themselves to remain on a rigid and demanding schedule suffer more from depression. Good advice from Alaska, where there is less light in winter than you'd ever want to know!

The Outer Planet Transits and Loony Tunes

The outer planet transits correlated with an increase in emotional stress as the lunar supports have been eroded. The rates for emotional illness, suicide, and crime are climbing. We've discussed the conflicting and often impossible expectations women face, and the scarcity of supports as we try to meet those expectations. As we'll see in the section called "Women as Lunatics," more women are breaking down under this strain.

We are taught that there is something WRONG with us if we feel. We are looked down on as weak, irrational, and "feminine" if we grieve over ties lost due to geographic mobility; if we are angry at our powerlessness; or if we are anxious over our high pressure jobs. We are expected to be detached about such conditions, to rationalize them so they don't bother us. If you

---

[4]Robert N. Moreines, M.D., *Light Up Your Blues* (New York: Berkley Books, 1989), pp. 12–14.

can't fit in (i.e., if your emotions are uncomfortable for others), you are told you need tranquilizers or *in extremis* a little therapy. You can only suppress your feelings for so long before you blow up or break down. There is still another consequence—psychosomatic illnesses may develop as unexpressed feelings damage our bodies. The disease cancer, for instance, has been linked with repressed emotion. One contributing cause of Chronic Fatigue Syndrome can be prolonged stress. In such situations, taking a stress reduction workshop and learning relaxation or deep breathing techniques can help break the cycle.

What is repressed becomes obsessional, and the outer planet transits correlated with the growth of psychology and psychotherapy. Freud was forming his theories of the unconscious and the childhood origin of neurosis from 1910 to 1920, when first Neptune, and then Pluto, were passing through Cancer. The Pluto-in-Cancer era was the beachhead of psychoanalysis, and transits since then have made the unconscious a preoccupation. Having become too detached, we turn the intellect toward the study of feelings, creating psychology departments in universities everywhere.

It is an analytic commonplace that we form "transference relationships" to our therapists—that is, they come to represent our mothers and fathers. Yet, what kind of parents are therapists? They are usually detached, rational, and undemonstrative. They aim to teach us about feelings, yet are traditionally constrained against showing any of their own. The appointment system is like feeding on schedule rather than on demand. (The newer transpersonal therapies, thankfully, do not always fit this model.)

No doubt the self-help movement is partially a response to the distance and detachment of traditional therapy. The movement is continually growing, and there are self-help groups for every conceivable problem. There are shelves of these books in nearly every bookstore, and hundreds of articles appear monthly (mostly in women's magazines). Talk shows on television and call-in shows on the radio have become a kind of lay psychotherapy for the exhibitionistic. Turned off by the coldness of experts, we are learning to think for ourselves, to choose the ideas that help us while discarding the rest. (The U.S., with its Aquarian Moon, is in the forefront of the movement.)

Many people find astrology a powerful self-help tool, giving new perspective and insight into emotions and behavior. Astrology can help your growth because it identifies habitual emotional responses that can be self-destructive. In chart analysis, you may focus on one issue at a time, such as partnership. Tracking transits can put an emotional crisis into perspective. (Chapter 15 will discuss transits to the birth Moon.)

Women as Lunatics

Sex Role Stereotypes and Mental Health: We've spoken of the harmful effects of rigid sex role stereotypes that symbolically relegate men to Mars and women to the Moon. One focus here will be the damage women suffer because the culture confines their avenues of expression so predominantly to lunar modes. The Moon rules emotions, and women more frequently than men show emotional disturbances in response to the stresses of living in modern America. In many studies, women comprise two-thirds of adults in outpatient mental health facilities and about 60 percent of psychiatric inpatients. This was not always the case. The past thirty years have brought a sudden, sharp increase in the number of women seeking psychiatric help. We have more awareness of role discomforts than we used to, and we seek a palliative for these social ills in therapy or pills.

The very roles and traits identified with femininity mitigate against our effectiveness as human beings. In several studies, the traits associated with masculinity and femininity were identified, with a high degree of agreement by different kinds of people. These same traits were then ranked as healthy or neurotic, without reference to gender, by others from the same groups. Participants ranked ten out of fifteen of the traits associated with maleness as mentally healthy, while ten of the fifteen traits associated with femininity were characterized as unhealthy. If we fit the feminine stereotypes we are trained for, we are not being healthy adults.

Women in Therapy: Sigmund Freud himself saw women as inherently more sick than men. He admonished his followers not to pay attention to the feminists of his era:

> For women, the level of what is ethically normal is different from what it is in men. We must not allow ourselves to be deflected from such conclusions by the denials of feminists who are anxious to force us to regard the two sexes as completely equal in position and worth.[5]

Maddened by this put down, I sought the astrologer's revenge, and looked up Freud's chart, which is reproduced as Chart 2. Freud's problems with women are apparent from his 8th house Gemini Moon squaring Neptune in the 4th. Talk about an Oedipus complex! His understanding of women and emotions was limited by disowning his own lunar side. I'm not going

---

[5]Phyllis Chesler, *Women and Madness* (New York: Avon Books, 1972), p. 76.

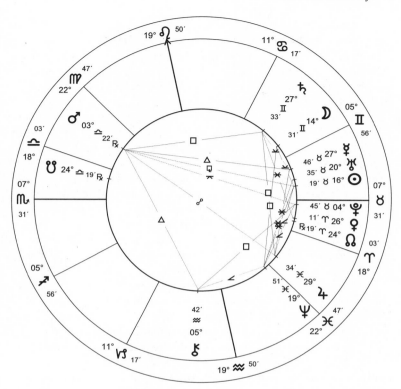

Chart 2. The horoscope of Sigmund Freud, born May 6, 1856, 6:30 P.M. LMT in Pribor, Czech Republic. Information from his father's diary. Placidus houses are used here. (Source: Father's diary, quoted by Phillip Lucas in Mercury Hour, *1979. Courtesy of Lois Rodden, AstroData II. San Diego: Astro-Computing Services, 1980.)*

into an analysis of Freud's chart here, but interested students can at least look up his lunar descriptions in the various Moon sign sections.

If we women are discontented with the lunar roles, male experts label us neurotic and maladjusted. If we show too much Mars energy, we are considered castrating. When you choose a therapist, be very conscious of his or her orientation toward women, as an unwritten goal may be to fit you back in the lunar mold. Danger—mental health may be damaging to your mental health! The higher statistics on women in treatment may be a reflection of the symbiotic way we are raised and the lack of support for our lunar needs. We are particularly vulnerable to upheavals at the various lunar thresholds we will be discussing, such as puberty, childbirth, and menopause. At the times when we most want our lunar support systems— mother, sisters, aunts, and women friends—we may be bereft of them due to the increase in geographic mobility.

We are also raised to believe we can't exist without mother or her replacement, so we are thrown for a loss when ties are broken by death, divorce, or distance. We may become depressed by the losses and seek a surrogate in the therapist. The condition for maintaining the therapeutic relationship is to stay sick, so we may attach to our negative patterns as a resistance to getting well. We become therapy junkies, unable to do without our weekly fix. Yet, therapy's effectiveness is not dependent on its length— the greatest impact and growth can come in the first few months. If you've been in therapy for a considerable time and don't see significant recent growth, set concrete new goals, or try some new form of therapy. For instance, switching to a group or to body work may be in order.

Another reason for women's greater prevalence in mental hospitals, nursing homes, and other facilities is men's inability or unwillingness to fill the lunar roles themselves. Many have so much difficulty dealing with their own dependency that it is hard for them to deal with dependency in women.

When the woman in his life requires care and can no longer take care of him, a man may react with overt or covert hostility, often rejecting or abandoning her. The man who is incapacitated by depression, alcoholism, or other emotional problems is likely to be cared for at home by his wife. When a woman is incapacitated, her husband is more likely to sign her into the hospital.

The increased statistics may also represent a backlash against women who do not fall into line. Women who are certified insane, according to Phyllis Chesler's unsettling classic, *Women and Madness*, are either being aggressive, or are no longer able to function in their nurturing role. In astrological terms, being aggressive is a Mars problem, and being unable to nurture is a Moon problem. If you are either too Mars (showing rage) or too Moon (too emotional), you are said to be having a breakdown and you are put away. They numb you with drugs so you won't feel anything, and so you can resume your lunar functions without rocking the boat.

Women and Depression: Depending on the study, anywhere from two to six times as many women are diagnosed as suffering from depression as are men. The passive-dependent roles we are taught make it hard to mobilize ourselves to change situations that make us unhappy, according to *The Book of Hope:*

> The cultural roots for depression among women center around learned helplessness and a position of self-effacement. It is those cultural roots which create the conflict women now experience in striving toward changing their assigned roles and realizing and asserting their own needs.[6]

A very feminine source of depression is anger turned inward, a consequence of having to suppress Mars. We saw that the premenstrual blues arise from inverted anger, and serious depression is similar in origin. Angry (Martian) women face heavy pressure to get back into the lunar fold, such as being called dykes, or even dealing with physical retaliation. Since we can't safely express our rage, we turn it inward. Depression is a safer outlet, one that brings more sympathy and social approval. It is more "feminine."

The ultimate expression of rage turned inward is suicide. Women make three times as many suicide attempts as men.[7] Another factor in depression is impossible standards of perfection coupled with hopelessness about living up to them. Working full time and struggling with the complex demands of modern life haven't changed the demand that we be "perfect women." Failing to live up to these standards lowers self-esteem and makes us more prone to depression.

Women and Mood-Changers: One self-destructive response to anger or the resulting depression is the abuse of alcohol, tranquilizers, cigarettes, food, or other mood altering drugs. Narcotization is a common response of people who have relatively little power in society. Liquor was used consciously to tame and emasculate Native Americans and African Americans, resulting in high rates of alcoholism and drug addiction continuing into our times. Today doctors widely prescribe drugs like Prozac to women to numb their anger and discontent.

Consistently over the past twenty years, research studies have shown that when men and women go to the doctor with the same complaint, women are far more likely to receive prescripitons for psychotropic drugs.

[6]Helen A. DeRosis, M.D., and Victoria Y. Pelligrino, *The Book of Hope* (New York: Macmillan, 1976), p. 3.
[7]Due to using more active methods, men are more often "successful" at suicide than women, but the "success" rate for women is rising sharply.

As detailed in an unsettling book about women and medicine, *Outrageous Practices*, women prescription abusers outnumber men three to one, and doctors prescribe 83 percent of antidepressants and over 70 percent of psychotropic drugs to women. One complicating factor in the medical establishment's propensity to narcotize women is that studies on safe dosage levels for most medications are conducted exclusively on men. Women are routinely excluded because of the belief that our hormonal makeup will contaminate the results. Yet, it is specifically because of medication's interactions with our hormones that safe dosage levels need to be tested on women. Men's generally larger frames and lack of these hormones mean that the recommended dosage may be too strong for us, creating a substantial risk of overdosing or harmful side effects. Women have twice as many fatal drug reactions as men and, with psychotropic drugs, have a seventeenfold increase of risk of fatal heart attacks.[8]

Women additionally use food to narcotize themselves, making eating disorders mainly a female problem. As many women as men drink today, and the rate of alcoholism among women is rising. Women also smoke as much as men now, and more teenage girls than boys are smoking. In earlier times, smoking and drinking were socially unacceptable for women, and even today the social stigma of female alcoholism is far greater than for men. Women with drinking problems, therefore, are likely to hide the addiction rather than seek treatment. Here again, men cannot handle our incapacitation. Statistics show that the majority of men leave their alcoholic wives, while most women stand by their alcoholic husbands.[9]

Differences Between Men and Women: There are some sexual differences in emotional expression—most due to differences in the way we are raised, but some possibly innate. Psychological studies show that girls are far more reactive to other people's emotions than boys, particularly to their mother's. Signe Hammer notes the consequences of this greater sensitivity:

> A mother's emotions have a powerful effect on a daughter and are part of the glue that binds a daughter to her mother. Small children tend to relate everything that happens to themselves, and

---

[8]Written by Leslie Laurence and Beth Weinhouse, *Outrageous Practices* should be required reading for all women who have to deal with the medical establishment (New York: Fawcett Columbine, 1994). See page 276.
[9]Statistics from various sources, including the Secretary of Health, Education, and Welfare; the National Institute of Drug Abuse; the U.S. Tobacco Journal.

when a mother explodes in rage or cries, a little girl thinks she's responsible.[10]

The process of identification is another reason women's emotional responses are also more shaped by their mothers. Finally, because of codependency, we are also more threatened by the withdrawal of love when our feelings don't meet with mother's approval.

In Western cultures, "real men" are not supposed to be afraid or reveal their vulnerability, so they may cover up such responses by aggressiveness or a cultivated indifference. On the other hand, women who show their anger or strength are often shamed or shunned for it. They are rewarded instead for helplessness, tears, or docility. While these stereotypes are changing, we often receive mixed messages. We encourage men to be sensitive to their feelings—but those who are sensitive may be regarded by both men and women as wimps.

If you've been feeling that this presentation is one-sided, that surely, given the pressures of our society, men must suffer from emotional problems as well, you are right. Due to the pressures to be Mars-oriented, however, men's emotional distress manifests in more outer-directed ways, such as aggressive behavior. Crimes of violence, which are committed by men in four out of five cases, aren't noted as mental health statistics, although they should be. It is enormously damaging for men to be confined only to the Mars traits (competitiveness, action, and aggression). Many men respond to stress in aggressive Martian ways, being drawn to crime, violence, or accidents. They even commit suicide in more active ways than women—gunshots or jumping off bridges. Women take more passive routes, like overdoses of pills. Thus, although the next section, about the Moon signs and emotions, is true of both sexes, men do express their Moon signs and emotions differently. In chapter 13, we will see how Moon signs influence male sex role stereotypes, emotional expression, and other lunar matters for men.

What Kind of Lunatic Are You?

Your Moon shows many facets of your nature. It shows the emotional tone of your early childhood, particularly how your mother dealt with her own reactions and yours. It shows how you react in a crisis. For the astrologically knowledgeable, Table 5 (page 66) shows how the Moon's aspects and houses

[10]Signe Hammer, *Daughters and Mothers/Mothers and Daughters* (New York: Signet, 1975), p. 36.

TABLE 5. CORRESPONDENCES BETWEEN MOON SIGNS, HOUSES, AND ASPECTS.

MOON SIGN	SIMILAR TO ASPECTS BETWEEN	HOUSE PLACEMENT
Aries	Moon and Mars	None
Taurus	Not strong	Second
Gemini	Moon and Mercury	Third
Cancer	(Double lunar energy)	Fourth
Leo	None	Fifth
Virgo	Moon and Mercury, somewhat	Sixth
Libra	Moon and Venus	Seventh
Scorpio	Moon and Pluto	Eighth
Sagittarius	Moon and Jupiter	Ninth
Capricorn	Moon and Saturn	Tenth, Midheaven
Aquarius	Moon and Uranus	Eleventh
Pisces	Moon and Neptune	Twelfth

may also affect your emotional makeup. I have used a system of correlations based on Dr. Zipporah Dobyns' teachings, with a few modifications suggested by my experience over the years. For instance, when the Moon is in the 1st house, I don't particularly find it like the Moon in Aries. Instead, particularly when it is within ten degrees of the ascendant, it is more like Cancer rising. Depending on the Moon's sign, it can be even more lunar than Cancer rising, qualifying as an additional lunar type.

The Moon's major aspects are more often more like the sign than the sign itself. Moon-Neptune aspects can be like Pisces in spades; Moon-Pluto aspects can beat out Moon in Scorpio any day in the intensity sweepstakes. Thus, if you have Moon-Neptune conjunct in Libra, you may find you identify more with the readings for Moon in Pisces. If you have Moon in Leo conjunct Pluto, then check the Scorpio readings to see why you're not perpetually sunny.

The house placements don't necessarily match the personality traits of the Moon sign, but matters crucial to that sign are also major issues for that house placement. For example, financial security is important to Taurus Moons and it is generally crucial for the person with the Moon in the 2nd. Depending on the sign, however, the 2nd house Moon may not share the good, grounded commmon sense in financial matters that we see with Taurus Moon. Just for the purpose of understanding how the house positions work, we will consider these positions separately later in this chapter. In future chapters, however, they will be combined with their planet and sign equivalents.

Using the table, make a list of the correspondences that apply to you and tuck it into the book somewhere. In the readings that follow, we will repeat these correlations next to the Moon signs, so you'll see how to use the list. In other chapters where Moon sign readings appear, consult the additional readings that apply to you, as given here.

Moon in Aries: (Moon-Mars aspects) This person was taught to assume a masculine denial of emotions. Neither parent believed in sitting around crying about a situation. When a crisis arises, the response is to take action, even if it's a rash action that further complicates the matter. Aries also tends not to finish things, and this often happens when feelings get too stirred up by the project or by coworkers.

Another Aries Moon defense is aggressiveness or a short fuse. Anger or irritability are often coverups for less welcome feelings. Feelings of inadequacy might make an Aries Moon person become competitive or else abandon the task as not worth the effort. Likewise, the Aries penchant for sexual conquest can become a coverup for anger, anxiety, fear of closeness, or dependency.

Dependency is particularly difficult for the Aries Moon individual to accept. Often, the parents were openly hostile when the child showed weakness. Thus, when the individual feels needy, she may rely on any of the defenses outlined above. Women who have this Moon may feel inadequate as a traditional female and may be convinced that it is better to be a man. They may defend their own softer feelings by being fiercely self-sufficient.

Moon in Taurus: Unless there are difficult aspects to this Moon, such as a square to Pluto or Uranus in Leo or an opposition to Neptune in Scorpio, the early home environment tended to be fairly serene. The mother was well-grounded and able to deal solidly with crisis. The person with this Moon, therefore, is not easily rocked off center. Like the bull that symbolizes Taurus, however, the individual can be extremely stubborn, especially if asked to adjust to change in a hurry. It is important that he or she have time to chew over feelings, much as the cow chews its cud. In today's fast-moving world, the Taurus Moon may react to pressure like a raging bull when the lunar areas, such as security, the homelife, or the children are threatened. The Moon in Taurus person also deals with the insecurity of modern life by amassing material possessions.

Moon In Gemini: (Moon-Mercury aspects) The early home environment provided mental stimulation and placed great value on communication.

Humor was both a gift and a defense against less pleasant feelings. The child was rewarded for intellect and discouraged from purely emotional responses. The mother may have responded to emotional outbursts by trying to reason with the child, to prove the reaction wasn't logical. There was an overt or a subtle withdrawal of love unless the child remained good-humored.

A Gemini defense would be to clown around in emotionally charged situations. Granted, humor is one healthy way of dealing with emotions, but when done compulsively, it is an escape. The primary Gemini response to a crisis is to reason everything out and make the most logical choice, rather than taking feelings into account.

Moon in Cancer: This placement shows an extremely strong attachment to the mother. A very emotional person, her outbursts may have been overwhelming to the child. The Moon in Cancer person tends to cling to emotions and take them very seriously. Neediness and dependency are powerful, and when there is no release from them, food may be used for comfort. Alternately, the person may be fiercely counterdependent, the tough Cancer shell used as protection. Insecurity and anxiety are frequent when the person lacks a strong home base. Crying is overwhelming to others, so can be used to manipulate and control, but also to create distance; it's part of the Crab's shell.

As lunar types, Cancer Moons react strongly to the new and full Moon, and women of that sign react to the premenstrual phase. Consistently following the transiting Moon would help make sense of those constant mood swings. Meditation daily and at the full Moon can keep the lunar hemisphere clear, for better balance.

Moon in Leo: The early home environment may have been lively and boisterous. The mother may have been theatrical, adept at projecting emotions for effect. The child learned that the only way to be taken seriously is to upstage everyone. Because the mother was a sort of prima donna whose attention was mainly focused on herself, the child grew up hungry for attention and approval. Tantrums became a tool for getting this much craved response. As a result, the Moon in Leo person performs rather than communicating feelings. What starts out as genuine may get lost in thespian efforts. Wounded pride is a particular trigger point, especially when the Leonian doesn't recieve the appreciation, respect or admiration he feels he deserves. Sometimes, too, the professed feeling may not be the real one, but simply one that is more dramatic. To act injured, for instance, is more dramatic than revealing inadequacy or vulnerability. In a crisis, the histrionics can be turned on full force. Nonetheless, since Leo wants dignity and a regal bearing, the histrionics may be more internal than external, or may be carried on solely in the royal bed chamber. (Special note: those with Moon conjunct Pluto in Leo may combine these qualities with traits of Moon in Scorpio.)

Moon in Virgo: (sometimes Moon-Mercury aspects) The early home environment may have been a rather cold one, in which significant adults worked hard and had little patience with a child's needs. Often the mother was working, or overloaded with other children and household duties. Because parents were critical of any emotional display, the child grew up guilty and self-critical about feeling anything. An upsurge of self-criticism is often a mask for other feelings, such as anger at not having dependency needs met. Interestingly, many Catholics who come to me have been as profoundly influenced by the nuns in their parochial schools as by their mothers. Often the Moon in Virgo or Virgo rising shows this influence.

Another prevalent Moon in Virgo defense against unwelcome feelings is illness. Psychosomatic illnesses are common, since the disallowed emotions go into the body, and since it provides a legitimate reason to be dependent. Hypochondria also distracts one from feeling, and lends a reason for the responses. The response to crisis is self-blame for allowing a problem to develop, obsessive analysis, and then working compulsively to avoid the problem.

Moon in Libra: (Moon-Venus aspects) Often there were marital problems between the parents, and the child acted as a buffer. Therefore, conflict threatens peace of mind, and the person will bend over backward to avoid it by people-pleasing. Anger must be kept down by being sweet, or by professions of love. The person may try to suppress negative emotions in a relationship to make it resemble a Hollywood romance.

Emotional balance is so important to the Libran that the usual ambivalent feelings about people or situations are threatening. She may act impulsively to resolve conflict, only to find she hasn't taken both sides into consideration. This Moon sign must develop patience with decision making, since the feeling of indecision is a tormenting one. We cannot MAKE decisions with our minds, we can only COME to decisions by trusting our true feelings about a situation.

Moon in Scorpio: (Moon-Pluto aspects) The early home may have had an uptight and suspicious atmosphere with hostile undercurrents. Because this was nonverbal, the child became adept at reading unspoken emotions to survive. Thus, many of these people have a gift for psychology. The mother, in particular, may have been strongly controlling of her own emotions and of the child's. The child learned to hide emotions and to feel guilty for any Mom wouldn't like.

Due to this background, the adult with Moon in Scorpio keeps feelings hidden and may feel no one would understand his feelings, that he is an alien creature. Others sense that much is hidden and may not trust him, increasing the isolation. The more feelings are controlled and kept secret, the more powerful they become, in a self-reinforcing cycle. Work on the lunar hemisphere is important so the person is not consumed by intensity. Group therapy would be particularly useful, if these patterns are pronounced, for the person could learn to risk sharing feelings with others. (My book *Healing Pluto Problems* would be a good one for Scorpio Moons to read.)

Moon in Sagittarius: (Moon-Jupiter aspects) This is another sign that intellectualizes feelings, rather than confronting them directly, because this was the mother's defense. Nonetheless, these natives have a drive to learn from emotional situations and thereby aquire wisdom. There is an optimism that says that no matter how bad today is, things are going to work out—a philosophy Mom imparted. Very often, things work out as we unconsciously believe they will, so this mind set is not necessarily destructive. Sag Moons use humor, both in a healthy way and as a defense against feeling. There may be concern about ethics and about what they "should" feel in a given circumstance. It may be difficult for these people to admit to uncharitable or "un-Christian" feelings. Punitive actions, pursued in the name of religious conviction and righteous indigation, may actually be an outlet for anger.

Moon in Capricorn: (Moon-Saturn aspects) The early environment was often melancholy and lacked warmth. The mother may have been depressed or weighed down by duty. This melancholy becomes part of the person's outlook on life even as an adult. The mother either worked, had heavy family responsibilities, or may have been older, and thus had little patience with the child's needs. There may have been an atmosphere of poverty and hardship, where survival depended on burying feelings and taking care of the task at hand. Because the family was critical, this person may be tormented by self-hate or shame. This contributes to depression when the individual cannot live up to her own impossible standards. In a crisis, the Moon in Capricorn puts aside emotion and performs like a trouper, becoming the rock of Gibraltar for everyone involved. This Moon sign is sometimes found among alcoholics, because drink is often the only release for depression and the harsh, perfectionistic demands this person places on herself. (Additionally, the gene for familial alcoholism and the gene for hereditary biochemical depression are on the same strand, so many alcoholics drink to self-medicate chronic depression.)

Moon in Aquarius: (Moon-Uranus aspects) The early home environment was doubtlessly an unsettled one, with frequent moves or losses of important ties. Often in such families, conflict simmers beneath the surface and erupts periodically and destructively. The mother may have been erratic, or cut off from feelings, and may have withdrawn when the child expressed emotions. The adult Aquarian Moons often cut off contact whenever conflict or other unpleasant emotions arise in relationships. The tendency is to deal with people and situations in a highly intellectual manner to minimize the emotional content. The repressed emotions, however, may erupt in sudden and shocking ways, to the dismay of the person who has this Moon—and everyone around.

It is very important to work on being conscious of emotions and respecting them as valid rather than detaching from them or acting out erratically. Work with your lunar hemisphere regularly to be well balanced and not triggered by lunar stresses. If you needed therapy at some point, you might respond best to group therapy. Aquarius rules groups, and you might have less of an authority problem in that setting than in a one-on-one situation.

Moon in Pisces: (Moon-Neptune aspects) There was much confusion during this person's childhood, often due to a parent who was alcoholic, mentally or physically ill, or overly religious. The child has to deny the turmoil and live in his or her own dream world to survive. Thus the tendency to escape from feelings remains a defense, possibly bolstered by the same defenses the parents used—alcohol, psychosomatic illness, or other escapes.

Because of suppressing emotions so long, this person is afraid of being overwhelmed. When repressed so persistently, emotions can indeed be overwhelming and come out in "crazy" ways that make them even more frightening. The more alarming they seem, the more repressed they will be, and a difficult pattern can get set up that many need help to break.

Another consideration is that the person with this aspect is extremely psychic, and absorbs the emotions of others. Perhaps this arose as a survival mechanism in a dysfunctional family environment, and the child had to be extremely alert and perceptive to stay out of trouble. It is important that this person learns to differentiate psychic perceptions from his or her own true feelings. Meditation, dream work, and other tools for getting in touch with feelings will help differentiate personal emotions from others'. Techniques for psychic shielding can be learned from psychic development courses or from books. Times of quiet retreat are a great solace.

The Effect of the House Placement of Your Moon

The house placement of the birth Moon is also important, for it shows where you try to get your lunar needs met. This area acquires a heavy emotional charge, and it is often a source of upset when things are going badly. You may also notice that it is an area of heightened activity and emotion each month when the Moon comes back to the same place as in your birth chart—your lunar return. (Beginners, look at the Cancer Rising Wheel—Figure 2, page 27—for an understanding of how the houses are arranged and what each house signifies. The signs around that wheel are typical of those with Cancer rising. If you have a different rising sign, your own wheel would have different signs on the cusps.) Combine the Moon sign readings with the house position, for the sign illustrates your personal style of dealing with lunar concerns.

Moon in the 1st house: Especially if it is within ten degrees of the Ascendant, this birth placement qualifies you as a lunar type. The Moon's meanings dominate your face to the world—starting with the powerful impact your mother had in shaping your interactions with the world. You may even look a lot like her. So, you may be either intensely maternal or intensely dependent, but the world at large confuses you with Mom. If your Moon sign is so inclined—say a water sign—you project emotions strongly. No one around you could miss knowing how you feel. Depending on the Rising and Moon signs, your body is likely to be lunar, but tending toward the extremes. You may have large breasts or be flat-chested, you may be overweight or anorexic. Your digestion and menstrual cycle may be highly sensitive to outside stimuli and the food you eat.

Moon in the 2nd house: This position is a bit like Moon in Taurus, in that money and material goods go a long way toward giving you a sense of well-being. You may be gifted at earning money, perhaps in some old-fashioned and domestic ways. Emotional turmoil comes up when your bank balance is threatened. The similarity ends here, because your Moon sign tells more about how you operate with money. A Capricorn Moon will be economically conservative, watching the bottom line and making sure there is plenty in reserve for retirement. A Pisces Moon, however, may spend addictively and unwisely to keep unpleasant feelings at bay. Despite the sign, Mom is a big influence in money matters, either by model or else by keeping you somewhat dependent on her financially.

Moon in the 3rd house: With this placement, siblings, aunts, uncles or cousins may have taken on parental roles, often due to the mother's immaturity. Sometimes it's you who acted *in loco parentis*, sometimes they were the ones. At any rate, it results in a powerful and influential tie that lasts well into adulthood. Whether the tie was essentially positive, or not, depends on the Moon's sign and aspects. With Moon in Aries, there was likely to be a strong sibling rivalry and incessant conflict. With Moon in Libra, it was likely to be a very loving connection. At best, you are likely to have the equivalent of two Moms, one much younger and longer-lived, and you are likely to have a strong and supportive extended family.

Moon in the 4th house: This is another lunar type. The Moon's meanings are double-strength here, just as they would be with Moon in Cancer. Home, Mom, family, and the past are powerfully emphasized and deeply important for security and well-being. Again, the Moon sign and aspects may modify it. A Sagittarian Moon might as well buy an RV and live in it, because that wanderlust will make it hard to keep the roots planted to any depth. A Moon in Taurus might spend its waning years on the old family homestead, still using the dishes dear old Gram brought from the old country.

Moon in the 5th house: Here relationships with children or romantic partners are a main source of emotional fulfillment. When they are going well, there's nothing like it for pleasure and satisfaction. When they're going poorly or changing, as they may under an outer planet transit, the resulting emotional whirlpool can temporarily take over your life. In cases where these relationships replace a disappointing or difficult family of origin, a powerful and easily dysfunctional dependency can result. Perhaps you act as parent, yet rely on them for emotional gratification in a way that's not always healthy for either. Again, consider the sign. Moon in Scorpio may keep them dependent in order not to feel so alone, while Moon in Capricorn insists that they grow up and take responsibility for themselves. At best, there is a deep and lasting emotional bond here which makes the world a better, friendlier place.

Moon in the 6th house: Here, many needs are met in the workplace. When work is going well, you are likely to be much happier—and healthier—than when things are stagnant or going poorly. Generally, the Moon in the 6th tries to establish a family atmosphere in the work place—maybe bringing home-baked cookies or other goodies as treats. However, take the sign into account. Suppose your Moon is in the 6th house but in Sagittarius. Coworkers would be less likely to get home-baked cookies than a Joseph Campbell tape or a Greenpeace flyer. If it were in Virgo, you might be warning them about the sugar and fat content of cookies while dishing out vitamins and herbal remedies instead. Be aware, however, that it is not always appropriate to treat the boss as your parent and your co-workers or supervisees as your children. It can get in the way of adult functioning on the job.

Moon in the 7th house: Here the closest and most committed relationships are lunar, very possibly codependent unless you've absorbed every word John Bradshaw ever spoke. Your mate is likely to serve as either your parent or your child, but seldom as an equal. Men with this placement are often so deeply attached to Mom that they either don't marry while Mom is still around, or their wives have serious in-law problems. (No doubt the same could be said of women with this position as well.) At best, the mate is a deep source of security and well-being, and family ties are paramount to the partnership. The sign and aspects modify the picture. With Moon in Gemini, there is a sense of the mate as a brother or sister, and the communication and mental stimulation the mate provides is deeply rewarding. With Moon in Scorpio, the ties are typically murky and intense, with possessiveness and battles for control likely to dominate the relationship.

Moon in the 8th house: Many with strong 8th house Moon placements fail to develop their own resources because Mother encouraged and even manipulated them to remain dependent. This prolonged dependency can take many forms—financial as well as emotional, caretaking as well as enabling. At each level, Mom taught you that you needed her or other women because you couldn't do it yourself. Your emotional responses to this dependency vary with the Moon sign. The Moon in Pisces can experience a deep sense of shame and worthlessness about it and yet feel helpless to undertake more than the most menial of jobs. The Moon in Aquarius may feel justified in redistributing the family wealth as some sort of political statement. With the Moon in the 8th, there can also be an obsession with the sexual side of femininity. It becomes enmeshed with security and survival—as we will see in O. J. Simpson's chart in chapter 13.

Moon in the 9th house: This is generally not such a difficult position, being somewhat like the Moon in Sagittarius. Mom and other family members highly valued religion or education, so you pursue them—or reject them—in a deeply emotional manner. You believe in higher education for women and look to them as teachers—sometimes teachers have filled the gap for a mother who was less than supportive. If you feel secure in your philosophy and intellectual development, you are content. If there is a challenge to your belief system—let's say you find out that a mentor or guru has feet of clay—then you are deeply unsettled until you have sorted things out.

Moon in the 10th house: This house describes our authority figures, and the Moon here generally shows a mother-dominated home and even a matriarchy going back several generations. Often, the father was a lunar type. Like Moon in Capricorn, mother and her ambitions shaped the person's career choices or life path, often leaning toward a nurturing profession or role. The work may involve women, the public, the home, or other lunar concerns. The career and its waxings and wanings are a source of immense satisfaction, if it is going well, or of immense stress and upheaval if it is not. (Based on the work of the Gauquelins, this description applies even if the Moon is in the 9th, but within ten degrees of the Midheaven.)

Moon in the 11th house: Here the family of origin may have been sparse, bolstered by complimentary aunts and uncles among old family friends. In adolescence and beyond, the person creates a new family among friends or groups. Women friends become maternal substitutes, or the person may take on a maternal stance toward friends or groups. In adulthood, mother, herself, may become a good friend, depending on the Moon's sign and aspects. The person may periodically be disappointed to find out that her best friend is no better than Mom was at understanding and supporting her. There can be an inappropriate expectation of perpetual nurturance and emotional caretaking as a requirement of friendship.

Moon in the 12th house: Both the Moon and the 12th house tend toward repression, so the combination makes remaining conscious of your emotions a real and continuing challenge. Probably maternal figures were unable to deal with your upsetting feelings and may have withdrawn support when you expressed them. (I say maternal figures, as with this position there are sometimes losses, fluctuations, or emotional distance with the birth mother, and the person is likely to have found surrogates.) Conscious connections with lunar issues of all kinds may prove elusive and puzzling, until the individual tackles them directly and consistently.

When placed in the 12th house, even the usually hyper-lunar Cancer Moon may find them challenging, but the overly-cerebral Aquarian Moon hasn't a clue! The all-time champion of denial must have been the client with Moon in Aquarius in the 12th square Neptune in the 3rd. He informed me that he most certainly did not have emotions, although he did have fantasies. I suggested he haul himself back whenever he felt himself drifting into daydreams and ask what might have just happened that he'd be upset about. At best, the person with a 12th house Moon finds security and serenity in meditation and the spiritual path.

$$) \ ) \ ) \ ) $$

The readings about the Moon's sign and house placement focused on problem patterns to help us become more conscious of unhealthy defenses and change them. Yes, there are healthy emotional patterns and there are also times we need our defenses. However, when we freeze unwelcome feelings, they don't just go away. They simmer in the unconscious and come out in disguised, self-destructive ways, especially premenstrually or at the new and full Moon. To be alive is to feel. When we lack the courage to face difficult feelings, we deaden ourselves and settle for living less fully than we could.

Do You Use Emotions to Get Nurturing?

Emotions are tied to nurturing in that we may unconsciously use them to get nurturing. They are sometimes used to control people and situations. If we are depressed, for instance, no one can "blame" us for our condition, yet it entitles us to special care and concern. Mental health workers call these the *secondary gains* of an emotional or physical illness. The development of this pattern can go all the way back to mother. Many little girls learn that if they cry they will be hugged and held, maybe even given a cookie. Little boys, after a certain age, are scorned for crying. As we have seen, women are far more prone to depression than men, and rewards for crying may be one cause. Men learn other mechanisms for dealing with their pain—they may fight or drink because crying is considered unacceptable.

If emotional storms are embarked on to get nurturing, then find other ways to nurture yourself if you want to break the pattern. Otherwise, despite the very real pain involved, you will be seduced into repetition whenever you are particularly needy. If you suspect that you may sometimes go off the deep end to be nurtured, try the Cancer rising wheel as an alternate solution.

You might also want to take stock of the costs. Not only are emotional storms physically and emotionally devastating, but the nurturing you get under such circumstances is usually poor. Other people resent having to take care of you, because at some level they know something dishonest is going on. They sense that you aren't being out front about your feelings, such as the anger that underlies most depressions. The treatment women receive under the care of a hospital or clinic is often questionable. If you frequently need nurturing for emotional illness, you are not likely to be treated as an adult equal. If losses and deprivations lead you to seek caretaking this way, the quality of care is unlikely to be very satisfying, perpetuating the problem.

Learning to Cope Without Dope

Dope, of course, isn't just drugs, it's anything we use to deaden ourselves so we don't have to feel. It includes stuffing ourself with food, stopping for a few drinks after work, smoking a couple packs of cigarettes a day, watching four or five hours of TV a night, or taking tranquilizers for your nerves. These are all ways "respectable" people narcotize themselves, and many of us rely on more than one habit. We live in an anxious age where our lunar needs are unmet and where we suffer frequent losses. It is socially gauche to feel too deeply, so dope is becoming a way of life. Yet, most kinds of dope, used compulsively, are bad for your health, as are repressed feelings that express themselves psychosomatically.

In the end, dope doesn't solve the problem but only postpones it, and often makes it worse. You ultimately have to confront the issue; you eventually have to face the grief, or rage, or whatever you're avoiding. By not facing issues at the appropriate time, however, we complicate our lives. The situation gets worse because when we aren't paying attention to our real feelings, we act in neurotic or self-destructive ways.

We have to reeducate ourselves to feel. Meditation, keeping a journal, astrodrama, or dream work can help us tap into our lunar hemisphere. More techniques will be given in the final chapter. Following the Moon through your astrological chart, as you will learn to do in chapter 6, can be another useful aid. Greater self-awareness can come by using the full and new Moon phases and the premenstrual phase consciously.

Unexpressed feelings can be painful, so it is important to develop a supportive network of friends or a formal group where you can let feelings out safely. In certain self-help groups they say, "No pain, no gain," but it is important to use your pain as a stimulus for growth. If you remain stuck in self-defeating patterns that only perpetuate the pain, the temptation to use dope is overwhelming.

Some of what has been said so far sounds right off the Cancer rising wheel, doesn't it? Gemini on the 12th and Taurus on the 11th show some answers. As you go around the wheel while working through other lunar difficulties, you will find your emotional balance getting better. The processes outlined in this book will put you more in touch with your feelings. This awareness is only helpful if you are willing to work on things you can change—mainly your own harmful ways of treating yourself and others. Unless we are willing to grow, we will be at a loss in a rapidly-changing society.

It is especially important to learn to nurture yourself and to work regularly on clearing the lunar hemisphere. Throughout this book, we will consider clearing and balancing techniques. A variety of tools will be presented, since not all of them will suit the individual reader. You are invited to try them and work with the ones that suit you. In the next chapter, we will meet a very special tool to help in this work, the flower remedies.

CHAPTER 5

The Twelve Moon Signs, Their Emotional Habits, and the Flower Remedies

Some folks aren't happy unless they're sad. Others need anger to keep them pumped up. For some people, dwelling on self-pity or victimization become well-worn grooves that occupy an emptiness they would not otherwise know how to fill. Here I'm talking about the feeling tone that typifies each of us. "Delores is always depressed. What a sad sack!" "Bob would rather bite your head off than say hello. He's always in a foul mood."

Although a broad range of emotions is possible, most of us experience and express a very narrow range. The content and breadth of that range vary with the individual and are shown by the Moon in your chart. The Moon rules emotions, habits, and the unconscious. I made many discoveries by looking for connections between Moon matters. One such discovery was that many negative emotions that torment us persistently are bad habits we learned very early. We are no longer conscious of why they arose, so these tapes switch on automatically in stressful situations. In a crisis, we play the same tapes, only louder.

Understanding Emotional Habits

First, what is a habit? It is a learned pattern of behavior, repeated so often and for so long that it is strictly automatic. It is a personal ritual engaged in because it makes you feel secure. It works most of the time and produces results, so you don't even think about it. An *emotional habit* is a learned pattern, an unconscious and automatic response to emotion-producing circumstances. When people or situations push your buttons, it makes you feel safe. It works well most of the time, so it is no longer conscious. In a sense, it is a defense mechanism.

Emotional habits are familiar and comfortable, whereas unfamiliar feelings rock the boat too much. While the selected feelings tend to be unpleasant, they are still less difficult to handle than others that threaten the status quo. When uncomfortable reactions come up, many people unconsciously and rapidly call on the habitual ones. These become multi-purpose tools used—and overused—in many situations to keep from confronting the real feelings.

Many strong but recurring emotions should be seen as suspect, as all too often they are a distortion of the true response. The conversion may be made so quickly that people don't even allow themselves to recognize emotions they regard as unacceptable. For instance, those who don't wish to acknowledge their need to control may instantly convert it into guilt and walk around feeling guilty much of the time. Guilt may not be pleasant, but they believe it makes them a nicer person than someone who wants to dominate others. Those who find guilt too ego-wounding may convert it into blaming others.

Those who are uneasy with anger may immediately turn it into depression or anxiety. They may even say—and believe—that they never get angry. Anger, again, isn't nice. People around them, however, may sense the underlying anger in their words and deeds and react to it. Haven't you noticed how irritating depressed people can be? Others are far too comfortable with anger, using resentment and brooding to keep from experiencing a variety of feelings, such as powerlessness, or grief over their losses.

For someone else, anxiety may be a habit. In each new or challenging situation, anxiety gushes up from an endless pool underneath. The person spins into a state of fear that becomes all-consuming. Just as the depressive person automatically settles into the funk, the anxiety-ridden person unthinkingly allows his nervousness to become his total reality. In both cases, these habits can be defenses against other feelings.

Our habits both protect and limit us. These old-shoe patterns serve as defenses against less comfortable or less familiar emotions. Not that these familiar patterns aren't painful, they are just easier to cope with than feelings we don't know how to handle. Depression, for instance, is often anger turned inward, when anger is too threatening to express openly. For others, anger itself can be a defense against fear—one which men, in particular, are prone to use when they feel threatened. The important thing to know is that many of our habitual emotions are smoke screens, but we take them so seriously they assume a life of their own.

Some Common Bad Emotional Habits and How to Break Them

Your own habits may not be so extreme, but most of us have a small repertoire of feelings that get triggered repeatedly. Few respond spontaneously to the situation at hand. The various sections on Moon signs should give clues to your own patterns. The habits covered below do not have exact astrological correspondances, but individual Moon signs are more prone to some of them than to others. Here are some techniques that can help you stop falling into negative patterns. Although your formal introduction to flower remedies will come later, I can't help but mention the ones for these habits.

The Habit of Worry: I once kept a worry box. Each time I was consumed with anxiety about some situation, I wrote it on a piece of paper. I prayed over it and dropped it into the box, making a conscious effort to let go of the fear. At the end of six weeks, I opened the box and read the slips. Out of 26 worries that had been my total reality for hours or days, only one had happened. The other 25 were dimly remembered figments of my imagination. This exercise gave me a new perspective on my anxieties. After that, I was much more able to say a prayer and let go of the fear. (Bach's **White Chestnut** is helpful for worry, while **Aspen** is for anxiety.)

The Habit of Self-Pity: Self-pity is different from honest pain about your life situation. Poor-me-ism is a set up for self-indulgent behavior that ultimately becomes destructive. One way out is to stop believing you're a victim. Find out whether you've created your own painful reality and allowed people to victimize you. Working your way out of such situations would be important for your general well-being. (Bach's **Centaury** is very helpful for those who allow others to take advantage. The true victim, of domestic violence for example, needs the help of others outside the situation, but might find strength in Desert Alchemy's **Ephedra**.)

Making a list each day of the things you're grateful for is a constructive habit to offset self-pity. At first you may not be able to think of any, but the habit of a gratitude list is a great uplift. Another excellent way to combat it is to spend time doing something for someone who's even worse off than you are. Bach's **Heather** can help the pattern.

The Habit of Guilt: Many of us live in a pervasive aura of worthlessness with nothing concrete to justify it. We might see this situation with a strongly Plutonian person. The gnawing guilt, no longer consciously attached to any particular misdeed, becomes a way of life. It's there, waiting to fasten onto some current misdemeanor and magnify it. "I shouldn't have snapped at John. I feel so guilty." "Why didn't I offer to drive her home? That was selfish." If no current transgression can be found, the person who is dogged with guilt can drag something out of the past to chew over. (This type would benefit greatly from a few months of taking Bach's **Pine**.)

An antidote for this pattern would be to take an inventory of your life, as recommended in the Twelve Step programs. Write down each deed you feel was wrong, no matter how trivial or how long ago it was, and make a list of the persons you feel you've harmed. If it wouldn't cause further harm to you or anyone else, try to rectify the situation. This should be done with judgment and discretion, because sometimes more harm than good can be done by revealing secrets or stirring up the past. A real benefit from the exercise is that once you have become aware of the actual parameters of your guilt, it loses its global quality. You can see exactly what you have done and do something about it.

Chances are, you'll find you're not such a terrible person after all, that you acted out of immaturity and ignorance, and that you've grown enough not to make those mistakes again. Ask whatever form of deity you believe in to forgive you—even if you don't believe, pretend and do it anyway. Most important, work on forgiving yourself. (Alaskan Flower Essences' **Mountain Wormwood** and **Alpine Azalea** can help you come to self-forgiveness.) After these exercises, you'll experience a karmic clearing so you no longer carry such a load of guilt or unworthiness.

The Habit of Negativity: This habit casts a cloud over your every thought and paralyzes your efforts to have a better life. You create your own reality by your thought patterns. For instance, if you believe you won't get the job you're applying for, you will behave in such a self-deprecating way that prospective employers will think twice about hiring you. Metaphysical studies can help substitute positive thoughts for negative ones. Delete words like CAN'T from your vocabulary. (The word WON'T is often closer to the truth.) You will need to work consistently on your thoughts if you wish to overcome a lifetime of negative programming from your parents and culture. (Pegasus' **Pennyroyal** and Bach's **Larch** are helpful here.)

The Habit of Depression: With a predominant habit of depression, generally the original source is long since repressed. There is a reservoir of sadness in the depressive personality that can be tapped any time. A simple disappointment, like the newsstand being out of your favorite magazine, or an overcrowded subway, is enough to send you into a funk for hours. Depression is as habitual and comfortable as a well-worn shoe, easy to slip into, safe and predictable.

According to Dr. Helen A. DeRosis, there are two main sources of depression: 1) anger turned inward, and 2) impossibly perfectionistic standards that the person fails to uphold. When depressed, ask yourself what you're angry about, or what impossible standards you have set for yourself.[1] You also may profit from assertiveness training, because by standing up for yourself, you have less need to get angry in the first place. Anger, in itself, is not a bad thing. Mars is both anger and action. Once you get in touch with your anger, you can use it to mobilize yourself for constructive action to change the situation.

Serious or chronic depression, of course, is more than a bad habit or smokescreen for anger. You are seriously depressed if, for more than two weeks, you have several of the following symptoms: 1) sadness, hopelessness, and not caring about life—or these feelings alternating with elation; 2) loss of interest in food, sex, or other normal appetites, or else obsession with them, such as food binges; 3) either being unable to sleep or sleeping for unusually long periods, coupled with great fatigue and lethargy; 4) sudden trouble in concentrating, sitting still, or making decisions; or 5) a sudden upsurge of guilt, discouragement, self-hate, or feelings of great neediness.[2] Serious clinical depression needs treatment and won't go away just because you took some flower remedies. Addictions like those to food or alcohol are often attempts to self-medicate a chronic depression.

There are other emotional bad habits. You may have some we've discussed and some that are your own personal brand. Coming to see them as the bad habits they are, rather than the gospel truth about your life, is a step toward

---

[1] Helen A. DeRosis, M.D. and Victoria Y. Pellegrino, *The Book of Hope* (New York: Macmillan, 1976), p. 34 ff.
[2] Maggie Scarf, *Unfinished Business: Pressure Points in the Lives of Women* (New York: Doubleday, 1980), pp. 71–72.

changing them. With work, bad habits can be broken and positive new ones established. When the old tape starts playing, stop it sharply by saying, "NO! That's not the truth! I deserve better than that!" Become aware of emotions you were conditioned to feel, like hopelessness or self-flagellation, and look beyond them to your real feelings.

Our personal range of safe, old-shoe emotions often correlates with the Moon's sign and aspects in the birth chart. The patterns characteristic of the twelve Moon signs are often no more than habit. As we go along, we will learn about the reactions typical of the twelve Moon signs. For example, most Moon in Aries people aren't comfortable with fear or neediness, so they may react aggressively instead. Moon in Virgo individuals, on the other hand, may avoid strong emotions by turning them into psychosomatic illnesses, or by overworking.

Incidentally, this approach reveals clear distinctions between the Sun sign and the Moon sign. The differences are not so much in the behavior, but in the underlying motivation. For instance, Sun sign Virgos and Moon sign Virgos may both overwork to the point of exhaustion. Sun sign Virgos do it, however, because their self-worth is bound up in their work. Many of them identify strongly with their productivity. They don't feel good about themselves unless they put in more hours and get more work done than anyone else on the job. It's almost a form of one-upmanship. Moon sign Virgos, on the other hand, overwork as a way of avoiding feelings, especially about some ongoing issue or condition. When there is too much conflict in their primary relationship, they may absent themselves by working long hours. Or, when there is no relationship, they may overwork to avoid going home to an empty house and confronting the loneliness. Sun sign Virgos, on some level, are still trying to please Dad or his equivalents, while Moon sign Virgos are modeling themselves after Mom.

How Do We Learn Our Emotional Habits?

The next question is, where do these habits come from? We learn them, to a certain extent, from our culture's values and taboos. Unwritten rules of a nationality or ethnic group determine what is acceptable. In some cultures, it is bad form to weep at funerals, while in others you are considered heartless unless there is a dramatic display of grief, like fainting or rending your clothes. Many Native American tribes would smother their babies' wails until the babies learned not to cry. The reason was that a crying child could reveal their hiding place to an enemy.

However, within a given culture, why do we not all react the same to similar circumstances? The answer lies in another meaning of the Moon— the mother. (The word "mother" in this discussion includes any female who consistently had caretaker responsibilities.) Because they sleep so much, small babies spend much of their time on the astral plane, where emotions are a strongly active force. The psychic connection between mother and infant is powerful. At that stage, mother must constantly attend to the baby, and the infant's world is still very limited. It is almost as though you bathed in the sea of emotions your mother experienced most strongly as she took on the responsibility of parenthood.

Your mother's predominant emotions become part of your outlook on life. They govern how you feel about being in the world and whether it seems safe and trustworthy. You also tend to be most at home with those emotions. They may or may not have been characteristic later, but were her primary state in your first year or two. The Moon also symbolizes the unconscious, and most of this conditioning happened before you could consciously understand what was going on. We absorb and imitate our mother's emotional state during the first year or so, and it becomes part of our outlook on life. An anxious mother transmits her anxiety to the infant, who then comes to see the world as unsafe and frightening.

Early home conditions, as suggested by the Moon in a horoscope, can set the emotional tone for an entire life. For instance, I have often found that the person with a Moon-Pluto aspect, Moon in Scorpio, or a strong Pluto was born into a household of mourning. Shortly before or after the child was born, there was a significant death that upset the family, especially the mother, so the child's normal needs were unmet or secretly resented. The child takes on this mournfulness, and it becomes a strong part of his or her response to life.

Because these states are unconscious, it requires a great effort to become aware of Moon habits and break them. Therapy and other insight-producing situations may help if these habits are making your life miserable. However, conscious awareness is a good beginning, and it can come through studying the Moon in your horoscope. The Moon's sign and aspects relate to the mother's state during the child's first year of life. For example, with Moon in Capricorn, the mother was probably depressed or very somber in the child's earliest months—perhaps even suffering from postpartum depression. Living in this emotional bath, her offspring's reactions to the world may be shaped by depression, even in adulthood. Moon in Scorpio may show a woman who was more than reluctant to care for a baby then. She may even have become pregnant in the midst of a power struggle with her husband. Her resentment of the infant's needs may imprint the child with a strong tendency toward brooding and real ambivalence about nurturing.

Apart from the tone of your earliest contacts with mother, she shaped your emotions in the same way she shaped a great variety of behaviors you take for granted. She trained you—just as she did in toothbrushing and table manners—by giving her approval or withholding it. Like anyone else, Mom had a narrow comfort zone of emotions. If she gave attention or approval for showing particular emotions, they would tend to increase. If she withdrew—or even punished you—when you displayed others, you quickly learned to suppress them or mask them behind the ones she could accept.

For instance, the mother of a child born with Moon in Aries typically has little patience when the child is whining, clinging, or afraid. She may respond with impatience and even rage. On the other hand, some such mothers have a sneaking admiration for spunky little displays of independence, of assertiveness, or even of temper. You can guess which of these qualities she suppressed and which she rewarded. In addition, rage is contagious, so if she was irritable and impatient in handling the child, the result could be an irritable child.

Contrarily, the mother of a Moon in Capricorn child may respond with stern discipline to temper tantrums, but reward the "stiff upper lip" approach. The child's anger threatens to trigger her own suppressed rage, which she defends against at all costs, so the child has to be stopped. She may spank or withdraw when her child shows anger.

A child who is repeatedly punished for showing anger will soon become afraid of feeling it, due to its unpleasant consequences. When anger arises, the child will quickly push it down or turn it inward. Yet, psychologists point to anger turned inward as a major cause of depression—and depression is often a recurrent feature of life for the Capricorn Moon individual. If Mom, herself, was often depressed, she could accept and respond to sadness in her child more readily than to anger. As the child gets more sympathy for depression, that response increases. A similar process of learning, through reward and punishment by key parental figures, holds true for other emotional patterns as well.

Siblings within the same family may have different Moon signs and aspects. This reflects how differently each may have experienced the mother, due to changes in her life circumstances, the family structure, and her emotional state. For instance, she may have been anxious and insecure about her ability to handle the first child, but was an old hand at mothering by child number three. Thus, the first child might have Moon in Cancer, while the third might have Moon in Taurus.

Why Change Your Emotional Habits?

Although we can gain insight by identifying our own personal emotional habits, why would we want to change them? If they seem safer and more comfortable than unfamiliar or threatening ones, why would we risk the discomfort? If it works, why fix it?

Like any habit relied on too frequently, emotional habits can become an impediment. When we react like robots, we lose authenticity and live a falsehood. There is always a deadening of experience—a price to be paid—for such lies. We also lose the chance to improve the emotion-provoking situation. Uncomfortable feelings motivate us to change and to grow more readily than comfortable ones.

Suppose that anger is hard for you to deal with, so you convert it to depression. If you are in an irritating situation over any length of time and continue to convert the anger to depression, you can become immobilized. Depression is a passive state, whereas anger calls for an active response. (Remember that Mars signifies both anger and action.) When you suppress anger, you ignore the valuable signals—the red flags or flashing red lights—that alert you that a situation needs to be addressed. Allow yourself to recognize the anger, as unsettling as it might be. The discomfort can motivate you to assert yourself or otherwise take action to resolve the conflict.

Furthermore, any habit can become a compulsion or an addiction in times of stress or in a chronically difficult life situation. We all know people who are addicted to suffering, and, unfortunately, we all know a rageaholic or two—people who are continually in a rage. The more the disallowed feelings arise in response to a difficult situation, the harder we evoke the acceptable ones. Ultimately, they themselves become a continual torment. Suppose your pattern is to cover up anger with anxiety. When an enraging circumstance persists, you are likely to become more and more anxious until you are no longer able to function.

Eventually, under some outer planet transit, suppression and substitution no longer work. The emotions you expend so much energy to keep at bay break through, all the stronger for being so long suppressed, and you have to face them anyway. During transits to the Moon by Saturn, Uranus, Neptune, or Pluto, in particular, we confront unfamiliar and unacceptable feelings that we must learn to integrate. For instance, under a hard aspect of transiting Neptune to the birth Moon, old defenses often dissolve, inundating people with feelings they had previously hidden from themselves. During this transit, people often fear they are having a nervous break-DOWN, because of this breakTHROUGH of forbidden feelings. (We'll go deeply into outer planet transits in chapter 15.)

When someone habitually suppresses anger, a major transit to Mars can bring that long-suppressed anger to the surface. This means that the individual must face the backlog of anger and do something with it—hopefully something constructive. The individual who continues to suppress anger during such transits may well attract unwelcome people or circumstances to force a confrontation with the disowned rage.

Ultimately, the hard work of suppressing uncomfortable emotions and substituting more comfortable ones is not cost-effective. At the very least, it would be useful to have a choice whether to know your real feelings or not. Therefore, we also will explore tools to help you become aware of and break undesirable habits, in order to become healthier.

How Can You Change Unwanted Emotional Habits?

For each Moon sign, we will see undesirable emotional habits—undesirable, that is, when people evoke them rigidly and compulsively. We also will look at a positive new habit you could develop, drawing on the more positive qualities of that sign. This new behavior can help you integrate a broader range of feelings. Especially during major transits, old habits may cease to work. You may need to find healthier responses like the ones that will be suggested.

I also will suggest a healing tool—the flower remedies—to mitigate bad habits and develop positive ones. I have written about these remedies—also known as essences—in several books, but in detail in the *Flower Remedies Handbook* (Sterling, 1992). For those who are not familiar with them, these liquids help to catalyze healing and self-awareness in a gentle, natural way. Not to be confused with aromatherapy or herbal preparations, the flower remedies are more akin to homeopathy. The energy field or essence of the plant affects your own energy field, releasing emotional backlogs and repairing damage.

Those with a scientific bent may wonder how the remedies work. I don't know how, any more than I know how astrology works. However, long experience has convinced me that both astrology and flower remedies not only work, but work far beyond the power of suggestion. The Bach remedies have been clinically tested for over sixty years throughout the British Commonwealth. Both Bach and several of the more modern companies have been used in the U.S. for twenty years and longer. Third world countries, such as Brazil and Argentina, are embracing them enthusiastically; there are over 3000 certified practitioners in Argentina.

Beyond that, you may be reassured to know about a tightly constructed research study that demonstrated the Bach remedies' effects were statistically significant. For his doctoral dissertation, Michael Weisglas selected three groups of people. One group received a mixture of four remedies, one got seven remedies, and one was given a placebo bottle (it contained no remedies but was indistinguishable from the others). He gave a psychological test to all participants before they took the remedies, then after three weeks, and again after six weeks. The placebo group did not change, so the power of suggestion was ruled out. The group receiving four remedies improved significantly in self-esteem, well-being, creativity, and other positive qualities. The group receiving seven remedies had more difficulty.[3] (I believe that this was because the participant's remedies were not individually selected, which would become more important the greater the number of remedies in the mix.)

Let's be clear that the remedies do not take feelings away. They are not liquid Prozac. They help you become aware of your true feelings and work through them more quickly, neither stuffing nor holding onto them. For instance, remedies for grief, such as **Hackberry** by Desert Alchemy, or **Bleeding Heart** by the Flower Essence Society, will not take away your grief. However, they will help you work through bereavement without either getting stuck in any of the stages, or freezing the grief, only to have to confront it years later. They also help resolve difficult emotions and experiences in a healthy and frequently spiritual way. The remedies help you come to terms with that death. You may become willing to let go of the person, so you both can continue in your evolution.

One thing to know about remedy work is that sometimes with a new mixture—especially your first one—you may experience a catharsis in the first day or so. Suppose you wanted to work on your indignation about the way your boss treats women, so you take Bach's **Vervain**. Rather than chilling out, you might just be more incensed for a few days, as the upset you

---

[3]From *The Flower Essence Journal*, v.1:1, 1980, pp. 11–14. Published by the Flower Essence Society.

have been suppressing to get by on the job is evoked. This phenomenon, called a healing crisis, is seen in many healing efforts, up to and including conventional psychotherapy. Sometimes it is a needed catharsis—like a spat that clears the air in a relationship. Sometimes it only seems worse because you have chosen to face your emotions head-on, rather than hiding from them any longer. The remedies don't cause anything that isn't part of you already, but they can increase awareness of those parts. I often suggest that working people start a remedy on the weekend, when they would have more private time to process any reactions.

At any rate, it doesn't happen to everyone or all the time. If it does, cut back to one or two doses a day until you feel better. Your days off are often a better time to start a remedy because it gives you a few days to work your reaction through. In the case of **Vervain**, as it takes effect, the remedy won't make you stop caring about the discrimination, but it can help you see more clearly what actions to take. You will also be able to pursue those actions calmly, with less danger of losing it.

Often, while working through an important issue with the flower remedies, layer after layer will emerge, so that more than one mixture may be needed. Grief frequently contains components of shock, sorrow, guilt, resentment, or the wish to follow the loved one into death. Subsequent mixtures can address each new layer as it arises, while continuing to work on issues that are not completely resolved. The remedies are not a magic bullet or a quick fix, but they do catalyse change. For a better idea of what they do and don't do, here's an excerpt from a rap song I wrote and recorded about the Bach Remedies.

> I don't mean to imply
> that it's all clover,
> you just pop some drops
> and your troubles are over.
> It's not like that—
> you still have to work.
> You have to keep going
> and you cannot shirk
> your responsibilities
> for your own healing.
> No, that'd be stealing.
> But if you use these drops,
> it goes a lot better.
> Your consciousness grows

and you shake off the fetters
of your old patterns,
and you come to see
that your thoughts are prisons,
and you get free.

Flower remedies are not for everyone, certainly, so if they are just too much of a stretch for you now, skip over the flower remedy sections in various chapters. You may find yourself coming back to them later, when the strangeness of the idea recedes. As for this chapter, don't miss out on the description of your own emotional habits, listed under your Moon sign, at the end.

Finding and Using the Flower Remedies

The oldest and best-researched of these remedies are those by the Bach Company, developed in the early 1930s and documented since then. The Bach remedies are available in many health food stores, particular the well-known **Rescue Remedy** for emergencies. Besides Bach, we will draw on several companies here. One major source is the Flower Essence Society (or FES), makers since the 1970s of the so-called "California remedies." FES conducts excellent training seminars, and many of the other companies also hold workshops, so get on their mailing lists if you are interested. Addresses for several companies appear at the end of this chapter, so that you can write for catalogs with a more detailed description of offerings.

A company that is coming into its own in the 1990s is Desert Alchemy, which makes essences from cacti and other desert plants. These plants, which survive great heat and drought, have a very strong life force, which the essences draw upon. Water represents the emotions, and the desert is anything but wet. Nonetheless, these essences can be very helpful in dealing with emotions. My watery clients—i.e., the overly emotional ones with important planets in Cancer, Scorpio, or Pisces—seem to find these essences helpful. In taking them, they more quickly—and with less upheaval—release feelings and patterns they would have previously held onto. Along with individual essences, we will mention Desert Alchemy's premixed combinations.

When you purchase a flower remedy, most likely it will be in concentrate form, called "stock." If so, you will need to get a one ounce amber dropper bottle—the type nose drops come in—from the drugstore or the flower remedy companies. Add four drops of each concentrate to the bottle, along with an ounce of spring water. Shake the bottle 100 times to disperse the mixture. Take four drops of the mixture four times a day, unless your intuition guides you to take fewer doses. (If you'd feel more secure having an expert select your remedies, most of the companies do consultations by mail for a fee.) With this tool, less is definitely more. You get the optimal response by taking the diluted version rather than the concentrate. The exception is during a healing session or ceremony. In one to three bottles of the mixture, you will undergo a process of gaining greater awareness of your feelings and insights into their causes. You will release emotional backlogs and gradually develop healthier ways of handling these emotions.

In a severe depression or other serious emotional difficulty, naturally, you would want to consult a qualified psychotherapist. You would also want to get a complete physical evaluation, since physical imbalances can produce emotional imbalances. The remedies do not replace psychotherapy, health care, or medication when needed. However, many therapists find them a helpful adjunct to the process. Although I will suggest helpful remedies throughout the rest of the book, the descriptions will necessarily be brief. To learn whether a particular essence applies to you, consult the companies' catalogs and literature for a fuller description.

Flower Remedies of General Use in Dealing with Emotions

Here is where differences between the Bach and more modern remedies become obvious. The British of Bach's era were also of the stiff upper lip school, so I find no remedies of general use in integrating the emotions. However, there are remedies for specific responses like fear, discouragement, and anger. Because Dr. Bach developed his remedies in the climate of fear and discouragement that accompanied the Great Depression of the 1930s, they contain a detailed spectrum of remedies for these two emotions. Until encountering the Bach kit, I never realized there were so many distinct types of discouragement. It's almost like the Eskimos, who have dozens of words for different kinds of snow.

On the other hand, FES developed many of their remedies during the Human Potential movement of the 1970s. At that time, masses of people were first going to therapy or studying psychology and applying these ideas to themselves. You may find their remedies applying more to the issues of the inner planets. They also provide support for constructive expressions of Neptune, like creativity and psychic development. (The Bach remedies, on the other hand, include many for the full spectrum of expressions of Mars, Saturn, and Pluto.) Concerning the Moon, the FES kit contains several important remedies for understanding, processing, and integrating the full emotional spectrum. They can be taken along with remedies for specific emotions.

Their **Black-Eyed Susan** helps people who resist looking at emotions, especially the less acceptable ones. **Fuchsia** is for those who mask their true feelings with generalized hysteria, hyper-emotionality, or psychosomatic illness. Their **Scarlet Monkeyflower** is for those who bottle up feelings until they explode. The essence helps them stop this cycle in favor of one where they examine and deal with their reactions honestly as they arise. Throughout this discussion, I will refer to the explanations given in their *Flower Essence Repertory*, a valuable reference for anyone working with the Bach and FES remedies.

Desert Alchemy also has several remedies of general usefulness in changing emotional habits. Here I quote from the catalog descriptions written by cofounder Cynthia Kemp, with her permission. (Astrologically sophisticated herself, Cynthia has suggested remedies throughout this chapter.) For instance, **Violet Curls** helps in recognizing and processing feelings as they arise, so as not to create a backlog. It relieves congestion in the emotional body and balances it to function in harmony with the physical and mental bodies. **Ocotillo** is useful for those whose subconscious feelings erupt in uncontrolled ways. It helps people understand and accept their feelings without being victimized by them. **Cardon** releases powerful energies for change as repressed feelings are unlocked, so that the shadow side becomes a source of strength. Two of their combinations are also helpful: **Experiencing One's Feelings** and the **Emotional Awareness Formula**.

These remedies from FES and Desert Alchemy help expand your emotional range. They can be especially useful during psychotherapy or healing work. They support the process by working through the layers of feeling more quickly and with less tendency to get stuck in various layers. They would be useful to take along with the remedies for specific emotions. Suppose you are working on releasing a backlog of guilt, so you take **Pine**, by Bach. Adding **Black-Eyed Susan** would help you be more at ease with your shadow side. Thus, you could more easily face and deal with actual transgressions, so that you wouldn't be so likely to hold onto the guilt. The end result is spiritual, in that you don't lose your conscience or stop feeling guilty when it is appropriate. Instead you more quickly recognize when you have done something you aren't proud of, and work to correct it. You learn from mistakes, but are no longer haunted by guilt.

Emotional Habits of the Twelve Moon Signs

Let's look at the Moon signs and their habits. In addition to your Moon sign, check the signs ruled by any strong aspects to your Moon, particularly conjunctions. You learned how to find these correspondances in the last chapter. Leo Moons born while Pluto was in Leo may have Pluto conjunct their Moon. Many of them are far more like the description of Moon in Scorpio. Some Cancer Moons born with Uranus in Cancer may find that they identify strongly with the patterns described under Moon in Aquarius. Libra Moons with conjunctions to Neptune may have some Piscean characteristics. A hard aspect from Mars may give you some Aries Moon traits, and a conjunction of Venus to the Moon can give you some Libran qualities.

For each habit, remedies from various companies will be listed in paren-thesis. To give complete descriptions of their uses would take a book, but each helps resolve the pattern in question. The lists are only suggestions, and may or may not be correct for any given individual with that Moon sign at a particular time. For a more complete understanding of various remedies, consult the catalogs and literature of that company, or my own book on the subject. Check your selections with a pendulum, muscle reflex, or other test, if you know how. Add remedies for emotional integration like **Fuchsia** or **Violet Curls** to enhance the mixture and speed the healing. Some patterns and remedies apply to more than one sign, usually within the same element.

Moon in Aries: A typical emotional habit is to respond to crisis or challenge with anger, rather than unwelcome feelings like fear, neediness, or inade-quacy. (Suggested remedies for this pattern would include **Impatiens** by Bach; **Scarlet Monkeyflower**, **Tiger Lily**, or **Snapdragon** by FES; **Compass Barrel Cactus** or **Mala Mujer** by Desert Alchemy.)

Another habit is leaping into action—compulsively doing, to keep from feeling at all. This is different from Virgo's compulsive working, in that Aries do not necessarily value productivity, only action. Any action will suf-fice, even purposelessly driving around for hours at top speed. (Remedies that would help this pattern include Desert Alchemy's **Fairy Duster**, **Jump-**

ing **Cholla Cactus**, and their combination formula, **Unwind—Integrating Being and Doing**.)

A POSITIVE NEW HABIT for Aries Moons to cultivate: tackle your feelings with as much courage and vitality as you tackle all new undertakings.

Moon in Taurus: A strong tendency for Taurus Moon, when confronted with crisis or unwelcome feelings, is balking, with a stubborn refusal to change. (Remedies that help are **Chestnut Bud** by Bach, for those who refuse to learn from their mistakes; **Cayenne** by FES; **Desert Willow** by Desert Alchemy, to create emotional flexibility and to accept change, and the **Wind and Storm** combination by Desert Alchemy.)

Taurus Moons also ward off feelings by the Shop 'Til You Drop ploy or by overeating. A particular emotion they avoid in this way is deprivation or fear of lack. This pattern includes compulsive spending to fill the emptiness. (Useful remedies here are **Hedgehog Cactus** by Desert Alchemy and **Hound's Tongue** by FES.)

For Taurus Moons, a POSITIVE NEW HABIT would be to tend your feelings as lovingly as you tend your garden.

Moon in Gemini: One habit is getting on the phone or the modem and talking for hours about anything that comes to mind. Compulsive talking can be a way of warding off emotions—or intimacy, for that matter. (**Cosmos** or **Calendula** by FES can help the chatterer, as can **Foothills Paloverde** by Desert Alchemy.)

As mentioned earlier, Gemini Moons also rationalize their emotions away. They can often talk articulately about feelings, analyzing and labeling them. Naming them is not the same as feeling them. (For this pattern, try Desert Alchemy's **Emotional Awareness Formula**, or **Foothills Paloverde**, or **Isopogon**, by Australian Bush Flower Essences.)

A POSITIVE NEW HABIT would be to have a dialogue with your feelings. Writing them out would help. Get curious about them.

Moon in Cancer: While tears may be legitimate expressions of emotion, frequent crying may serve as a defensive maneuver. Just as Moon in Aries people often rage when they need to cry, Cancer Moons cry when they need to rage. "I'm not angry, I'm just hurt." (The crier may need **Fuchsia** by FES, **Windflower** by Pacific Essences, or **Milk Thistle** by Pegasus. The **Water Formula** or **Emotional Awareness Formula** by Desert Alchemy may be helpful to all water signs in regulating and balancing emotions.)

Living in the past is another common theme, as a way of avoiding the emotions brought out by today's difficulties. Nostalgia or homesickness may serve as an escape. (**Honeysuckle** by Bach is the primary remedy for this pattern, but Desert Alchemy also suggests **Arizona White Oak** or **Lilac**.)

Like Taurus, many Cancer Moons turn to overeating as a way to avoid feelings, especially anger or neediness. (Remedies to help are **Milkweed** and **Mariposa Lily** by FES; **Hedgehog Cactus**, **Milky Nipple Cactus**, or the **Inner Mother Formula** by Desert Alchemy.)

A POSITIVE NEW HABIT for Cancer Moons would be to nurture yourself, while exploring your feelings. One nurturing act would be to tend your nest, as attention to the home can make you feel better when you're blue or bereft. (**Angel Wing Begonia**, by Desert Alchemy, can help you tend your nest.)

Moon in Leo: A primary pattern is putting on a good front, and hiding one's feelings so that others won't know. Laughing on the outside, dying inside. (To let go of the facade, try **Agrimony** by Bach, or **White Desert Primrose** or the **Embracing Humanness** combination by Desert Alchemy.)

Conversely, creating drama or uproar is a way of getting attention while focusing it away from the real issues and the quieter and less dramatic feelings. (Remedies to offset these patterns include **Chicory** by Bach and **Crisis Formula** or **Fairy Duster** by Desert Alchemy.)

A POSITIVE NEW HABIT: Use psychodrama or gestalt techniques to let those quieter feelings be heard.

Moon in Virgo: Criticizing and finding fault, especially about small matters, can serve as a smoke screen for other feelings, such as disappointment. (To change the habit of being too critical, try **Beech** by Bach, or **Mala Mujer**, **Strawberry Cactus**, or **Recognizing and Releasing Judgment and Denial** by Desert Alchemy.)

You won't be surprised to discover that working too hard is one of Moon in Virgo's bad emotional habits. Workaholism is often a convenient escape from confronting important issues in their personal life and of avoiding unsettling emotions. (Those who work too hard can find relief in **Aloe Vera** by FES, **Rock Water** or **Oak** by Bach, and the combination formula **Unwind—Integrating Being and Doing** by Desert Alchemy.)

When other defenses fail, these natives get sick. The Moon in Virgo person may express feelings through psychosomatic ailments, often having one or more vulnerable organs that malfunction. (Those with psychosomatic ailments can learn to integrate their emotions by using **Fuchsia** and

Self-Heal by FES, or **Strawberry Cactus** or **Star Primrose** by Desert Alchemy.)

Virgo Moons, many of you have such good work and health habits, but here is one to try for your emotional health. Work as hard at allowing yourself to feel—and to feel thoroughly—as you are capable of working on any other worthwhile endeavor. (Try the **Embracing Humanness** combination by Desert Alchemy.)

Moon in Libra: One knee-jerk response is preserving the peace at any price, so they suppress conflict and any other emotions that might rock the boat. They also try to smooth over the situation by exercising their considerable charm. (Helpful remedies might be **Agrimony** by Bach, **Trumpet Vine** and **Goldenrod** by FES, or **Hoptree**, or **Canyon Grapevine** by Desert Alchemy.)

Compulsively looking for love and affection can become an addiction used to take away fear, sorrow, and other painful emotions. (Try **Pink Yarrow** by FES, **Centaury** or **Chicory** by Bach, and Desert Alchemy's formulas: **Unconditional Love and Support**, and **Making and Honoring Boundaries**.)

A POSITIVE NEW HABIT for Libra Moons to cultivate would be to make peace with even the negative feelings. Learn to balance all those warm and wonderful feelings with others that are more difficult to accept. (Use **Cardon** by Desert Alchemy.)

Moon in Scorpio: Resentment can be more than a habit, it can be a life style for these people. Going over and over their grudges and the wrongs done to them can be a way of hanging onto the person they once cared for. It also avoids processing the underlying grief at the loss. (**Willow** by Bach, is an important transformative tool for resentment. It is often followed by remedies for grief such as FES's **Bleeding Heart**, or **Yerba Santa**, or Desert Alchemy's **Hackberry**, **Crown of Thorns**, or **Compass Barrel Cactus**.)

For some, getting even can be a knee-jerk response. Retaliating, or holding onto the idea of revenge for years afterward, is a still more toxic level of resentment. One is reminded of the Scorpion's sting. (A very important—and life transforming—remedy to take would be **Holly** by Bach, or **Mountain Wormwood**, for forgiveness, by the Alaskan Flower Essence Project. Desert Alchemy's **Inmortal** or **Compass Barrel Cactus** can also help.)

Another well-established habit may be to withdraw and isolate, so no one will see them in an emotional state. They are also protected from further conflict or vulnerability. (Remedies against isolation include **Shooting Star** or **Mariposa Lily** by FES, and **Mesquite** and **Teddy Bear Cholla** by Desert Alchemy.)

A POSITIVE NEW HABIT would be to transform the negative feelings by allowing them to flow through you rather than holding onto them. In the process, they will transmute into something else. (Remedies to support this stance would be the **Water** or **Emotional Awareness** formulas by Desert Alchemy.)

Moon in Sagittarius: Philosophizing about upsetting situations, rather than experiencing and truly processing them can become a habit. If the reactions are not cosmic or enlightened, they must go! Jupiterians are especially prone to pushing feelings—especially the downbeat ones—away by projecting a falsely optimistic outlook. (Try **Star Primrose** by Desert Alchemy or **Agrimony** by Bach.)

Gambling, overindulging, or taking excessive risks can be an addictive or compulsive way of avoiding feelings or issues. (For patterns of excess or ill-considered risk-taking, try **Four Leaf Clover** by Pegasus, **Cherry Plum** by Bach, or **Harmonizing Addictive Patterns, Klein's Pencil Cholla**, or **Hedgehog Cactus** by Desert Alchemy.)

A POSITIVE NEW HABIT: Recognize processing your emotions as a tool for expansion and growth. Find out what the latest personal growth guru is saying and see how it applies to you—but don't teach others until you've truly mastered it yourself.

Moon in Capricorn: A primary habit, although a painful one, is depression, especially as a way of avoiding anger. Depression can be addictive. (If anger is the suppressed emotion, test for **Scarlet Monkeyflower** by FES. Bach has many remedies for depression. Consult the books to find out which one applies to the specific situation. Desert Alchemy offers **Inmortal, Rainbow Cactus**, and **Experiencing One's Feelings**.) Again, chronic or clinical depression may require treatment.

Capricorn Moons work hard for status and security, just like Capricorn Suns. However, when unwelcome emotions arise, they may respond by working even harder. (**Rock Water** by Bach, is a primary remedy for workaholism. Like Virgo Moons, they may benefit from **Aloe Vera** by FES or the formula **Unwind—Integrating Being and Doing** by Desert Alchemy.)

Taking control is a habit for both Capricorn and Scorpio Moons, although they do it for slightly different reasons. For Scorpio, the issue is power versus powerless, while for Capricorn control ensures safety and proves one's competence. (Try **Vine** by Bach, or **Strawberry Cactus**, or **The Universe Handles the Details** by Desert Alchemy.)

A POSITIVE NEW HABIT to develop, with all the discipline Capricorn can muster: rather than getting stuck in depression, bite the bullet and allow your real feelings to come out. (**Hackberry**, by Desert Alchemy.)

Moon in Aquarius: A primary habit is to intellectualize, as a way of shutting down feelings. This is similar to Moon in Gemini, but more brainy—rather like Gemini with a Ph.D. Raw emotions are just not enlightened enough for them to own. (Helpful remedies include **Nasturtium** by FES, **Isopogon** by Australian Bush Essences, and **Foothills Paloverde**, or **Embracing Humanness Formula** by Desert Alchemy.)

Aquarians are different from ordinary, garden variety humans and often get negative feedback about not conforming. To avoid feelings of social insecurity, rejection, or shyness, they often become aloof or withdrawn, or react by feeling superior. (Try **Water Violet** by Bach, or **Teddy Bear Cholla**, or **Mesquite** by Desert Alchemy.)

Having stuffed and denied their feelings too long, people with this Moon may periodically explode to release them. This is very different from the drama of Leo Moons, in that an audience is not of positive value—in fact, there can be embarrassment at having blown one's cool. (Particularly helpful would be **Ocotillo**, or **Recognizing and Releasing Judgment and Denial** by Desert Alchemy, perhaps in combination with **Scarlet Monkeyflower** by FES.)

A POSITIVE NEW HABIT: Grant your emotions equal rights to exist, rather than always favoring the intellect.

Moon in Pisces: One major pattern for this Moon sign, when confronted with unwelcome emotions, is spacing out. This may take the form of daydreaming or fantasizing—or a nebulous, lost in space feeling. When confronted with an upsetting situation, they can react like a lens going out of focus. Often, they haven't a clue why they suddenly feel so crummy. They instantly convert it to, "This world is a terrible place, and I don't belong here. Why was I born. Angry? Oh, not me, I'm much too spiritual to get angry." (Bach's **Clematis** is a precise remedy for this type. Also helpful can be **Fawn Lily**, **St. John's Wort** by FES, or **Sacred Datura** by Desert Alchemy.)

Getting high or drunk can become a habit, and even, when relied on too frequently, an addiction. (Though no one would claim flower remedies alone can cure addictions, some helpful essences are **California Poppy** and **Morning Glory** by Pegasus, and Desert Alchemy offers **Morning Glory Tree**, and the formula called **Harmonizing Addictive Patterns**.)

Feeling sorry for yourself can become a bad habit or even an addiction. There are narcissistic gratifications for the martyr type, but it keeps you from taking effective action to improve the situation. (When this pattern comes up, take **Chicory** or **Heather** by Bach, or **Inmortal** or **Woven Spine Pineapple** by Desert Alchemy.)

What POSITIVE NEW HABIT can you cultivate? As a way of gaining perspective on your feelings, give service to others with the same or similar problems. Listen to them tell their stories, and you will often find that your own feelings are very similar. Self-pity may disappear as you hear about people who are even worse off than you are. (**Larkspur** or **Trillium** by FES can support the development of positive leadership and service.)

Addresses of Flower Remedy Companies

Now that you've learned some habits and patterns of your Moon sign, I hope that you will venture to try the flower remedies to help you recognize your true reactions and deal with them in a healthy way. For those who are curious enough to try them, remember that the remedies are not a magic bullet, but they can be a catalyst to change. The Bach flower remedies can be found in most areas in a variety of health food and new age book stores. Addresses for the other companies mentioned here are as follows:

Alaskan Flower Essences
P. O. Box 1369
Homer, AK 99603-1369
(907)235-2188

Desert Alchemy
Box 44189
Tuscon, AZ 85733
(520)325-1545

Healing Herbs
P. O. Box 65
Hereford HR2 0UW
England

Pacific Essences
Box 8317
Victoria, BC V8W 3R9
Canada
(250)384-5560

Australian Bush Flower Essences
8A Oaks Avenue
Dee Why, NSW 2099
Australia

Flower Essence Services
Box 1769
Nevada City, CA 95959
(800)548-0075

Living Essences
P. O. Box 355
Scarborough 6019
Perth, WA
Australia

Pegasus Products
Box 228
Boulder, CO 80306
(800)527-6104

What can you do if you aren't ready to order bunches of bottles of remedies—maybe you want to sample one first, or maybe remedies from several different companies appeal to you? An excellent resource is Centergees, which carries over 1,900 different flower and crystal essences. Contact them at:

Centergees
2007 Northeast 39
Portland, OR 97212
(503)284-6603

Suggested Reading About the Remedies

Chancellor, Dr. Philip M. *Handbook of the Bach Flower Remedies.* Saffron Walden, England: The C.W. Daniel Co. Ltd., 1976.

Cunningham, Donna. *Flower Remedies Handbook.* New York: Sterling Publishing, 1992.

Flower Essence Society. *Flower Essence Repertory.* Revised Edition. Nevada City, CA: Flower Essence Society, 1994.

Johnson, Steve M. *Flower Essences of Alaska.* Homer, AK: Alaskan Flower Essence Project, 1992.

Kemp, Cynthia. *Cactus & Company: Patterns and Qualities of Desert Flower Essences.* Tucson, AZ: Desert Alchemy, 1993.

Pettitt, Sabina. *Energy Medicine: Pacific Flower and Sea Essences.* Victoria, BC: Pacific Essences, 1993.

Vlamis, Gregory. *Flowers to the Rescue.* Rochester, VT: Healing Arts Press, 1988.

CHAPTER 6

Tool Time—How Following
the Moon Can Make Life Easier

No, we're not settling down to watch an episode of Home Improvement. However, we *are* getting out our tool kit, full of astrological wrenches and ratchets. Life is much easier if you ride the lunar currents, rather than trying to swim against them. The solar world teaches you to beat up on yourself when you can't produce at the same high rate every day, rain or shine, summer or winter. When you don't meet your Should Quotient, you wonder what's wrong with you—why you're having trouble crunching numbers when the Moon is in Pisces, for instance. Self-flagellation doesn't improve productivity, but it does increase stress. You need to know the best times for doing things. You need to know when the best thing to do is nothing at all. You need to know when to rest. There's no manual for that in the solar world, but astrology does have one. It's called an ephemeris.

Making Use of Lunar Rhythms

Be aware of the phase the Moon is in and how it relates to the body and mind. When we are not attuned to these phases, we can overextend ourselves so much we become exhausted or demoralized. Activity during the waxing phase is balanced with rest and reflections during the waning phase.[1]

---

[1] Kathleen Rathbone, "The Lunar Calendar as Symbol and Affirmation," *Womanspirit,* v. 2:8, Summer, 1976, p. 51.

The Moon passes through the twelve signs of the zodiac in its monthly orbit. You can track it through an astrological calendar or an ephemeris. Clearly, a calendar is no match for the kinds of social problems we are facing, but it can be a helpful stress reduction tool. Following the Moon's monthly and yearly cycles helps us keep on an even keel emotionally, so we can cut our stress levels. We have seen how powerfully the Moon, as a physical force, affects our rhythms and emotions. To work with these natural rhythms, it would make sense to pay more attention to the Moon. *Resistance* and *friction* are ideas from physics that are useful in astrology, too. Doing things during a Moon sign alien to what you want to accomplish builds up inner friction that can be wearing. When you work against the flow of lunar energies, you work harder and less effectively than when you work with them.

The Moon's cycle has two parts: 1) the *waxing* Moon, the period from new to full Moon, while the Moon increases in light; and 2) the *waning* Moon, the period between the full Moon to the next new Moon, while the Moon is decreasing. The waxing phase is supposedly best for activity on new projects, spontaneous physical and instinctual activity, and mundane matters. The waning Moon is best for evaluating and completing work begun in the first half of the cycle. It can also be used for creativity, planning, rest, and reflection.

Many astrologers feel the best days to make decisions and launch new projects are just after the new Moon, as the greatest clarity comes after the reflective waning Moon phase. (The day of the new Moon itself is not recommended. Instead, wait at least 24 hours.) Activities and patterns initiated then tend to persist throughout the cycle, so be conscious of the seeds you plant. If you are aware of the new Moon's sign and the house it activates in your chart, planning can be even more attuned to natural rhythms. (The second half of this chapter describes a method for using the new and full Moons to your advantage.)

The full Moon is spiritually powerful and can bring great insight if used for meditation or other spiritual pursuits. (Remember the precaution about meditating in groups rather than alone at the full Moon, for better balance.) Both the full and new Moon are good for work on lunar issues. Astrology helps pinpoint problem areas but even the general reader has doubtlessly identified pressing concerns while reading various chapters.

One time-keeper is the Table of Planetary Hours, known to astrologers since antiquity as a way to schedule activities for the best outcome. Each planet is related to a day of the week and to certain hours of the day. It is considered most effective to pursue Moon matters during Moon hours, or on Monday. Since the hours are counted from sunrise, the exact Moon hour depends on the season. (Almanacs or astrology magazines, like *Dell Horoscope*, often publish a current table.)

There is a substantial body of knowledge about the best Moon signs to pursue a variety of common tasks. Housewives and farmers once relied heavily on this lore and got better results in gardening and other important domestic activities. Llewellyn's annual Moon Sign almanac is full of articles about these practices, in addition to providing the best and worst dates.[2]

Astrologically-derived appointment calendars, such as Jim Maynard's *Celestial Influences*, or Llewellyn's *Daily Planetary Guide*, give the Moon's sign and major aspects each day. (You can buy one in a metaphysical book store or ask them to order it.) The word *zodiac* is Greek, and means "belt of life," so the circle formed by the twelve signs encompasses all areas of life. Watching the daily Moon sign helps you attune to inner rhythms, the ebb and flow of energies that we all experience. By observing yourself as the Moon moves through different signs, you can learn the best times to tackle various activities. Following it through your birth chart would produce the best results. Even without that, you can get useful information from the Moon's position each day. Over time, observe how each Moon sign affects you personally, including your best ones and those where you are at a disadvantage. This is a highly individual matter, stemming from the natal placements of planets in signs and houses.

A very special calendar which is individually generated, based on your birth information, is Astro Numeric Service's Cosmic Window engagement book. Designed by Philip Levine, this handsomely bound marvel shows and interprets your daily and slower-moving transits, rates your stress levels, and gives your best and most difficult days for a variety of activities. It doesn't show the Moon's aspects to your chart, but contains the usual monthly ephemeris and daily Moon signs and void of course periods. The twelve month calendar can begin on any date you specify, not just January 1st (great birthday gift!).[3]

As the Moon goes through a sign, it seems to produce events, emotions, and urges that fit the nature of the sign. For instance, I was in three separate discussions of death in one day. Afterward I discovered that the

---

[2]You can find *The Moon Sign Book* in metaphysical book stores, or call 1-800-THE-MOON. Similar information can be derived from Matrix Software's amazing shareware program for PC's, The Electric Almanac. At only $14.95, it contains an astrological clock which shows the current planetary positions, biorhythms, the I Ching, and does a Tarot reading. To order, call 1-800-PLANETS.

[3]It costs $39.95 at the time of this writing, but you couldn't get an astrologer to plot all this for you by hand for anywhere near that amount. To order, call 1-800-MAPPING.

Moon was in Scorpio, a sign much concerned with death and its meaning. The media often carry stories that match the nature of the Moon's sign, especially at the new and full Moons. Pisces rules the feet, and, once upon a full Moon in Pisces, there was a story about a burglar who broke into a home and forced the residents to suck his toes! Observing the events of daily life, you'll see constant examples of these sign traits.

One clue to understanding the Moon signs is the repetition of the four elements (fire, earth, air, and water) throughout the twelve signs. Signs within the same element share basic energy patterns and concerns, as shown in Table 6. To summarize, while the Moon passes through the water signs (Cancer, Scorpio, Pisces), people are more emotional and introspective. The fire signs (Aries, Leo, and Sagittarius) put people in a more energetic, lively, assertive mood. When the Moon transits the air signs (Gemini, Libra, and Aquarius), communication and mental pursuits are highlighted more than feelings. As the Moon travels through the earth signs (Taurus, Virgo, and Capricorn), people focus on practical, down-to-earth concerns. Understand, however, that these patterns go around in a circle, rather than a straight line.

As you learn the nature of each sign, avoid wasting energy by taking advantage of its most constructive qualities. For example, the Moon traveling through Cancer seems to put many people in a domestic mood. They may enjoy working around the house, cooking, visiting family, or just being quietly at home. A Cancerian who goes off on a business trip might feel especially homesick. Taurus, Virgo, or Capricorn—the earth signs—are good

TABLE 6. THE SIGNS IN EACH ELEMENT.*

FIRE SIGNS	EARTH SIGNS	AIR SIGNS	WATER SIGNS
Aries	Taurus	Gemini	Cancer
Leo	Virgo	Libra	Scorpio
Sagittarius	Capricorn	Aquarius	Pisces
THEIR MAJOR CONCERNS			
FIRE SIGNS	EARTH SIGNS	AIR SIGNS	WATER SIGNS
Initiating	Organizing	Communicating	Evaluating
Action/Energy	Consolidating	Feedback	Creating
Movement	Practicality	Disseminating	Reposing

*Note that the natural zodiac reads across the table, while the elements read down.

for taking stock of your financial situation, or for embarking on small business endeavors. A party? Moon in Leo, Libra, Aquarius, or another outgoing fire or air sign.

Wanting to organize the closets or files? Try Moon in Virgo. If you did it while the Moon was in Pisces, you'd probably never find anything again! Moon in Gemini isn't the greatest for closets either. You'd spend the day on the phone and at the end shove everything back in a worse mess than before, but at least you'd catch up on the gossip.

This technique can help with much more important issues than that pile of junk at the back of your closet. I'm using these small matters to show how much more productive it is to work with the zodiac than against it. To give an example, the Moon in Gemini produces the urge to communicate. Being stuck at home alone with dreary, routine tasks will only create frustration and restlessness. It's a good day to do lunch with someone you'd like to know better. If you're homebound at a time like that, ditch the routine and pursue worthwhile Gemini activities. Catch up on correspondence, or write that story that's been rumbling around in the back of your mind. If you do want to write, I'd suggest you deliberately block off communication so the verbal energy will pour out in words on paper rather than in a big phone bill.

Ah, but you say, "If I butterfly under Gemini, how will those dull household tasks get done?" The zodiac to the rescue! The Moon goes into Cancer next and you'll feel more like tending the home fires. That's the fascinating and profound thing about the zodiac—the sequence of the signs seems to take care of problems like these. If your thinking about an issue is too rigid and traditional while the Moon is in Capricorn, wait a day or so. When the Moon goes into Aquarius, you'll be more innovative. Moon in Pisces got you dreamy and a bit lazy? That's because you need to rest, regroup, and be in touch with your spirituality. Don't worry or feel guilty. The Moon hits Aries next, and you'll spring into action with all those creative ideas you dreamed up under Moon in Pisces.

Signs following each other are related in meaningful ways. Let's say the Moon is in Scorpio, and you've withdrawn into yourself, analyzing some problem. The apparent solution hits you, and BAM! You're off into BIG IDEA Sagittarius, all fired up with enthusiasm for a few days. Next, the Moon moves through Capricorn and brings you back to earth so you can sort out the practicalities. While the Moon is in Aquarius, you talk it over with your peers and get some feedback. As the Moon moves into Pisces, you're a bit disillusioned with the grand plan. You drift off to Never-Never Land for a few days, while your unconscious sorts out what's happened. But another fire sign, Aries, comes next, and you're reenergized. Around and around we go, through all four elements and all twelve signs but there is perfection to the pattern, a logic all its own. (My book, *Moon Signs*, has several chapters about the daily Moon signs and their uses, as well as the new and full Moons.)

A major influence on the prevailing emotional winds occurs when the Moon aspects other planets. Watch those aspects with astrological calendars or an ephemeris. Their effects seldom last longer than half a day. The most powerful modifications are produced as the transiting Moon crosses over the outer planets. The energy then corresponds to the nature of the outer planet rather than the sign. By 1996, Uranus will be firmly entrenched in Aquarius, and Pluto will be in Sagittarius, where they will remain for over a decade. Neptune will shift from Capricorn to Aquarius in 1998.

Even by observing the public mood, you may be able to guess that the Moon is touching off the current position of a planet. If the phone is ringing off the wall and people are talking a mile a minute, the Moon may be aspecting Mercury, the planet of communication. Moon-Venus aspects often put us in a warm, sociable mood, since Venus is the planet of relatedness. If it's one of those days when everyone is irritable, the Moon may be aspecting Mars, the planet of anger. If people are rebellious or erratic, it's probably Uranus. Moon-Neptune is spacey, so watch out for drunken drivers. Moon-Pluto is a decided case of the heavies—the climate is often intense and brooding.

Would these principles work equally well for everyone? The Moon has different effects on different people. Some are profoundly affected, others scarcely seem to feel it. Most strongly impacted are the lunar types—people who have the Sun, Moon, Ascendant, or several planets in Cancer, the Moon near the ascendant or midheaven, and those born at the full or new Moon. So, sometimes, are the people who live with them! I once lived with an unconscious lunar type born on the full Moon who claimed to be unaffected by it, yet I found myself atypically screaming and slamming doors each month when the Moon was full.

The individual's chart also modifies the Moon's effects. Suppose you have Mars and Saturn in the sign Libra. Generally, Moon in Libra should be good for relationships. However, when the Moon passes over your Mars and Saturn, your love life can hit a nasty—but all too familiar—snag. Follow the Moon for a few months to pick out the highs and lows generated by your natal planets.

The houses of your chart also modify Moon transits. The Moon going through your 4th house energizes the home life. The Moon moving through your 6th can bring the necessity to work hard, and the Moon in the 8th may emphasize sex. Natal planets modify house transits. If you have Neptune in the 4th, you'll do more daydreaming than housework while the Moon goes through that house. The 11th house is friendship, but if you have Pluto there, a Moon transit might make you withdraw rather than reach out. Watch the course of the Moon through your own houses until you see how you generally respond to the pattern.

Observe yourself to see which parts of the Moon's monthly cycle are significant—both the good signs and the consistently bad. One healer found that she reacted badly to Moon in Scorpio, becoming resentful and withdrawn. She blocked off those days on her calendar and didn't see clients, knowing that she wasn't at her best. Instead, she used that time to good effect for inner work and self-healing. An astrology speaker found that he was most eloquent when the Moon passed through Sagittarius and formed a grand fire trine with his natal planets. As often as possible, he scheduled his lectures and workshops under Moon in Sag.

I'm not advocating that you become a slave to astrology, so that you won't even go to the hairdresser without consulting your astrologer. But do develop the willingness to let things slide until the time is ripe, rather than being hounded by the "shoulds." When you do things at the wrong time, it takes longer and much of the effort is wasted, spinning your wheels. As you discover your own lunar highs and lows, you can plan more effectively and reduce stress.

The Void of Course Moon—A Lunar Sabbath?

Another lunar phenomenon to be aware of is the *void of course Moon*, which you can track by using an astrological calendar. While the Moon passes through a sign, it aspects the transiting planets. When it comes to the place where it forms no more *major* aspects before leaving that sign, we consider it void of course. Under the date, the calendar will give the Moon sign and say something like, "Moon v/c 12:46 P.M." (Calendars may list either Eastern or Pacific times, so adjust for your zone.) These periods shift continually as the inner planets move through the signs. They can last anywhere from half an hour to a day-and-a-half.

Cancerian Al Morrison was the first modern astrologer to popularize the void of course Moon. It is not considered a good time to initiate important efforts or make important decisions, for, "nothing will come of it." Astrologers pay varied amounts of attention to this factor—anywhere from indifferent to hysterical. One of our most talented astrologers, Michael Lutin, won't even go grocery shopping, for he says the food goes to waste. Michael is a very hardworking guy, and I frankly think he uses the void of course Moon to rationalize some much-needed down time. Whatever it takes!

I'm more moderate (and more absentminded) about these periods, but believe you can save yourself stress and wasted effort by not starting anything major then. Never knowingly mail off a manuscript, or make an important business contact or agreement with another person in those intervals. Instead, tackle routine, undemanding work like housekeeping, filing, or trying to organize your desk. For your convenience, Table 7 provides the top ten list of things *not* to do on a void of course Moon.

Like Michael, I do lots of mooning around the house, listening to music, or vegging out in front of the television when the Moon is void. I also deliberately use it for things that *should* come to nothing—like every bit of work on my taxes. You may be able to think of other matters you hope will come to naught—like responding to nuisance complaints, threatened legal actions, or invitations from people who bore you to tears. Let's say the personnel office wants to meet with you about those lengthy lunch hours. You fully intend to reform, but for protocol's sake they must cuff your ears. Go when the Moon is void. Keep a file on your desk of things to do purposely in those intervals. Fill in the void with tasks like tedious memos you're supposed to respond to, senseless regulations that you can't ignore, or your monthly statistics. Used creatively, the void of course Moon can be a hedge against the time-guzzling, but trivial, pursuits the solar world thinks we should spend our days doing.

TABLE 7. THE TOP TEN LIST OF THINGS NOT TO DO ON A VOID OF COURSE MOON.

1. Begin a class or conference.
2. Start a project.
3. Try to sell something.
4. Initiate new business contacts.
5. Start a job search or a job.
6. Make an important agreement.
7. Sign a contract.
8. Buy a car or house.
9. Get married or take on a partner.
10. Ask Michael Lutin to make a commitment.

How about some more uplifting applications for this phase? It is good for meditation and inner work on emotions. Plato said that the unexamined life is not worth living, and these phases are good for contemplation. Where possible, it is a time to be laid back and lunar. Although the solar world judges us on our productivity, action isn't always useful. In creative pursuits, a period of seeming inactivity when you read a steamy novel or play gin rummy for hours on the computer often produces a fresh burst of inspiration. Just as there is a solar sabbath on *Sun*days, the v\c Moon can function as a lunar sabbath where we attend to our lunar hemisphere and emerge refreshed.

Would having the Moon void in the natal chart have any effect? I've only known one—a Cancer Moon, no less. I hated eating out with him, because we couldn't get fed. He had dozens of food prohibitions and a very suspicious nature. He would drag me from restaurant to restaurant, scrutinizing the menus and interrogating the cooks. We'd finally wind up in some perfectly dismal hole where the food was tasteless but fit his diet. Why didn't I cook for him instead? I did cook a few meals, but always managed to add just that one minor ingredient he couldn't eat, so I stopped. That lunar I'm not!

Finding Balance by Following the Lunations

We've seen how the Moon's monthly orbit around the zodiac creates a full cycle of major human concerns and varieties of experience. Another complete cycle is the yearly array of full and new Moons, which are called *lunations*. This cycle highlights each of the twelve signs and houses in your chart in turn. We will make a map of the lunation cycle, so you can use the new and full Moons to the best advantage. Like the arrangement of the zodiac, there is perfection in the order of the houses, each laying the foundation for the next, or providing balance. Each new Moon energizes one house. If you consciously work on the areas governed by that house while it is highlighted, you will do much better at keeping your life in order. The house where the lunation occurs can become the focus of energy and emotions for anywhere from a week to a month.

If there is turmoil, you should not fear the emotions or feel that the Moon is causing them. Chances are, the emotions and conflicts were already there, but they come out all the more strongly because you've avoided them. Dealing with them allows growth—better than allowing them to fester underneath and deteriorate further.

For instance, if the new Moon falls in your 4th house, you could conceivably argue with your mother, say about the fact that she still treats you as a child. If the disagreement forces you two to deal with hidden resentments, at least it is possible to make a new beginning in this important relationship. Thus, a lunation that brings emotions out into the open is really an opportunity to make life better. In some years, a particular house will have two new Moons or more than two full Moons. When that happens, it is a signal that the concerns of that particular house need more attention for now. Close by, there is probably a house that has no lunations. You get a free pass in that area, no doubt because you've managed it well.

At the new Moon, the Sun and Moon are standing together in one house and sign. For example, a new Moon in Aries happens when the Sun is also in Aries, between March 20th and April 20th each year. Each new Moon focuses a strong jolt of energy in one department of your life. It can then become a productive area to address. If the lunation also aspects a natal planet, the energy may seem even stronger. (The orb of the lunation as it aspects a natal planet would be approximately 3 degrees.)

At the full Moon, the Sun is traveling through a particular sign and house while the Moon occupies the opposite sign and house, so both signs and houses are emphasized. There is tension between these areas, each demanding your attention. The key is to learn how to deal with both in a balanced way, without neglecting either. For instance, a full Moon across the axis of the 6th and 12th houses shows tension between the demands of the work life and the inner life. A full Moon across the 1st/7th axis would show conflict between your own interests and those of your partner, demanding to integrate the two. The affairs of each house pair can conflict unless there is cooperation, but they can also lend mutual support and wholeness when they are integrated. During a typical year, the full Moons will tie in each of the six house pairs twice, producing opportunities to balance every major area of life.

Eclipses and Their Effects

Throughout history, we have been awed by eclipses, and ancient astrologers made their reputations by being able to predict when they would occur. Now we all know when they are happening, and we're able to watch them on television, direct from wherever the totality occurs. Eclipse buffs will even fly halfway around the world to see them in person. (The solar world does have its wondrous features!) In the olden days, eclipses were so mysterious that they were considered powerful and often unfortunate omens. Today, most astrologers would agree that they aren't necessarily destructive. They are an indication of a heightened focus of energy, so most astrologers do track the chart areas where they occur.

When you make the lunation map later, consider the eclipse picture. They are shown on the top row of each table by an *E* next to the date. In 1996, for instance, there are solar eclipses on April 17th and October 12th, and lunar eclipses on April 4th and September 27th. Solar eclipses occur at the new Moon and block out the Sun, while lunar eclipses occur at the full Moon and block out the Moon. The transiting nodes, which determine where eclipses fall, travel backward at the rate of one sign a year. A complete nodal cycle will impact all twelve signs and houses of your chart in turn.

If you have followed eclipses, you may have noticed that some are intense and others are mild. The more intense ones often involve aspects between the Sun and Moon and a transiting outer planet, or they may set off a major pattern in the birth chart. For instance, the solar eclipse on April 17, 1996 at 28 Aries forms a close square to transiting Neptune at 27 Capricorn. Seldom have I seen lunar meltdown at an eclipse unless important outer planet transits have already acted on the same area for a while.

Joanne Wickenburg also points out that the Moon's nodes are necessarily involved in eclipses. She feels that an eclipse at the north node is going to be different—more productive, generally—than one at the south node, which involves more necessity to let go of things. It would take an ephemeris to know this, but the April 4, 1996 eclipse finds the Sun in Aries on the south node, with the Moon near the north node in Libra. (The Sun and Moon can be some distance away from the exact aspect to the nodes, for they are only exact at a total eclipse.)

What can you expect if an eclipse triggers off one of your natal planets? For at least six months afterward, it highlights the house involved, but especially the matters concerned with any planets it aspects. These are periods of special tension between the solar and lunar hemispheres. They are particularly powerful windows for healing work or flower remedies, for a great clearing can occur. When an eclipse affects you in a major way, you may experience conflict in the houses involved. For six months or longer, you will need to concentrate on balance in those areas. Sometimes the eclipse six months later will be in the same house, so there is a repeated emphasis.

An eclipse that aspects a natal planet can trigger an upheaval in the functions of that planet. If so, it's not the Moon's fault. Over time you have allowed those matters to deteriorate or to build up a backlog of tension that must be discharged. Suppose a solar eclipse conjuncts your natal Saturn in the 11th. Perhaps you've been carrying too much responsibility for a friend for far too long—or allowing a friend to assume too much responsibility for you. The eclipse hits, and the friendship is in jeopardy. Don't curse Hecate—you set this up, and now you have to clean it up.

If an upcoming eclipse is going to fall in an area where you feel vulnerable, use this knowledge preventatively. Begin to take stock of the issues, examine what your true feelings are, and then work to improve the situation. When the eclipse happens, you will already have let off some of the tension and resolved some of the problems. It won't be as hard on you as it would be if you'd hid your head in the sand.

Creating Your Own Yearly Lunation Map

Beginners, you may be out of luck with this technique, as no computer service offers this feature. If you've got a pal who's studying astrology or if you happen to have a professional astrologer on retainer, you might twist their arm to do it for you. If you at least know your rising sign, put that on the horizontal line that begins the 1st house. Continue putting the signs of the zodiac on each house counterclockwise around the circle to house number 12. Then follow the instructions given below. Otherwise skip ahead to the next chapter for now.

If you've studied astrology, you'll be able to plot the lunations on a chart wheel. A sample chart blank, which you can photocopy if you want to use it more than once, is given here as Chart 3 (page 115). Begin by placing your natal house cusps around the outside rim, with the exact zodiac degree if possible. (For simplicity's sake, you could photocopy your birth chart. It would be crowded, but you'd easily see lunations that form aspects to natal planets.)

Plotting the New Moons: Use Table 8 (page 116), which shows the dates and degrees of the 1996 new Moons, and follow the instructions below. Once you have plotted the new Moon for each house, consult the readings in the last section of this chapter. You'll be able to design monthly projects and activities that would best suit you. (New Moon tables for 1997–2004 appear in the appendix.)

If you know your rising sign, find that sign on the left side and follow the horizontal row across the table. For instance, if you have Aries rising, the January 20th, 1996 new Moon is in your 10th house, the February 18th new Moon is in your 11th house, and so on. If you have Taurus rising, the new Moon on January 20th would fall into your 9th house, the new Moon

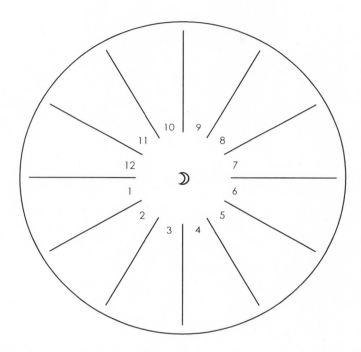

Chart 3. A chart blank for your use.

on February 18th would fall into your 10th house and so on. Plot each lunation into the proper house on your own map. Find the house the January 20th new Moon falls in and continue counterclockwise around the circle. (You won't be starting with the 1st house, unless your rising sign happens to be Capricorn or late Sagittarius.)

The houses in the table are not precise, for if you have the last few degrees of a sign rising, you might do better to follow the row for the next rising sign. (For example, if you had 27 degrees Taurus rising, the Gemini rising wheel would give you more accurate results for this purpose.) The table is just a working example. In one year, you would experience one complete cycle of your houses.

TABLE 8. NEW MOON TABLE FOR 1996.

This table lists the new Moons and the houses they affect for 1996, according to your rising sign.

	1996 NEW MOONS AND THE HOUSES THEY AFFECT											
Date:	1/20	2/18	3/19	4/17E	5/17	6/16	7/15	8/14	9/12	10/12E	11/11	12/10
Rising Sign:	29CP45	29AQ36	29PI07	28AR12	26TA51	25GE12	23CN26	21LE47	20VI27	19LI32	19SC03	18SG56
Aries	10	11	12	1	2	3	4	5	6	7	8	9
Taurus	9	10	11	12	1	2	3	4	5	6	7	8
Gemini	8	9	10	11	12	1	2	3	4	5	6	7
Cancer	7	8	9	10	11	12	1	2	3	4	5	6
Leo	6	7	8	9	10	11	12	1	2	3	4	5
Virgo	5	6	7	8	9	10	11	12	1	2	3	4
Libra	4	5	6	7	8	9	10	11	12	1	2	3
Scorpio	3	4	5	6	7	8	9	10	11	12	1	2
Sagittarius	2	3	4	5	6	7	8	9	10	11	12	1
Capricorn	1	2	3	4	5	6	7	8	9	10	11	12
Aquarius	12	1	2	3	4	5	6	7	8	9	10	11
Pisces	11	12	1	2	3	4	5	6	7	8	9	10

E = Solar Eclipse

Note: See appendix for additional years.

TABLE 9. 1996 FULL MOONS AND THE HOUSES THEY AFFECT.

Date:	1/5	2/4	3/5	4/4E	5/3	6/1	7/1	7/30	8/28	9/27E	10/26	11/25	12/24
Rising Sign:	14CN48	15LE07	15VI06	14LI31	13SC19	11SG37	9CP36	7AQ32	5PI41	4AR17	3TA26	3GE10	3CN20
Aries	4-10	5-11	6-12	7-1	8-2	9-3	10-4	11-5	12-6	1-7	2-8	3-9	4-10
Taurus	3-9	4-10	5-11	6-12	7-1	8-2	9-3	10-4	11-5	12-6	1-7	2-8	3-9
Gemini	2-8	3-9	4-10	5-11	6-12	7-1	8-2	9-3	10-4	11-5	12-6	1-7	2-8
Cancer	1-7	2-8	3-9	4-10	5-11	6-12	7-1	8-2	9-3	10-4	11-5	12-6	1-7
Leo	12-6	1-7	2-8	3-9	4-10	5-11	6-12	7-1	8-2	9-3	10-4	11-5	12-6
Virgo	11-5	12-6	1-7	2-8	3-9	4-10	5-11	6-12	7-1	8-2	9-3	10-4	11-5
Libra	10-4	11-5	12-6	1-7	2-8	3-9	4-10	5-11	6-12	7-1	8-2	9-3	10-4
Scorpio	9-3	10-4	11-5	12-6	1-7	2-8	3-9	4-10	5-11	6-12	7-1	8-2	9-3
Sagittarius	8-2	9-3	10-4	11-5	12-6	1-7	2-8	3-9	4-10	5-11	6-12	7-1	8-2
Capricorn	7-1	8-2	9-3	10-4	11-5	12-6	1-7	2-8	3-9	4-10	5-11	6-12	7-1
Aquarius	6-12	7-1	8-2	9-3	10-4	11-5	12-6	1-7	2-8	3-9	4-10	5-11	6-12
Pisces	5-11	6-12	7-1	8-2	9-3	10-4	11-5	12-6	1-7	2-8	3-9	4-10	5-11

E = Lunar Eclipse

Note: See appendix for additional years.

The table shows the degree of each lunation under the date. Those who have an accurate chart and are able to follow it can put the lunation into the proper house. Since many who will read this book are beginners, the abbreviations for the zodiac signs are used in these tables rather than the glyphs. The abbreviations are as follows:

AR = Aries	LE = Leo	SG = Sagittarius
TA = Taurus	VI = Virgo	CP = Capricorn
GE = Gemini	LI = Libra	AQ = Aquarius
CN = Cancer	SC = Scorpio	PI = Pisces

The New Moon for 1/20/96 is at 29CP45, which means 29 degrees, 45 minutes of the sign Capricorn. Suppose the cusp between your 5th and 6th houses is 28 degrees Capricorn. The New Moon will fall into your 6th house. If the 6th house cusp is 0 Aquarius, the New Moon would fall into the 5th house. Some years there are two new Moons in a house or sign, indicating the need for more work on those issues.

Adding the Full Moons: For some, the part of the map already completed will be enough. However, remember the effects of the full Moon, and how it can challenge you to find balance between competing areas of your life. If you are a lunar type, and especially if you do notice that the full Moons can throw you off, you will want to include them. To plot in the full Moons, go to Table 9 (page 117), and add them to the map. For example, if you have Aries rising, the full Moon on January 5, 1996, listed as 4-10, should be noted in both the 4th and 10th houses. There are usually two full Moons in each house, because six months later another one falls across the same axis. Accordingly, if you have Aries rising, the full Moon on July 1, 1996, listed as 10-4, should also be plotted into the 4th and 10th houses. (Full Moon tables for 1997–2005 appear in the Appendix.)

Understanding Your Lunation Cycles

Now that you've (hopefully!) constructed your lunation map, let's look at the meaning of the lunations in each of the twelve houses of your chart. At the full Moon, consult the readings for the two opposite houses, which will be listed in the full Moon table. I'll also suggest flower essences to support the activities of that month. Though several are listed, it's a good idea to take only one or two for a full month's cycle. In general, FES suggests starting a remedy mixture at the new Moon and taking it throughout the lunar cycle. It would be even more effective, then, to select remedies related to your own personal lunation for that month. To choose, consult the companies' litera- ture for a fuller description than can be given here. For the week of the full Moon, as you concentrate on balancing the two houses, you may wish to add a remedy from the list for the opposite house. Desert Alchemy also has combination formulas for the house pairs—The 1st House–7th House For- mula, The 2nd House–8th House Formula, and so on.

Lunation in the 1st House: The 1st house, including the rising sign, shows pat- terns of relating you learned as a child to survive in your family. You carry these patterns into adulthood. Some of them hold you back, and some are your own personal charm. The rising sign and any planets in the 1st describe the image you present to the world. When the lunation falls in this house, consider whether you are presenting your true self and feelings, or hiding be- hind a facade. If that facade keeps your needs from being met, think about how to express them more openly. Ask yourself whether these defenses are functional in adult life and how to let your real self shine through. Since the 1st house also describes your appearance, check to see if your style reflects the changes you've made in the past year. If it doesn't fit, you may want to update your image. (At the full Moon, the 7th house emphasis shows a concern for integrating your desires with those of your closest relationships.)
    YOUR MONTHLY BOUQUET: **White Desert Primrose**, by Desert Alchemy, helps you see through projected images to find modes of self- expression more in harmony with your essential self. Their **Mariola** helps you let go of a false persona.

Lunation in the 2nd House: Practical economic matters may capture your at- tention now. Attend to security by taking inventory of your assets, debts, and cash flow. Making a realistic, but not overly severe, budget may help put your finances in order. Assess what you are spending in various areas and trim the waste in order to meet neglected needs or desires. Set achievable fi- nancial goals; e.g., the trip you've always wanted to take or that new car you'll be needing. Then devise a plan of savings, however modest, to fulfill them. You may also wish to explore new ideas about lucrative sidelines. Money is an emotional issue, so examine how your emotions and insecuri- ties get in the way of sound fiscal practices. (At the full Moon, the 8th house is also emphasized. Thus, a new balance must be established between rely- ing on your own resources and those of others.)

YOUR MONTHLY BOUQUET: To put finances in a new and more solid perspective, try FES' **Hound's Tongue**, Pegasus' **Four Leaf Clover**, Pacific Essences' **Polyanthus**, or **Abundance Essence and Oil**, or Desert Alchemy's **Celebration of Abundance**. (But don't spend too much on essences!)

Lunation in the 3rd House: Communication is a major focus when the lunation falls here. Spelling out your true thoughts, needs, and feelings can improve your clarity of expression. If you ask for feedback, you may be amazed to discover that what you thought you said is not what people received at all. Unwritten rules in relationships may be revealed as areas of confusion where you need to be more direct. This is a productive period for catching up on correspondence or calls to people you've neglected. Since the 3rd house is one of learning, the lunation is ideal to begin a new class or to pursue an intriguing new interest. Writing, *per se*, can bring growth now, so you might want to begin a journal or another form of writing that would lend clarity. (At the full Moon, find a balance with the 9th house, which helps you to find answers through books, classes, or other new input.)

YOUR MONTHLY BOUQUET: Communication can be enhanced by FES' **Cosmos** and **Calendula**. Mental clarity can be enhanced by FES' **Peppermint**, and their **Madia** can help concentration and focus.

Lunation in the 4th House: Keeping the home fires burning is a concern this month. You may find yourself wanting quiet, cozy evenings at home so you can relax and reflect. This can also be a period of work on family relationships and getting to know your family again by spending quality time together. If your home life is ripe for an explosion, this could be the month when you have to look seriously at what's gone wrong and take some action to fix it.

You may devote energy to decorating or repairing your living space so that it reflects your personality and becomes a comforting haven. Take time for nesting and making your home and family as warm, supportive, and rewarding as possible. Attention to your home life provides a solid base of security to meet the demands of a world that often leaves us anxious and drained. (At the full Moon, you'll be called upon to balance domestic concerns with career or other major life directions, represented by your 10th house.)

YOUR MONTHLY BOUQUET: Tackle closets and clutter with the help of Desert Alchemy's **Staghorn Cholla** and Bach's **Honeysuckle**, which also help with nostalgia for the past.

Lunation in the 5th House: Learning to play and to lift life out of its dreary routine is the keynote now. It is often a good month for a vacation, but even if you can't do that, take a long weekend or go on a little trip. Best of all, learn to take a five-minute vacation at least once an hour. If you've neglected leisure interests or creative pursuit, get back to them, and if there's something fun you've been wanting to try, do it. Listening to the playful inner child can enhance another of this month's concerns—children. If you have children spend time learning who they are and what is on their minds. Get away from the house with them individually to mend or deepen the relationship and to improve communication.

Another area ruled by the 5th house is romance, so devote some thought to enriching this part of life. Even if you're married—ESPECIALLY IF YOU'RE MARRIED—get to work on putting the romance back in the relationship, lest you or your partner be tempted to seek it elsewhere. We all want romantic attention, and isn't that what brought you together in the first place? Make this month an annual honeymoon. (At the full Moon, the 11th house is also heightened, showing the need to find time for friends or groups.)

YOUR MONTHLY BOUQUET: Maybe a literal bouquet of flowers for your lover would do more for romance this month than knocking back drops! For connecting with the inner child, try **Zinnia** by FES, or Desert Alchemy's **Strawberry Cactus**, or their **A Way to the Elf** combination.

Lunation in the 6th House: After a month of play, you will be more in the mood to settle down to work, which is the domain of the 6th house. Reorganizing to find more effective ways of handling daily routines can be productive now. If you want to change positions, this is generally a good window for updating the resume and answering ads. (Don't hand in your resignation, however, without checking transits to your Midheaven.) If you have a job, this is the time of the year to take stock. Is your work performance up to par? Can you improve relationships with your coworkers? Is the job a source of growth, or has it become stagnant? Is it time to move on? You get out of most jobs what you put into them, so perhaps you can find more challenging ways of using your talents and abilities right where you are.

Since health is another 6th house matter, this may be the opportune moment for a physical. If you've wanted to lose weight or pay more attention to nutrition, now is a good moment to embark on a new food plan. If you've neglected yourself in some way, such as not getting regular dental checkups, or not exercising, you'd be more likely to sustain the effort if you began at this lunation. If you're not feeling well, your body is saying something in its own language. Track down the life issues or suppressed emotions that may be coming out psychosomatically. (At the full Moon, both the workaday 6th and the more spiritual 12th house are calling for your attention. Meditation or a retreat may help restore the balance between the spiritual and the mundane.)

YOUR MONTHLY BOUQUET: FES' **Filaree** helps sort out essentials and priorities; Bach's **Elm** bolsters those who are capable but overwhelmed; FES' **Manzanita** grounds you so that you pay proper attention to your body.

Lunation in the 7th House: Lunations bring hidden emotions to the surface, so during this new or full Moon either you or your partner may uncover buried feelings about the relationship. Use this opportunity to get conflicts out into the open and work on them. Likewise, it's important to talk about unfulfilled needs. One or both partners may be feeling insecure, so devote time to your relationship. If you're not involved with anyone, you may be feeling the desire for closeness. That yearning is good motivation. Think about any self-defeating patterns of relating and work on them. Experiment with reaching out or going places where you'd be more likely to meet someone. (At the full Moon, the 1st house emphasis causes you to examine how your image may put off other people or interfere with relationships.)

YOUR MONTHLY BOUQUET: **Pink Monkeyflower** by FES helps you open up to closeness, and their **Calendula** helps you listen better; **Teddy Bear Cholla** by Desert Alchemy helps with deep fears of intimacy.

Lunation in the 8th House: Two additional facets of close relationships can come into focus in this four week period—the sexual partnership, and the joint use of resources. It's important to reestablish a balanced give and take so neither partner feels drained. Look for interdependence, rather than one being overly dependent on the other. A one-way flow eventually creates resentment and distorts the relationship. If feelings are running high about financial dependency, it's time to get that act together. Another area deserving attention is debt—plan how to get out of debt and restrict the use of credit to be more secure. (The full Moon also highlights the 2nd house and will draw you into taking stock of your assets and looking for ways to earn extra cash.)

The lunation can bring neglected needs to the surface in the sexual area. Working on them now can make your relationship more fulfilling. Make sure you and your partner spend time together, no matter how busy you are. Those evenings spent together can bring new warmth and interest in each other. If you're not involved with anyone, sheer physical deprivation may push you to reach out to someone responsive.

YOUR MONTHLY BOUQUET: **Sticky Monkeyflower** and **Hibiscus** by FES help with sexual barriers; Desert Alchemy's formulas, **The Helpless Siren**, and **Giving and Receiving Support** help establish a better balance between your own resources and those of others.

Lunation in the 9th House: You may feel an itch to find new meaning in life and to reexamine your philosophical underpinnings. If you've been a lapsed churchgoer, you might find it renewing to go back for a month. If you've rejected traditional religions, explore other philosophies that appeal to you. You may also be drawn to develop your mind by trying some advanced course of study. Read at least one serious book. Changing your thinking in one area can reverberate to many other areas. It's time for an intellectual challenge, for stretching your mind, for looking beyond everyday, humdrum existence.

Part of stretching your mind might be a trip to some distant place where you gain a different perspective. If this is beyond your reach, a foreign film, a trip to a museum, or even inviting a foreign exchange student to dinner, can expose you to new ideas and broaden your horizons. (When the Moon is full, both this house and the 3rd are energized, for a real mental boost.)

YOUR MONTHLY BOUQUET: **Sacred Datura** by Desert Alchemy gives you new vision and supports you in going beyond the known; FES' **Shasta Daisy** is excellent for synthesizing ideas learned in various studies. Pegasus recommends **Ylang** and **Yucca** for adjusting to new environments when you travel.

Lunation in the 10th House: Once a year, take stock of your life direction, particularly regarding career. Focus attention away from the short range and toward the long range perspective. (The sequence of lunations is helpful. That trip you took last month, or the new ideas you absorbed, have no doubt given you a different outlook on your career and long range goals.) What progress have you made since last year? Are you headed in a direction you want to go? Set priorities and then plan concrete actions to accomplish them. These might be goals for the year to come or for the distant future. If you lack certain skills to get ahead, take definite steps to acquire them. If you are uncertain about your goals, explore some appealing possibilities. See if they are realistic, and arrive at an informed decision. This month, a reading from a professional astrologer could lend clarity about vocational concerns. (At the full Moon, the 4th house is also emphasized, reminding you that you need a secure home base before you can shoot for the Moon.)

YOUR MONTHLY BOUQUET: Bach's **Wild Oat** helps those whose career path is uncertain. Authority and confidence problems can be eased by **Sunflower** and **Saguaro**, made by Pegasus, FES, and Desert Alchemy. Desert Alchemy's **Soaptree Yucca** helps keep long-term goals in sight with faith and perseverance.

Lunation in the 11th House: After devoting yourself to career concerns last month, you now want good friends to encourage and appreciate you. Visiting old companions can be rewarding, or you can also gain from reaching out to new people this month. If friendship is a difficult area, analyze and begin changing your approach to people. After all, you must be a friend in order to have a friend. On the other hand, if you're giving far more than you're getting, begin now to develop a better balance. If there's a blowup with a chum this month, examine yourself to see how you contributed and what has to change.

The 11th house also deals with groups, and this month you might want to seek one out for an area of your life you'd like to enrich. Often a group can help you do what you cannot do alone. It might be devoted to business or leisure interests, a self-help meeting of people with similar problems, or purely social. If you're on-line with your computer, the Internet has thousands of special interest forums. Whatever your need, there is doubtlessly a network of people somewhere who share it. Your local library should have lists of local or national organizations for any purpose. If you're aleady involved up to your ears and feeling drained, stock-taking may be in order. (At the full Moon, the 5th house adds additional dimensions of recreation or intriguing romantic complications.)

YOUR MONTHLY BOUQUET: Essences for working with groups would include FES' **Violet** and **Trillium**; more and closer friendships can result from taking their **Pink Monkeyflower**, **Mallow**, or **Nicotiana**.

Lunation in the 12th House: After the social whirl is over, you're ready for a retreat to examine your inner self. No doubt the year has left you with many questions to mull over, many knots to untangle. Recognize that you have a valid need to withdraw and regroup now and then. The 12th house deals with the unconscious and the spiritual and psychic realms. Tapping these deeper levels of self requires peace and quiet. If you venture out in the world more than necessary now, it can be wearing. You also may lose an important opportunity to develop self-awareness.

By pursuing dreams, meditation, writing, or other roads to self-knowledge, you can move out into the world again next month in a more centered way. You will be less likely to repeat self-defeating patterns. If it is an emotionally difficult period, it may be because repressed feelings or self-destructive habits are coming to the surface. It is important to acknowledge them, because otherwise they can cause neurotic behavior or psychosomatic illness. (When the Moon is full here, there may be tension because the 6th house demands you attend to work or health concerns.)

YOUR MONTHLY BOUQUET: You can find support for dream work, meditation, and other spiritual practices with **Mugwort** or **Lotus** made by Pegasus and FES. Pegasus' **Angel of Protection** essence is highly recommended for 12th house matters. Desert Alchemy's combinations to support spiritual growth include **A Way to the Godself**, and **Angel Love**.

☽ ☽ ☽ ☽

As you read all twelve lunations, you may have sensed the perfection in the pattern. They form a complete cycle in which one house leads logically to the next. By conscious attention to the concerns of the twelve new and full Moons, you can make substantial improvements in all areas in a year. The lunations can also put you in touch with emotions, either because you consciously work on them or because they pop to the surface demanding attention. Despite the reputed moodiness of lunar types, the regularity of the Moon's cycles ensures that the concerns of all twelve signs will be given their proper due in the Moon's monthly, yearly, and eclipse cycles. Perhaps we are only excessively moody because it has become so difficult to remain in touch with these natural rhythms. Working with them consciously can lead you to wholeness and balance.

Lunar Lore Meets the Solar World

In most jobs, you can't tell your boss that the Moon is in Pisces so it's not such a good day for that client presentation, or that you don't want to make sales calls because the Moon is void of course. Nor would your supervisor be terribly sympathetic if you wanted to wait two weeks so you could start a project on the new Moon. What can you do if you're locked into a rigid 9:00-5:00 schedule with little autonomy over your tasks? Follow these guidelines as much as you can, organizing your tasks to fit the Moon sign. However, if you're stuck doing a presentation while the Moon is in Pisces, use the Capricorn Moon a few days earlier to perfect it. Also take the ideas brought up during that client meeting under advisement, creative as they might seem, and think them through more carefully later. Still, most of us have some discretion in organizing our work and certainly our personal lives. Using an astrological calendar as an appointment book keeps knowledge of current conditions at your fingertips.

CHAPTER 7

MOON PHASES, LIFE CYCLES,
AND MAMA'S LITTLE GIRL

In the Old Religions, the Moon was worshiped as the Great Mother. Sexist or not, due to the way we are raised in our culture, the Moon is often more important to us women than the Sun. By combining astrological insights with those gained from modern psychology, we can better understand why our mothers have such a powerful influence on us. It doesn't matter if we never see her or even whether she is still alive, because she lives on inside us. She is imprinted at such an early age we don't even remember it. The older we get, and the more we take on traditional lunar roles, the more we usually behave like her, no matter how we try to be different.

Popular astrology coyly calls people born under the sign of Cancer Moonchildren. In a larger sense, all women are Moonchildren—daughters of our mothers and shaped in their image. We cannot be whole until we are no longer the child of our mother or father, but our own person—until we have broken the links in the cosmic chain and stand free. We can love our mothers even when we do not like them, but we cannot be ourselves until we untie the mother knot. When we do that, we are no longer Moon*children* but can integrate the Sun and Moon in a positive and balanced way.

Men, I don't mean to neglect you here, I just don't know enough to write about your mothers' effects on you. No doubt there are parallel effects on the phases of a man's life, but there also must be differences, because mothers deal differently with sons than with daughters. Perhaps some male reader will be inspired to write something that will enlighten us. Meanwhile, you might read this chapter to see how it applies to you. Know, however, that it's not the same. The culture does not pressure you to be lunar as it does women, but instead pressures you to suppress your lunar side. ("Aw, Mom! Don't hug me in front of the guys!")

The Mother/Daughter Bond

We will trace the mother's influence at the lunar thresholds—childhood, the teen years, going out on our own, and becoming mothers ourselves. At each step, the Moon's astrological meanings illuminate the subject. Transits or progressions to the natal Moon generally accompany these phases. You may wish to add to these brief explorations by reading about and working on these phases in more detail, discovering how they apply to you and analyzing your birth chart.

The Mother and the Young Girl: The Moon in our charts describes the care we got early in our lives from our mothers or their surrogates. By its sign, house, and aspects, the Moon shows whether our mothers gave us security and basic trust of our world. The Moon rules the breast and stomach. There is evidence that even in an area as basic as feeding, girls may be treated differently than boys. For instance, in a study of infant care in Italy, Belotti found that almost all boys were breastfed, while only two thirds of girls were. Mothers weaned girls earlier and spent only half as much time feeding them.[1]

In India, girls are breast fed for one year while boys are breast fed for two. Female infanticide by starvation reduces the number of female infants in that country to only 80 for each 100 males.[2] The latest technology further contributes to the uneven ratio. There is a big business now in India of testing pregnant women to determine whether they are having a male child. They often choose abortion over having a girl.

In the United States, a smaller number of women breastfeed their children, but feeding differences between boys and girls still exist. Homemakers often save the choicest meats and morsels for their husbands and growing sons. (Chapters 11 and 12 have more to say about food and its meaning in the mother-daughter relationship.)

Mothers keep girls closer to home and raise them to be more dependent than boys, again emphasizing the importance of the Moon. Boys are

[1]Susie Orbach, *Fat Is a Feminist Issue* (New York: Berkley Books, 1978), p. 18.
[2]Gloria Steinem, "Politics of Food," *MS*, February, 1980, p. 48.

encouraged to be more adventurous and self-reliant—"Be a little man"—while girls are taught to be afraid to try new things and wander about alone. Because of the way their mothers train them, girls are more likely than boys to remain attached in a smothering type of closeness called *codependency*. In learning to be codependent, women come to believe they can't survive on their own. This stage of development is legitimate in childhood but continues as a way of life for many women. If we are overprotected as little girls, we grow up afraid of trying to do things alone. We often remain tied to our families longer than our brothers, switch the dependency to our husbands if we marry, and raise our daughters the same way. The Moon represents dependency, and due to the fears instilled in us, women are generally more dependent than men.

Emotions and how we handle them are another area described by the Moon. Again the Moon looms large in a woman's chart because women are allowed to be more emotional, and we learn from Mom what to do with our feelings. How our mothers react to our anger, joy, pain, and other feelings will determine whether we feel free to express them. It also decides how we, in turn, react to other people's feelings.

In all these areas, a mother generally treats her daughter as her own mother treated her, so the links in the cosmic chain are forged from generation to generation. Often, in tracing a family's history through astrological charts, you'll find that the women's Moon signs and aspects are similar. For instance, a mother who has Moon in Capricorn might give birth to a daughter who has the Moon and Saturn conjunct.

The Moon and Images of Femininity: Another way the Moon is important in women's charts is that our mothers teach us early in our lives what it means to be a woman. We identify and pattern ourselves after her in feminine pursuits. Boys, on the other hand, imitate their fathers to a greater extent, another reason the Moon decreases in impact in a man's chart. This patterning makes it difficult for women to achieve a sense of where we leave off and mother begins. We may feel guilty or unfeminine acting in ways other than what our mother's words or behavior taught us.

The sign, house, and aspects of the natal Moon show what kind of woman our mother was, and what ideas about femininity she taught. My mother was far from ruffles and curls as a role model. She went hunting with my dad, helped him build a house from scratch, and could change a tire in nothing flat. My Moon in Aries in a trine (a harmonious 120 degree aspect) with Mars shows her as an atypical but resourceful female. With her as an example, I'm not exactly Vanna White myself. In the next chapter, when specific Moon signs and aspects are shown, you'll see the images of womanhood you may have picked up from your mother. (As we'll see in the chapter on men, they also absorb their ideas about what a woman should be from their mothers. This information is coded in their Moon but is usually acted out with the women in their lives.)

The Mother at the Menarche: By age 5, we've already learned most of what our mothers have to teach us about womanhood. However, the ideas remain abstract—"I'll find out about that when I grow up." After we develop breasts and begin having periods, such ideas are no longer abstract. We become women biologically in the physical and emotional crisis of puberty. (The progressed Moon may be opposite the natal Moon at this point.) Young men don't develop either breasts or periods, but instead develop a Martian physiology—a deeper voice, more body hair, and muscles.

The *menarche* (a girl's first period) is the rite of passage into womanhood, a dramatic confirmation that we have joined the ranks and can become mothers ourselves. Up to that point, we are treated as children and given some freedom, allowed to run with the boys a bit. Now the pressure is on, and we are expected to behave as our culture demands. We must be seductive, but ladylike; no longer competitive with men, but instead interested in catching a mate, learning to keep house and raise a family. We are expected to be like mother—more lunar with every passing month. (Desert Alchemy's combination, **The Miracle at Menarche**, helps teens going through this passage, but also helps adult women with any difficulties left over from this introduction to the menstrual cycle.)

The Mother and the Teenage Girl: Mother is the main instructor and enforcer of society's demands, which causes a crisis in the mother-daughter relationship at adolescence. Some of us escape direct pressure from our more enlightened mothers, but society still surrounds us. It is a rare mother who is not at least subliminally affected by the programming. In particular, she worries that we may get pregnant, so she tries to bind us closer to home and supervises our dating. If she is uncomfortable about her own sexuality, we sense it. This adds to our turmoil and becomes part of our feelings about being a woman. (The flower remedy, **Alpine Lily**, from FES, helps when the programming from our mothers about the female body and sexuality has been negative.)

Teenage rebellion can partially be explained by the change in the relationship with our mothers that our newly female bodies cause. We may resent the restrictions and the expectations. Simultaneously, we see that our mother's fate may be our own—that we, too, are lunar creatures. We come to identify all the more with her, and yet we must rebel and break away to become women rather than children.

Astrology lends some interesting insights into the teenage years. Uranus and Aquarius are associated with adolescence. Either the mother-daughter dependency must be broken in the teenage years or else that is the death of the girl's struggle to become an individual. Uranus rules Aquarius and has much to do with independence and autonomy. Adolescence, with its Uranian upheavals, marks a turning point in the mother-daughter tie. At that age, we begin to turn from Mom to the peer group for validation and guidelines. Feeling shut out, she may try all the harder to control.

The Young Adult Woman and Her Mother: The young woman's growth into adulthood continues the struggle between autonomy and codependency. Either she becomes more Uranian (a single, autonomous person on her own path) or she becomes more lunar (settling into the traditional roles with a husband and perhaps children) or some balance between the two. The planet Uranus rules rebelliousness, separations, breaks, and independence. It is abrupt in its effects. For many women, the quest to become a free-standing individual is marked by one sudden moment of rebellion in which she says she intends to live by her own rules from now on. This is a personal Declaration of Independence. If our mothers could only see it, our declaration means independence for them, too—no longer being tied to mothering us.

Nancy Friday, who wrote the classic *Our Mothers—Our Selves*, feels that our separation from our mothers is only external. As we separate more, we may well find ourselves doing things Mother's way. The female image we got from her now becomes even stronger in the unconscious, because having mother inside us makes the journey to adulthood seem less fearsome. Geographic mobility may actually make separation harder. Distance is no real resolution of this normal stage of development, for it may bind us more tightly to our mother's ways unconsciously.[3]

We spoke in an earlier chapter of the growing anti-Mom sentiment and the social pressures that label us neurotic if we remain close to our mothers. Since the Cancer transits have correlated with the erosion of other supports for our lunar needs, the mother/daughter bond becomes a focus of heightened emphasis. Our mothers may be the targets of displaced anger when our unmet needs surface enough to realize that we are angry at all the

[3]Nancy Friday, *My Mother/My Self: The Daughter's Search for Identity* (New York: Dell, 1978).

demands and losses. This angry rejection of our mothers, pushing them away, is a counter-dependent defense. The truth is, the mother/daughter bond can be constructive, something to sustain both women through our difficult times. Only when the tie is codependent rather than sustaining does it prevent both parties from growing.

Daughters who have bought into the Myth of the Perfect Mother become angry when mothers cannot live up to it. When we accept responsibility for our lives and understand the stresses our mothers are under, then we can work through to the only real resolution of the tie, which is forgiveness. (A section in the next chapter can help with this process.) Then we have the possibility of becoming friends with our mothers, in a relationship between two equal, independent adults.

In a sense, we are never free of our mothers until we can see them as separate, and understand the circumstances that shaped the way they dealt with us. At age 30, one of my friends finally learned a family secret that explained much of her mother's difficult behavior. The secret was that her parents divorced because her father had beaten her mother. Once she knew this, she understood many of her mother's reactions to her and to men. She reacted in a loving way by sending her mother a dozen roses. Only by gaining empathy for our mothers as lunar people like ourselves, can we ultimately be free and separate.

Over the years, I have done chart readings for thousands of business and professional women whose mothers did not have a career. Especially when the vocation involves competition and leadership rather than nurturing, these women have often drawn more on their fathers than their mothers as role models. In their professional lives, they typically express their Sun and its aspects and their 10th house and Midheaven, more than their Moon. They identified strongly with their fathers in career patterns and strategies, including both his strengths and his dysfunctional behaviors. They tend to follow his lead and try to live up to his expectations. They are often held back by his weaknesses and failures, which they tend to repeat. If Father valued sons more than daughters, striving to live up to his model is tough. (**Saguaro**, and **Sunflower**, by various companies, and **Red Helmet Orchid**, by Australian Bush Essences, are helpful in working through authority and identity problems related to the father.) This pattern will change as more girls have career mothers for models, so that both the Sun and Moon can be drawn upon.

Daughter Becomes Mother—Another Link Is Forged: In chapter 9, we will discuss the process of becoming a mother, and the intense emotional crisis that accompanies it. The birth of a new generation changes the bond with our own mothers. She now accepts us as adults, but only because we have finally taken on a lunar life path. We may become closer because we have more in common now and can identify with her more. Simultaneously, however, Mom often steps up the pressure to be just like her—to mother the baby the same way she mothered us. A second Declaration of Independence may be needed to set Grandma straight.

Often, we simply follow suit, as we have absorbed her mothering style without conscious awareness—we live what we learn. Try as we might to be different, the mother we had is often the mother we become, unless we work consciously to transcend any unwanted patterns. The birth of a child also gives our personal Moon new influence—a woman without a child usually has less necessity to limit her life to lunar functions and can be more Venusian. This is another point where the Moon is less important in a man's chart. Very few men have the primary responsibility for raising children.

Not only does the Moon in your chart show what kind of mother you had then, it also shows what kind of mother you are likely to be! Often, the more we bend over backward to be different, the more we wind up creating the same effect. The section, "What Kind of Parent Would You Be," in chapter 9 will explore the Moon signs from this perspective. Also, as you read the Messages from Mom section in the next chapter, you may find messages from your own Mom. If you have children, you may also be dismayed to recognize yourself and messages you could be giving your own daughter. **Ancestral Patterns Formula** by Desert Alchemy can help clarify and release these unwanted repetitions.

Mother Becomes Child—Her Declining Years: Another stage in the life cycle, and one that may seem far-fetched now, is mother's senior years. If she lives long enough to become feeble and in need of our caretaking, we may find ourselves experiencing a difficult jumble of reactions. We may feel loving and tender, especially if the relationship has been good, but these feelings are still often tempered by annoyance or downright resentment. Moms are never supposed to get sick or old! Viewing her fragility, we may feel strangely bereft of the omnipotent figure she became in the unconscious as we grew up. Still, there is often a healing and forgiving that takes place, seeing her as just another human being, as fallible and vulnerable as ourselves.

Many men who have avoided integrating their lunar side find it especially hard to handle their mother's decline. They may shut off and avoid visiting or calling her, often relegating her care to their wives. The more lunar male may find his nurturing side coming to the fore as he helps care for his mother, even if only emotionally.

The Mother's Death: If it hasn't happened yet, it will someday, unbelievable as that may seem right now. If you've loved your mother and found her a deep source of support, the loss can be a gaping heart wound that takes a long time to heal. On the other hand, the more difficult the relationship, the greater the feeling of loss may be. All the "if onlies," the regrets for what we never had, come up strongly and need to be worked through. With Aquarius on the 8th house of the Cancer rising wheel, we tend to abandon the dying and the bereaved. We distance ourselves so we don't have to feel anything about this greatest lost. We're too modern to beat our breasts or rend our clothes, and no emotional displays at funerals either. If you avoid dealing with the bereavement, you may do major lunar damage to yourself. Stuffing strong feelings about the loss can lead to a general emotional shutdown or more generalized depression.

If your mother has passed on and your bereavement was short, you may find that it wasn't as complete as you thought some years later, when you have an outer planet transit to the Moon. One friend who had been adopted said he experienced very little grief when his adoptive mother died. Yet when the cat he'd lived with for years died, he went into deep and inconsolable mourning, not only for the cat, but for his mother as well. (My friend was having a Neptune quincunx to his 12th-house Gemini Moon.)

The mother's death, however, is a major, and not altogether negative, rite of passage. We may fully emerge from her shadow and stop molding our lives to please—or displease—her. In the first year after her death, we may find that we let go of acting out *her* neuroses and hangups, which she transmitted psychically to us as long as she lived. We may take surprising actions in several lunar areas of life, striking out on our own as more individuated beings. This phase may lead women to discover new expressions of the female roles. For men, it may change their relationships with women and with their own feminine side. If the mother knot was too tight, her passage may allow them to bond more closely with their partners.

Essences that help work through this process—but do not keep you from feeling grief—include **Bleeding Heart**, and **Golden Eardrops** by FES, **Starfish** and **Purple Crocus** by Pacific Essences, and **Wolfberry** by Desert Alchemy. Essences help you to be present for your own grief and that of others. Useful to the dying in their transition, and to the survivors in feeling the connection afterward, is **Angel's Trumpet** by FES, and **Transitions Formula** by Desert Alchemy.

Lunar eclipse—when Mom wasn't up to her job: We've been talking about fairly ordinary mothers up to now. Our relationships with Mom can be stormy enough when we're dealing with the ordinary garden variety—well-meaning and caring, but emotionally illiterate. However, the difficulties are compounded when there are serious family problems, such as an alcoholic or abusive father, or when Mom herself was addicted, abusive, or mentally ill. Dysfunctions like these make the mother knot harder to untie. Young children of abusive mothers, for instance, work all the harder to please them and cling all the more loyally and tightly. When we see Mom as a victim— let's say of father's abusiveness or a serious chronic illness—we experience guilt at needing to separate and helplessness at not being able to do anything for her. (For this, you might try what I call the Rescuer's Remedy—mix a combination of **Pine** and **Red Chestnut** by Bach, and **Red Clover** and **Pink Yarrow** by FES.)

If Mom dies while we are growing up, the grief and anger at being abandoned can go on for years. Since the solar world restricts mourning, these feelings can become unconscious and all the more potent. Fortunately today there are tools to help heal mother problems like these— flower remedies, books on dysfunctional families, workshops, support groups, and knowledgeable therapists. There is no one flower remedy that magically dissolves wounds from dysfunctional family backgrounds. They are not magic bullets but supports for other recovery work. If I were to mention just one that has proven powerful in codependency work, it would be Desert Alchemy's combination **Making and Honoring Boundaries**. Other important flower remedies for those from dysfunctional family backgrounds would be FES' **Echinacea**, **Evening Primrose**, **Mariposa Lily**, and **Golden Eardrops**. To make working with the essences smoother and more effective in cases like these, however, you might want to consult an experienced essence practitioner along with your other recovery efforts. The companies listed in chapter 5 can provide services or recommend someone in your area.

Dysfunctions or interruptions in mothering often appear in the birth chart as hard aspects to the Moon from Mars, Saturn, Chiron, Uranus, Neptune, or Pluto—usually the conjunction, square, or opposition. Serious difficulties are more likely when the Moon has more than one hard aspect. Some Moon signs are also prone to family dysfunction—Scorpio, Capricorn, and Pisces—but generally only when the Moon has negative aspects. The Moon in the 8th or 12th house sometimes signifies losses or interruptions of mothering. Pluto, Neptune, or Saturn on the Ascendant, Midheaven, or IC may also show problematic parents or family conditions. An example of serious maternal dysfunction and the codependency that generally results from it will be explored next.

A Study in Codependency—
Liza Minnelli and Judy Garland

Codependency has been a buzz word of the nineties, and I wrote of it at length in a chapter of *The Consulting Astrologer's Guidebook*. However, it is an important idea here, as it speaks so much to the excessively binding mother-daughter tie. Codependency is a relationship addiction in which we allow the other person's needs and behavior to rule our lives, often with an obsessive focus. We are in a joined-at-the-hip symbiosis that is not the same as love, but, instead, is fear of not surviving without the other. It is a com-

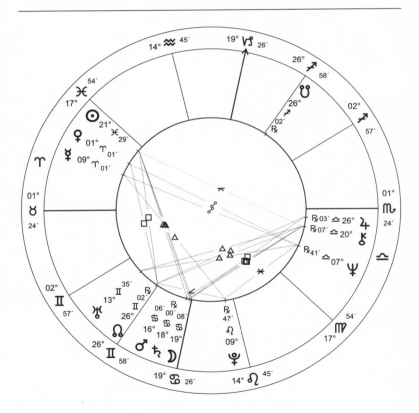

Chart 4. The horoscope of Liza Minnelli, born March 12, 1946, in Los Ange-les, CA at 7:58 A.M. PST. Data from the birth certificate supplied by Ruth Hale Olivier in Dell *No. 12, 1966. Reprinted by permission from Lois Rodden's* Pro-files of Women *(Tempe, AZ: American Federation of Astrologers, 1979).*

mon relationship pattern among those who grew up in alcoholic and other dysfunctional families.

The charts of Liza Minnelli and her mother, Judy Garland, are shown here (See Charts 4 and 5.) While Judy was at her alcoholic and pill-addicted worst, Liza took on the parent role toward her mother. From age 10, she begged food for the two of them and conducted suicide watches over Judy. She would sneak out of hotel rooms to find another place to stay when they couldn't pay the bills. She finally left for New York at 16 with less than $100 in her pocket to try for a musical career. Despite their stormy relationship,

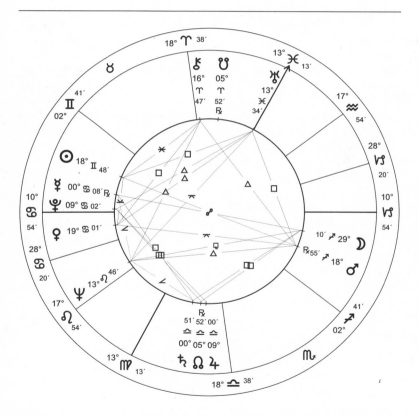

Chart 5. The horoscope of Judy Garland, born June 10, 1922, in Grand Rapids, MN at 6:00 A.M. CST. Data from the birth certificate collected by E. Steinbrecher. Reprinted by permission from Lois Rodden's Profiles of Women *(Tempe, AZ: American Federation of Astrologers, 1979).*

she has remained loyal to her mother and to this day will not talk about her in interviews.

We won't go into all the astrological or psychological signatures of adult children of alcoholic or dysfunctional families here, except to say that both Neptune and Pluto figure heavily. What is relevant, however, is that I also discovered a strong emphasis on the sign Cancer in such charts. In this example, neither Liza nor Judy has Sun in Cancer. However, Liza has a conjunction of the Moon, Mars, and Saturn in Cancer, and Judy has her Ascendant, Mercury, Venus, and Pluto in that sign. (All of those planets are in the Gauquelin sectors—i.e., ten degrees either side of the four angles—and thus are very strong influences.)

Not all Cancerians come from dysfunctional families—some come from very fine families, indeed. However, it seems to be a case of, "when it is good, it is very, very good, and when it is bad, it is horrid." Given the strong Cancerian emphasis on home, family, and nurturing, it must have been extremely painful and frightening for Judy and Liza to live that way. Like Judy, Liza wound up addicted, no doubt partially in response to these lunar deprivations. However, she has been in treatment and her life has been better for it.

Fortunately, we are now in an era of much greater awareness and treatment of both addiction and the results of growing up in a dysfunctional family. In such families, there is deep distortion in the lunar areas of life—mother, home, family, security, and emotional management. If you came from such a family and are working to balance your lunar hemisphere, do take advantage of the recovery tools and programs that are available, for it is difficult to be whole without them. The counter-dependent stance we have been discussing is common among those who have come from such backgrounds, but do not feel you have to do it alone. Read the books, go to the meetings, and find therapists and healers who are knowledgeable.

Flower Remedies for the Phases of Women's Life Cycles

I would be remiss if I didn't take this opportunity to write about Desert Alchemy's **Celebration of Womanhood** Flower Essence Kit. Since Desert Alchemy's special contribution seemed to be its fine essences for women's issues, I nudged and prodded Cynthia Kemp into developing this kit. It includes essences for many phases of the woman's life cycle: **Thank Heaven** for Little Girls, The Miracle at Menarche, New Mother's Formula, and Woman of Wisdom. Moontime Harmony helps with PMS, Birthing Harmony is a support during pregnancy, and Unlocking Sexual Grace allows gentle exploration of feminine sexuality. The Wild Woman is for the woman who runs with the wolves, and Helpless Siren is for those who believe they can't do anything on their own, so they must seduce others into doing it for them. Giving and Receiving Support helps balance nurturing with receiving nurturance. Saguaro-Queen is for a good weaving together of our male and female strengths—integrating our solar and lunar hemispheres. The kit also includes Making and Honoring Boundaries, The Inner Mother, and Single Mother's Formula. It could be regarded as a self-help kit for women, since at various times of our lives we (or our women relatives and friends) may need almost all of these combinations. If you are a practitioner who focuses mostly on women's needs and issues, you may find this kit invaluable. These essences may also be purchased individually. (No, I don't get a percentage, I just find these remedies exceptional.)

Moon After Moon After Moon . . .

A trip through the stages of our lives, seen from the perspective of our relationship with our mothers, inevitably recalls the endless cycles of the Moon. Your life, your mother's life, her mother's life, and all the generations before and after repeat the phases, over and over.

At each major threshold in our lives and hers, from our weaning to her death, we face the demand for greater autonomy. As we approach these thresholds, we must increasingly say goodbye to Mother as our caretaker and nurturer. We must increasingly say hello to her as another human being, equal to ourselves in her stresses, insecurities, yearnings, and needs.

Many of us do not want this equality, and we do not feel adequate to the demands of the next threshold. We become afraid, and in defense against the fear, we become angry—at her, at ourselves, and at the world. The world is a challenging place, with precious little to offer in the way of wombs and security blankets. As adults, we must build our own wombs, we must knit our own security blankets, and we must know when to leave them behind.

CHAPTER 8

HEALING THE MOTHER KNOT

Here we're going to get up close and personal, exploring your relationship with your own mother. The Moon in your natal chart, the 4th house, and any planets in the sign Cancer describe your mother. The aspects to your Moon also show her effect on you, as we will see. We will go through exercises from my mother-daughter workshops so you can do them. We also will identify flower remedies that can clarify and ease the mother knot. Although these exercises are primarily designed for daughters, sons may also find them helpful, especially those who were abused or rejected by their mothers.

Messages from Mom

In a daughter's chart, the Moon has a great deal to do with the messages we got from our mothers about certain important areas of our lives. These messages taught us what it means to be a woman, what we should do with our feelings, whether it's okay to need others, and how we in turn should behave when we join the ranks of mothers. Some messages came in loud and clear ("Listen to mother, dear.") and some messages were in code. The messages that were in code are more crazy-making because we aren't consciously aware of them and yet they rule us all the same. We can decode the messages if we work at it—and astrology is one way of doing it. They show up loud and clear in the aspects to your Moon and its sign and house.

In the readings that follow, I have used the form of make-believe letters from Mom in response to an imaginary situation where you might call for help. Maybe you never got such a clear-cut letter and maybe your Mom never verbalized these sentiments. The letters are exaggerated for effect, but I'll bet the programming was there to some degree. No doubt several will apply. Read the one corresponding to your Moon sign, but if you can't identify with it, the major aspects to your Moon may be overriding the Moon sign. Consult the letters for any major aspects, as explained in chapter 4. If you have Moon in Libra, but it also aspects Saturn, then Libra's "My Dearest" may be less accurate for you than Capricorn's "Honor thy Mother and Father." This is particularly true of outer planet aspects, even the traditionally easy ones. If a letter doesn't apply, mark it "Not at this address," and drop it back in the box.

Men who are reading this, you got letters from Mom, too, but it's not on this route. Still, open the mail and see if it shows something about how Mom influenced your idea of women and what to expect from them. Does the letter under your Moon sign, for instance, remind you uncannily of your wife? I think I hear the postman now. . . .

Moon in Aries

Daughter,

As usual, you come crying to me when you're in trouble. What does crying accomplish? Size up the situation, think of a plan of attack, and then hop to it! If there's nothing you can do, there's no point in moping around. Get to work on something else—you'll feel better with a trophy under your belt.

If us women go to pieces, the whole shebang will fall apart. Men are useless creatures—unless you take charge and keep pushing, nothing gets done. I've been both mother and father to you kids, worked, and still had plenty of energy left over for running the house. I know not everyone is as strong as I am, but how would it have been if I'd caved in just because I felt a little down? It's time you started doing things for yourself—I won't always be around to pick up the pieces.

Write when you get it all straightened out. No news is good news.

Ma

Moon in Taurus

Dear Daughter,

I'm sorry to hear you're having a problem. I don't want to say I told you so, but I did think you were getting a bit too far away from the old, tested ways of doing things. If I do it the way my parents did it, there has to be a good, practical reason. Don't change something if it works!

But some things never change, and one of them is that I'll always be there when you need me. A good mother is like money in the bank—something you can count on. And, speaking of money, what will it cost to get you out of this mess? I do hope you've been putting money aside, but if you need a little help, let me know. After all, what's a mother for?

Love,

Mom

Moon in Gemini

Sissie,

I heard through the grapevine that you're having *un petit ennui.* I won't reveal my sources—I know it's supposed to be hush-hush, but Mother always finds these things out.

What bothers me most is that the perfect communication we've always had—more like sisters than anything—seems to have broken down. I've always felt a girl should be able to talk to her mother about anything. I know you were hurt that I told your dad about the abortion, but I don't believe secrets are good in a family. He'll write you back into the will eventually. People do get over these things.

So call me, darling, and we'll talk it all over and get it into a rational perspective. Besides, I have some amusing gossip to share with you. You'll die laughing!

Hasta luego!

Jane

Moon in Cancer

My Baby!

If only you hadn't wandered so far from home, this never would have happened. I tried so hard to raise you just the way my mother and father raised me. I've given my whole life to being a real mother, to meeting your every need, and somehow that wasn't enough. I'm hurt and upset at what you've done, but a mother never turns her back on one of her children when she is needed. Even at a time like this, I can't imagine life without you kids. I shall never forget this, not to my dying day, but I shall never speak of it again. Please, darling, come home!

Your mother

P.S. Tuesday is Daddy's birthday, and it would mean so much to him if you called.

Moon in Leo

DARLING!!

How AWFUL! Of course Mama Cat will come to the rescue, but under one condition. You must do exactly as I say, and word of this must NEVER leak out. I'd be so HUMILIATED, I couldn't hold my face up in this town. Think of our social position! We are a PROUD family!

Don't let me catch you looking down about this in front of the others, either. A woman should always be sunny, bringing others up rather than dragging them down. After all, people want to have a good time, and THE SHOW MUST GO ON!

Smile, darling, you will always have . . .

YOUR MOTHER!

P.S. Honey, when you come, can you bring me some of that divine perfume?

Moon in Virgo

Dear Daughter:

Sorry you're in trouble, but now you see what happens when you ignore the moral precepts I taught you. Under separate cover, I'm sending you my analysis of the situation, showing where you went wrong, and with detailed instructions on how to get out of this mess you've made. Not to be critical, dear, but what were you thinking? I'm always glad to be useful. That's what a woman ought to be—a model to her children and an inspiration to those who are mired in the none-too-perfect flesh. A good mother never thinks of herself.

I'm sorry if you're upset, but the truth is, you've made your bed and now you must lie in it. Speaking of bed making, I've neglected my housework to write this, so now I must go.

As ever,

Mother

P.S. Let me know if you're still troubled by irregularity, as I've found an amazingly effective herbal remedy.

Moon in Libra

My dearest,

How sad Mama is to hear that you're having a problem. On the other hand, how glad I am that it is bringing us closer. I love you so much, I would do anything for you. I've always tried to put you first in my life—especially since things have not worked out with your father the way a woman dreams. We women do tend to live for others—too bad people so seldom return the consideration.

And so you, too, are finding disappointment in one you love. No one could love and appreciate you the way I do, and no one is quite good enough for you. Lovers may come and lovers may go, but you'll always have your mother. Do come back to me soon, sweetheart.

All my love,

Mother

P.S. Don't return the diamond. You deserve to keep it.

Moon in Scorpio

My own Little Girl,

I'm writing this because you're old enough now to know the bitter truth about men and life. It's better you learn it from me than from some stranger, because other people don't have your best interests at heart the way I do. I don't often speak my mind right out in the open, but you are at an age where I am concerned about you and sex. You have been too eager around men from the time you were small. I've always been afraid you'd be promiscuous, so I've kept you close, to protect you from your carnal nature. The only place sex has in life is in procreation, if that's your thing. It wasn't mine, but I was a little wild when I was your age and that's how it worked out. Not that I begrudge the sacrifices I've made for you kids—after all, motherhood is the only thing that gives a woman's life its real meaning. Still, I can't pretend I didn't want something very different for myself.

It's all worth it, though, when I think that I will go on living through you and your sisters after I'm dead and gone—which won't be long, the way I've been feeling. I wonder how you'll get along without me around to set you straight. Get it through your thick head that the only one you can trust is me—

—Your Mother

P.S. Burn this—it's just between you and me.

Moon in Sagittarius

My Dear Fellow Traveler,

I know you are my daughter, but I see you as you truly are, another human being with as much capacity for wisdom as I have. I am older and more experienced, and that's why I offer you advice.

You are very upset over the situation you are in, but to choose to be in emotional turmoil solves nothing. I've always tried to teach you to look on the bright side and see the good that can come of a bad time. That's what women are for, if you look at history—to uplift, inspire, and encourage. We may have to give a little more, but 'tis more blessed to give than to receive, as some wise old philosopher once said.

A year from now, you'll see this event in a whole different light. There's a lesson to learn from it if you only will. It's never good to dwell in your emotions. Lose yourself in a good book, learn something new, or even go away on a trip. You'll see that I'm right. (As usual—Ha! Ha!)

That reminds me of a funny story—oh, but it's time for me to teach my Sunday school class. I must run.

Mom

Moon in Capricorn

Daughter:

It's my duty to warn you that you are ruining your life. Consider the long range effect, rather than snatching at some momentary pleasure. Take it from someone who's been through the school of hard knocks, you've got to keep your shoulder to the grindstone and your eye on the main chance in order to survive.

I've sacrificed everything and worked two jobs to give you every opportunity, and now you want to chuck it all for love? It's not any harder to love a rich man than it is a poor man—men just aren't that easy to love, period. A woman has to think about security and establish a solid financial position, because sooner or later, she'll wind up with all the responsibility in her lap. Look at what happened to me with that worthless father of yours. Do you really expect it to work out any different with your young man?

Sometimes it seems like I'll never see light at the end of the tunnel. But if you accomplish something, then I'll feel that all my sacrifices were worthwhile. I've got to go now. I brought a little work home from the office. I do wish you'd write more often—Honor Thy Mother and Father, it says in the Good Book.

As Always,

Your Mother

Moon in Aquarius

Hi Pal!

Glad you've finally got your modem up and working so we can e-mail back and forth. It's so much faster.

Sorry to hear of your little calamity. I wasn't surprised, because my astrologer warned me Uranus was making an aspect in my fifth house. It just wasn't in the stars for it to work out, that's all.

You know, our self-help group had a speaker last month who was talking about this very thing. You're not unique. He says it's common among young single women in our society today. So, instead of feeling sorry for yourself, why don't you start a group to help other women who are in the same predicament? How else will this world ever change, unless we women get active and involved in the things that concern us?

If nothing else, you'll make some new friends. Friends are so important—conditions change constantly, it's an insecure world, but as long as you have friends, you have a full and rewarding life. I hope you'll think of me as your friend, too, not as your Mom. Those diaper days are over now, and we should relate as peers.

Isn't it liberating to be so modern, not to have those suffocating codependent ties like John Bradshaw talks about? His programs on PBS have really opened my eyes to how we've enabled you, so I've persuaded your dad to stop sending you those monthly checks. I know times are rough for you but then they're rough on everybody. You'll thank me later for setting you free from that last bit of codependency, so we can truly be friends.

I have no more time for you now. My women's group is tonight, and I'm up for chairperson. I have some new ideas for how it should be run.

Love and Light!

Mother

Moon in Pisces

My wonderful, perfect, darling baby,

I just knew something was wrong—even before you called I got the vibrations and I was so worried! I know you are suffering terribly and I hurt for you. I wish I could be there with you, the way a good mother should. But, unfortunately, I have to go back into the hospital for another operation. The pain is intense, and I am so depressed I can hardly think.

Of course, your father is no help. Why are men so insensitive and women always the ones to carry the burdens of life? When you were little, I worried so about you that I couldn't sleep nights, but your father just didn't seem to care. (Thank God my fears never materialized . . . at least not yet. I won't worry you by speaking of them.)

So, my baby, once again I've failed you as a mother. The good Lord knows I've tried, but when you've had as many sorrows as I've had in my life, maybe you'll understand. And maybe—just maybe—you won't judge me so harshly for taking a pill or two to make life bearable.

My eternal love and concern,

Your Hopeless Mother

The Dead Letter Office

Some days it doesn't pay to open the mail! For some of you, the letters might have matched, line for line, a letter or three you actually got from Mom. Others might be protesting, "Mom would never answer me like that! She was always in my corner." Maybe she was—what GOOD mother isn't—but did some of the rest of it come through in code? Maybe she loved you all the way to the end of the letter and then killed you in the P.S. Did she say one thing and do another?

What can you do if the letter was right on target? Do you answer the mail? Refuse to accept delivery? Return to sender? Put it in the circular file? The problem is not the letter you got in the mail, but the letter inside your unconscious, the file that's still on the computer. That file is made up of all the thousands of messages from Mom, verbal and nonverbal, that you got daily in the eighteen or so years you lived with her. They were so constant and, sometimes, so subtle, that you probably no longer remember where they came from. You have absorbed them into your thinking, no longer questioning them.

For that kind of message, you may need reprogramming. Therapy, self-help groups or workshops, flower remedies, and astrology can contribute. You'll learn a great deal from the exercises from my mother-daughter workshops. With such methods, you can be assured that some day the destructive messages will no longer get to you for they will wind up in the dead-letter office.

Flower Remedies for the Mother Knot

In chapter 5, we learned about the flower remedies and how they can help us deal with our emotions. There are also some deeply healing essences to help you work with problems arising from the relationship with your mother. One of the most important is **Mariposa Lily**, by FES. It is a balm for those who were deprived of a positive bond with the mother, particularly where there was a lack of nurturing or a separation. Their **Golden Ear Drops** helps release unhappy childhood memories. For those who have suffered rejection by their mothers, **Evening Primrose** may be a longterm remedy. (Adoptees who feel abandoned by their birth mother may also find this essence healing.)

Barnacle is an essence made from a sea creature by Pacific Essences. It enables those who felt abandoned by their mothers to find nurturance within rather than forever seeking it outside. **Milky Nipple Cactus** by Desert Alchemy helps transform dependency into autonomy. (Yes, that really is its name!) Their **Organ Pipe Cactus** is immensely comforting and nurturing. Their combination, **The Inner Mother**, enhances a deep sense of inner security. If you'd like to stop blaming and judging your mother, try their formula, **Recognizing and Releasing Judgment and Denial**. Boundary issues you may have with or because of Mom respond remarkably well to their formula **Making and Honoring Boundaries**. Where the wounds from a dysfunctional family background have been severe, you might wish to consult my chapter on healing the past in *The Flower Remedies Handbook*. Use the recommended essences as an adjunct to other healing work. In such instances, healing is a process that the remedies will support, but other assistance such as therapy or self-help groups are usually needed.

A Do-It-Yourself Momectomy

The exercises that follow could be done in one day or spread out over several weeks. It is helpful to find others to work with, because sharing the experience is healing. I have separated the psychological exercises from those requiring a knowledge of astrology. They are especially helpful in combination, because the astrological information adds depth and objectivity to the psychological exercises. If you aren't familiar with the astrological techniques, skip over the second section or go to a kindly astrologer. Good timing for doing this work would be at an appropriate new or full Moon—say one that falls near your birth Moon or in your 4th house. Outer planet transits to your Moon or IC would be especially strong times for the work, although the nature of the experience would reflect the nature of the planet involved.

Part One: Psychological Exercises _____

Exercise One: Write a description of what your mother was like as a person. You might look back to see what she was like as you were growing up and write about that, as well as about what she is like today. Try to see her as a separate individual, rather than writing about how she treated you, which you will do later. What was her personality? What kinds of things did she enjoy doing? What were her talents and abilities? How did she approach people and situations other than her children? In a few words, what was her philosophy of life? Was she happy? Able to love? Fulfilled or frustrated? What were her dreams? (I have done all the exercises in this series several times, and this one particularly helps me see my mother more and more objectively.)

Exercise Two: Describe your mother as if she were a young woman of today just starting out, without a husband and family. What would she be doing and how would she react to today's social conditions?

Exercise Three: Another woman's moccasins. Again, it is best to do this with a partner if you can. Breathe deeply, and focus your attention in the area of your heart. When you feel calm, pretend that you are diving and swimming underwater, except you are pulling yourself downward to deeper and deeper levels of consciousness. Tell yourself that you want to experience your mother's state of mind at some crucial age in her life. Such ages might include when she left home, became a mother, or at the time of some important event in her life. With that same swimming motion, imagine that you are moving backward in time to that event. Pretend that you are your mother, and answer the questions your partner asks about what it is like for her.

Begin by asking for information: Who are you? Where do you live? Who's in the family? What are your parents like? Are you poor or well-off? and so on. It will soon become more than an intellectual exercise, for you may actually begin to experience what life was like for your mother. Try being her at different periods, including when she was young, when she was a teenager, when she left home, and so on. If you're really brave, go forward to the period when she had you to contend with, and see how those eras felt for her!

Exercise Four: In the same vein as the "Messages from Mom," concoct an imaginary letter that your mother would have written to you on the subject of what it means to be a woman or when you were in a crisis. This is a strong exercise, both amusing and painful.

Exercise Five: Go back to Exercise One, the written description of your mother as a person. Ignore the surface differences—e.g., that she lived in the country and had four kids, while you live in the city and are single. Apart from that, does the description fit you? Most participants have had to say that the character traits are uncannily similar. We take on many of our mothers' traits, especially those we dislike.

Exercise Six: Make a list of the POSITIVE traits you got from your mother. We love to blame her for our hangups, but we don't often give her credit for our strengths. For example, perhaps your mother over-emphasized money and thrift. Yet, because of that exposure, you gained a capacity to deal with money in a practical way without having to devote much attention to it. Myself, I have come to bless my mother for my strong constitution. She gave us a healthy start with the vegetables she grew, preserved, and insisted we eat. I didn't appreciate being on garden detail, as it cut into my time with my friends, but I can see now how the garden contributed. (HINT: Think about the positive qualities of your Moon sign.)

Exercise Seven: Write about how you experienced the connection with your mother at different ages—childhood, teen years, and now. Here you need not be objective, since what we want is your subjective, internal experience of this key relationship.

Exercise Eight: To complete the process, write an imaginary letter to your mother, saying all the things you would want to if you could communicate honestly with her. Can you show the love and appreciation as well as the hurt and anger? What would you have wanted from her, or what could she do to make things feel right between you? What do you wish you had done differently? If you can, finish by trying to forgive and asking to be forgiven for any wrongs either of you might have done to the other, so you can live free of guilt.

Part Two: Astrological Exercises _____

The following exercises are intended for those who have some understanding of astrology. They are arranged in order of difficulty, with advanced techniques at the end. If you aren't familiar with some of them, consult a professional, your teacher, or the books recommended in each section. You probably would find it helpful if you had a fellow astrology student to work with, but you can do it completely on your own. You are less likely to be objective, but the experience will still be valuable. Astrology, ruled by Uranus, is a powerful aid for detachment. (When working with a partner, it might be useful to tape the readings so you can continue to work with what you learned from the exercises.)

Exercise One: The Moon and its aspects, the 4th house, and planets in Cancer all show the mother's influence. With your partner, exchange readings on these factors in your charts, without reference at this point to your mother's chart. What kind of mother is shown in your chart? (The various discussions of the Moon sign and the mother's effects in this book and in my *Moon Signs* should be helpful.) Remember that your mother has made contributions to your life as well as the not-so-constructive effects. After all, the Moon is not a malefic.

Exercise Two: Calculate your mother's chart—with the birth time where possible, or a solar chart if you only know her date of birth. (To draw up a solar chart, place the Sun on the Ascendant and use equal houses around the zodiac from there, then fill in the planets from the ephemeris.) Exchange readings with a partner again, this time using the mother's chart. Listen to your partner's description of your mother as a person without describing her aloud yourself. Perhaps some of your frustrations can be explained by astrological incompatibilities—or, for that matter, similarities.

For instance, early in my studies of astrology, some of the heat of my anger toward my mother diminished when I discovered that she was a Leo, for that explained her bossiness and opinionation. I had to back down even further off my high horse when I found out that *I* had Leo rising and thus was more like her than I'd care to admit.

Exercise Three: Compare the reading you have been given with your written description from Exercise One in Part 1 (page 150) and with your own experience of her. Are there differences between how you see her and how she was described by your partner? Might they be caused by the fact that you saw her from a dependent child's point of view rather than that of an outsider who might be more objective?

Exercise Four: For greater understanding of your mother as a person, look at the factors in your mother's chart that describe HER mother. This would include her Moon and its aspects, her 4th house, and any planets in Cancer. (Obviously, her mother is your grandmother. You may be surprised to find a vast difference in how your mother experienced her as a mother, and how you experienced her as a grandparent.) By doing this, you can see what kind of mothering *she* got, and how that in turn influenced the kind of mothering she was able to give you. For example, a student I will call Margaret had an accurate birth time for her mother. The resulting chart had Pluto at 10 degrees Cancer, on the Midheaven. When this woman was 10 years old, her mother (Margaret's grandmother) died, and the prominent Pluto shows the powerful effect of the mother's death. Margaret's mother didn't know how to deal with Margaret after age 10 because she lacked a role model, so adolescence was more difficult than usual.

If you are in the mood for more explorations, trace your mother's outer planet transits at key ages, or at the time of key events in her life. This would provide additional clues as you work with Exercise Three in Part One (Another Woman's Moccasins). Your birth chart, of course, shows her transits at the time of your birth and the circumstances surrounding it.[1]

Exercise Five: Again with a partner, if possible, do the synastry (also called chart comparison) between your chart and your mother's. Determine which planets in each person's chart make aspects to planets in the other's.[2] If you are less experienced in astrology, or just want a different perspective, order a computer printout or get a reading.

Keep in mind that both of you contributed to any problems that existed in the relationship—the planetary energies flow both ways. Since the energies flow both ways, we may have influenced our mothers nearly as profoundly as they influenced us. That idea was confirmed by an interesting article in *Psychology Today* some years back called, "Bringing Up Mother." It discussed how the personality of the young mother can be shaped in response to the demands and the personalities of her individual children.[3]

Exercise Six: If you have accurate birth times for both you and your mother, make a composite chart or have it done by computer. The composite describes how both parties experience the relationship.[4] Again, the less experienced—or hopelessly biased—may wish to order a computer printout.

Another student, whom we will call Jane, was working with the composite of her chart and her mother's. She was amazed to see that anger—Mars—was not heavily stressed, although she had experienced that as the major dynamic. Instead, the problem was unrequited love (Venus in the 12th house, with a conjunction to Saturn the only aspect). She had to con-

---

[1]Two excellent books on transits are Robert Hand's *Planets in Transit* (Alglen, PA: Whitford Press, 1975), and Betty Lundsted's *Transits: The Time of Your Life* (York Beach, ME: Samuel Weiser Inc., 1980).

[2]A good book on the subject is Frances Sakoian and Lewis S. Acker's *The Astrology of Human Relationships* (New York: HarperCollins, 1989).

[3]Julius Segal and Herbert Yahres, "Bringing Up Mother," *Psychology Today,* November 1978, p. 90.

[4]The classic work is Robert Hand's *Planets in Composite* (Alglen, PA: Whitford Press, 1975).

sider that the composite chart describes how the relationship feels to both parties. Jane's mother may have felt as unloved and abandoned by Jane as Jane felt by her mother. After all, Jane was the one who put 3,000 miles between them and seldom visited or called.

Forgiveness—the Final Frontier

Why is forgiveness the final frontier? If your life has been based on hating and blaming your mother for what she did or didn't do, forgiving her can open the way to new adventures and explorations. If your worldview has been limited by your childhood experiences, you will discover new possibilities in both the inner and outer world—new facets of yourself. Hate binds you to the past, while forgiveness frees you to move ahead.

If your relationship with your mother was toxic, letting go of your resentments may be the last thing on your mind. You've grown attached to them, and you enjoy the righteous indignation at how bad and wrong she was. It may feel like winning—but as long as you hold onto it, you're still locked into the war. There are better pleasures. They say the best revenge is living well, and you can't live well if you're full of hate. If she can still trigger you into rage, you're giving her too much power.

Forgiveness is for your sake, not hers. She may or may not deserve to be forgiven—only you can determine that. But you deserve to forgive, for only then are you truly free. You don't even have to be willing, at this moment, to forgive, but it helps if you're at least willing to be willing.

And, no, forgiveness doesn't mean allowing her to continue to abuse, manipulate, or control you—it doesn't mean being a doormat or a victim. (To stop being a victim, Bach's **Centaury** and Desert Alchemy's **Ephedra**, and **Making and Honoring Boundaries**, are strong catalysts.) When you've worked through the intricate knot of hate, guilt, powerlessness, and grief, you may find you're able to set better limits. Not convinced? It's a process, not a single act. Premature and phony declarations of peace only stuff the anger deeper. For many, it's a place to arrive near the end of their journey to recovery from family wounds.

Still, the journey would be lighter if you let go of some of the baggage. There are things you can do to further the process. Work on clearing the chakras is helpful, especially the root, solar plexus, and heart. There are flower remedies aimed at this work, the most powerful being **Mountain Wormwood** by the Alaskan Flower Essence Project.

My first experience of **Mountain Wormwood** was a moving one. A therapy client had been working for over a year on resentments toward her family. Her sister was to be married, and my client was the matron of honor. A couple of weeks before the wedding, my client pleaded, "I don't want to spoil this wedding with my attitude. Please, can't you do something?"

In desperation, I gave her **Mountain Wormwood**, since **Holly** and **Willow** hadn't helped. When she came back the next week, she had a remarkable story to tell. She had talked with her mother and worked up to courage to ask if she had been a difficult child. Her mother replied, "My goodness, no! You were a wonderful child. But when you were little I had terrible migraines, so I was irritable a lot." Seeing the situation from an adult perspective, my client realized what physical pain her mother must have endured and how difficult it must have been for her to be patient with children. Mother and daughter wept and hugged, and a loving new bond was forged.

The trouble with **Mountain Wormwood** is its lack of specificity. If you take it, you may just find yourself forgiving people indiscriminately—not just the person you had in mind, but *all sorts* of people. They really should put a caution on the label—WARNING: This product may be hazardous to your grudge list. Other good remedies to include are **Salal** by Pacific Essences, **Alpine Azalea** by Alaskan Flower Essences, and **Black Kangeroo Paw** by Living Essences. **Holly** and **Willow** by Bach can be helpful in letting go of character traits that create resentment and hate in the present. However, in all my years of work with abuse survivors, adult children of alcoholics, and other dysfunctional families, I have never seen either of these remedies result in true forgiveness. It was only after I started using **Mountain Wormwood** and **Salal** that I really got results.

Another helpful technique is based on the work of Sondra Ray and others. It consists of writing the same statement seventy times a day for seven days—seventy times seven being a magical number of completion. It's not a gooey affirmation about love and abundance, but a statement designed to help you release some piece of programming that keeps you locked into the war with Mom. It may have been a decision you made along the way, e.g., "I can never forgive her for what she did." The statement you are writing creates a RE-decisioning, and it is helpful if it contains the words "I release," or "I allow myself to." Here are some possible statements, but you would need to tailor them to your situation.

I release my need to hate and blame my mother.

I let go of all negative programming from mother.

I forgive my mother for anything she may have ever done to me.

I accept forgiveness for anything I may have ever done to her.

I release my mother from all karmic obligation.

It's better to do only one of these affirmations at a time, to avoid burnout. You may type them on the computer, if you're comfortable with it, but don't cheat and use the repeat function or it doesn't work! You may also skip a day at times, so long as it is seven days total. Another potent statement, that covers not just Mom, but any and all karmic links, is the following: "I negate all vows of poverty, chastity, and obedience."

Are you wondering about astrological timing for beginning this work? There are no end of good times. The very best is a trine or sextile from transiting Neptune to the natal Moon or IC. Neptune dissolves hardened defenses and brings compassion. I observed forgiveness occuring spontanteously with clients having this transit, so I began recommending it to other clients and found that it worked well. Conjunctions, squares, oppositions, and even semi-sextiles to the Moon will also work, if less smoothly. Transiting Pluto's aspects to the Moon or IC would be my next choice, but often Pluto and Neptune will both make a series of aspects to these points. You might also try the new Moon in Cancer or Scorpio or the 4th house, the transiting Moon conjunct natal or transiting Neptune, the Moon hour of the Moon day, or any combination of the above—but not the void of course Moon.

~

December 24, 1995
Christmas Eve

Hi.

I'm Donna's Mom, and if I were ever going to stick my oar in, this would be the place. I don't know where we went wrong, but Donna and I just couldn't be close. She was always mad at me. It's really hard to be a Mom—you don't know how hard. It's so much work and you get so little support. I made many mistakes, but you know Leos can never apologize.

I was into astrology long before she was, although she seldom acknowledges it. She thought I was crazy at first, then almost despite herself she got interested. When she was doing so well at it, I could never tell her how proud I was, as long as I was alive, and now that I've crossed over, it's hard to get my message heard. But Dell Horoscope was my favorite magazine, and it's making me pop my buttons that she's got that Dear Abby column there now.

I try to make up for some of my mistakes by helping her as much as I can from the other side. I think she has fully forgiven me. As for me, I never really held it against her that she had to create so much distance in order to make something of herself. If you have hard feelings against your mother and she's still alive, please work on forgiving her. You've only got one Mom, and life is too short to miss out on being close to her.

Zelma Hedges Cunningham Baker

P.S. Look at this, will you? I finally got in the last word!

CHAPTER 9

THE PASSAGE INTO PARENTHOOD

Becoming a parent for the first time is an intense emotional experience—a profound lunar threshold with life-altering aftermaths. For women, all the meanings of the Moon are involved, and all bring conflict. The new mother must become protective and give the infant a sense of security at a time when she herself may feel insecure and vulnerable. She has to give up much of her own dependency because she now has a helpless creature dependent on her. She goes through a crisis in her relationship with her mother and gains a new identity as a lunar type. Not until she is a mother is she regarded a "real woman," and yet motherhood is extremely stressful in modern life, where so many lunar supports have vanished. Men also face adjustments and dilemmas when they become fathers. We'll examine the Moon signs again for clues to the kind of parent you might make. The Cancer rising wheel will suggest ways to relieve the stresses of parenthood.

The Aquarian Moon and Parenting Options

Aquarius symbolizes freedom and conscious choice. One exciting development in the transition to the Aquarian Age is the growing freedom to choose whether we will be parents. Even twenty-five years ago, non-parenthood was unthinkable. A woman without children was pitied as "barren," and one who openly said she didn't want them was considered unnatural. Some of these attitudes persist, especially in rural areas, but there is enough latitude that we do have a choice.

As a result, both men and women are making conscious decisions about whether to have children, how many, and when. Many women are choosing to delay parenthood until they accomplish career goals. Some men and women consciously go into a nurturing profession such as teaching, rather than having children. There are nontraditional family arrangements, and in some families, fathers take a more nurturing role. Many divorced couples are challenging the assumption that mother should have custody by sharing equal responsibility for caretaking, or having the father take the children. Some single women consciously decide to have babies, and single men and women are adopting children. For these situations, the public library should have information about support groups and organizations that you could join.

Advances in birth control and obstetrics have contributed to this freedom. Although some forms of birth control have harmful side effects and there haven't been any noticeable advances since the first edition of this book, there is hope of perfecting methods that don't harm us. The current methods have at least given us the consciousness that biology is not destiny. Those who were previously infertile also have more choice, as new methods make conception possible.

When one is faced with an unwanted pregnancy, the issue becomes a deeply emotional one. The adjustment to parenthood is difficult, even when entered into freely. To be locked into lunar roles unwillingly can engender deep resentment that can damage both parent and child. On the other hand, abortion can also be a sad experience for those who are in touch with their lunar nature, stirring up conflict and guilt.

The 27th-28th degrees of Cancer seem related to birth control and reproductive freedom. Pluto was at that degree in 1937–1938, when the AMA first came out in favor of birth control and when estrogen was synthesized. When Uranus formed a 90-degree angle, at 28 Libra, the U.S. Supreme Court made its pro-abortion decision, on January 22, 1973. In the mid 1990s, as Uranus and Neptune approached the opposition, Right-to-Life groups became powerfully politically active and even violent. Yet, with the U.S. Moon in Aquarius, American women will not readily relinquish their freedom of reproductive choice, once having won it. They may find this an even more compelling issue to organize around than suffrage was.

My choice of a lunar heroine for this chapter is birth control crusader Margaret Sanger, whose chart is shown in Chart 6. A nurse on New York's Lower East Side early in this century, she was moved by the plight of poor immigrant women whose health and lives were at risk by yearly pregnancies

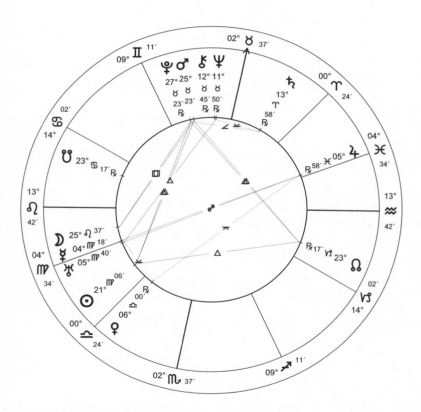

Chart 6. The chart of Margaret Sanger, born September 14, 1879 at 2:30 A.M.
LMT in Corning, NY. (Data from the Church of Light, published in Rodden:
Profiles of Women, *Tempe, AZ: American Federation of Astrologers, 1979.)*
Sanger generally lied about her age, giving the year as 1883, but if she were to-
tally politically correct, wouldn't you hate her? We assume this data is speculative.

that doomed their families to poverty. Although disseminating birth control information or devices was a criminal offense and was considered scandalous, she established a clinic and wrote a sex education column for a socialist newspaper. She was jailed for her efforts in 1917, but returned to them immediately on release and ultimately won her cause. She is as much a Plutonian as a lunar type, since her 1st-house Moon in Leo squares a close Mars-Pluto conjunction in the 10th house. Her courage, fiery temperament, and fierce advocacy for women result from this emphasis on fire and on Mars. If you are back in body, Margaret, please remember who you are. We are going to need you.

Birthing Under the Aquarian Moon

The Moon rules the stomach and mothering, and the most obvious signs of pregnancy are the nausea of morning sickness and the prominent belly. Did you know that the real purpose of belly dancing was to strengthen the abdominal and pelvic muscles for childbirth? Women danced together in private, and only later in history was the dance performed before men.

Pregnancy can be a crisis, particularly for the first-time parent. It is a time of adjusting to a new identity, of looking toward the lunar roles. The parent-to-be anticipates relinquishing freedom and independence for this child who will be totally dependent for several years. Any residual dependency, any conflict over nurturing others, is evoked. For women, hormonal shifts add further emotional upset, as do feelings about loss of control over the body, as the belly grows and other changes occur.

Physically and emotionally, the pregnant woman is vulnerable. Earlier in our history, the expectant mother was sheltered, made few public appearances, and was regarded as delicate because she was "in a family way." After delivery came a 40-day period of confinement or "lying-in." The new mother was recognized as needing more care and assistance from her partner and female relatives. She was given time to get over the physical shock of childbirth, adjust to parenthood, and learn to care for the baby. Often her own mother was there to help. That presence must have had a different effect on the subsequent mother-daughter relationship. It must have produced more closeness than when the only contact may be long-distance calls. Since the young mother's lunar needs were met, her adjustment was not as hard.

Today, the pregnant woman is expected to function in a highly independent way and gets very little special treatment. She may not even be given the courtesy of a seat on the bus. Out of economic necessity, she may work up to a month before delivery, and come back to work a month or two later. Due to our geographic mobility, she may go through the process of pregnancy, delivery, and recovery without the aid of relatives or friends. She is expected to bounce right back, physically and emotionally. The proud self-sufficiency of the modern woman causes her to ignore her special needs at these times. Even the woman who wants to stay home with her infant may think twice if she also has a career to consider. A recent study showed that women who returned to work within six months of the birth of the first child had a lifetime career advantage over women who stayed home longer, including higher wages.[1]

The Cancer transits have affected childbirth. The average woman no longer gives birth at home in the bosom of her family. Instead, she gives birth with strangers in a sterile, scientific environment as little like home as possible. Not all the change is negative, of course, because maternal and infant mortality have nose-dived in this century. Yet, the United States' statistics are not as good as other Western nations that make fewer intrusions on women's bodies during pregnancy and delivery.[2]

The birth moment is profoundly spiritual and emotional, and may figure heavily in the bonding between mother and child. Many midwives have described the birth process and the flow of spiritual energies accompanying it in very moving ways. Often the baby's father is present and, by his loving caresses, helps the mother to relax and participate more fully in delivery. The high point is a rush of spiritual energy, perceivable to all, as the baby is born and ecstatically wakes to conscious awareness.

Sadly, the proclaimed health care reforms of the mid-1990s are having a negative impact on lay midwifery, which is not recognized in the new laws, and therefore not covered by health insurance. Doctors are also less willing to rely on them due to new malpractice insurance provisions, despite the fact that home deliveries by midwives have far lower complication rates than hospital births.

Women who use anesthesia during childbirth may lose the beauty and satisfaction of this powerful moment that initiates them into their lunar role. When birthing becomes sterile, it is easy to lose awareness of its spiritual dimensions. The usual hospital delivery methods are shocking to the in-

---

[1]David Shapiro and Frank L. Mott. "Long-term Employment and Earnings of Women in Relation to Employment Behavior Surrounding the First Birth." *Journal of Human Resources,* Spring 1994 (v.29:2), pp. 248–276.
[2]Gina Corea, *The Hidden Malpractice* (New York: Jove, 1978), pp. 209–248. Her entire chapter on childbirth is an eye-opener.

fant's nervous system. The child is yanked suddenly into a noisy room with harsh bright lights, spanked, and roughly handled.

Induced labor is unnecessary up to 90 percent of the time and is primarily for the convenience of hospital staff. It can have severe consequences for both mother and child. Contractions are longer and harder than they need to be. This can result in so-called "minimal brain damage syndrome" like reading disorders or hyperactivity.[3] The rates of cesarean sections are also on the rise. That this may be related to economic motives rather than medical ones is substantiated by a study reported in the New England Journal of Medicine. Although poor women may be at higher risk in childbirth, due to nutrition and other factors, higher income women had 75 percent more cesareans.[4]

The first few days after birth are crucial in bonding, and much of that time the baby is in a mostly metal, harshly-lit nursery away from the mother. Baby animals become attached to their mothers in the first few hours after birth in a process called imprinting. Although scientists disparage the role instinct plays in human life, the intermittent separation of mother and infant in those first few days may cause us to miss crucial bonding. This lack can affect both the child's trust in the mother and her adjustment to motherhood. Thus, this practice may contribute to milder versions of the disease of non-attachment discussed in chapter 3.

Matrescence—The Process of Becoming a Mother

> The myth of the Maternal Instinct says we are all born mothers, that once we are mothers we will automatically love our children and always do our best for them. If you believe in the maternal instinct and fail at mother love, you fail as a woman.
>
> Nancy Friday[5]

When we spoke of Neptune in Cancer, we saw that the myth of the Perfect Mother has become an impossible ideal, crushing the self-esteem of women who try to achieve it. Part of the myth is that childbirth leads automatically

---

[3] *The Hidden Malpractice*, pp. 224–228.
[4] Jeffrey B. Gould, Becky Davey, and S. Stafford-Randall. "Socioeconomic Differences in the Rates of Cesarean Section," *New England Journal of Medicine*, July 27, 1993, v.321:4, pp. 233–240.
[5] Nancy Friday, *My Mother/My Self: The Daughter's Search for Identity* (New York: Dell, 1978), p. 33.

to unconditional love of the infant, and proficient knowledge of how to be a mother. Nothing could be further from the truth. The first year of the child's life is a maturational crisis for the mother, as she learns mothering skills and wrestles with feelings about taking on the lunar role. It is a crisis for the father as well, which we'll discuss next.

In her book, *The Tender Gift: Breastfeeding*, Dana Raphael coined the term *matrescence* (literally, *becoming a mother*), for this process. It is a period of transition, of adjusting to new demands. In earlier times, women had plenty of support from other women in this process and could identify positively with them. In today's world, because of geographic mobility, many women are thrown back on their own resources and may spend their day alone with the infant. This increases stress and leaves them needy, drained, and often angry that their own lunar needs aren't being met. Because motherhood has decreased in prestige, new mothers have even less sense of pride and importance just at the very time they need recognition for their hard work. It is normal for the new mother to be in emotional turmoil, uncertain, and anxious. The relationship with the baby takes as long to develop as any other important relationship—perhaps longer, since the infant is unable to give back very much. It is rarely love at first sight; the day-by-day contact builds the tie.[6]

Post-partum depression, which is glibly labeled "the baby blues," is part of the process for up to half of new mothers. Depression is often anger turned inward, and it is a common female response to the stress of conforming to lunar expectations. Hormonal shifts and fatigue also contribute to the emotional upheaval of the post-partum period, but the myth says we must be radiantly happy with the baby.

The result of the myth can be another emotional split. As described by Nancy Friday in *My Mother/Myself,* the mother feels the mixture of love and resentment, affection, and anger for her child, but she cannot afford to know it. The split between what mother says and what she feels leaves her unsure of herself. As Friday says, the glorification of motherhood demands that when her child is born, a woman's autonomy over her emotions must end.[7]

Adjusting to parenthood is a process, rather than something inborn. It takes at least one year, and maybe twenty, since each stage of development means adjusting to new requirements. There are tremendous physical and

---

[6]Dana Raphael, Ph.D., *The Tender Gift: Breastfeeding* (New York: Schocken Books, 1976). No longer in print.

[7]Nancy Friday, *My Mother/Myself: The Daughter's Search for Identity*, p. 35.

emotional demands, years of 18-hour days. How can you put out so much lunar energy and not wind up in the loony bin? It is a tribute to our strength that women do adjust and put out that energy consistently year after year. Nonetheless, it is hard, and the Cancer rising wheel given later holds some ideas for helping to alleviate the stresses. Desert Alchemy's **Birthing Harmony** and **New Mother's Formula** can be wonderfully supportive.

What About Fatherhood?

We're devoting most of this chapter to matrescence, but what about *patrescence*? What do men go through in becoming fathers, and what can help them make stronger bonds to their children? Are they as capable of loving, nurturing child care as women are supposed to be? Certainly we have grown in the last decade or two in terms of allowing men to take on some caretaking roles. Now more divorced fathers have primary custody, and some single men adopt children. Both categories are more the exception than the rule—unusual enough that they are still remarked upon as special and viewed with ambivalence. However, partly due to the economy, in 1991, one-fifth of preschool children were cared for by the father while the mother worked outside the home.[8]

There are a few studies that shed light on men and parenthood. They found that fathers who participated in childbirth classes and assisted in the birth were later more involved in childcare. The experience strengthened the bond of father to baby, just as being awake and aware during birth strengthened the mother's bond to the baby. By the age of one month these infants responded differently to their fathers than to others in the environment. It could be argued that men who are willing to participate in these experiences are inherently more lunar, but perhaps most men are simply not allowed to develop that side of themselves. It took an act of congress in the 1970s to force hospitals to allow fathers into delivery rooms in the U.S.—before that it was illegal.

Another study involved rhesus monkeys, who have an inflexible culture with strong sex role stereotypes in which the males are detached and indifferent toward the infants. Psychologists took little monkeys away from their mothers at the age of one month and put them in a cage with adult

---

[8] *Information Please Almanac, Atlas, and Yearbook, 1995* (Boston and New York: Houghton and Mifflin, 1995), p. 436.

males. The males quickly became devoted fathers and spent as much time fondly grooming and playing with the babies as their female counterparts.[9] If you've ever watched documentaries on primates and their young, you can imagine the grief of the devoted mother monkeys whose babies were taken. At least we did learn from the study that males are not biologically prevented from being nurturing.

Becoming a father for the first time can evoke many ambivalent feelings. Men who like children may welcome them and yet be daunted by the responsibility of both rearing and supporting this new being for the next 20 years or so. For many, fatherhood means giving up dreams of pursuing creative talents or their yearning for adventure in favor of a safe career path that they may come to detest. It means a greater degree of commitment to their partner, often at a point when they haven't been together all that long. Just as mothers do, fathers lose much of their freedom in taking on the parental role. Many men today are opting out of that commitment altogether. Taken collectively, this trend leaves behind a large number of women who yearn for children, yet aren't allowed to have both a child and their relationship.

When parenthood is not chosen but imposed, being confronted with a pregnant partner may evoke hopeless anger and frustration in men who do not want the child. One battered woman in three is pregnant at the time of the battering.[10] Add to this the number of men who abandon women when they become pregnant, those who enter into affairs while their wives are pregnant, and those who physically abuse their offspring, and it is clear that this threshold is a lunar crisis for men as well. Most men cross this threshold successfully, yet there are a significant number of catastrophes. And, yes, mothers do also physically abuse their children. It is a wonder that more of them don't, considering how ill-suited, poorly prepared, and unsupported many of us are for the exhausting daily demands of being the primary caretaker.

First-time fathers cross a particularly difficult lunar threshold when the baby is born. Especially if they have mostly relied on women to supply their lunar needs rather than explore this dimension themselves, they can feel bereft and cheated. If they've had their partners' undivided attention up to now, men may experience a sense of loss as the focus of the woman's attention shifts from them to the baby. There is no longer so much intimate time,

[9]Both studies from Mark Gerzon, *A Choice of Heroes* (New York: Houghton Mifflin, 1982), pp. 205–208.
[10]*Information Please Almanac*, 1994, p. 436.

as the woman is often preoccupied and exhausted. The most fundamental lunar patterns are temporarily in upheaval. Sleep is disrupted, meals may be scanty or erratic, and even the living space, itself, is altered. There may also be a shift in the relationship with Mom. She now diverts some of her love and attention to her new grandchild and may bond more closely with the new mother.

Yes, the greater part of the upheaval is temporary, and men can adjust and even come to love their new role. Still, that first year is as much of a crisis for men as for women. Men, like women, need support in preparing for and adjusting to their new role, and yet the macho stereotypes mitigate against asking for help or talking it out. **Red Helmet Orchid** by Australian Bush Essences is a great healer for those who had a poor bond with the father and is also helpful for new fathers in bonding with their own children.

Breasts, Breastfeeding, and Mother Love

Consider that, for millions of years, mammals had been breast-feeding. Then, in just a moment in time, the human animal changed this. We just turned off the breast! Never in the evolution of the human species has a bodily function been pressured into such a sudden and dramatic change.

Dana Raphael[11]

Breastfeeding and Mother Love: The Moon rules the breasts, food, and mothering. Until the early part of this century, the infant had a direct physical connection with the breast that simultaneously soothed and fed. In several ways, breastfeeding promotes the natural rhythms of both mother and child. It gives the infant optimal nourishment on demand. It stimulates the production of hormones that are thought to be related to maternal feelings (prolactin and oxytocin). These hormones also suppress ovulation, so breastfeeding acts as a natural form of family spacing, which is effective so long as the baby's diet isn't supplemented by other foods and until menstruation returns.[12]

---

[11]Dana Raphael, *The Tender Gift: Breastfeeding*, p. 47.
[12]Kathy I. Kennedy and Cynthia M. Visness, "Contraceptive Efficacy of Lactational Ammenorrhoea." *Lancet*, January 25, 1992 (v.339:8787), pp. 227–231.

The end of breastfeeding as a general practice may well have contributed to the strains of motherhood. Nursing helps ease the transition from pregnancy to motherhood, as it keeps mother and baby closely connected. Part of the direct satisfaction of caring for an infant is the pride of knowing the food your body made contributes to the child's growth. An experiment was performed in which microphones were attached to nursing babies and to bottle-fed babies, both held in similar ways by their mothers. The bottle-fed babies only drank quietly, while the breastfed babies gurgled and made other contented noises. The difference in the recordings was striking. The researchers concluded that the effect of breastfeeding a child was very positive, and that the good feelings coming from the baby also increased the mother's satisfaction.[13]

Synthetic Mother's Milk: Pluto's transit through Cancer correlated with the introduction of synthetic formulas in the 1920s, and their rise to almost universal use. This was partially due to a joint campaign by corporations and the government, claiming that mother's milk was contaminated. (Similarly, one formula-maker, Nestle, recently widely published ads warning that you can transmit HIV through breastfeeding.) The popular use of pacifiers—artificial plastic nipples—and the skyrocketing number of smokers may be attempts to make up for oral needs the breast used to satisfy. Many synthetic formulas are high in sugar, and early exposure to them may set us up for sugar addiction. There are differences between human milk and cow's milk, with implications for bone formation. Mother's milk also contains antibodies that help protect the baby from disease.

The entrance of women into the labor force in masses has made breastfeeding extremely difficult, yet even non-working mothers rejected breastfeeding in awesome numbers. Not all women need to be mothers, but those who choose to have children might want to reconsider breastfeeding. The nursing mother needs support, or she may not be able to produce the necessary milk, leaving her with a sense of failure as a woman. A study showed that women who received home visits and instruction after delivery were much more likely to continue breastfeeding than those who did not.[14]

The All-American Breast Fetish: Breasts are one of the best advertising gimmicks, selling everything from cars to chewing gum. The mass media also

---

[13]Ingrid Mitchell, *Breastfeeding Together* (New York: Seabring Press, 1978), p. 34.
[14]Paula Serafino-Cross and Patricia R. Donovan, "Effectiveness of Professional Breast Feeding Home-Support." *Journal of Nutrition Education*, May-June, 1992, v24:3, pp. 117–122.

shape women's self-image, because we measure ourselves against the young, firm, voluptuous breasts showcased in the media and find ourselves wanting. Our national fetish for breasts has made women painfully self-conscious. We are rarely satisfied with our breasts, believing they are too big, too little, not shaped right, or not firm enough. The woman who is well-endowed, however, is treated as a sex-object rather than as a person. We feel inadequate if our breasts aren't perfect, and we judge our attractiveness and femininity by them.

On some unconscious level, I believe this insecurity is due to the cessation of our breasts' natural function. Breastfeeding put us in touch with our womanhood in ways that were deeply satisfying emotionally and instinctually. As the outer planets transited Cancer, and as breastfeeding disappeared, we not only got the myth of the Perfect Mother but the myth of the Perfect Breast as well.

A sad demonstration of women's willingness to endure nearly anything to feel more attractive is the story of silicone breast implants. One to two million American women (that's MILLION!) got them before the FDA restricted their use in 1992. Now doctors are finding that the silicone can leak and migrate to other parts of the body, contract and disfigure the breast, and create serious immune system problems, chronic pain, and fatigue. They also obscure mammographies, making it difficult to detect breast cancer.[15] Furthermore, there are numerous reports of infants who breastfed after their mothers had implants, who developed a thickening of the esophagus, making swallowing difficult, as well as experiencing recurrent abdominal pain.[16]

Men are powerfully moved by breasts, and not purely for sexual reasons. Breasts unconsciously represent the fulfillment of dependency needs. Lacking the deep bond with Mother that breastfeeding provides, men may feel a similar lack of bonding to the subsequent women in their lives. The fetish for breasts represents a fantasy return to the comfort of being held at Mama's breast. As modern life and changes in women's roles erode the lunar supports men once relied on, men's magazine covers highlight bigger and bigger breasts.

Preventing Breast Cancer: Although men may love our breasts, they don't take very good care of them—at least the predominantly male medical establishment does not. Leslie Laurence and Beth Weinhouse documented this and

---

[15]Leslie Laurence and Beth Weinhouse, *Outrageous Practices: The Alarming Truth about How Medicine Mistreats Women* (New York: Fawcett Columbine, 1994), pp. 186–191.
[16]"When Breast Feeding May Be Bad." *Women's Health Letter*, 11/94, p. 7. Subscriptions to this newsletter may be ordered from (714) 693-1866.

many other upsetting ways medicine neglects or mistreats women in *Outrageous Practices* (New York: Fawcett, 1994). For example, a pilot project on breast and uterine cancer conducted by Rockefeller University *used only males as research subjects!* Although women comprise 51 percent of the population, only 13 percent of the 1987 National Institute of Health budget was spent on diseases that affect predominantly women, including breast and uterine cancer, pregnancy, contraception, fibroids, endometriosis, and PMS. NIH then had only three gynecologists on staff, but 39 veterinarians.

Laurence and Weinhouse noted that breast cancer rates increased about one percent per year between 1940 and 1986, but four percent a year since then. In 1960, one in fourteen women had a lifetime risk of getting breast cancer, while now it's one in eight. In treatment, at least 90 percent of women with breast cancer are eligible for lumpectomies, but more than half will undergo mastectomies.

In addition, women don't always take good care of their breasts. Our conflicts and embarrassment about this emotionally-laden part of the body persists, no matter how well-educated we are. At a conference I attended about breast cancer, a speaker asked how many women regularly examined their own breasts for lumps and changes. Several hundred health educators, nurses, and other medical personnel were present. Only a few raised their hands, despite their knowledge of breast self-examination and its life-saving potential. The thought of any threat to this symbol of our femininity is enough to make most of us blank out. Another factor is that we have also been taught to avoid touching the very parts of our bodies that make us women!

Many Moon-related concerns covered in this book play a role in breast cancer, including estrogen, overweight, diet, and family history. One-third of all breast cancers are estrogen-dependent. Anything which prolongs our exposure to estrogen increases the risk—early menstruation, many pregnancies, birth control pills, fertility drugs, late pregnancies, late menopause, and estrogen replacement therapy after menopause.[17] Overweight women have more estrogen in their bodies to begin with, and the fat acts as storage for the estrogen. It is recommended that we strictly limit fats in our diet, because there is a connection between fat intake and breast cancer rates. Women who breastfeed for long periods, on the other hand, are less prone to breast cancer, according to the World Health Organization.[18]

---

[17] *Let's Live*, April, 1979 issue, p. 88.
[18] "Breast Cancer Cause: Is It Too Much Fat?" *National Health*, October, 1979, p. 1; Oliver Cope, M.D., *The Breast* (Boston: Houghton Mifflin, 1977), pp. 38–48; and Dana Raphael, *The Tender Gift: Breastfeeding*, p. 85.

If you feel you are at risk, breast self-examination and having regular checkups could be crucial. Metaphysically, the disease cancer is said to be a disease of resentment, and the affected body part reveals what is resented. Breast cancer, therefore, can show resentment of one's own mother, filling the mother role, or other lunar functions.

What Kind of Parent Would You Be?

Again, consult your list of the Moon's sign, house, and aspects, as explained in chapter 4. Since your Moon represents both the mother you had and the parent you become, the Letters from Mom may have some relevance to you as a parent. Much of the pattern is unconsciously transmitted. By becoming more conscious of these patterns, and by working through the mother knot, you can learn to be a different kind of parent than your mother, if you aren't happy with your model. Of course, not everything our mothers transmitted was detrimental or we wouldn't have grown up at all. The Moon in your chart, its sign, house, and aspects, shows how you feel about nurturing others and your reactions to those who are dependent on you. It may not always show your actual behavior in the parental role, but more how you inwardly feel about it.

Moon in Aries: You may have considerable anger over needs that were not met, and thus may respond with irritation when you have to take care of others. Most likely, your mother pushed you to be extremely independent, so you want others to be independent as well. Your own sorrow or neediness as a child was often met with scorn or the withdrawal of love. You may, therefore, become impatient when a child cries or clings, even if you don't act on it. (**Impatiens**, by Bach, is a great antidote to Aries' characteristic irritability.) Work to develop more patience with your child's emotions and needs, and with your own.

On one hand, you have excellent leadership ability, but on the other, you can be a bit bossy and get angry when not obeyed. You are an active person and feel frustrated if confined only to the home, so it is important to find ways of having more freedom. Physical activity is an excellent outlet, releasing anger and providing for a valid need on your part. When old enough, the child can participate in your activities and would learn from them. You will impart to your child your vigorous, eager approach to life, as well as your admirable self-sufficiency.

Moon in Taurus: This is supposedly the "best" Moon sign—the sign of the Moon's exaltation in traditional astrology. Unless there are difficult aspects to your Moon, you may be old-fashioned and contented in the parental role. Your own dependency needs were met by a stable home environment and you find it natural to do the same for your own children. The rapid changes in our civilization can throw you off-base, so you might invest too much energy in your children as a form of personal security. (**Walnut** by Bach, or **Transitions Formula** by Desert Alchemy, can help you cope better with change.) It would be soothing to raise some of your own food, grow plants in your home, and you can impart your gift for growing things to your child. It is important that you give your child the opportunity to manage some money. However, do not place too much emphasis on the material things of life—a good, commonsense balance is needed. (**Hound's Tongue** by FES can help establish such a balance.) You will pass on to your children your own steadiness, practicality, and capacity for rich enjoyment of sensual pleasures. (If your Moon aspects Pluto in Leo, this mellow picture may not be true of you—try Moon in Scorpio as well.)

Moon in Gemini: If you're a typical Gemini Moon, you were raised to be uncomfortable with emotional displays, so you may try to talk your child out of his natural fears and frustrations. Know that unpleasant feelings are part of life. Your child can adapt to these feelings as long as they aren't banished from consciousness. (FES's **Nasturtium** can help you stop living in your head so much.)

Your own mother was probably on the move constantly, and like her, you are a restless, active person, wanting a good deal of mental stimulation and conversation. If you neglect these pleasures, you can feel squelched and bored. You probably can concentrate on two things at once. Get a cordless phone and learn to manage your chores quickly to make time for your own interests. You would make a fine teacher, and your capacity to stimulate your child intellectually is a plus. Reading to your child or telling stories can be enjoyable and will give him a love of books. Humor is another asset, and teaching your children to laugh can be a legacy that stands them in good stead throughout life.

Moon in Cancer: You are the true lunar type. The parental role can hold great satisfaction, yet you may also become a smotherer. (**Red Chestnut** by Bach is the perfect antidote to smother love.) Because you may have some residual dependency, establish nurturing relationships with other adults in order not to feel depleted by your family. Outside interests and relationships can also keep you from fixing too much attention on the child. Finding safe outlets for your strongly emotional nature will keep the child from becoming the focus of too much emotion. The techniques for keeping your lunar hemisphere regulated are important in your dealings with your children.

Connections with older and more experienced parents will reassure you as the child goes through normal stages of growth. Children live through scrapes and emotional tailspins with great resilience, so don't overreact. (**Red Clover** by FES can help you remain centered when family members are upset.) Child psychology books can put your child's development in perspective, so that you need not be anxious. If this is an only or youngest child, you might want to form play groups so the child is not too dependent. The exercises and readings suggested earlier to de-intensify your tie with your own mother will help you in turn prevent a symbiotic attachment to your children.

On the plus side, many of you have a great natural understanding of children and are extremely nurturing. Your capacity for emotional understanding and intuitive perception makes you keenly sensitive to your child. You also have the capacity to foster this emotional sensitivity and intuitive awareness in your children.

Moon in Leo: If you had a rather narcissistic mother, your own wish for attention was never properly met, so you may still hunger for attention in your adult life. (Bach's **Chicory** or **Heather** help if this is the case.) The tasks of childrearing, where all attention has to be focused on someone else, absolutely must be balanced by outside activities. Make sure the child has an acceptable substitute—e.g., a play group. You have a strong drive for significance, which could be met by work or community activities where you gain a sense of importance and accomplishment. Otherwise, you may seek attention vicariously by becoming too involved in the child's accomplishments. No doubt, you'd like be an absolute ruler. Constant obedience is neither necessary nor desirable, if you want a child who will grow up to be able to think for herself. Learn not to take the child's emotions so seriously—they do dramatize situations, and these incidents pass quickly.

On the positive side, you have a fun-loving, childlike streak, so if you allow yourself to enter your children's world and play with them, you can share delightful times. You might enjoy making up and acting out stories. By recognizing and loving your inner child, you can share your children's world in a way most stuffy grownups never do. (**Zinnia** by FES can enhance this connection to the inner child.)

Moon in Virgo: Because of the example of your own mother, who may have been somewhat of a martyr, you want to be the perfect parent. You are a hardworking, well-motivated person, but inclined to be far too hard on yourself. Learn to let go of perfectionism, since you may apply the same critical standards to your children as well. As you learn to love yourself and not demand perfection, your criticism of others will ease off, too. (**Beech, Rock Water**, and **Pine**, all by Bach, can be immensely helpful in learning not to be so hard on yourself.)

When it comes to maintaining the house, guilt and compulsivity are your enemies. Delete "should" from your vocabulary, and take time to smell the flowers with your children. Being able to eat off the floor is no substitute, in a child's world, for having an understanding ear when needed. You will transmit to your children your strong sense of order, your wish to be of service, and your conscientiousness. Your practicality and your many useful skills can also be a legacy.

Moon in Libra: There can be a warm parent-child bond with this position and an excellent capacity to share with your children. It is important, however, that you have loving interchanges with other adults so the bond is not overemphasized. If you are having marital difficulties, work at them, so the child doesn't feel pressed to mediate or to make up for your lack of companionship. If you are divorced, find intimate support networks, so that you don't focus too much attention on the child as an outlet for your desire for closeness. (Bach's **Chicory** helps those who become too possessive out of a need for closeness.)

You may also be threatened by conflict and cover it with sweetness and light. Only by learning to deal with anger and conflict can you teach your child how to manage basic human emotions. You will impart to your child your own sociability and love of people and beauty, plus the capacity to see the other person's side of things.

Moon in Scorpio: Due to unmet dependency needs, you may feel burdened and somewhat resentful of the parental role. However, you would feel guilty over not being a perfect parent, so you may work yourself into near-exhaustion. (Bach's **Pine** and **Rock Water** can help you ease up on yourself.) The section on burnout would be important, because you can sometimes become drained from trying so hard to be perfect.

You have also been taught, and taught well, to control your feelings and needs and to believe you have no right to them. When you are angry at your children's demands, or are needy, you may become even more guilty and try to hide it. You can wind up feeling all alone in the world, bearing family responsibilities by yourself. (This is a counterdependent position for the Moon.) Learn to express your own needs and emotions in a supportive atmosphere so that you do not become bitter and transmit your resentment to your family.

You periodically require quiet and privacy to regenerate and refuel. Having had a very controlling mother, you may manage your children tightly, rather than letting them have freedom to explore life's possibilities. Or, you may bend over backward not to be like her, so you may wind up being permissive and overindulgent. It is important to work on letting go— to live and let live. (A couple of months on Bach's **Vine** will loosen up even the most extreme control freak.) Doing your lunar hemisphere housekeeping can keep emotions from spilling over into your homelife. On the plus side, you look deeply into human nature and hear what your children verbalize as well as what they don't. You will transmit to your offspring your analytic abilities and this gift of going deeper than the surface of human interactions.

Moon in Sagittarius: Your motto may be, "Do as I say, not as I do." Don't preach at your children, or find a moral in every story, but listen and communicate. You are by nature an optimist, yet may too quickly point out the bright side, not really listening to your children's fears and concerns. (Bach's **Agrimony** helps those who cover over difficult feelings by projecting a cheerful front.) You are mentally active and curious, and it is important to find intellectual outlets, lest you feel stultified. Don't neglect your mental growth. Libraries and educational TV can be a haven for you. You can be self-taught in any area of interest, even if you can't take time to go to school just now. You will impart to your family your desire to learn and grow, your love of education, your quest for wisdom, your optimism and your philosophical approach to life.

Moon in Capricorn: You're another one who can be tormented by the perfect parent image and can be very hard on yourself if you fall short. (Like Virgo, you could use Bach's **Rock Water** and **Pine**.) Work on releasing unrealistic standards of perfection for yourself, your housework, and your children. You do have needs, which you tend to feel guilty about and override. Find ways of replenishing yourself to avoid depression or fatigue. Respect your emotions, because you can't build walls against your feelings or protect your children from theirs.

Unless you feel the satisfaction of achievement, you may focus on your children's endeavors, pushing them toward accomplishment. It is certainly possible to combine career and parenthood, especially given your genius for organization. When you try to be perfect at either, you only succeed in making yourself and your family miserable. Women with this Moon, in some respects, might be happier as career women, working toward accomplishments in the outside world. (**Pomegranate** by FES helps establish a feminine balance between home and career.)

On the constructive side, you will teach your children your own conscientiousness and your wish to improve the world around you. You have a strong sense of responsibility, and will impart your own sense of right and wrong. You will also pass along your self-discipline and sense of order.

Moon in Aquarius: If you have this Moon, recognize that you will never fit totally into the traditional marriage and family roles, that something within you rebels against them. You may wish to experiment with other life styles and parental options that allow more freedom while still providing for your children's needs. (FES's **Goldenrod** helps you remain comfortable with your convictions despite outside disapproval.) You have a strong drive for intellectual stimulation and involvement with the world at large. There is nothing that says your children can't participate, even in such simple activities as stuffing envelopes or recycling.

If you respect the necessity for a certain amount of freedom and mental stimulation, you can avoid the difficulties of this position. Work on conscious awareness of feelings will help balance your needs with those of the family. You will impart to your children your own wonderful concern for humanity and a wider view of life, affording them a degree of freedom and independence that is rare in a traditional childrearing pattern. Like you, they will come to question what is and have the courage to forge their own path, not bound to stereotypes.

Moon in Pisces: If you try to live up to the image of the Superparent, you may wind up feeling down on yourself and a martyr to the cause. You have a deep urge for spiritual exploration and fulfillment. In order not to be depleted by parenthood, meditate regularly and find your spiritual center. (**Lotus**, made by a variety of companies, is as important spiritually on the essence level as the flower itself, and Pegasus' **Angelica** helps you attune to the angelic realms.)

Doing your lunar hemisphere work will be helpful because you tend to hide from your feelings and to try to get your children to hide from theirs as well. This is partly due to your extreme sensitivity and receptivity, so much so that you feel your children's pain. This is a good trait, but when carried to an extreme, you may overreact. Children have great resiliency and quickly get over hurts. Their emotions may be strong one moment, only to be forgotten moments later, while you are left in a stew. (**Red Chestnut** by Bach, and **Red Clover** and **Pink Yarrow** by FES, would help you keep these ups and downs in perspective.)

You will impart to your children your sensitivity and compassion toward others and your spiritual nature. These qualities serve not only as an example to them, but also can sustain you through the stresses of parenthood.

☽ ☽ ☽ ☽

As these readings show, every Moon sign and aspect has pluses and minuses in parenting. By maximizing the positives and working consciously on the negatives, you can make the most constructive use of the sign. The more balanced your lunar hemisphere, the less likely you are to overdo the negative aspects, and the more likely you are to enjoy parenthood's positive contributions. Have compassion for yourself as a lunar type laboring under the strains of the solar world. Remember that your capacity for nurturing can be strained by the social changes we have discussed.

Using the Cancer Rising Wheel to Avoid Parental Burnout

Up to now we have focused only on the lunar threshold crossed by the first-time parent. We haven't acknowledged the day-in, day-out lunar drain that parenthood can entail. BURNOUT is a buzz word in the helping professions. Everybody who is anybody has it—doctors have burnout, social workers have burnout, nurses have burnout. Victims of this dread disease take it very seriously. There are workshops, programs, and counselors to get you fired up again or else to help you make a midlife career change.

What nobody recognizes is that mothers have been having burnout for centuries, only when a mother has it, they hint you're unfit. If it's bad enough case of burnout, they say you've had a nervous breakdown. Men can have parental burnout, too. They may express it in a variety of ways, like spending more and more time away from the family, or glued to the television. The Cancer rising wheel is a great tool, not only for diagnosing whether you have parental burnout, but also for alleviating it.

The symptoms? Let's go around the wheel. You have burnout if you're feeling that your house is a hard shell around you (Cancer on the 1st), if you're overspending to get out of the dumps (Leo on the 2nd), if you constantly analyze and criticize your performance or your family's (Virgo on the 3rd), and feel married to your home responsibilities (Libra on the 4th). Suspect that you may have it if you sometimes want to kill the kids (Scorpio on the 5th), and if you overindulge in food, alcohol, or other substances because you feel so tired and drained (Sagittarius on the 6th). If you can't remember why you married this stranger who lives with you (Capricorn on the 7th) and feel cold and distant in bed because you resent living this way (Aquarius on the 8th), the cause may be burnout. If you feel your life is a prison (Pisces on the 9th), and you're vaguely angry at the whole world (Aries on the 10th), if you dream of getting rich as an escape route (Taurus on the 11th), and feel your mind has been on vacation since heaven knows when (Gemini on the 12th), then the diagnosis of burnout is 100 percent certain!

The Cancer rising wheel teaches us that parents also need nurturing in order to keep on giving to their children. Since t.l.c. is not that easy for adults to come by, the message is that you need to learn to nurture yourself, without guilt at being "selfish." Otherwise you will feel depleted and begrudge the nurturing you must do. Let's go around the wheel again to get concrete suggestions on how to avoid deadly burnout.

Cancer on the 1st: Besides learning to give yourself t.l.c., this placement suggests the need for consciously establishing connections with older women who can give you advice and emotional support, and who can act as mother figures for you. There is no shame in this—we all need it, and it can be mutually rewarding. If you can develop a friendship with your own mother, through processes like those in the last chapter, much emotional nourishment can be gained. Because of her blood tie with your children, she might also like to help with them at times. Remember, however, that grandmothers can resent being taken for granted, just as mothers can.

Leo on the 2nd: It is important that you gain a sense of self-esteem for the contribution you are making to your family. Parenthood is possibly one of the most exacting life paths you could select, one that forces you away from self-centeredness into selflessness, and you deserve recognition for it. Take pleasure and pride in the fact that in your own personal castle, you are the queen or king, and that's a job that would challenge any administrator. Also, to avoid the consequences of lunar stereotyping, you need to develop a sense of your worth and abilities as an individual apart from your parental role.

Investing a bit of time in your creative abilities keeps you from depletion and gives you a SELF to return to, a center.

Virgo on the 3rd: If things aren't going right in some area of your home or your family life, analyze why and then get to work on it with that great Virgo practicality. Virgo is efficient, and there may be more efficient ways to organize your work so you are less tired and have more time for your own needs. For example, some of the housekeeping we have been programmed to believe is essential is time-wasting perfectionism.

Virgo on the 3rd also suggests that if you have the means to have someone else clean your house, even once a month, it would relieve you. It costs less than the hour at the shrink you'd need if you worked yourself into a really bad case of burnout! Call it preventive psychiatry, and file it under medical expenses. The 3rd house is neighbors, and you might find a young person among your neighbors who'd like to earn some money and would clean for you for a reasonable price.

Libra on the 4th: This placement suggests the need to balance the scales in your marital relationship. We are programmed to think men can't learn to do household tasks or care for children. Sharing responsibility for the home more equally requires communication and consistent self-assertion, but eventually your efforts will take hold. Children can also share in the work and are better prepared for living on their own if allowed to learn basic household skills. Libra on the 4th also shows the need for a balance between working at home and having some contact with the outside world that would replenish you.

Scorpio on the 5th: There is an absolute need for you to have time alone to relax and pursue your own interests, even if only half an hour a day. If you establish a firm rule about your quiet time, your children will accept it as unquestioningly as they do any other firm rule. If you are ambivalent and guilty about it, however, the children will sense it and will manipulate your guilt. You make the rules, and unless you establish your right to some time of your own, your inner resentment will pollute the atmosphere of your home. If you do take time from your children when you need it, you will come back refreshed and be able to give without such resentment.

Sagittarius on the 6th: Apply some new ideas to your work with your family, by reading some of the vast array of books on family life and child care. Be cautious, however, about accepting "expert" advice full of "shoulds" that only burden you with more guilt. Many good books now are written by your peers in a down-to-earth and even humorous manner.

Capricorn on the 7th: We've already considered the helpfulness of developing relationships with older women and of sharing more equal responsibility with your partner. Women are programmed to treat men in two different ways. We treat them either as absolute authorities or as little boys, when really they are only fellow human beings struggling toward wholeness just as we are. The chapter on men will doubtlessly challenge some of your ideas. Working toward a more equal relationship is difficult, yet must be undertaken if you are to survive the kinds of strains we all face as lunar types in a solar world. If there is no partner, work seriously at developing support systems.

Aquarius on the 8th: Take a break, as often as you must, to regenerate yourself. No matter what you've been programmed to believe, the kids are not going to die from it. In fact, they might develop more independence through some benign separations. Separations don't always have to be traumatic. They are only that if you've neglected yourself so long that you get sick, or if you've become so resentful that you cut off coldly and abruptly in an Aquarian way. Absence makes the heart grow fonder, and if you can get away regularly for a few hours or even for a weekend by yourself, the relationship with your family will be better for it.

Pisces on the 9th: Taking a course at a local college can be a wonderful escape, and it can also give you new inspiration, so you don't feel like you're in jail. Spending time reading books on spirituality or studying meditation can broaden your perspective on what your life is really about. There is also a spiritual component to parenthood. Spiritual pursuits cannot only help you appreciate what your work does for yourself and your family but can also help you impart more spirituality. In the difficult times they face in our rapidly-changing world, these spiritual teachings will be extremely helpful.

Aries on the 10th: Developing self-assertiveness and being more open with anger can relieve the fatigue and depression that usually accompany burnout. Aries is leadership, and your children will respect you more if you provide clear leadership and rules to live by, rather than playing the martyr. Overly permissive child-rearing creates problems for both the parent and the child. Children need firmness and rules to live by in order to feel secure. This is different from being a harsh disciplinarian, but without limits and direction, they become anxious and constantly test you. Someday, the big cold world is going to say "no" to them. Discipline at home can help them develop the discipline they need for later life.

Taurus on the 11th: There are support groups and self-help organizations to meet practically any situation, from new parents groups to Tough Love groups for families of troubled teens. If you join or form one, and invest your efforts in it, it will pay off handsomely by grounding and nurturing you. If money is a problem, one answer might be bartering with friends for the skills you have. Baby-sitting exchanges in neighborhood pools are one method many young parents have found useful.

Gemini on the 12th: Learning to tap more consciously into your intuition can provide personalized answers to family problems that no book or expert can give. Daily meditation, even if you have to get up half an hour earlier, can help you reach deep wellsprings of energy. Getting in touch with your real emotions can help you deal with your family in a more balanced way. You can avoid losing your center and developing the distorted relationship patterns, fatigue, or depression that repression can produce.

CHAPTER 10

THE MOON AND THE MENSTRUAL CYCLE

Why devote a whole chapter of an astrology book to menstruation? Yes, it's ruled by the Moon, but it's an embarrassing, messy, and sometimes painful part of women's lives. We'd just as soon no one knew when it happens, and it's certainly not a subject for mixed company. When a Japanese television crew interviewed me about *Moon Signs*, I was told I must not mention the word. (Male readers probably closed this book with a bang the minute the *M* word hit their eyes!) If you don't want to deal with the topic, you're certainly welcome to skip this chapter. If you suffer from PMS, food addictions, or other lunar dysfunctions, however, you might just find some answers here. The menstrual cycle is important in integrating the lunar hemisphere. Women's monthly periods are one way the body balances, heals, and cleanses itself. When we ignore and override the special needs we have at that time of the month, our physical and mental well-being suffers.

As women entered the work force, economic necessity forced them to downplay their menstrual care. In order to survive, working women try to suppress their lunar nature and function like machines at that time of the month. You may not be promoted if you are too obvious about dysmenorrhea. Still, we can't totally ignore these functions—cramps account for the greatest number of lost work hours—140 million annually in the U.S. Not every woman who calls in sick with cramps is actually ill. Many are exercising that privilege to get out from under the pressures of the solar world.

Menstruation, Myths, and the Moon

Apparently, human reproduction follows a lunar, rather than a solar, clock. One large research study showed that more women began menstruating at the full and new Moon than at any other time. Since the average pregnancy is nine lunar months, there are also more births at the full and new Moon. The average length of menstrual cycles is the same as the lunar month—29 days.

In many languages, the words for Moon, month, and menstruation have similar roots. For instance, *mens* is the Latin word for Moon, and thus its English derivative, *menstruation*, literally means change of Moon. Native Americans say that a menstruating woman is "on her Moon." The words we choose to refer to the period tell a great deal about our attitudes. Whether it's a "friend" or a "curse," "falling off the roof," or "that time of the month"—all have different connotations. Contrast that with the Chinese, who call it the heavenly waters.

All over the ancient world, myths and practices connecting the Moon and menstruation were strikingly similar. In many cultures, the new Moon was connected with menstruation, and the full Moon was worshiped as a fertility symbol. The word estrogen is related to *oestrus*, the period of heat for animals. A high estrogen level, such as women experience at ovulation, can increase sexual desire. Thus, ancient fertility rites at the full Moon may have had a biological basis.

Louise Lacey, author of *Lunaception*, read scientific research and concluded that old beliefs about the Moon were not symbolic, but factual. Her theory is that originally all women were fertile at the full Moon. They menstruated at the dark of the Moon, secluded in menstrual huts. Thus, women's relationship with the Moon's cycle was direct and basic to our feminine nature. The power of many women going through these changes in unison would have been magical, part of the appeal of the Moon goddess cult.

Of course, women lived in close proximity in tribal life. Even today, a Native American healer named Oh Shinnah says that in her tribe all the women menstruate at the full Moon. It is considered a sacred and powerful time. The women segregate themselves and meditate so that they are able to give guidance to their people. This isn't just true of women living in tribes, however. Various studies confirm that the biological connections between women are so strong that when they become roommates, coworkers, or friends, their periods often synchronize. Close ties are apparently part of the reason. Women who live in the same dorm or next door who are not emotionally close do not synchronize.

Why are women's cycles no longer so tied to the Moon's phases? The pineal gland apparently times ovulation and is light-sensitive. When the Moon was the main nighttime illumination, the light of the full Moon triggered ovulation in masses of women. Lacey feels artificial lighting has thrown it off. During the outer planet transits, electric lighting became nearly universal, so ovulation is more individual. Located in the brain, the pineal gland is also considered the seat of the third eye. Thus, artificial light may produce subtle disruptions in other lunar matters as well.

PMS—Temporary Insanity or the Real You?

If we women have emotional outbursts any time of the month, the scornful rejoinder is, "Are you having your period or something?" The message is that it's not okay to be either a woman or an emotional being, that both should be squelched. We are conditioned to regard PMS as a form of temporary insanity—proof of the irrationality and weakness of the female. The psychiatric establishment apparently agrees. In 1993, they proposed to classify PMS a mental disorder. With this kind of feedback, we learn not to take ourselves seriously. If we are blue or irritable premenstrually we dismiss it as, "Oh, I must be getting my period," and disregard what we are feeling as "crazy."

Our premenstrual feelings are our REAL feelings and we dare not ignore them. We are more tapped into the lunar hemisphere then, and any imbalance becomes critical. We are also more connected with our real needs and reactions to our situation. Perhaps the emotions are exaggerated because we've suppressed them all month—or perhaps they aren't exaggerated at all. Nonetheless, we stew about basic issues—the things that really bother us. If we work on these issues, rather than dismiss them, we can ultimately become better balanced.

The now-familiar Cancer rising wheel gives many insights into the menstrual cycle. It is printed again as figure 3 (page 186), but this time the inner wheel shows how the house/sign combinations correspond to PMS. You will find all the typical symptoms—from increased appetite and hypersensitivity, to irritability. Later, we will revisit the wheel for some clues about healing ourselves of premenstrual upheavals.

Cancer on the 1st house of the wheel shows how much more out in the open our feelings are at that time of the month. Nonetheless, this is one reason our periods should be seen as friends. If we pay attention to the emotional states that come up each time, we can address and heal their causes. A

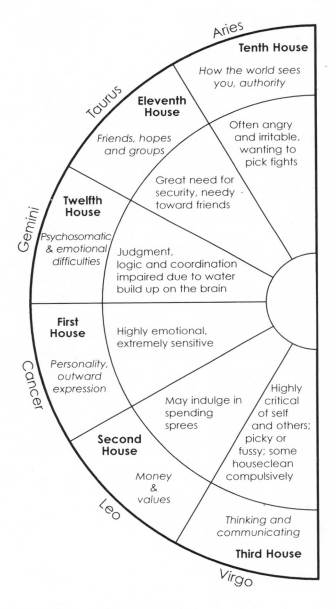

Figure 3. Another version of the Cancer rising wheel.

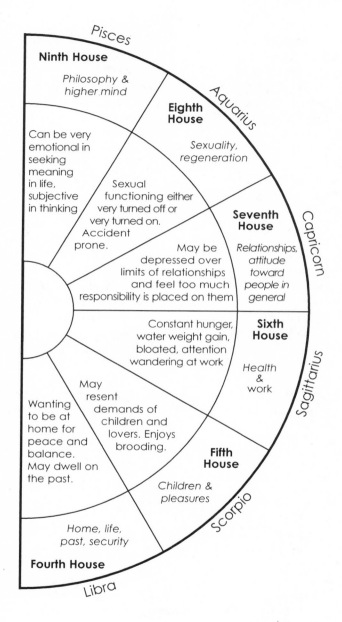

Ninth House

Philosophy & higher mind

Can be very emotional in seeking meaning in life, subjective in thinking

Eighth House

Sexuality, regeneration

Sexual functioning either very turned off or very turned on. Accident prone.

Seventh House

May be depressed over limits of relationships and feel too much responsibility is placed on them

Relationships, attitude toward people in general

Sixth House

Constant hunger, water weight gain, bloated, attention wandering at work

Health & work

Fifth House

May resent demands of children and lovers. Enjoys brooding.

Children & pleasures

Wanting to be at home for peace and balance. May dwell on the past.

Home, life, past, security

Fourth House

Pisces

Aquarius

Capricorn

Sagittarius

Scorpio

Libra

special journal where you record recurring feelings and issues would help identify them. Making changes in these areas involves doing our lunar hemisphere housecleaning all month long. That way things don't pile up to such an extent that our balance can be toppled by the added stress of this phase.

These periodic upheavals are also a natural mechanism for regulating emotions. If we cry or explode, we discharge backlogs that could cause damage if not released. We must give ourselves permission to feel and express those feelings rather than suppress them. Of course, some women rather childishly use their periods as an excuse to have tantrums and to avoid responsibility. I am not recommending that. Learn healthy and constructive ways of expressing feelings or in the long run, you and those you care for will suffer.

One feeling women go through premenstrually that is routinely dismissed as "crazy" is anger. If we express any, we get hostile feedback. The ultimate male putdown of a woman is that she is "on the rag," a remark that is only directed toward us when we are angry or assertive. We are expected to be nurturing, not aggressive—Moon, not Mars. If you are irritable premenstrually, what are you irritable about? Sure, the dirty socks on the bedroom floor, the upturned toilet seat, the trail of snack plates are the focus of the anger.

However, you may really be angry about what those things represent—your role in the family, on the job, or among your friends. Mars is anger, and Cancer rising puts Mars-ruled Aries on the 10th house. The 10th describes authority and our status in the world. Aries there suggests that many premenstrual women are more consciously angry at authority and at their status. We often resent others' demands that we neglect ourselves and take care of them. The demands are constant, but irritation about them may surface more urgently at that time of the month. If so, you may have to change relationships where you don't get much back—where there is dependence rather than interdependence.

Many women are not aware of being angry. Since female anger is frowned upon as "crazy," dangerous, or unfeminine, they take the more socially approved approach. They turn the anger inward and become depressed during that part of their cycle. We who take this route wallow in the blues, wondering why we were born or whether life is worth living. When the period is over, we emerge from the storm relieved, but wondering where that came from. We conclude that, yes, we must be crazy after all, and we dread the next one even more.

Anger or depression may not be the main emotion connected with your period. The Moon's sign, house, and aspects in your chart show what those primary feelings are. A woman with Moon in Cancer might have a powerful nesting urge at that time, while a Moon in Sagittarius woman might have a restless yearning to leave the rat race behind and travel. A Moon in Pisces woman might feel spiritually lost—or, if she's handling her lunar hemisphere well, she might feel spiritually illuminated. Based on the birth Moon, your typical reactions will put you in touch with your lunar needs, true feelings, and what it means to you to be a woman.

Some women experience ravenous hunger premenstrually. This is partly due to hormone shifts, but there are also emotional reasons. With Cancer rising, uncomfortable feelings come to the surface. To suppress them, we may eat, drink, or resort to mood changers—a Moon idiom. Our society scorns feelings, and considers food a woman's province, so women are likely to overeat rather than take care of themselves. The crab needs a protective shell. If we don't create a protective environment for ourselves premenstrually, we may create a protective layer of fat. (The relationship between women and food will be considered in the next chapter.)

Cancer rising puts Gemini on the 12th house, showing that writing about your feelings at that time of the month can help identify problem areas. After a few months, certain patterns will emerge. (I used to have feelings of hopelessness premenstrually that I christened my "end of the world" syndrome.) Gemini on the 12th suggests other helpful techniques like meditation or paying special attention to your dreams. Any physical, emotional, or spiritual tools that usually help you should be especially productive now. Respect the "irrational" feelings or "nonsensical" notions that arise. If you examine them, you will find clues to important issues. Once you've confronted the truth, you may find it uncomfortable to keep things the way they are and might have to make some changes. You see where it leads—today a tampon; tomorrow the world.

Menstrual Taboos—Superstition or Wisdom?

Like other myths about the Moon, the ones about menstruation may contain many truths. Similar taboos were found in far-flung areas of the globe. Menstruating women were secluded in special huts, avoided sexual contact, and were prohibited from cooking and touching food or other items. Were these customs superstition and bias against women, or did they—like so many folk traditions—contain ancient wisdom? Over the centuries, there would have been distortions and elaborations. Still, at the core of these practices, women may find connections with their lunar nature. To discover the purposes of the taboos, consider the Cancer rising wheel.

The Seclusion of Menstruating Women: Since the practice of secluding men-struating women was worldwide, there must have been good reasons. The wheel suggests that women may require some seclusion each month to get in touch with instincts and emotions. Cancer needs a protective shell. Aquar-ius on the 8th, the house of regeneration, shows that separation during this phase can be healing. The menstrual hut, like lying-in after childbirth, gave women much-needed quiet. Rest and privacy around the period are impor-tant in maintaining emotional balance. Discomforts like cramps and PMS arise as suppressed feelings affect our bodies and force us to pay attention.

Periodic retreats from the world are also a 12th house pursuit, which suggests spiritual gains. Some psychics say that women are extremely psychic premenstrually and during menstruation. Since the solar plexus tends to be wide open, we are easily thrown off balance by negativity. This vulnerabil-ity may be one reason we seem moody and irrational during our periods. We are psychically perceiving and reacting to others' emotions and unconscious motives. Seclusion may protect the highly-sensitized intuitive woman. It also provides time to meditate, experience the lunar hemisphere, and return to right alignment with it.

The **Yarrow** essences are good for psychic protection—white being for general protection, pink effective against drains by loved ones, and gold being specifically for the solar plexus. Almost all companies who make flower essences recognize the importance of the yarrow family and make remedies of it. Wiccans also put dried yarrow around the home to protect it from nega-tivity. **Pennyroyal** by Pegasus is another strong cleanser. **Sea Urchin** by Pacific Essences strengthens our capacity to protect ourselves in this manner. I often put several of these remedies in a plant mister, along with uplifting ones like **Lotus**, and spray my home and workspace regularly to clear the energies.

Isaac Bonewits presented a less positive view of women's occult powers. A Ph.D. in ritual magic, he sat on the dividing line between science and the occult. He believed menstruating women put out negative energy that inter-fered with ritual magic. While this seems to contradict women psychics' views, perhaps our powers should be directed into tasks other than rituals at that time. If we are out of touch with our lunar hemisphere and don't meet our special needs, the resulting turmoil may affect psychic energies negatively. A retreat can help us relearn to use these energies as they were meant to be.

Fasting and Food Taboos: Other common practices such as fasting or not touching food may have been due to poor hygiene in primitive circum-stances—or perhaps not. The menstrual flow is a way the body sheds toxins, one reason women are healthier than men, and live longer. Biochemists have found that this blood contains poorly metabolized proteins because our liver functions are impaired at that time. Premenopausal women have far more gallstones and liver ailments. Dr. Burton Coombs, a liver specialist, links women's susceptibility to liver problems with the estrogen in our bodies. In the Cancer rising wheel, stress on the liver is shown by Jupiter-ruled Sagittarius on the house of health. Jupiter governs the liver. Estrogen, the main female hormone, is broken down in this organ. Many cultures prescribe fasting or special diets during the period, no doubt to give the liver a rest. Anyone with a personal or family history of liver problems might try it.

Sexual Abstinence: If the menstrual retreat is valid, other universal menstrual taboos may also be wise, such as the prohibition on sex. The 8th house signifies sexuality and regeneration. Detached Aquarius is there on the Cancer rising wheel. Perhaps at this phase of the cycle, detachment from sex promotes both higher consciousness and regeneration. Abstinence may also protect us from infection. The entry to the uterus is more open during the period than at any other time. The blood may act as a culture medium for bacteria or STDs.

Astrologer Bob Mulligan offers a spiritual justification for the sexual prohibition. Like Alice Bailey's followers, he says there is a powerful female deity connected with the Moon. Celibacy is required for invoking her and for spiritual exercises to overcome Moon-related obstacles. Abstinence at menstruation, when the solar plexus is open, may actually serve to increase spiritual power. Whether or not one accepts a female deity, intermittent celibacy is recommended in many spiritual practices.

If women's cycles once correlated with the Moon's phases, then the full and new Moon must have been spiritually powerful. Group meditation and ritual increase psychic energies, so you can imagine the impact of numbers of celibate women, secluded in menstrual huts and involved in spiritual work. How far from that power we came by divorcing ourselves from natural cycles! By paying attention to this rhythm we can regain some of it.

Menstruation and Feminine Identity

The birth Moon shows women's self-image. Menstruation is connected with self-image because the monthly cycle clearly marks the phases of a woman's life from menarche to menopause. During the outer planet transits to Cancer, the average age of the first period fell from 14 to 12 1/2, while menopause has been delayed. In earlier times, our reproductive history must have been closer to progressed Moon aspects to its natal position. Using the day-for-a-year method, the Moon's 28-day cycle becomes a 28-year cycle. The four quarters become seven, fourteen, twenty-one, and twenty-eight years, with a new phase every seven years after that. These phases correspond with changes in lunar areas of life.

The lower age of menarche may not seem important on the face of it. However, a 14-year-old is better equipped than a 12-year-old to deal with the breast development, rise in hormones, and sexual attention puberty brings. Girls are capable of motherhood years before they have the maturity for it. It is no longer unusual for 11- and 12-year-olds to be brought to abortion clinics, and there is an epidemic of teenage pregnancies. Parents who "solve" the problem of a teen's sexuality by putting her on the pill endanger her hormonal balance, which is quite delicate at that age. The extra hormones contribute to adolescent emotional upheaval.

Men have no such clear-cut entry into manhood, but for women the first period or menarche is the rite of passage into womanhood. Until her periods begin, the young girl may not fully identify with adult women. It is the first major lunar threshold and sets the stage for all that follow. Our experiences at that crucial point color our perceptions of womanhood. From the reactions of important adults, we find out whether this part of ourselves is dirty or natural. We learn whether it is a joyful thing to be celebrated or a shameful thing to be hidden. Customs, such as the Jewish slap in the face at the first period, convey messages about what it means to be a woman. Contrast that with the one day or even week-long celebrations of a girl's first period in many native cultures. (Lacking culturally-sanctioned puberty rites, perhaps teen pregnancy is partially intended as a rite of passage—an "in your face" statement that, "now I am a woman.") If you'd like to design a ritual for your daughter or some other young lady, Marcia Starck's *Women's Medicine Ways* is full of cross-cultural examples and hints.[1]

Each period may bring the heterosexually active woman a moment of either relief or regret that she has not conceived. Many of us have primitive fears or longings about our fertility, using it at some level to decide whether we are "real women." Women going through the menopause or a hysterectomy often have strong feelings about this change, including fears that they are losing their femininity. Our female identity and sense of self-worth are bound up in these functions, regardless of our capabilities and achievements. No matter how liberated or educated we are, they remain mysterious

---

[1]Marcia Starck, *Women's Medicine Ways* (Freedom, CA: Crossing Press, 1994).

and powerful. We have strong emotions about the body parts that most clearly define us as women—the breasts and the uterus. These Moon-ruled organs can arouse feelings of inadequacy, fear, or shame. Men also react powerfully to them.

What Does Mom Have to Do with Menstruation?

A major factor in women's identity is our tie to our mothers, and Cancer rising shows a strong maternal influence. The mother makes an especially powerful emotional imprint at the first period. Studies show that her reaction, which is often negative, shapes how we feel about being women. Often she regards it as a threat. Now the daughter is sexual and on some level a rival, while the mother is the older woman in the house. She may be near the other end of the reproductive cycle—menopause. The end of her own periods may represent aging and the threat of losing her femininity. This is especially true if she defined herself in lunar terms—as a mother rather than a total person.

Our mothers greatly influence how we function during our periods and what discomforts we experience, according to Brenda Sobel. She is a Brooklyn therapist who specializes in menstrual distress. She believes cramps are an "organ habit" resulting from fear of menstruation, and maintained by getting sympathy and extra attention for them. If the girl's mother teaches her to fear menstruation, the girl anticipates the menarche with anxiety. The uterus naturally contracts during menstruation to expel fluid. At first, the contractions can be especially strong and somewhat uncomfortable. The girl's fears are fulfilled, and the resulting uterine tension adds to the discomfort. The more uncomfortable we are, the more we tense up. The more we tense up, the more painful it becomes. Sobel uses biofeedback techniques to break the cramping habit.

Your Chart and Your Menstrual Cycle

The story of your own puberty and how your mother handled it is coded into your birth Moon. These stories are more than dim memories. In microcosm, how this first major lunar threshold was handled reveals a great deal. It sets the scene for your adult relationship with your mother, feelings about your feminine body parts, and ways of dealing with your period.

As an example of how revealing these stories can be, one shy 12-year-old with Moon in Aquarius opposite Pluto was going to camp for the first time. Her mother, a secretive and uncommunicative woman, apparently noticed staining in the girl's clothes and thought she might be about to have her first period. She said nothing to the girl about this possibility nor did she teach her anything about menstruation. Instead, she gave sanitary napkins to the scout leader and warned her to observe the girl. The first period did arrive while the girl was at camp. Ashamed and frightened, she hid what was happening and muddled through on her own. When she later discovered that her mother knew it was coming and didn't prepare her, she felt betrayed. The incident solidified an already-developing resentment and alienation from her mother, which lasted until her mother died. Only when we discussed it in therapy years later did she realize how important the event was, and how shame-based her mother's behavior must have been. Her own shame and disgust about her female organs and her menstrual cycle were a direct result of this experience.

Writing your menarche story and comparing it with the condition of your Moon can be revealing. With new consciousness of that critical time, you can work on healing any current difficulties resulting from it. Desert Alchemy's formula **The Miracle at Menarche** helps resolve emotional residues of that stage. **Crab Apple** from Bach eases shame or disgust about bodily functions. FES's **Alpine Lily** helps release shame or negative programming about the female body from the mother. Their **Mariposa Lily**, over time, can heal wounding from a poor bond with the mother.

Your Moon sign and aspects also show your reactions to menstruation and your feelings about this part of being a woman, because of what your mother taught you. Those with Moon in Taurus might see it as natural, and care for themselves properly, knowing how to conserve their energy. A Virgo Moon might hate the mess but use psychosomatic symptoms to get a break from workaholism. A Moon in Scorpio woman might regard it as part of her feminine power—or, less positively, may resent it as a reminder of women's subordinate position. Astrology students may find it interesting to pursue this exploration further.

One correlation I found is that many women with Moon square Mars have severe PMS or cramps and also suffer from headaches. Women with Moon trine Mars, on the other hand, rarely have either cramps or headaches. My sample is small—how often can you bring this topic up in polite conversation? A Moon-Mars square can show tension between the male and female parts of our psyche. It can also suggest difficulty in dealing with anger and dependency, so these conflicts may add to PMS. A Moon-Mars trine (or sextile) shows harmony between these parts of ourself and less ambivalence about going after the things we lack. I have no information on the opposition, so maybe it doesn't result in physical difficulties during menstruation. Perhaps it is acted out in relationships instead, as oppositions so often are.

Hormones—the Lunar Link?

We are always mind, body, and spirit, so emotional upheaval has physical correspondences. Female hormones are responsible for events which make us female: the menstrual cycle, development of breasts, ovulation, and lactation. Hormonal changes at various phases of women's lives—the major lunar thresholds—often bring emotional upheavals in their wake. At puberty, a notoriously stormy time, the levels increase as the body adjusts to menstruation. Hormone shifts contribute to PMS and to post-partum depression. Major hormonal adjustments add to the turmoil women go through at menopause or after a complete hysterectomy. In fact, female hormones seem to be an underlying link between many of the Moon's meanings. Men have only minor amounts of these hormones, another reason the Moon is less influential in their charts.

A primary factor in the emotional roller coaster is estrogen. It builds to a peak at ovulation and premenstrually, then drops rapidly. Remember that women are stronger than men in the lunar hemisphere. If estrogen affects the lunar hemisphere, this is another reason we are easily thrown off balance premenstrually. It also hints that synthetic estrogen can create emotional difficulties.

Water is symbolic of emotions in many occult teachings, and fluids and emotions are strongly connected. Premenstrually, fluids build up throughout the body, increasing pressure on the brain. In *The Lunar Effect*, Lieber associates changes in what he calls the body water with the premenstrual phase:

> Transient fluid buildup and electrolyte imbalance during premenstruum could result in physical and behavioral consequences. . . . Women are more susceptible to physical illness and erratic behavior in the few days before the menses, and hospital admissions, psychiatric illness and violent crimes are more frequent then.[2]

---

[2] Arnold Lieber and Jerome Agel, *The Lunar Effect* (New York: Anchor Press, 1978), p. 54.

Gemini on the 12th house in the Cancer rising chart suggests impairment in judgment, logic, and coordination during this phase—all documented statistically. They are mainly caused by fluid build-up in the brain. Estrogen acts strongly on salt, and salt binds up to 70 times its weight in water. Lieber recommends eliminating salt two weeks before the period. Because male hormones are not so involved with fluid balance, Lieber says there is no male counterpart of premenstrual tension.

Every organ is affected by unnecessary exposure to estrogen—more than 50 metabolic changes have been recorded. Physical complications include liver disease (Sagittarius on the 6th), blood clots, high blood pressure (Aquarius on the 8th), infertility, and cysts on the ovaries and uterus. Serious emotional consequences can arise as well. Depression is a frequent complication, and chemical interactions with psychiatric medications may further compound the damage. In the next chapter, we'll explore ties between estrogen, appetite, and weight.

Estrogen was synthesized in 1938, the last year Pluto was in the sign Cancer. Pluto is connected with the disease cancer. We've known since 1932 that estrogen is linked with cancer, especially in the Moon-ruled breast and uterus, and a conclusive link was shown between estrogen and cancer in 1971. Nonetheless, OB-GYN doctors continue to promote various forms of synthetic estrogen, the birth control pill being only one. New mothers are given estrogen to dry up their milk if they don't want to nurse. Synthetic estrogen is used in Estrogen Replacement Therapy (ERT) to delay menopause.

Diethyl-stilbestrol or D.E.S. is the chemical name of synthetic estrogen. D.E.S. had alarming publicity as a cause of cancer, endometriosis, and other reproductive problems in about 50 million daughters and sons of women who took it during their pregnancies in the late 1940s and early 1950s. The use of D.E.S. was widespread during the conjunction of Pluto and Saturn in Leo in 1946–1948, as doctors hailed it as a panacea for optimal pregnancies. Women who have that conjunction in health-related placements—i.e., in the 1st, 6th, or 12th house or aspecting their Moon or Sun—might want to get pap tests and breast exams regularly.

The four Cancer planets in the 2nd house of the U.S. chart show an economy that profits from exploiting women. Reducing aids, cosmetic surgery, and planned obsolescence in the clothes closet are just the beginning. Synthetic estrogen is a multimillion dollar industry. Hysterectomies are the second most common surgery, and as many as one in three are unnecessary. Hysterectomies bring on sudden, severe hormonal shifts, causing changes in the body and emotions. They should therefore not be casually recommended by doctors or readily accepted by women without second and even third opinions. It is painful to know that women's position in society may subject us to bodily and emotional hazards from the medical establishment, which is predominantly male. (In 1980, 95 percent of OB-GYN doctors were male—hopefully that ratio has changed.)

The Cancer Rising Wheel and PMS

If the ideas in this chapter apply to you personally—for instance if emotions or eating habits make your life unmanageable premenstrually—what can you do to get back on an even keel? Become more aware of your lunar needs and minister to them. The Cancer rising wheel not only shows problems associated with the menstrual cycle, it also contains some solutions.

Cancer on the 1st House: Nurture yourself with a protective shell, so you don't feel tired and drained. As far as feasible, schedule quiet time alone. Things are not going to fall apart if you have an afternoon or two off a month. Allow your feelings to come up rather than suppress them. Nourishing contacts with other women are also a comfort.

Leo on the 2nd House: This is a good time to focus on the self and on developing your own inner resources. If you can afford it, it is not amiss to spend a little money on yourself.

Virgo on the 3rd House: Pay attention to health, proper nutrition, and whatever physical ailments are beginning to show up. Like your emotional reactions, your physical difficulties may come out in an exaggerated form at this phase. Paying attention to them in a constructive—rather than hypochondriacal—way, can prevent serious health problems later. With Virgo on the 3rd, analyze your daily routine for efficiency to have more time for yourself. Many women are struck with an urge to clean house premenstrually. If it's not too exhausting, this might be a tension reliever. Housecleaning can make you feel closer to your roots.

Libra on the 4th House: Harmony and peace are necessary in the home environment. A heart-to-heart chat with your partner might strengthen the ties. You can build into the relationship that it is okay for you to be more dependent during this time. A mature relationship recognizes that each has times of greater and lesser needs. The 4th house is the past, so examine your own part in any past difficulties to get better balanced emotionally. You might also want to beautify your home by splurging on flowers or other decorative items—even if it means a garage sale binge.

Scorpio on the 5th House: You might find it fulfilling to pursue creative efforts on your own. Quiet pleasures like reading mysteries, occult materials, or self-help books can be healing and refreshing. Since children can be irritating now, send them to a baby sitter or relative in order to luxuriate in some solitude. A neighborhood baby-sitting exchange can serve the same purpose if you are fresh out of money or relatives.

Sagittarius on the 6th House: Avoid overindulgence in food, sugar, or alcohol, for they affect women's livers badly at this time. If you have to be on the job, at least avoid the pressure of detailed work, for mistakes are more likely. Instead, get an overview of where your work is going, then fill in details later. If you are restless, do any required running around, rather than chain yourself to the desk.

Capricorn on the 7th House: You may want some reserve and distance from others now. While you are off on your own, take a serious look at how you function in relationships. You contribute as much to the problem as the other person. If you are feeling like a victim, you may be allowing yourself to be victimized. If you don't like what you see, give some thought to how you can change it.

Aquarius on the 8th House: We discussed celibacy during menstruation as potentially regenerative and promoting higher consciousness, but naturally that is an individual decision. Also, Aquarius rules breaks. Taking a break from routine during this phase can be restorative, bringing a fresh new perspective.

Pisces on the 9th House: Meditation during this phase can give a new understanding of your place in the scheme of things and the meaning of your life. Intuitive answers rather than book learning should be stressed, but if you wanted to read, something spiritual might inspire you.

Aries on the 10th House: Earlier we saw that premenstrual irritability relates to the role we are assigned as women. It doesn't help to store anger until you are premenstrual, then blow off steam. If this is a problem (or, if you turn your anger into depression), work on being more assertive and direct.

Taurus on the 11th House: Develop a solid support group of women you can fall back on when stressed out by your period. Such friends might help you sort out feelings, exchange baby-sitting or other services, or even form a meditation or ritual group. Taurus is your wealth, and investing in friendship will pay off when you are more needy.

Gemini on the 12th House: Keeping a special period journal where you record your feelings, dreams, and thoughts can make you more aware of issues you need to work on and ways to keep a better balance. Carrying on a dialogue with troubled parts of yourself (as in Gestalt techniques or NeuroLinguistic Programming) can help integrate split-off parts that have been causing difficulty.

Alternative Means of Dealing with Menstrual Woes

Since estrogen and the lunar hemisphere are so closely connected, the vulnerable may wish to avoid synthetic estrogen, whether in pill form or in the food we consume. Salt increases water retention, so watch salt intake. We are also extremely sensitive to sugar and alcohol premenstrually. Overindulgence in either of them can create an emotional roller coaster. These precautions help with the physical side of PMS, but we must also consider the emotional and spiritual sides through some of the tools already given.

Among the flower remedies, Desert Alchemy offers **Moontime Harmony** as part of its women's kit, although it may also be ordered separately. Kathleen Otley reported in my now-defunct essence journal, *Shooting Star,* that she used Pegasus' **Onion** essence with many coworkers and friends who had PMS. When the causes were emotional, or due to dysfunctional family backgrounds, as opposed to structural problems, the results were excellent. FES's **Fuchsia,** for repressed feelings that are acted out hysterically or psychosomatically, is another remedy to consider.

Naturally, structural problems—i.e., malfunctions or misalignments of the uterus and vagina—cannot be cured by flower remedies. If lower back problems contribute to pelvic congestion and pain, the combination of chiropractic and massage can create an easier menstrual flow. A local herbalist, Zylpha Elliott suggested some gentle, nontoxic herbs that support circulation of the blood through the internal organs and especially the uterus. Many of them also serve to cleanse the blood and liver. They include angelica, rosemary, ginger, licorice, flat-leaf cedar, and burdock root. Those that also help with cramps are lavender, mugwort, and cramp bark (viburnum). The Chinese herb dong quai is well known in the western world for its effects on various menstrual problems, but should be used with caution if you are debilitated. Consult your local herbalist for personalized suggestions.

Acupuncturist Linda Joy Stone explains that in Chinese medicine, menstrual blood is considered a function of *jing,* translated as vital essence. This is one of the finest substances in the body, produced by the kidneys.

(In men, it is the ejaculate.) When you are a girl, your blood and chi—the yin and yang energy—are not strong enough to handle the menstrual blood flow, but by age 14, you are strong enough. Women have seven year cycles—like the phases of the progressed Moon—while men have eight year cycles. This culminates in the menarche around age 14 (2 x 7) and the menopause around age 49 (7 x 7).

In a healthy woman, there is a superabundance of blood which brims over about every 28 days unless she conceives. Also at the menses, there is a release of heat and toxins, a natural purging. In the Chinese medicine system, the spleen, kidneys, and heart are responsible for producing blood. The spleen also rules thinking and is affected by worry. The kidneys rule willpower and are affected by fear. The heart rules the mind/spirit and is affected by joy and sorrow. Thus, negative emotions like worry and fear indirectly have their effect on the menstrual cycle. The acupuncture system called Five Element Theory focuses more specifically on balancing the emotions as well as the body.

The liver chi is responsible for moving the blood and energy through the body. (As we saw earlier, Western medicine also recognizes that estrogen has a strong affinity for the liver.) The liver rules the psychospiritual system and is affected by anger. Any stagnation or constraint of the liver chi, often due to stress or emotional problems, can weaken other systems, creating cramping, anxiety, headaches, or depression. The liver is seen as responsible for the regularity, volume, and flow of the menses and for the blood's nourishment of the tendons and body tissues. Anything that disrupts liver function is likely to disrupt menstruation. Thus, acupuncture not only works to reduce pain but also to restore liver function.

Menstruation—Curse or Friend?

Did you have any idea the menstrual cycle was so interesting or so crucial to women's well being? Many hints on how to be more comfortable during your period can be drawn from this material. If we women work with our lunar hemisphere consistently and meet our lunar needs, we won't be so precariously balanced that this phase throws us into a tailspin. The menstrual cycle is not just something to ignore or put up with. It is a key to balancing body, mind, and spirit. If we pay attention to our cycle and care for ourselves properly, we can achieve a much better and more even emotional tone. We can also reclaim and exercise our spiritual power as women. No doubt this is why Chinese medicine calls it the heavenly waters.

CHAPTER 11

THE MUNCHIES AND THE MOON

Weight is an almost universal female concern, and even women who are not particularly overweight struggle with food daily. If you listen to conversations around you, you hear many women talking about how they "pigged out" the night before so they aren't eating today. They agonize and suffer from low self-esteem for being "bad" when they indulge in sweets, or even in salad dressing that isn't low-calorie. Or, they are starting their diet tomorrow because they blew it today. Many count the calories in every bite, guilt robbing them of any real pleasure in food. While learning why overeating is mainly a female problem, we will go around in our usual lunar orbits, touching on the mother-daughter bond, estrogen, emotions, and the pressure on women to be primary nurturers.

The Moon rules food and security, and because of losses and disruptions during the Cancer transits, many people have become extremely insecure and oral. We have something in our mouths all the time—food, cigarettes, coffee, soda, or alcohol—anything to fill us up when we feel empty and deprived. In seeking insight into the problem, we will trace the relationships between food and other lunar concerns, discovering how deeply tied they are. We will discover what our Moon signs can teach us about our eating habits. We will see how those transits have changed our diets and the consequences of the changes. Finally, we will explore how society programs us to despise ourselves, and others, who fall short of an ideal body. It's only fair to warn you that the intent of this often unsettling material is to deprogram you so you can regain your self-respect where food and weight are concerned.

Food and Mood

We are profoundly emotional about food, a substance that is our first on-going experience of the outer world. Through being fed as infants, we experience relief of tension. We form a primary attachment to the one who feeds us—she becomes our mother. Eating is our first conscious act, our first dim awareness that we can take action to get our needs met. By eating, we take in the outside world and decide whether we can trust other people. Any breach of trust can lead to problems with food and digestion—many abuse victims develop eating disorders.

The stomach, which is ruled by the sign Cancer, is the seat of our earliest, most primitive emotions and needs. The public makes an intuitive connection between the stomach and emotions. We talk of gut-level feelings, and when something is disgusting, we say we can't stomach it. People who are upset or seriously depressed may not be able to eat. (Often this appetite loss goes along with the loss of someone or something they've been dependent on.) Under emotional stress or lunar deprivation, depending on our basic nature, we may either overeat or lose our appetites. When people sense you're upset and don't know what to do, they try to feed you. "Eat something. It'll make you feel better."

The difficulty, the addictive hook, is that we often DO feel better when we eat. The reason is a chemical in the brain called *serotonin* that profoundly affects behavior, emotions, and consciousness. A high-carbohydrate and low-protein meal sharply increases the serotonin level, so we feel drowsy after a starchy meal or a rich dessert. This stupor-inducing property may be one reason people become addicted to sugars and starches. When we don't have enough serotonin, we can become depressed or aggressive, lose sleep, and suffer from poor judgment. Doesn't that sound like you a couple of weeks into your last serious diet? Typical diet foods are low in serotonin.

Personality disturbances can result from prolonged dieting. In one study, normal, healthy women who dieted for three months became hostile, anxious, and suffered memory problems. In another, normal, healthy men dieted for six months. They changed from fun-loving, idealistic people to cynical neurotics. Both studies involved non-neurotic people who didn't have the personality problems associated with food addictions, but they became disturbed due to nutritional deficits.[1] Considering the vast number of

---

[1] All the foregoing material is from two sources: Gene Bylinsky's *Mood Control* (New York: Scribners, 1978), the chapter "Food and Mood," and, Richard Wurtman, M.D., "Brain Muffins," *Psychology Today*, October 1978, p. 140.

women who perpetually diet, undernourishment could have much to do with women's high rates of depression and emotional problems discussed in chapter 4.

If we lacked proof that dieting produces serotonin deficiency, we only have to look at the growing use of Prozac. It is regarded by all too many doctors (and the public) as the miracle drug of the 90s. It is often prescribed for eating disorders. Prozac works by indirectly increasing the serotonin levels in the brain. We are under immense pressure to cut out carbohydrates and be svelte—then when rigorous dieting makes us depressed, they put us on Prozac. The solar world has a solution for everything—and every solution extracts a price. The cost of Prozac? At this writing, it's about $70 to $100 a month. However, I'm really not talking about the out-of-pocket cost so much as the flattening of emotions that can cause you to deny, and thus delay, working on lunar issues.

The ideal is a balanced diet (including sufficient grain to keep serotonin at an optimal level)—not so much that you nod out or become addicted, nor so little that you wind up irritable and depressed. If you realistically need to reduce, your reducing plan should be a balanced one that includes some grain. (Vitamin B supplements are also important, because a low-grain diet can deplete this ingredient that is so vital for the nervous system.)

Like starch, sugar powerfully influences the emotions and can become addictive. It has a multitude of negative effects on the body and mind, including addiction and serious depression. Sugar seems very much a Moon-related substance. It is the most yin (feminine) matter we generally consume, and is grown around the Tropic of Cancer. It is broken down in the pancreas, another Moon-ruled organ. The effects of sugar on the lunar hemisphere have not been documented. However, sugar addiction may be an attempt to deaden upsets to that side of our nature. If there were any question that sugar is lunar, those Cancer transits produced a ten-fold increase in the amount used in the United States. Having created a sweet tooth, the food industry then made another fortune on reducing aids and "sugar free" products.

To digest sugar or starch, the pancreas secretes insulin, so people who habitually consume too much sugar, starch, or alcohol produce excess insulin. Since sugar gives us a quick energy "high," we use it to boost low energy levels caused by poor nutrition, excess caffeine, overwork and improper rest. The pancreas secretes insulin, dropping the blood sugar level even lower, and we feel even more exhausted and blue. More sugar may be taken to boost us up again, and the circle goes around and around. If we habitually abuse sugar, we neglect important nutrients, gain weight, and ultimately develop an addiction.

Chronically producing too much insulin can lead to hypoglycemia, a prediabetic condition related to a number of emotional disturbances. Dr. Philpott of Oklahoma City tested schizophrenics and found many of them hypoglycemic. When they were treated by diet, their mental condition improved greatly. A study of murderers showed that 90 percent suffered from low blood sugar or vitamin deficiency. A probation officer tested offenders and found that 82 percent suffered from hypoglycemia. A change to a highly nutritious diet improved their attitude and appearance greatly.[2]

Sugar and starches are lunar in nature and have a powerful effect on our lunar hemisphere and emotions when abused. These two Moon meanings—food and mood—are related, and there is a physiological aspect of food addiction; namely our sensitivity to starch and sugar. (The emotional component of food addictions will be dealt with in the next chapter.)

Family, Food Habits, and Weight

The family we grew up in shaped our food preferences and eating habits. Most habits and feelings about food are unconscious—Moon areas often are. Any suggested change in diet meets great resistance because of the emotional associations and the sense of security connected with food. Some family therapists even observe family meals to diagnose family problems. What goes on at supper is a microcosm of the relationships and conflicts within the family. At this near-ritual meal, children learn age and sex roles, what is expected of family members, what emotional expressions are permitted, and other values. Since such highly-charged interaction occurs at the main meal of the day, it is not surprising to find food and feelings so intertwined.

Holiday meals are a special case. The sign Cancer is greatly concerned with tradition, and the traditional holidays are times when we generally stuff ourselves. We either get together with family—or else feel pain that there is no family to visit. Unpleasant memories and unresolved conflicts about family members and the past are evoked. The mountains of food so close at hand push feelings down. Holiday blues are commonplace, with sharp increases in the number of suicides, homicides, and thinly disguised suicidal

---

[2]These studies reported in Martin Zucker's "Diabetes and Allergy: An Investigation Worth Pursuing," *Let's Live*, April 1979, p. 65 (zucker is the German word for sugar!); and in Bylinsky, *Mood Control*, pp. 52–53.

impulses in the form of traffic accidents. These reactions testify to our sorrow and rage over lunar losses.

The Moon rules instinct, and eating would be healthier if governed by instinct rather than poor family training. Most animals, if their owners haven't hopelessly corrupted their diets, know what is good for them to eat and when they've had enough. A sick animal will not eat, but sick people are cajoled into eating when fasting might be better. Children are also born with sound food instincts. In one study, toddlers were given free choice of a range of foods. Their diet may not have been balanced on any one day, but over time it balanced out perfectly. Families teach children to override their instincts by forcing them to eat more than they want, to eat on schedule rather than when hungry, and to eat heavily sweetened processed foods.

Research shows a definite connection between weight and family influence. A team at the University of Michigan took histories of nearly 3,000 children. The more overweight the parents were, the more likely the children would be overweight and the more overweight they were. Nearly 40 percent of children from obese families were obese, where only 15 percent would be by chance. The daughters were the most affected, which makes sense astrologically due to the Moon and the mother-daughter bond. By age 17, if both parents were overweight, the daughters were more than seven times fatter than daughters of lean parents.[3] Severe obesity is apparently a recessive gene. That is, it has to exist on both sides of the family for it to be transmitted, and then you have just a one in four chance of inheriting it.[4]

If you have a weight problem, you may be saying, "Then it's just my bad genes!" While not denying that heredity may play a role, the team also studied adopted children and found that those adopted by obese parents had the same tendency to obesity as those born into the family. Their pets even had a high rate of obesity. The Moon shows early learned habits. What these studies suggest is that overeating is a habit, a mechanism learned through exposure to parents who overate. The Moon rules emotions, and much serious overeating is a learned familial defense against unwelcome emotions.

[3]Stanley M. Garn, Patricia Cole, and Stephen M. Bailey, "The Effect of Parental Fatness Levels on the Fatness of Biological and Adoptive Children," *Ecology of Food and Nutrition*, 1977, pp. 91–93.
[4]R. Arlene Price, Roberta Ness, and Peter Laskarewski, "Common Major Gene Inheritance of Extreme Overweight," *Human Biology*, December 1990, v62:6, pp. 747–766.

What Your Moon Sign Shows About You and Food

Your Moon sign and aspects show a great deal about how you were fed and therefore how you tend to feed yourself and others. Let's take a quick look around the zodiac for some hints. Remember that strong aspects to your Moon—the list you made in chapter 4—modify your experience. In addition, Cancer placements can override your Moon sign when it comes to food, as can a highly-emphasized Moon. Strongly lunar types have a powerful connection to food and tend to use it to cope with deprivation or stress in the lunar areas of life. Consider how the chart reflects your mother's ways of dealing with food and how you in turn learned to deal with it. (If it wasn't Mom who fed you, for some reason, but maybe Grandma, these readings could refer to the real cook.)

Moon in Aries children may have had mothers who were impatient about meals and nurturing, wanting to get it over with as soon as possible. The grown Moon in Aries may eat too fast to enjoy the food, or to let satiation signals kick in, so they may eat too much. *Moon in Taurus children*, except those with difficult aspects to their Moon, may have had a real apple pie type of Mom who made food a joy. Many of them love their food and have cushiony bodies.

The Moms—or older sisters—of *Gemini Moons* were better at reading stories or playing games than dealing with food. These people may grow up considering mealtimes no more than a reason for good conversation. Food fads and gadgets interest them, but day-to-day cooking does not. Most *Cancer Moons and other lunar types* were deeply involved with food and Mom growing up, and remain so in adulthood. However, there is a tendency toward either extreme in weight.

Many *Leo Moons* had mothers who did great dinner parties with showy dishes, but considered ordinary meals a bore. If they could afford a cook, fine. If not, it was catch as catch can while Mom did her own inimitable thing. (Remember that a Moon-Pluto conjunction in Leo is more like Moon in Scorpio.) With *Moon in Virgo*, Mom worried about nutrition and health, maybe because many of these children had food sensitivities. She would be critical of overeating, which is neither frugal nor healthy.

Those with *Moon in Libra* had mothers who indulged a bit of a sweet tooth, but cared too much about appearances to let weight become a problem. Remember that Libra's symbol is the scales. This Moon sign may confer with the scale each morning, perhaps alternating between binging and fasting to keep the weight down. On the one hand, a *Moon in Scorpio* child's mother may have resented cooking. On the other hand, she may have half feared the child or the family wouldn't survive without her efforts. Thus, her messages about food could have been very crazy making, and a power struggle over food may have ensued.

Sagittarius Moons may have had Moms who overindulged out of sheer *joie de vivre*, thinking they were blessedly exempt from the risks and the rules. As adults, Sag Moons also ignore health risks related to food and weight. Hardship or sparse nurturing may have been the lot of *Capricorn Moons*, and many of them are thin by nature or to maximize their chances for success. They tend not to be able to eat when they are depressed or anxious, which happens frequently.

Aquarian Moons may have had erratic mealtimes growing up, with a Mom who tended toward the quick and easy approach to food. As adults, they probably had the first microwave in their peer group, and may be the queens and kings of the takeout meal. Some people with the *Moon in Pisces* come from dysfunctional family backgrounds, and food may or may not have been Mom's drug of choice. In adulthood, it may be a haven when confusing or unmanageable feelings come up.

These are only some possible expressions, and maybe the scene around your dinner table was different from the one pictured here. Maybe the differences were only external—some families use paper plates while others dine on fine china. It's the emotional experience of food that counts. If these readings don't ring a dinner bell, try the ones related to the hard aspects to your Moon, as given in chapter 4. For instance, if you have Moon in Libra, and that scale is tipping way, way over, maybe you have a Moon-Neptune conjunction in that sign—that is, if you were born between 1942 and 1957. Or, if you are a Leo Moon born between 1938 and 1958, consider that Pluto was in that sign. If your Mom wasn't the hostess with the mostest, but instead was an isolate, you probably have a Moon-Pluto conjunction.

What if your Moon sign or aspects show a propensity to eat not wisely but too well? Your food upbringing does not doom you to a weight problem, any more than your genetic makeup does. It merely means you must take a conscious approach to food and be sure not to use it as an emotional outlet. There are many tools in this book to help soothe the lunar beast so that you don't have to deaden it with food. Additionally, the Moon sign calendar can be a friend. The transiting Moon sets off fluctuations in feeding cycles for everything from the most primitive organisms to human beings. By following the transiting Moon around your chart regularly, you can discover when you are most vulnerable to binges. At those points of the Moon's cycle, call more heavily on your support systems and on the tools learned here. In addition, the more you work to balance your lunar side over the course of time, the fewer food catastrophes you should have. (The next chapter is intended for those with serious eating disorders.)

Women and Weight

Fat is a social disease, and fat is a feminist issue. Fat is *not* about lack of self-control or will-power. Fat is about protection, nurturance, sex, strength, boundaries, mothering, substance, assertion, and rage. It is a response to the inequality of the sexes.[5]

In the U.S. today, over half the women are estimated to be overweight. Women buy 90 percent of the billions of dollars worth of reducing products and programs sold each year. All those health spa memberships, those "light" foods, those low-fat recipes, those diet programs, and those diets of the month in women's magazines are not necessarily being snatched up by obese people, but more often than not by "normal" women. The price women pay to be thin is as painful as the price of being overweight in a society that bases our acceptability on our appearance. Struggling with food is part of life for women in this weight-obsessed world of ours.

We may wonder why a nation like the United States, with four planets in Cancer, makes such a fetish of thinness. In many underdeveloped countries, largeness is a sign that you are a person of substance, while thin people are considered poor and unhealthy. It was not until the 1920s—as Pluto crossed over the U.S.'s four planets in Cancer—that thinness became the rage. Now, fashion designs clothes that will only look good on the emaciated and makes stars of models who are anorexic. These supermodels represent a flat-chested, hipless ideal that is seldom seen in nature after puberty. In short, we are admonished to remain little girls rather than to become women. Even if our weight is in proportion to the bone structure of the body, we are made to feel miserably fat.

It gets even stranger, for men additionally want us to have large breasts. In terms of nature's design of the female body, this does not compute. In nature, you either get the rounded, well-padded frame with large breasts, a la Rubens, or you get the ballerina type, whose ribs you can count, and who is flat as a board, but you don't get both ribs *and* big boobs. The impossibility of the demand does not sink in, only the fact that you, personally, do not

---

[5]Susie Orbach, *Fat is a Feminist Issue* (New York: Berkeley Books, 1978), p. 6.

meet the ideal. The solar world has the technology to override and conquer nature. Now many women starve themselves into a ballerina frame, with maybe a little liposuction to treat the fat deposits that don't respond, and then get breast implants.

To be fair, men are also under pressure to look good, both to attract women and to succeed, especially in jobs where public contact is important. Rather than being about weight (the Moon), however, men's struggles seem centered on being more Mars—hairier and more muscular. Many are working out, pumping iron and even taking dangerous steroids to increase their muscles. By early adulthood, those who need them will get contact lenses and braces on their teeth, since women don't go out with geeks or dorks. Baldness—a homone-related condition—is definitely out, so they're rubbing in the Minoxidil or undergoing hair transplants to halt their receding hairlines. A friend who is a vocational counselor informs me that he has a difficult time placing short men in jobs, and that many of them wear platform shoes to look taller. (Short women are merely seen as petite, a positive—or at least cute—attribute.) Still, unlike women, men may be seen as even more attractive as they age, and overweight men are not necessarily out of the running in the matrimonial sweepstakes.

Concerns about appearance aren't so much a Moon and Cancer issue as they are a Venus and Libra issue. I feel that the increased obsession with appearance and rejection of the lunar body type over the last several decades resulted from transits to Libra, which form squares to the sign Cancer. Neptune in Libra, from 1942–1957, started the process, as the movies (Neptune) held up ideals of glamor and romanticized relationships. The generation born then has struggled mightly to meet those ideals, with only intermittent success and many painful failures. They programmed their children, born with Uranus (1968–1975) and Pluto (1971–1984) in Libra, to demand physical perfection of themselves and their potential mates. Uranus, however, is the rebel, and many with that placement rebelled by developing their own unique style—the punkers with half a head shaved and the other half dyed purple come to mind.

Of all of them, the Pluto in Libra people are likely to be the most obsessed and the most likely to take drastic steps to be accepted—a damn-the-consequences, do-or-die transformation of the body. In some regards, anorexia is a morbid escalation of our fetish for thinness. As they come into adolescence and young adulthood, it is the Pluto in Libra generation which has had the most anorexia among the girls, and the most steriod addiction among the boys. This generation demands cosmetic surgery at an early age and regards Reeboks as an entitlement.

How are you doing with all this? Pretty scary stuff, isn't it? My intention in writing this isn't to demoralize you, but instead to shock you into sanity. The solar world is insane in the way it handles food and appearance—you'll doubtlessly come to agree as you read on. Only by looking squarely at the lies versus the truths, the programming versus the realities, can we all go sane again. Hang in there through the end of the chapter. If you do, I promise that you'll never look at your weight in quite the same way again and you'll have more compassion for yourself and for people who are in worse shape—figuratively as well as literally—than you are.

How Women's Roles Increase their Food Problems

Pressures about appearance aside, women's roles set them up for trouble with food. Women are still largely responsible for cooking. Preparing coffee for the men is part of many women's jobs—an expectation not limited to waitresses and secretaries. While men are more free to cook than they were earlier, their contribution to family meals is seldom close to half. Mothers are expected to put feeding and caring for themselves last, only after doing these things for their husband and children. Their needs are ignored, while they are expected to devote enormous energy to the needs of others. If they feel empty, they may turn to food to fill themselves. Food is how many of our mothers showed love, so women eat when they feel unloved. The more our lunar supports are eroded, given the social conditions we have been discussing, the more other lunar needs are denied. The more we ignore the lunar hemisphere to succeed in the solar world, the more food looms as a fast, available, comforting, and legal solution.

Once children arrive, being a mother can become a woman's main identity, and food can be considered an expression of motherhood. Because mothers show love through feeding the young, overeating can get hooked into the mother-daughter relationship. Susie Orbach, who wrote *Fat is a Feminist Issue*, feels a mother's personal powerlessness may make her reluctant to give up her power over her daughter. She may unconsciously consider her daughter as an extension of herself. Control over the daughter's weight can become a battleground for control of the daughter.[6]

As a girl grows and learns to feed herself, she feels more independent, yet Orbach says that by rejecting the dependency she is also rejecting the

---

[6]Susie Orbach, *Fat is a Feminist Issue*, pp. 3ff.

mother and her role. By feeding herself too much, the girl is rejecting her mother's role, but also showing her mother up for not nurturing her enough. At the same time, she may be trying to retain some sense of identity with her mother. Overweight can be a rebellion against mother's pressures on us to be desirably thin. So can anorexia (excessive thinness), which is the other side of the coin. Anorexia also can be a rebellion against Moon-ruled matters—such as the development of breasts and menses—and against fitting into lunar roles, like becoming a mother, herself, someday.

Orbach feels that the overweight woman is also rebelling against a society that sees her only as a sex object, a piece of meat. In the Cancer rising wheel, the rebellious sign Aquarius is on the house of sexuality. Fat is a way of removing herself from the meat rack and avoiding her sexuality, yet she does this at the price of becoming the earth-mother stereotype. Because of her round contours, people associate her with mother, and with the feminine skills of caretaking and food preparation. The "mother to the world" stance is a draining one—they feed everyone and wind up very hungry. Yet women are expected to be either the mother (Moon) or the pretty plaything (Venus). The Moon rules instincts, and women are taught to ignore both instincts and physical responses to food and hunger in favor of what Mom, or the experts, tell us. We learn to override our body's signals and to eat when we're not hungry, or to override the hunger in order to be thin.

Many studies show that women in the lower economic strata are more likely to be overweight, while men's weights are not so connected to their social class. There are more poor women than men to begin with. Women's wages are generally lower than men's, and in the U.S., over three quarters of those subsisting on welfare are women and children. Poor Latin American and black women in the U.S. have a high proportion of severe obesity, compared with other groups.[7] These economic trends represent both cause and effect, in that today being overweight can disqualify you from many high-paying jobs. In fact, employed women who are 20 percent or more overweight earn about 12 percent less than women of ideal weight, while weight does not affect men's wages significantly.[8]

---

[7]"Prevalence of Overweight for Hispanics—United States, 1982–84," *Journal of the American Medical Association*, February 2, 1990, v263:5, pp. 631–633.
[8]Charles A. Register and Donald R. Williams, "Wage Effects of Obesity Among Young Workers." *Social Science Quarterly*, March 1990, v71:1, pp. 130–142.

The Menses and the Munchies

The lunar hormone estrogen is inextricably tied to women's struggle with weight. The hypothalamus area of the brain not only regulates estrogen but also provides signals for hunger and satiation. Since estrogen and the hypothalamus are connected, any estrogen imbalance may increase the appetite. Table 10 (page 213) shows how estrogen and weight are naturally related in major phases of a woman's life cycle, from the menarche to childbirth through menopause. From 15–30 percent of the normal adult woman's body is made up of fat, while a normal man's body is only 10-15 percent fat. Whether or not we ever become pregnant, this layer of padding stays with us throughout our childbearing years. Many of us spend our lives vainly trying to diet away that natural layer, while the body sends out distress signals of hunger to get the layer back.[9] This factor has a great deal to do with the yoyo weight syndrome.

Women who diet until they are too thin often lose both their periods and fertility, as the estrogen balance is affected. Not coincidentally, infertility has multiplied in the past decade as thinness became a fetish, and as synthetic estrogen has been used so routinely. Excessive or continual dieting may tamper with many of the body's delicate protective mechanisms. Ordinarily, premenopausal women have a natural health advantage over men in that they have higher levels of fat-protein compounds (lipoproteins) that protect against hardening of the arteries.[10] Diets which consistently exclude the building blocks of these compounds may contribute to health difficulties in later life.

The estrogen-based birth control pill affects both our weight and our ability to digest sugar and starch. Of women who use the pill one year or longer, 80 percent experience significant damage to their sugar metabolism and 13 percent will get diabetes. One in three becomes depressed. When antidepressants are added to the pill, the chemical combination can further interfere with sugar metabolism and create a tremendous weight gain.[11]

The synthetic estrogen (that the food industry and medical doctors so cavalierly dump into our systems) only compounds the difficulty in staying on an even keel. Estrogen is routinely used to fatten poultry and cattle for

---

[9]Two Sources: 1) *Maternal Nutrition and the Course of Pregnancy* (Washington, D.C.: National Academy of Sciences, 1970), p. 150; and 2) Dr. Barbara Edelstein, bariatric physician, Mt. Sinai Hospital, Hartford, CT, in private communication.

[10]"Lipoproteins: A Delicate Balance," *Science News*, v. 113, April 22, 1978, pp. 244–245. For anorexia, see Barbara Seaman and Gideon Seaman, M.D., *Women and the Crisis in Sex Hormones* (New York: Rawson Associates, 1977), p. 36.

[11]Seaman, *Women and the Crisis in Sex Hormones*, pp. 95–100.

TABLE 10. ESTROGEN AND WEIGHT IN WOMEN'S LIFE-CYCLES.

Here are some of the phases of women's lives when a change in estrogen level can affect appetite and weight:

AT THE MENARCHE: Estrogen begins building up in our system for the first time at the menarche. There is a short-term increase in appetite, as menstruation cannot begin until we reach a certain weight. We put on an extra layer of fat then, designed to cushion and sustain us through pregnancy.

DURING THE MONTHLY PERIOD: Women's estrogen-linked monthly cycles affect their appetite and emotions. Premenstrually, there is a rapid drop in estrogen level, and many women experience a ravenous hunger at that point in their cycle.

DURING PREGNANCY: Pregnancy is another time when the estrogen balance is altered. Many pregnant women experience both extreme hunger and emotional ups and downs, especially during the last trimester. Fat deposits formed during pregnancy are part of a storage system designed by nature for the months of breast-feeding and child care that would normally follow.

AFTER CHILDBIRTH: Women are given synthetic estrogen to dry up their breasts if they don't want to breast-feed. There is a natural hormonal imbalance following delivery, and the addition of estrogen at this point complicates matters even more, especially if the woman immediately goes onto the pill. Many women gain weight during pregnancy and after childbirth, especially the first child.

AT THE MENOPAUSE: Estrogen balance changes drastically during menopause, and menopausal women have a natural tendency to gain weight as part of the body's own provisions for itself. A layer of fat is laid down to manufacture and store estrogen, delaying the symptoms of menopause. The menopausal woman in our age-biased society, afraid of losing her attractiveness, may diet vigorously to remove this new protective padding. In ERT (estrogen replacement therapy), synthetic estrogen further disrupts the balance, affecting appetite, emotions, and weight.

greater profit. Since World War II, 85 percent of livestock are fed estrogen. How come the packing industry knows what gynecologists will not admit—that too much estrogen can make you fat! When women gain weight on the pill or during Estrogen Replacement Therapy at menopause, doctors are likely to attribute it to emotional causes such as anxiety over sex!

Due to complex interactions between sugar and estrogen, women are more sensitive to both sugar and alcohol premenstrually. (Alcohol is a highly concentrated form of sugar—the equivalent of seven tablespoons to one shot.) Since sugar throws us emotionally off-center, overindulging in either sugar or alcohol premenstrually contributes significantly to emotional turmoil in that part of the cycle.

As you can see from the points raised above, both synthetic estrogen and our efforts to be ultra-thin can play havoc with our physical and emotional health. However, excess weight also creates an excess of estrogen, so that obese women are more likely to suffer from diabetes, cancer of the breast and uterus, and liver disease. We apparently require a delicate estrogen balance to stay healthy and at a normal weight, so avoiding synthetic estrogen would seem to be a good strategy. In addition, using sugar sparingly and maintaining a normal weight through a balanced, healthy diet would relieve many of the difficulties of keeping on an even keel. High fat intake causes excessive secretions of estrogen, so reduction of fats would produce not only a gradual weight reduction but also a better estrogen balance. Perhaps because of the estrogen in livestock, a four to six week vegetarian diet has also been found helpful in decreasing excess hormones.[12]

Food and Fat in America—A Cancer that Spreads

The U.S. chart is very lunar, so we are emotionally attached to food—motherhood and apple pie are synonyms for patriotism. As the slow-moving planets transited our Cancer planets, our diets changed tremendously. Mass production, mass distribution, and mass media reshaped our eating habits. Table 11 shows the most important of these changes.

The more detached we are from the actual preparation of food, the less attention we seem to pay to our natural food instincts. The mass entry of women into the labor force brought the necessity to rely on fast-food chains, instant mixes, and flash-frozen items. Food is scientifically processed until the nutritional value is practically gone, and then advertising creates a market for it. This is not to suggest that a woman's place is in the kitchen, since men are capable of sharing this responsibility. It is to suggest that we be less concerned about who's minding the store and more concerned about who's minding the stove.

Our food habits are powerfully influenced by advertising. Giant food corporations spend billions a year on ads. It seems that Madison Av-

---

[12]Seaman, *Women and the Crisis in Sex Hormones*, pp. 59, 136.

TABLE 11. HOW AMERICANS' DIETS HAVE CHANGED SINCE 1900.

- In 1900, fresh fruits, vegetables, and whole grains made up 40 percent of our calories; now it's only 20 percent.

- The use of sugar rose from 12 pounds a person per year in 1810, to 128 pounds in 1975.

- In 1900, fats and processed sugar made up 40 percent of our calorie intake; now it's 60 percent.

- Around 1900, when we began using white bread, coronary thrombosis was virtually unknown; now it is a major cause of death.

- In 1900, there were virtually no artificial ingredients in our food; now there are 3000–5000.

- In 1900, there were no fast-food chains; in 1993 hamburger chains sold close to $35 billion with McDonald's sales rising 7 percent in just one year.*

*As reported in the September 19, 1994 issue of *Brandweek*, an advertising journal, p. 52.

enue ought to be ruled by the Moon. Its initials are MA, and it deals with lunar concerns—that is, it manipulates the public by appealing to emotions and insecurities. Women are the targets of, by far, the largest amount of advertising, powerfully shaping their desires and images of femininity. We are told what to eat (high calorie junk food) and what to weigh (be ultra thin). We never notice the contradiction, we just wonder what's wrong when we can't do both. As another clue that advertising is lunar, the Cancer transit correlated with the rise of advertising. It did not come into wide use until the beginning of this century, but grew rapidly after that.

Poor nutritional patterns reached their peak in the 70s, but from the mid-80s on, awareness of health and fitness began to restore the balance. (Pluto in Scorpio was trining any Cancer planets, and Uranus and Neptune in Capricorn opposed them.) Now mass-produced foods often feature reduced calories, sodium, and fat as sales points. Dieting and exercise became first habits and then obsessions for many. By the mid-90s, however, many of us had grown tired of the perpetual struggle, so beef, butter, and fat were slipping back into the American diet. A survey showed that people were also significantly less concerned with cholesterol, sugar, caffeine, salt, and additives in 1994 than they were in 1990.[13] The sales of fast foods, generally high in fats and calories, continued to rise.

Labor-saving devices also contribe to weight gain. Riding a lawn-mower or pushing a button on the microwave or food processor just doesn't consume the calories it used to take to plow the field, chop the wood, or knead the bread by hand. Accordingly, men now require only 2,800 calories a day and women 1,800 to maintain their weight, whereas twenty years ago men needed 3,500 and women 2,400. Even if our diet remained the same, we would gain weight. Excuse me, but if all these labor-saving devices mean we now must labor over exercise machines several hours a week, how much labor are we actually saving? Just checking. Dedicated fitness buffs are working out to compensate, even compulsively at times. The rest of us just beat ourselves up about exercising, and mental self-flagellation doesn't burn up many calories.

Sadly, we are losing the battle of the bulge, and losing it in a big way. Despite all the dieting, despite the "light" foods, and despite the health spa memberships, there is a steady increase in the percentage of Americans who are overweight. In 1970, some 70 million were 30 pounds or more over-weight and most of us were 1-14 pounds heavier than in 1960. The trend for a growing number of obese people continued into the 1990s. The number of overweight Americans increased by 8 percent from 1975 to 1991, and by 1991, over a third of us were overweight.[14] A great many of us, then, are attempting to fill our emptiness with food when other lunar supports are difficult to come by.

The good news is that we may not have to be as thin as we think we do. New statistics show that people who are 20 percent heavier than government standards live longer than people who are underweight. Accordingly, in 1991 Metropolitan Life replaced their old tables of ideal weights with tables listing healthy rather than desirable weights. The healthy weights are higher than the ideal weights given in earlier guidelines.[15]

---

[13]Julie Steenhuysen, "Consumers Overcome Their Food Guilt," *Advertising Age*, May 2, 1994, v65:19, p. 58.

[14]Robert J. Kuczmarsk, Katherine M. Flegal, et al. "Increasing Prevalence of Overweight Among US Adults," *The Journal of the American Medical Association*, July 20, 1994, v277:3, pp. 205–207.

[15]Charles Marwick, "Desirable Weight Goes Up in New Guidelines," *The Journal of the American Medical Association*, January 2, 1991, v265:1, p. 17; also, "Good News for Heavyweights," *USA Today Magazine*, January, 1992, v120:2560, p. 6.

Fat Hate—A Consequence of Our Losing Battle

Says Joseph McVoy, head of the Eating Disorders Program at a Virginia hospital:

> If Marilyn Monroe were taking a screen test today, she'd probably be told to diet and go to the gym.[16]

In a land where thinness is the Holy Grail, overweight people are second-class citizens. Standup comics who wouldn't dare to make a racial slur don't hesitate to ridicule "fat broads," while their audiences fall on the floor laughing. Young children include the word *fat* in their vocabularies, and they use it accurately, if not tactfully. Mere acquaintances who wouldn't say boo if you were cheating on your income tax or stealing office supplies think they have the perfect right to lecture you sanctimoniously on what you are eating. It is as though a new version of the Ten Commandments has been handed down from on high, no doubt on polyurethane tablets. It reads, "Thou Shalt Not Steal or Commit Adultery—not unless you can get away with it—but Thou Shalt Not, under any circumstances, Get Fat."

If they could pass laws against public obesity, as they have with drinking, you can bet they would do it. (Smoking, another oral habit, is also undergoing siege, with nonsmoking laws proliferating so fast it's almost like the Prohibition era.) And romance? Even if the obese found people who wanted them, there'd be all that flack from the peer group to discourage the suitor. In addition, job discrimination based on weight and age is an unacknowledged reality. If you're fat AND fifty, hold onto your job.

I know that what I am about to say is likely to sound anti-male, but please bear with me. We've seen that women suffer much more than men from weight problems. Much of the rage directed against fat people is therefore rage against women—and much of the rage comes from men. It is men who yell, "FAT PIG," when an overweight woman passes them on the street. It is men who dump girlfriends or wives who gain weight—women are more likely to stand by their man while cooking lower calorie meals to help them reduce. Male comics are the ones making mean-spirited jokes about fat people. Women comics—and a few overweight men—are more likely to joke about how fat they are, and about their own struggles with food.

---

[16]Joseph McVoy, head of the Eating Disorders Program at St. Alban's Hospital, Radford, VA. *Health*, 10/94, p. 38.

Why do men behave this way? As we'll see in chapter 13, men mostly disown their Moons, and assign women the responsibility for their lunar needs. When those needs are not met, when they suffer from the same lunar deprivations we all face, they turn their rage and frustration against women in general, and overweight women in particular. This male rage and contempt toward excess weight is a major reason women struggle so frantically to be thin.

Women also shame their overweight sisters, but in more subtle ways like, "You don't really NEED that piece of cake." Outside the larger cities, the shaming is not always so blatant, and thinner people may not even realize that they are doing it. They may couch their remarks in the guise of concern for your health, but in condescending tones, as though you were somewhat retarded. Or, when an overweight person walks into the room, many of the conversations somehow turn to dieting.

Where does it come from, this neobigotry, this fat hate? Well, let's look at life in the solar world. You were out there swimming with the sharks all day, and it looks like the company is downsizing. The commute home was a nightmare, and you were too exhausted to even pick up takeout. The house is a disaster, the kids are threatening to tear each other apart, and you're divorced now, so there's no one else to take up the slack. Your teenage daughter's eyes look funny these days, and you're afraid to ask why. So you order pizza rather than try to cook, and later while you're slumped in front of the television, you get a call from that ice cream in the freezer. You know it's bad, bad, bad, but you'll go back on your diet tomorrow, and maybe even dust the cobwebs off that exercise bike in the corner.

The next morning, your talking scale has a word with you, and you somehow start that diet, with black coffee and half a grapefruit for breakfast. When you finally make it through traffic to the office, dead tired, you are confronted with that chubby office mate, who is scarfing down not just one, but two, gooey pastries. She's not on a diet AT ALL, doesn't even seem to try. So, sure you hate her, but not a lot more than you hate yourself when you blow the diet again at lunch.

And that's the point of it—fat hate is really self-hate. The media hold up impossibly thin and gorgeous 16-year-olds we are supposed to compete with. We feel like failures when we can't do that along with everything else we're supposed to achieve. As remarked in discussing the sign Cancer, we as a people tend to scapegoat those who dare to be openly lunar, since we have all been subjected to painful deprivation of our lunar needs. Let's stop looking at overweight people as THEM and realize that we are all in this together. Our desperate collective struggle with food, to maintain a perfect appearance, can make us feel angry and deprived, and we turn it on those who are losing the battle. If you, yourself, are losing the battle or if you love someone who is, read the chapter on eating disorders, coming up next.

What can we do about the self-hate that underlies our fat hate? The first tool, as always, is awareness. We need to remain aware of society's impossible and often contradictory demands. Although it is hard to love yourself in a world that demands perfection, it helps to know that it's not you, but the world, that is off-base. Let's work at being compassionate with ourselves when we cannot always meet those demands and to work at deprogramming the ones that can't be meet. Deprogramming has been precisely the intent of this chapter and its many unsettling revelations. Let's also be aware of the stresses and lunar deprivations that drive us to eat for comfort. The second set of tools consists of the many ways this book teaches you to balance your lunar hemisphere. As you pursue them over time, food should have less power.

Finally, the third set is one we haven't discussed before—tools for self-esteem. Self-esteem is a solar, not a lunar function. The solar world is also damaging the solar side of our nature by its constant comparisions with those who are richer, more successful, more attractive, more educated, and just plain MORE. There are numerous workshops and books about loving yourself which you can consult. There are meditations and healers to help you work on the *solar plexus chakra*, the area of the aura around the beltline which governs self-esteem. There are also many fine flower remedies to help you love yourself more: **Sunflower, Buttercup,** and **Self-Heal** by FES; **Alpine Azalea** and **Mountain Wormwood** by the Alaskan Flower Essence Project; and **Rock Water, Larch,** and **Holly** by Bach. FES's **Pretty Face** is a solace when your looks are very different from the cultural ideal.

CHAPTER 12

EATING DISORDERS— MOUTH HUNGER AND MOTHER LOVE

Although Dr. Rubin has no place in his scheme of things for astrology, the following quote tells us that he is right on target.

> Overeating blocks peace of mind as sure as the Moon blocks the Sun in an eclipse, and certainly we overeaters long for inner peace.[1]

Overeating is a Moon problem, and it wreaks havoc with our emotional balance. Like the phases of the Moon, the food addict goes through endless cycles of fullness and emptiness—gorging and starving, bingeing and dieting, weight gain and weight loss. Full Moon/new Moon. Certainly the body of the obese person is very lunar. Cancer rules the stomach and the breasts, areas where the weight is usually concentrated. Both are connected with feeding, and their prominence proclaims to the world that the overeater has a strong need to be fed and nurtured. Their faces are also shaped like the full Moon, the weight masking individual features and creating a family resemblance of sorts. It is noteworthy that most diets start on Monday (Moonday) and rarely last more than one lunar month. Here, we will look at eating disorders as a lunar dysfunction and find suggestions about how to overcome them through ministering to lunar concerns. The prism through which we will view both the problem and the proposed solutions is the always-useful Cancer rising wheel.

---

[1]Theodore Isaac Rubin, *Forever Thin* (New York: Bernard Geis Associates, 1970), p. 339.

The Food Addict as Lunatic

People generally overeat for Moon reasons—to fill up when drained by nurturing others or when feeling insecure, needy, or emotionally upset. Anyone can overeat occasionally, but compulsive overeaters automatically turn to food as their primary response to all kinds of stress. They act on mouth hunger rather than true physical hunger and console themselves orally. Rather than solving the problem, this habit distresses the body, dulls the mind, and throws the emotions out of balance. Especially when consuming sugar, the overeater on a binge is at the mercy of uncontrolled emotions and wild mood swings. A binge intensifies negative lunar traits and throws the lunar hemisphere out of balance.

Not all eating disorders work this way, but food binges are a phenomenon described by many. To get an idea of the physical discomfort, recall that stuffed-turkey sensation after a holiday meal and intensify it. The emotional discomfort is even more painful. A dreadful hunger rises that is not biological—these folks rarely allow true hunger to surface. Instead it is an emotional and spiritual hunger, a cry for the emptiness to be filled and for the pain of living to be blanked out. The overeater is out of control, continuing to stuff food down even when it hurts or becomes repugnant. She feels compelled to devour everything she can get her hands on. It is a raging destruction where the food is at once the enemy to be attacked, the lover, and the breast at which the starving infant inside greedily sucks.

If this description sounds a bit insane to you, you are beginning to see how futile it is to tell her to use a little will power (a little Saturn) to lose weight. An eating disorder is a disease like alcoholism. Those who suffer from it have as little conscious control over eating as alcoholics do over drinking, and for many of the same reasons. They periodically go on diets, just as alcoholics periodically go on the wagon, and they just as regularly fall off when they do not address the underlying problems that create the addiction.

Of course, not all overeaters are like this description, and even the ones that are, aren't like this all the time. You aren't likely to be shoved in front of a subway train by someone who's having a Big Mac attack. Still, this is what the addiction is like at its worst—maybe at the full Moon, in the throes of PMS, or after suffering a major lunar loss. It's a composite picture, rather than any single overeater.

The public has begun to accept alcoholism as a disease, but still regards overweight people as undisciplined weaklings and objects of scorn. There is no National Council on Obesity, no New York City Division of Overeating, and still only a few rehab programs or treatment centers for the seriously obese, although they exist for alcoholics. Part of this is political—obesity is primarily a woman's disease, while alcoholism, until recently, has been primarily considered a man's disease. The things that go wrong with women are not taken as seriously as the things that go wrong with men.

Not all who overeat are heavy. Bulemics stay acceptably thin by alternating between bingeing and fasting, binge-vomiting, taking diet pills, or compulsive exercising. An eating disorder is a serious disease, not only in the health problems it can cause, but also in its devastating effects on those who suffer from it. You may be wondering if you have an eating disorder. If so, ask yourself these questions. Have you gone on diet after diet but always failed? Or, did you get the weight off but gain it back and a little more besides? Is your weight limiting or otherwise affecting the way you live? Do you stuff yourself secretly? Do you eat to escape anger, frustration, worries, loneliness, or other problems?

If you answered yes to several of these questions, you may have more than just a problem with your weight. You may have an eating disorder. For you, eating is as much a compulsion as drinking is for the alcoholic, and you can't stop just by exercising will power. If it were only a physical problem, any diet from a doctor or women's magazine would do the trick. It doesn't, anymore than detoxifying an alcoholic produces a cure. There is a physical component—the sensitivity to sugar, starch, or alcohol. However, these people primarily eat or drink to avoid unpleasant emotions or to fill the emptiness inside —i.e., for lunar reasons.

The most successful program to get alcoholics sober is Alcoholics Anonymous. Likewise, the most sustained success with eating disorders has been through Overeaters Anonymous, which uses the same principles, techniques, and teachings as A.A. Both programs believe their members suffer from a three-fold illness—physical, emotional, and spiritual. The programs encompass twelve steps to recovery. These steps contain much spiritual wisdom. They help members sort out emotional and spiritual difficulties and take action to resolve them.

The Anonymous programs and outside experts agree that alcoholics, drug dependent people, and severe overeaters have related problems, a character pattern called the addictive personality. This idea may be disturbing for the portly individual who would never touch port, much less pot, because she wants so much to be better than somebody. ("Maybe I do love chocolate a bit too much, but at least I'm not a drunk.") The drug of choice depends on coping patterns learned in the family, on subsequent exposure and experience, and even on the rise and fall in popularity of various drugs.

One proof is the frequent shift from one addiction to another. The overeater diets but goes on spending sprees, the alcoholic sobers up, but increases smoking to three packs a day, the chain smoker quits, but puts on weight, the junkie jazz musician goes off heroin, but winds up dying of alcoholism. No addict is "cured" who merely shifts his compulsion. It takes more than "will power," and it rarely works to do it alone.

Bulemia and Anorexia—The Thin Food Addicts

While much of this chapter is for those whose compulsions with food have visible results, there are also many people who struggle with food constantly, yet remain acceptably thin. Bulemics struggle in no less painful ways than obese people, with no less overwhelming self-hate. They may alternate between bingeing and starving themselves, like periodic drunks. The constant frustration and times of starvation only escalate the problem. They may exercise for hours a day, sometimes harming themselves physically. They may try to have their cake and eat it too, by vomiting or by purging themselves with laxatives and enemas. Although they remain relatively slender, this condition is no less dangerous than serious obesity. Death by choking or esophageal hemorrhaging is a real possibility, especially when vomiting is induced regularly. Anorexics and bulemics also disturb their hormonal balance and may lose their periods.

The obvious bulemia poster child is Princess Di. Diana, of course, was the Moon goddess, and we have tried to make a goddess of the Princess of Wales. We adore or deplore her every move. The press hounds her constantly, because any news item, any photo, is guaranteed to sell out an issue. While partnered with Prince Charles, she was subjected to intense pressures to be the perfect lady, wife, and mother in every public appearance. Pressures to look perfect were also intense. Photos do make people look heavier—and Diana's public adulation is as much due to her svelte good looks and fashion sense as to her personal virtues. (Contrast that to the continual ridicule "Fat Fergie" was subjected to when she was a mere size twelve—not exactly Lane Bryant country!) Mamma-in-law, Queen Elizabeth, is a Taurus, while Charles has a Taurus Moon, and you can't get more traditional than that. Even after the separation, she was not a free agent, but was still expected to uphold the royal ideals and responsibilities.

It's unfortunate, because although Diana is a Cancer, her Moon is in modern, freedom-loving, and unconventional Aquarius, with charismatic

Uranus in Leo forming a close opposition. We spoke earlier of the inherent tensions between Aquarius and Cancer, between the Moon and Uranus. Diana is a living example, and her bulimia, emotional breakdowns, and suicide attempts are all results of living with intense conflicts like these. In November, 1994, in response to public betrayals by the Prince and her former male friend, Major James Hewitt, the media reported that she had gone on Prozac. She was also reportedly in therapy with Susie Orbach, who did such ground-breaking work in her classic book, *Fat is a Feminist Issue.*

Diana's Moon/Uranus opposition is part of a t-square with Venus, the planet of love and beauty, in the 5th house. This combination represents her love of children and yet her ambivalence about the feminine roles. Pluto and Saturn's transits through this fixed t-square from 1992–1994 represented the final breakdown of her home. (See Chart 7 on page 226.)

Karen Carpenter, who with her brother Richard had many top records in the late 1970s and early 1980s, was a tragic casualty of anorexia. (See Chart 8 on page 227.) To illustrate the inherent conflicts between Cancer and Aquarius (or the Moon and Uranus), she had Uranus at 0 degrees Cancer only minutes from her Cancer Ascendant. Further increasing the stress on her lunar hemisphere, her close and emotionally intense Moon-Pluto conjunction in the 3rd opposed a highly mental Mercury-Jupiter conjunction in Aquarius. Tensions ran very high between the part of her that wanted nurturing, the part that rebelled against the traditional female roles, and against family pressures. Anorexia was an expression of these tensions. When Karen died, in early February, 1983, Uranus and Jupiter were conjunct in Sagittarius in her house of work and health, squaring her Pisces Midheaven. Jupiter expands what it touches, so the exaggeration of Uranian energies by Jupiter was physically the last straw.

My nominee for a lunar hero in the battle of the bulge would be Richard Simmons. Maybe he doesn't look like a hero to you, as he cheerleads you through his exercise video. A hero is someone with heart and courage and vision who leads and inspires the embattled to fight an overpowering enemy. If you ever saw one of the moving programs about Richard Simmon's volunteer work with the morbidly obese—the 400 and 500 pounders—you wouldn't doubt his heroism for a moment. He goes to their homes, which they haven't left in years, and personally escorts them to a hospital with an eating disorder ward. He calls them frequently to encourage them, and he visits to see how they are doing. Born July 12, 1948, according to the World Almanac, Simmons is a Cancer. What else could he be?

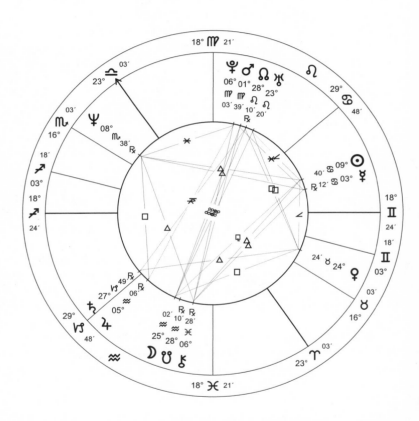

Chart 7. Princess Diana, born July 1, 1961, in Sandringham, England, at 7:45 P.M. BST. However, Lois Rodden reports that Diana has been quoted at different times as saying both 7:45 P.M. and 2:15 P.M. This time is from mother, according to Charles Harvey. Reprinted with permission from Lois M. Rodden's Astro-Data III *(Tempe, AZ: American Federation of Astrologers, 1986). The Placidus house system is used here.*

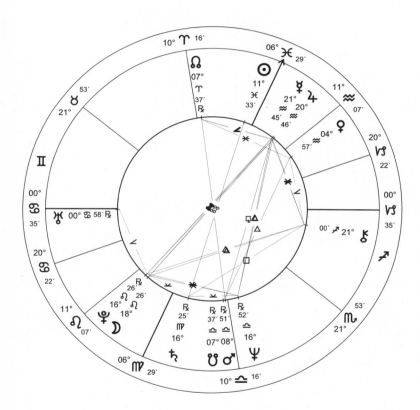

Chart 8. Karen Carpenter, born March 2, 1950, in New Haven, CT at 11:45 A.M. EST. Information from a hand-written note given to E. Steinbrecher from the registrar in the records bureau. (Reprinted with permission from Lois M. Rodden's Data News #18, August 1989.) The Placidus house system is used here.

The Obesity Matrix—the Cancer Rising Wheel

Psychiatrist Theodore Isaac Rubin talks about the obesity matrix, the syndrome of personality traits and defenses common to compulsive overeaters. (Rubin's excellent works, including *Forever Thin* and *The Angry Book*, are mostly out of print but worth rummaging around library basements and used book stores to find.) In my own observations of hundreds of overeaters, however, I am satisfied that the real obesity matrix is the Cancer rising wheel. It encompasses the characteristics described by Rubin, Overeaters Anonymous, and other experts in the field. (The word *matrix* is Latin for mother or womb.) Many with planets in Cancer have struggled with weight problems or food obsessions, although many Cancerians are also extremely thin. The extreme in one direction or another is typical. As we shall see, the personality of the compulsive overeater fits the less constructive traits of the sign Cancer, no matter what signs are present in the actual horoscope.

Astrologer Betty Lundsted made an interesting observation about weight problems in women. She saw many cases where young girls became overweight after suddenly developing large breasts earlier than others the same age and also where the menarche came early. This early development subjected them to wisecracks and sexual attention they weren't old enough to deal with. Perhaps their mothers were unable to explain this stage of growth, being embarrassed, confused or upset by the child's early development. The fat hid the girls' breasts and insulated them against sexual advances. Thus, the weight served defensive purposes that they carried unconsciously, long after they forgot this phase. We might also speculate that early breast development could accompany an upset in the estrogen balance, an additional predisposition to weight gain. As we've seen in chapter 10, a serious upset in the mother-daughter relationship at the menarche could contribute to insecurity in this new lunar role.

Like natives of the sign Cancer, people with eating disorders seem terminally hung up on their families, especially Mom. Anorexia often involves a destructive power struggle with the mother over appearance. Many with eating disorders still live at home or are in constant contact, perhaps even financially dependent. A good number gained weight at the lunar thresholds, when they moved away from home, lost their mother, or became mothers themselves. Even when the tie is ambivalent, tremendous energy is focused on either loving or hating mother for what she did or didn't do. In an opposite but related pattern, many eating disorders loudly profess their independence and total lack of connection with family in a counterdependent stance. They don't rely on others, proud souls that they are, but are addictively dependent on food to soothe and console them.[2]

A particularly loaded situation gets set up when the mother, herself, is obese. It is extremely difficult for her children to sever the symbiosis, given that smother love Mom can dish out along with her homemade ravioli. Losing weight can bring a terrifying identity crisis and a sense of losing mother or leaving her behind. Habits and emotions she imprints on food are very difficult to countervene because they are unconscious. If food was love to Mama, the child can feel deprived of love when dieting. Despite what she says to encourage you, successful weight loss on your part can threaten your mother's addiction, so she may resort to sabotage. In a situation like this, work hard on the mother-daughter tie to lose the weight permanently.

An additional impetus to overeating is the Mother-to-the-World stance adopted by many compulsive overeaters. They may do it because of low self-esteem, believing themselves unlovable unless they are ministering to other people. However, an emotional vacuum results from compulsive mothering. Not asking for or allowing help in return can increase the desire to overeat. Work toward interdependence, so giving and taking are in better balance.

Many obese women gained weight when they had their children. Hormonal shifts during pregnancy, and after, can contribute to weight gain, but the major factor is emotional. Nurturing is stressful to those who were never properly nurtured as children. It can create a good deal of unconscious rage and the tendency to eat in retaliation. In chapter 9, we saw how modern life makes the process of adjusting to motherhood a difficult one in which the new mother often lacks support. One way women try to fill up when they feel drained by children is with food.

Cancers hang onto the past, and what compulsive overeaters are hanging onto in those excess pounds are stored-up anger, resentment, trauma, grief, neediness, and other painful feelings. Dr. Rubin talks about the fat as a "slush fund" of feelings that melts as the weight is lost. Dieting becomes difficult when unresolved past conflicts rise to the surface as the dieter goes down the scale. Most diet doctors or programs pay little attention to emotions. If you get uptight, the doctor may prescribe a pill to make you comfortable.

Let's go around the Cancer Rising wheel, to see what insights we can gain. Later, we will make a second tour to find solutions.

---

[2]An illuminating book is Judi Hollis' *Fat is a Family Affair* (Minneapolis: Hazeldon, 1986).

Cancer on the 1st House: The 1st house shows the physical appearance, and overweight people's bodies are lunar. The first house also shows defenses and tools for keeping the world off our backs. The weight acts as a protective shell against coming too close to the outside world, particularly the opposite sex. Painful and humiliating as it is to the person trapped inside, excess weight is insulation against full participation in the demands of the solar world. It may also maintain dependency, since people often expect less of the seriously obese, stereotyping them as immature and even stupid. Getting thin may make the overeater feel exposed and vulnerable. FES offers **Golden Yarrow** and **Pink Yarrow** to help ease the sense of vulnerability, as well as **Poison Oak** to help shed that tough crabshell.

Leo on the 2nd House: The 2nd house shows what we value. Leo is thought of as a self-centered sign, and compulsive overeaters can be extremely self-centered at times. Many want the whole world to revolve around them. Thus it is hard to share food or the limelight, even if the attention is negative. (**Heather** or **Chicory** by Bach can help resolve this demand.)

Simultaneously, the self-esteem is low, so the compulsive demand for attention reflects a lack of self confidence. When others don't give them the attention they want, they fall back on food. Like alcoholics, overeaters can spend an enormous amount of money on their addiction, buying large amounts of food or high-end ice cream, or eating out. A frequent excuse for not dieting, however, is that diet food is too expensive.

Leo on the 2nd also shows the enormous value overeaters place on their pride. They feel asking for help, admitting to vulnerability, cheapens them, so they will go to any lengths to maintain their proud front. The price of false pride is that they are thrown on their own resources, a great strain in the end. Yet, what could be more damaging to the pride than being over-weight in a society where it is held in contempt, so this defense is a vicious circle. False pride can be offset by FES' **Sunflower** or **Goldenrod**.

Virgo on the 3rd House: The 3rd house shows communicating and thinking. Compulsive people are Virgo-like in this area—endlessly critical, particularly in assessing themselves. Perfectionism keeps them literally and figuratively in a stew, which they overeat to silence. Overeaters often indulge in negative thinking and being hard on themselves. "It won't work. This diet will fail like all the rest, so why try?" or "I'll never get thin." Thoughts like these reinforce hopelessness and self-hate, and they eat more to escape the feelings. One especially damaging Virgo pattern is self-deprecation. Overeaters put themselves down constantly, and when others buy the propaganda, it reinforces the negative self-image in a vicious cycle. (Bach's **Beech** is excellent for halting this self-critical pattern.)

Libra on the 4th House: Overeaters invest tremendous emotional energy in the past. The 4th house represents ties to the home, past, family, and mother, while the house Libra rules shows what we are truly married to. Thus the compulsive overeater is married to the past, and this is one marriage that rarely ends in divorce, although **Honeysuckle** by Bach is a good antidote. The real long-term commitment is to Mom and Dad or their inner representatives. Thus, it is hard for overeaters to break free and commit to an adult form of relating. Marriage takes on a nurturing quality beyond the usual. Those with eating disorders become a parent to the mate, who is seen as one of the children, seek a parent in the mate, or both. When we look for total security in someone or something outside us, we place a strain on the relationship. The 4th house is also feeding and nurturing, so Libra there shows that to the overeater, food is love. Libra is also famous for people-pleasing, which the overeater does compulsively. They placate people by nourishing them to get that desperately-craved love.

Scorpio on the 5th House: At its worst, Scorpio can be resentful, spiteful, and isolated. Applied to the 5th house concerns of love affairs, recreation and children, typical behaviors of overeaters are Scorpionic indeed. Every love affair takes on a life-and-death quality, and possessiveness often drives lovers away. They eat to forget old lovers, to make up for feeling deprived if no one wants them, or to spite potential lovers who insist they should lose weight. Scorpio is a private sign, and the weight isolates—and insulates—the overeater from romance. Eating, a solitary pursuit, then becomes the greatest pleasure, the lover and beloved.

Resentment is common among overeaters and frequently leads to binges. Yet overeaters can enjoy nursing a grudge—secretly, of course. They also eat out of spite, especially if they believe others are trying to control them. They then get great pleasure from saying internally, "See what you made me do?" (Revenge is sweet, but for the overeater, sweets are revenge.) When it comes to children, the overeaters can secretly resent the demands of parenthood and overeat to replenish themselves when it is too draining. (Good remedies for resentment and spite are Bach's **Willow** or **Holly**.)

Sagittarius on the 6th House: The 6th house shows illness, and Sagittarius' ruler, Jupiter, is the planet of growth and expansion. Some 50,000 Americans die every year from causes secondary to obesity. Jupiter rules the liver, and the mortality for cirrhosis of the liver in obese people, even those who don't drink, is 249 percent that of the nonobese. Yet, Sagittarius is the perennial optimist, so the overeater thinks, "It can't happen to me." (Pegasus' **Four Leaf Clover** is an excellent remedy for Jupiterians who push their luck in this and many other ways.) They may retain the old belief that plumpness is a sign of health and that thinness is sickly. If parents urged food on the sick child, overeaters may even eat more when ill, rather than eating lightly to give the body a rest. While their large size consciously makes them feel like second-class citizens, the child within remembers that the big people had all the power. Being big becomes equated with being powerful. This is especially true if Mom, Dad, or other crucial adults were obese.

Capricorn on the 7th House: Overeaters often look for discipline outside. They want someone else to control their eating and provide the security and structure they require to lose weight. When the other person healthily insists they take responsibility for their behavior, overeaters feel rejected at this "coldness" and eat for consolation. They love to blame the weight on others and their limitations. ("My husband doesn't understand me." "My boss is so demanding.") Those who project the blame onto others could be helped by FES' **Sage** or **Saguaro**. Capricorn on the 7th shows a wall between the overeater and other people, a wall reinforced by weight. It also shows sadness over the isolation and hopelessness about achieving a good relationship.

Aquarius on the 8th House: Aquarius is a rebellious sign. According to Susie Orbach, women with eating disorders are often rebelling against the role assigned to women in our culture. These women do not want to be seen primarily as sex objects or as vehicles for bearing children, so they rely on their shape to remove themselves from the marketplace. They may also fear intimacy and use weight to cut off sexual feelings. They are more apt to be seen as pals than as sex objects. This status is non-threatening for other women don't view them as competition. For the disassociation from the body that this position may entail, FES offers **Manzanita**.

Pisces on the 9th House: This house shows one's philosophy of life, and obese people feel like lost souls, imprisoned in the fat, and forever doomed to suffer. This may be a fairly good perception of the truth, unless they take action to change the pattern. Compulsive overeating is a compelling habit, though it may be arrested. Overeating is a spiritual and emotional problem rather than just a physical one. Unlike weight reduction programs that focus unsuccessfully on the physical aspects, Overeaters Anonymous is a program of spiritual and emotional recovery as well. Most essence makers offer remedies to support a spiritual awakening—for instance, FES' **Lotus, Angelica,** or **Star Tulip.**

Aries on the 10th House: Judi Hollis, a Ph.D. who specializes in eating disorders, feels that anger is a primary character trait of compulsive overeaters. Her book, *Fat and Furious,* is a powerful guide to healing oneself, which I would especially recommend to overeaters who believe they seldom get angry (New York: Ballantine, 1994).

Aries is ruled by Mars, the planet that symbolizes anger, and Aries on the 10th shows great anger toward parents, and the world. This anger, however disguised, may be picked up on by the world at large and is part of the reason overweight people are targets of public anger. Overeaters are extremely defiant toward authority figures, if often covertly. They carry on a private war against parents or supervisors with food as their weapon. The overeater also battles against society by gaining more weight in spite. When someone comments about their weight, or in any other anger-provoking situation, the response is, "I'll show them!" followed by a race to the refrigerator. Despite the fact they are angry, the wish to placate still exists (Libra on the opposite house). Therefore, overeaters are afraid to admit their anger, often even to themselves. They stuff anger down with food, convert it to depression or express it other distorted ways. The various remedies for anger discussed earlier can be helpful—especially FES' **Scarlet Monkeyflower.**

Taurus on the 11th House: The 11th shows our friendships and how we function in them. Due to low self-esteem, overweight people may feel they have to "buy" friends, whether with gifts, entertainment, or food. Or, there may be an underlying belief that if they want companions they have to pay for it by doing things for others. They can be possessive of friends. **Hound's Tongue** by FES and **Vine** by Bach can offset these tendencies.

Gemini on the 12th House: The 12th house shows hidden emotions that express in distorted and self-destructive ways. Gemini is communication, and with this sign on the 12th, we see how difficult it is for overeaters to show their true feelings. They communicate indirectly, through self-defeating behaviors like binges. Obesity, itself, is a form of communication, with a very 12th-house message, "Help me! I'm a sick person!" Self-pity drives them to eat more, which increases the problem, which increases the self-pity, and so on. In one of its traditional meanings, the 12th house is prison, and seri-

ously overweight people view their condition as a sentence of life imprison-
ment. **Heather**, by Bach, is an excellent antidote for self-pity.

The Crab Without a Shell—A Thin New You

Getting thin is the desideratum of every overweight person, no matter how
content they profess to be. They fantasize what it will be like—romance and
success falling at their feet. Well-meaning civilians reinforce these dreams
in an attempt to be encouraging. "You have such a pretty face. If you got
thin, you'd have to beat them off." Many overeaters postpone living their
lives. "I won't buy new clothes until I lose this twenty pounds." "There's no
sense going to the Bahamas in the shape I'm in. I'll do it when I lose the
weight." "I can't face the old crowd so much heavier. I'll skip the reunion
and go next time. By then, I'll be a size ten and really knock their eyes out."
Many such women put a moratorium on living, because self-hatred may be
so strong they feel they don't deserve good things. (**Polyanthus**, by Pacific
Essences, helps people feel more deserving.)

When they postpone living, the fantasies of what it will be like when
they get thin become overwhelming. They believe their lives will be transformed and all their problems will be magically solved. They fantasize that
suitors will clamor at the door and that they'll magically become perfect and
wildly successful. Many are shy with the opposite sex due to the many re-
jections because of their bodies. They can be uncomfortable in social situations and afraid of new demands, so getting thin becomes terrifying. The
fear is unconscious and the civilian world can't conceive of it, but it causes
the failure of many diets that are on the verge of success.

People who have lost a great deal of weight find it a frightening adjustment, a real identity crisis. They feel like a crab without a shell—fragile, unprotected, and self-conscious at finding their bodies uncovered. Many fear
the sexual attention they receive. Newly-thin people have to learn to live
without armor—and one way is to accept that life was never meant to be a
war anyhow (Aries on the 10th). Many things they thought they had to protect themselves from weren't real to begin with. (**Sagebrush**, by FES, works
to release outgrown or illusory self-concepts.)

To get thin and stay there, the overeater has to find ways of meeting
needs by nurturing herself, developing support systems, and balancing the
lunar hemisphere. One way to begin is by tackling negative patterns of eating disorders, as seen in the Cancer rising wheel. There are also construc-

tive qualities in each sign and in each house. A second trip around the wheel is in order so we can discover ways of climbing out of that shell. Again we see that astrology works homeopathically, that the problem contains the seeds of the solution. As we've already considered helpful flower remedies in our earlier trip around the wheel, we'll only mention a few additional remedies here.

Cancer on the 1st House: It would be especially healing, given the hunger for mothering, to learn to mother the child within. Somewhere inside you, there is a hurt child who never got the love she needed. Rather than spend life searching for someone else to fill that void, learn to consciously love and nurture the inner child yourself. Find out what she wants, then give it to her. Don't automatically feed her when she may want love, or rest, or something fun to do instead of working so hard. Love is the most common lack behind those food cravings, so give love to your inner child by reaching out to others rather than isolating.

You cannot give up the protective shell without at least temporarily protecting and sheltering yourself in other ways. You don't have to tackle things that make you anxious right away, just because you are now thin. Give yourself time to grow comfortable with the new person you are becoming. As one guideline, say no to anything that brings up the desire to eat. Eventually you won't be so anxious, but for today, be protective of yourself.

Leo on the 2nd House: The 2nd house is what we value and spend our resources on, and the primary concern of Leo is itself. To avoid overeating, you may have to adopt new ways of thinking that might at first appear selfish. Yet, if you destroy your life by overeating, you have nothing to give anyone else. To get thin and stay that way, learn to love yourself and be good to yourself, even if it costs a little money. Learn to value yourself and take honest pride in your capabilities, to gain a new self-esteem. (Work on the solar plexus chakra with the tools mentioned in chapter 11.)

Virgo on the 3rd House: Virgo, in its more positive expression, helps you analyze your thoughts, emotions, and behavior to change them. One of the twelve steps of O.A. is to "make a searching and fearless moral inventory of ourselves" to see the character flaws clearly and start cleaning house. Approach those flaws, not with self-criticism, but with that celebrated Virgo practicality—does it work or doesn't it? Maybe you have all the justification in the world for your behavior, but does it work for you or against you? If it doesn't contribute to happiness and self-worth, change it. (To help in taking an honest, but not self-battering inventory, work with **Henbane** and **Hyssop** by Pegasus, **Pine** by Bach, and **Black-eyed Susan** by FES.)

Libra on the 4th House: Strive for balance when it comes to the past, extracting out what is good and letting go of the rest. Be fair toward the people you believe harmed you—what did the situation look like from their viewpoint? What stresses might they have been under which caused them to act as they did? How did your behavior and attitudes contribute to the situation—e.g., did you invite them to treat you like a doormat? Looking at past hurts, you may come to see that you contributed equally to the problem. It takes two to tango. Guilt can also bind you to the past. The eighth and ninth steps of O.A. are concerned with freeing you from the past. It is done in a Libra way by making amends to people you have harmed, unless doing so would cause further harm.

Scorpio on the 5th House: Scorpio here suggests that you may need time alone to heal. Isolation is not always negative. You can find pleasure in self-transformation, so approach it playfully rather than dead seriously. Healing comes from ministering to the child within, learning to play, and developing your creativity as an emotional release. Sex, which Scorpio rules, can also be playful, not a life and death matter, making it less fearful.

Sagittarius on the 6th House: Apply the higher mind to bodily functions, by learning more about health and nutrition. Sagittarius is optimistic, and letting go of negativity improves your chances. Having faith that you can make it, and taking a positive attitude toward dieting can help you along. Even when you doubt you can do it, act as if. Affirmations help counteract your negative thoughts and past failures. (**Pennyroyal**, by Pegasus, is helpful in eradicating negative thoughts.)

Capricorn on the 7th House: Though you are responsible for yourself, you do need other people, the structure of a program, and a food plan to lose weight. You can learn to be interdependent in relationships, alternating between giving and taking. Then getting close will not be so anxiety-provoking, and you won't need that protective shell so much.

Aquarius on the 8th House: This non-conforming sign can help you reject cultural stereotypes about male and female roles. Once you find you have the right to free choice rather than being a sex object, you can be liberated from weight gained in rebellion and discover your sexual self.

Aquarius rules groups, and the 8th house symbolizes healing. Thus, belonging to a group is an important aid in healing eating disorders. They can give you emotional support through those rough times you once ate over. The new friends you make can help you see your problems in a more detached way. When you consider your problems as human ones, you discover that you're not alone.

Pisces on the 9th House: The second step of O.A. is, "Came to believe a power greater than ourselves can restore us to sanity." That's Piscean—both the recognition of the insanity of the pattern and the mystical surrender to something greater than the self. (FES's **St. John's Wort** can increase faith in the divine and their **Lotus** can help during spiritual awakening.) If you find it hard to accept any God figure, so do many O.A. members. For them the Higher Power is the group, itself. Most important is the admission of powerlessness over the eating disorder and the surrender to a spiritual way of dealing with it. As long as you believe you can do it your own way, that your will alone can stop the pattern, you'll be imprisoned in the addiction.

Aries on the 10th House: Anger that causes trouble is anger that is buried, misdirected, or distorted. Aries on the 10th shows a need to get anger more out in the open to stop overeating. Anger in itself is not destructive, only your misuse of it. You might find self-assertiveness training helpful. When you are able to speak up rather than allowing people to take advantage, you have less cause to get angry in the first place. (Flower remedies for dealing with anger are given in chapter 5.)

Taurus on the 11th House: Friends are a good investment, but only blue-chip friends who pay dividends by giving and taking equally. If your pals are takers rather than givers, cultivate new friendships. However, understand that a change in the cast of characters is not a real change unless you learn more balanced ways of relating. (For healthier patterns, call on Desert Alchemy's formula **Giving and Receiving Support**, or my personal favorite, **Making and Honoring Boundaries**.) Taurus is an earth sign, and friends can ground you in an emotional storm. The 11th house also concerns groups, and investing time in a support group can give you the security to relinquish that too solid flesh.

Gemini on the 12th House: Gemini is symbolic of communication, and the more you discuss those painful feelings, the sooner you can get through them. Every time you talk about things that trouble you, you cut them in half. You're only as sick as your secrets, and an Anonymous Program is a good place to spill it all and still let it remain secret. If no one is available to talk to, writing out your feelings can be a fine outlet. Gemini rules humor, too, and if you can learn to laugh at yourself rather than take everything so seriously, you won't resort to overeating.

$$) \;) \;) \;)$$

Eating disorders are tough, no two ways about it. If you have this problem, you will need more than this book and a bottle of flower remedies to change it. None of the flower essences or homeopathic remedies can cure this complex problem single-handedly. They can support you in working through the various layers of emotions that come up when you stop overeating, but you will also need the help of health care workers, counselors, and support groups. If a flower remedy could really stop eating disorders, it would cost $5000 dollars a bottle. The FDA would yank it off the shelves in ten minutes, and you'd have to fly to Europe to get it. (Many would go, though—there'd be charter flights.)

I do want to mention Bach's **Sweet Chestnut**, for that dark night of the soul when you are bottoming out, and their **Wild Rose**, when you've given up and have sunk into apathy. Pegasus' **Sugar Beet** and **Sugar Cane** are helpful in restoring physical and emotional balance if long-term sugar and carbohydrate abuse have created a functional hypoglycemia. (If you regularly get up at night and eat, this may be the reason.) Be aware that some of Pegasus' remedies are premixed into dosage rather than stock strength. Read the label for directions.

It is nearly as impossible for foodaholics to get thin and stay that way on their own as it is for alcoholics to get sober alone. The fellowship of Overeaters Anonymous provides emotional and spiritual tools for recovery from eating disorders. It also provides the support of a group to help you through rough times when you would ordinarily want to eat.[3]

To lick this disease, you will need every ounce of that famed Cancerian tenacity. Since overeating is a lunar problem, many of the tools described in this book are additional supports. You also need to develop a tough, crab-like shell to avoid being hurt by every bump and bruise life has to offer. And yet, not eating compulsively, being able to trust yourself, is the greatest security there is. You can do it, with help from others and love for yourself.

---

[3]To find the nearest meeting, check telephone information in your area, or write to Overeaters Anonymous, 4025 Spencer Street, Suite 203, Torrance, CA 90503, or call 213-542-8363.

Talking to the Moon—the Technique of Astrodrama

If losing touch with the Moon leads to eating compulsively, then getting in touch with it can be part of the solution. Astrodrama is an interesting technique for having a dialogue with your Moon. An astrology class or group can act out parts of a chart, each person taking on the role of a planet, so that the dynamics of a problem can be seen. The drama is an improvization, each participant saying things that reflect the traits of the planet being portrayed. As few as two can do it, dealing with a single aspect; or a small number can participate and focus on the planets most germane to the question. For instance, in dramatizing a Moon problem, such as compulsive overeating, the strongest aspects to the Moon can be singled out.

Astrodrama was used in a small group of astrologers who struggle with food. One of them gave me permission to share her astrodrama, so you can get a flavor of how it works. She is not seriously overweight, yet is often tortured by food. She overeats and then diets strenuously to stay reasonably thin, a pattern common to many with eating disorders.

If you are a general reader, the "cast of characters" that follows will explain the role played by each planet. The astrology student, however, might like to know a few details about the horoscope in this astrodrama. For reasons of confidentiality, the chart will not be reproduced. The aspects bearing on her food problem were:

1. Moon-Neptune conjunct in Libra in the 9th house.
2. Venus in Capricorn in the 1st house, square the Moon-Neptune conjunction.
3. Pluto in Leo in the 7th house, sextile the Moon-Neptune conjunction.
4. Saturn in Virgo in the 8th house, semi-sextile both the Moon-Neptune conjunction and Pluto.

The Cast of Characters: There were five participants in the astrodrama. Someone played the Moon, someone else played Neptune, and so on. Here are the qualities of each planet:

Moon: Dependency, security, emotions, food and feeding, the wish for home, family, and roots. With the Moon in Libra, she seeks security through a partner. In the 9th house, due to moving around often in childhood, there was increased insecurity, which the person intellectualizes away.

Neptune: A wish to escape emotions and harsh realities, suffering, confusion, illusion, and self-deception; a spiritual focus, a wish to unite with all there is. In Libra, there is a yearning to lose the self in some kind of ideal relationship. In the 9th house, this yearning is displaced onto philosophical concerns.

Saturn: Authority, achievement, and recognition; discipline, severity, and spartanness. In Virgo, Saturn is even more respectable and uptight, focusing on work and health concerns. In the 8th house, there is a strong tendency toward sexual inhibitions.

Venus: Beauty, attractiveness, the desire for love. In Capricorn, Venus is reserved and perfectionistic about appearances, convinced that only achievement will win you love. In the 1st house, the concern about appearance is heightened. There is a strong desire for attention—which may be achieved through beauty.

Pluto: Control, the wish for power, manipulation, guilt. In Leo, Pluto is somewhat narcissistic and demanding of attention, although this sign placement was true of an entire generation, now called "the me generation." In the 7th house, there can be a fear of closeness and a tendency to let the partner be the powerful one, denying one's own power.

Note that the statements made by each character are a synthesis of sign, planet and house—i.e., Venus talks as Venus in Capricorn in the 1st house, so the character consists of more than just Venus alone.

The curtain is going up:

MOON: I need, I need! I feel insecure. I wish someone would take care of me.

NEPTUNE: Why don't you just go to the movies? You'll forget your troubles.

MOON: I want popcorn then.

NEPTUNE: So have popcorn. Have some candy, too. You never got that as a child.

VENUS: Just be sure to do it the proper way. Only the best buttered popcorn and only have a little bit so you don't gain weight.

MOON: I don't think the movies will help, or the popcorn either. I need!

SATURN: You don't need. That's a bad, sinful thing. You've got to learn to discipline yourself.

PLUTO: Oh, but your partner's going to provide the discipline. You're doing it all for him.

NEPTUNE: Yes, I'll forget my own needs and suffer for the relationship. That'll make it work.

MOON: I still need, but I know what I'll do. I'll eat a big box of popcorn at the movies and then skip supper.

SATURN: You can't do that! It's terrible for your health!

PLUTO: Besides, you have to eat supper with your partner.

VENUS: All that matters anyway is that you look good. Wear a freshly pressed dress.

NEPTUNE: This is too overwhelming for me. I'm at one with all of you and I don't know who to listen to. I'll have lots of popcorn, and then I'll have dinner with my partner, but I'll wear a pretty dress and cook health food for him. That way, I'll make everybody happy and keep everything peaceful.

MOON: You're not making me happy. I just don't feel secure. We've moved around so much, two months here, two months there, that I don't feel like I have a home or any roots.

PLUTO: You just haven't met the right man. When you do, you'll settle down and have a home and feel just fine.

MOON: I need right now. I never get any mothering.

NEPTUNE: I'll just do yoga again today. Then I'll cry a lot.

MOON: But it's not just tears. I'm angry!

VENUS: You shouldn't be displaying all these nasty emotions. It's just not ladylike.

NEPTUNE: I'll write angry poems instead.

VENUS: But don't show them to anyone.

SATURN: Or else make sure they get published.

MOON: I don't feel at all comforted by that. I'm getting hungry again.

NEPTUNE: You're not real anyway. In yoga, we're trying to transcend you, so poof on you.

MOON: What do I have in the refrigerator? I need something immediate and direct. What I really need is love.

VENUS: You need too much love. It's unseemly.

NEPTUNE: GOD is the only love there is.

SATURN: You'll get love if you're successful.

MOON: Rum Raisin! Honey Haagen Daz!

VENUS: That's good . . . no additives.

PLUTO: But your partner likes chocolate better. Get chocolate to please him.

NEPTUNE: Have chocolate *and* rum raisin. You'll feel better.

MOON: To be perfectly honest, I don't feel satisfied. Not even if I have a gallon of ice cream.

SATURN: You never feel satisfied. You want too much.

NEPTUNE: There's no way to find satisfaction on the earthly plane anyhow, so get to a place where it doesn't matter.

MOON: Burp!

As you can see, astrodrama can be fun. It is also powerful and cathartic, as different parts of yourself appear and talk about the conflicts you carry around inside. They are easier to hear this way, since they are so often silenced by overeating or other defenses. Astrodrama can be used to explore many lunar issues, such as what to do with feelings, how to deal with the mother within, or how to resolve unmet dependency needs.

CHAPTER 13

MEN, MACHISMO, AND THE MOON

A 1994 New York Times best-seller proclaimed that men are from Mars and women are from Venus. The author, Dr. John Gray, never mentioned astrology, yet his descriptions are so close to traditional astrological teachings that one of three things must be true. One, he could be a brilliant and inspired observer of humanity who intuitively but independently arrived at the same conclusions astrologers did centuries ago. Maybe he reinvented the (chart) wheel. It happens. Once in a blue Moon. Two, he could be another of the "experts" who rip off astrology and don't give us credit. Or, three, perhaps he's simply a malleable writer whose agent or editor argued, "You've got a potential best-seller on your hands. If you mention astrology, nobody's going to take you seriously. Do you really want to take that chance?"

By the way, the bulk of this chapter appeared in the earlier edition of this book fifteen years ago, while Gray was probably still slaving over his Ph.D., so I haven't borrowed anything from him. I do recommend his book for its sane and gentle methods of helping men and women get along. However, Gray neglects to mention that most Venusians wind up relocating to the Moon after they marry.

In traditional astrology, Mars is said to rule men, and, due to the programming we receive, this teaching is right. How do men deal with the Moon? They generally do it in Martian ways and, as we will see, they pay a high price for ignoring their lunar functions. We'll look at men's Moon signs and the Cancer rising wheel for more insights and ways to heal the split between Mars and the Moon.

> Seen on a secretary's coffee mug: "If we can send one
> man to the Moon, why can't we send them all?"

Mars and the Male Mystique

In most areas of their lives, men do not feel they are being REAL MEN unless they are acting out the traits of Mars. It's not true to say that men ARE
Mars, but they ACT Mars because our culture believes that is what a man
should be. Mars was the god of war, and in a horoscope Mars has to do with
our warlike, aggressive instincts. Both medicine and pop culture have chosen the symbol for Mars ♂ to represent men.

Mars is machismo, virility, strength, and power. It's being cool, independent, the fearless leader, defending your territory against any infringe-
ment. Whether it's your woman, your job, or your top-dog position, you're
supposed to be ready to fight for it. It's being the jock, watching the game
every Sunday. The male version of the Ten Commandments was handed
down by the great god Mars. Don't cry, don't show weakness, and don't ask
for affection. Be steel, not flesh-and-blood, and take punishment without
flinching. Not all of them live up to these stereotypes or even want to do so.
Nonetheless, they may judge themselves and be judged by others on their
ability to live up to them.

Mars also symbolizes sex, and men carry very powerful and painful
myths about their sexuality. They're supposed to be ready all the time, to be
aggressive and conquering. As a result, many have tremendous anxiety about
their performance and potency. They are also hung up on size. Whether it's
the size of their penis, your breasts, their car, or their paycheck, the bigger it
is, the more powerful they feel.

Men are very involved with another Mars concern—competition.
They are taught that you're only worth something if you're a winner, and
anyone who isn't winning is a loser. They learn that any vulnerability, any
lack of competency is a failure. Consider the hard-driving Type A who has
a heart attack. If he has to curtail his activities, he feels he has failed and gets
depressed. Many men have tremendous self-hatred when they're not winning. Even as little boys, their dealings with others generally have a competitive edge.

It's hard for men to break out of these stereotypes because of heavy social penalties. They may suffer consequences ranging from ridicule (being

called a wimp or fag), to social and economic losses (they don't get recommended, don't develop business contacts), all the way to downright brutality. Women are also guilty of pressuring men to live up to Martian ideals, but more subtly. Then we blame them for being insensitive if they *are* Mars. In many ways, gay men are more free to express the lunar energy, yet they pay the price of ostracism. Most men are terrified to be thought the least bit feminine, and there are real reasons for this fear. Some patterns are slowly changing, but unless society evolves, those who try to break out of the mold will require plenty of support.

Unfortunately, we can't be whole and healthy unless we're free to express traits symbolized by all the planets. Men have a hard time expressing all the so-called female planets—the Moon, Venus, Neptune, and Pluto—due to the Mars model. They deny these traits and project them onto women. "I'm not like that. I don't need anybody. I'm cool. It's women who are like that." Anything repressed comes out in distorted ways, and men pay a heavy price for their roles, just as women do. If they act out their so-called feminine side, they suffer social and economic losses. If they don't, they suffer physical and emotional damage. Damned if they do and damned if they don't.

One of the consequences is that those who can't deal with their emotions and needs in healthier ways are prone to violence. Of those arrested for serious crimes in the U.S. in 1992, 80 percent were men. They represented 90 percent of the murders, 91 percent of robberies, 86 percent of the DUIs, 86 percent of drug arrests, and 85 percent of aggravated assault. Four times as many men as women commit suicide.[1] This staggering amount of mayhem is related to the damage done to their lunar hemisphere by the demand that it be suppressed.

Like nothing else, this very serious set of statistics underlines how damaging it is to all of us when men are kept from dealing with their emotions in healthy ways. When that hemisphere is ignored and rage is the only outlet for a variety of emotions, pressure builds up. The added stress of a new or full Moon can topple an already perilous balance, and set off a violent outburst. On a mass level, this results in a peak of assault, rape, and homicide at these phases of the Moon. Of course, the majority of men handle these stresses well enough that they aren't violent, just as most of us aren't sent off the deep end by the full Moon. However, as the lunar supports are eroded for all of us, crime rates keep rising.

---

[1]U.S. Bureau of the Census, *Statistical Abstract of the United States*, 114th edition. Washington, DC, 1994.

Men Who Come from Mars—or Krypton

Let's look at the charts of some famous men to see how their astrological makeup reflects these dynamics. The charts of many male sex symbols that our culture looks up to are heavily Mars and Aries. The Moon in Aries would be the most macho approach to the lunar areas. Some of our most classic tough guys—like Jimmy Cagney, Marlon Brando, and Al Capone—had Moon in Aries.

The ultimate symbol of machismo is Superman. He didn't come from Mars, he came from Krypton, but it must be a near twin. His birth records were smashed to smithereens when Krypton exploded, but I reasoned that the first radio broadcast was when he came to life for us. I dug

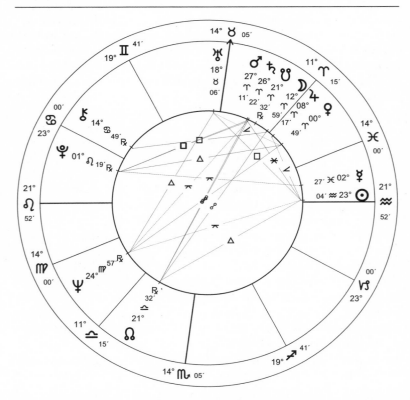

Chart 9. The horoscope of the first Superman broadcast. The radio program went on the air on February 12, 1940 at 5:15 P.M. in New York City. The Placidus house system was used for the chart. Data from the New York Times *archives.*

into the New York Times archives and found the data for the first broad-cast.[2] Chart 9 (page 248) is for the time the broadcast began. Considering transits for various events, the Midheaven seems about a degree off. (He probably didn't speak for a few minutes after the program started.) The chart definitely fits him. Having five planets in Aries is ultra-macho, espe-cially since the Moon and Venus—the main "female" planets—are among them. Leo rising adds to the fire, and Uranus, which is extremely detached, aspects his Aquarius Sun. A potent fantasy figure, he has all the Mars traits: invulnerability, strength, independence, and readiness to fight.

While the chart describes him well, a test of a chart's validity is whether transits fit the events. Astrology students might enjoy seeing how well the transits fit these Superevents: 1) the publishing of the first comic book in June, 1932; 2) the airing of the first television show on February 9, 1953; 3) the shutdown of the television production on November 27, 1957; 4) George Reeves' suicide on June 16, 1969 (he died of a gunshot wound to the head—Mars and Aries rule the head and guns); and 5) the release of *Superman, the Movie* on December 10, 1978.

Christopher Reeve played Superman in the modern sequels. According to a private letter from Lois Rodden, he was born September 25, 1952 in New York City. He told Terry Krall he was born at 3:30 A.M. EDT and told Linda Clark 3:12 A.M. EDT. At 3:30 A.M., his Ascendant and Midheaven are within one degree of the Ascendant and Midheaven of the Superman chart. That's one reason, no doubt, that he suits the part so well.

Most Men ARE from Mars, but Some Come from the Moon

After studying these Martians, I began to wonder about the lunar types. Franklin Delano Roosevelt, who helped Americans survive the strains of the Great Depression and World War II with his weekly fireside chats, had Moon in Cancer. (So did his wife Eleanor and their cousin, president Theodore Roosevelt. Moon signs do run in families.) Dr. Benjamin Spock, the pedia-trician who taught parenting skills to generations, also had Moon in Cancer, the placement that would be the most lunar. James MacNeil Whistler, most remembered for his painting of his mother, was a Cancer Sun. Lest you think Cancer men can't be macho, Ernest Hemingway was a Cancer Sun, with

---

[2]Date of broadcast from Grossman, *Superman: Serial to Cereal* (New York: Popular Library, 1976). Time of broadcast from the *New York Times*, December 12, 1940.

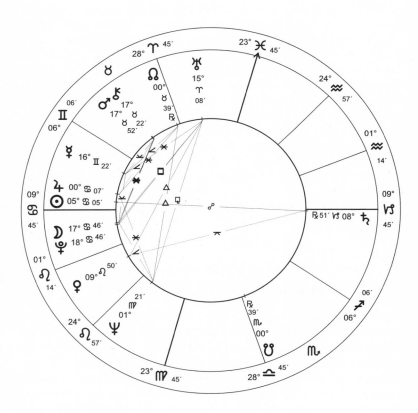

Chart 10. The horoscope of Ross Perot, born June 27, 1930, at 5:34 A.M. CST in Texarkana, TX. Data from the birth certificate, given in Michel and Francoise Gauquelin's The Gauquelin Book of American Charts *(San Diego, CA: ACS Publications, 1982). The Placidus house system is used here.*

tremendous sensitivity and emotionality hiding behind his tough shell. Arnold Schwarzenegger, with those awesome pecs, has Cancer rising.

Ross Perot (Chart 10), billionaire and would-be U.S. president, is a mega-lunar type. He is a triple Cancer—Sun, Moon, and Ascendant—with Jupiter in Cancer conjunct his Sun, and Pluto in Cancer conjunct his Moon. Triple Cancers are rare, as there are only about six hours in a year when they can be born. The same is true, naturally, of triples of any sign. (Actually, if you followed the material in chapter 2 on signs of long and short ascension, the correct figures would be about 6-1/4 hours a year for triple Cancers and 4-3/4 hours a year for triple Aquarians. In addition, many more Cancers are born than Aquarians, due to the seasonal birth rate differences we discussed.)

When Perot ran for president as a third-party candidate in 1992, Uranus and Neptune in Capricorn were opposite his Cancer Moon. Since the Moon rules the public, he was a sensation, appealing as he did to emotions and playing on family values. The country was in an insecure mood, yearning to return to the safety of the past and tradition. It wasn't enough to get him elected, but he was the man of the hour. He drew enough votes from each party to affect the outcome of the election, and retained enough of a following afterward to be a political force.

A love of the homeland is a Cancerian trait sometimes carried to extremes. As an example of Cancer's patriotism gone malignant, white supremacist David Duke has Sun in Cancer, Moon in Aquarius—the same combination that appears in the U.S. chart, and with all the tensions we've discussed before. (According to Issue #36 of Lois Rodden's excellent newsletter, "Data News," his birth certificate says he was born July 1, 1950 at 11:37 A.M. CST in Tulsa, OK.)

On the other side of the world and of the political spectrum, another Cancerian patriot is Nelson Mandela. South African astrologers now use the birth time of 12:54 GMT, as confirmed by Mandela himself. He was born July 18, 1918 in Umtata, South Africa, 28E47, 31S35. Noel Tyl worked with the chart and feels 2:54 EET (e.g. 12:54 GMT) fits the events well. Mandela's Moon is in Scorpio in the 12th house, and it is certain that he would have died for his country, had that sacrifice been required. His election to the presidency in 1994 came as Pluto in Scorpio trined his Cancer Sun and Uranus opposed it. He certainly qualifies as a lunar hero.

David Dinkins, New York's first African-American mayor, is a Cancer born July 10, 1927. He is a deeply caring man and a dignified advocate for his people, though not fortunate in his associates. The most moving moment—among many—we witnessed on TV occurred when he visited a ghetto grade school. A small African-American boy sat on his lap and asked him, "How's your job?" He answered, "It's a hard job sometimes, but it's a good one. If you study hard, when you grow up, you could be mayor too."

Lunar men *can* be wonderful! In the best of them, there's a quality of kindness and empathy. Not so egotistical as the solar types, they can be paternal without being paternalistic, protective without being patronizing. Bill Cosby, a Cancer Sun, appeals to us with his fatherly qualities, as seen in his delightful comedic interactions with children and in his book, *Fatherhood.*[3] Lunar men can remind us of home and a gentler time. The down-home style of Willie Nelson, who has Moon in Cancer, comforts those whose roots have been lost or damaged. Lunar men give great hugs, and lots of them are just big old Teddy bears. (Is this embarrassing you, guys? It's not like I was telling them how mushy you are.) If you were ever going to find a sensitive, New Age guy, you'd find him among the lunar types. Especially since they are not always well appreciated in the solar world, let's give them a vote of thanks.

O. J. Simpson—a Lunar Hemisphere Gone Ballistic

No doubt we all had our fill of the minutia of the Simpson case. However, O. J. Simpson's chart deserves another look, for he epitomizes the devastation of a lunar hemisphere gone ballistic. He has Sun, Venus, and Mercury in Cancer, so he's a lunar type (see Chart 11). As my friend Leya Heart discovered, his Mercury is only 11 minutes from an exact conjunction to the United States' Mercury, a retrograde Mercury in both instances. Transiting Uranus (television) and Neptune (scandal) opposed that degree during 1994 and 1995, while Americans watched in morbid fascination as the case unfolded.

O. J.'s Moon is in Pisces in the 8th house (sex, wealth, and death) squaring Uranus. Even more than Moon in Aquarius, Moon-Uranus aspects can be intermittently explosive unless the person consciously attends to emotions and keeps the lunar hemisphere balanced. So determined was O. J. to mold Nicole into his dream woman (Pisces Moon) he allegedly forced her to have breast implants. An unevolved Pisces Moon can escape from feelings through addictions. Since his Moon is in the 8th house, one of O. J.'s addictions was apparently women and sex. Uranus is self-willed, a law unto itself, so any opposition to his desires, any threat to the lunar realms,

---

[3]Bill Cosby, *Fatherhood* (New York: Berkley Publishing, 1994).

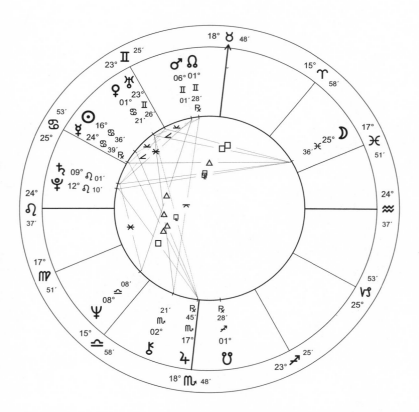

Chart 11. The horoscope of O. J. Simpson, born July 9, 1947, at 8:08 A.M. PST in San Francisco, CA. Information from the birth certificate. (Reprinted from Astro-Data II, *with permission of Lois M. Rodden. San Diego: Astro Computing Services, 1980.) The Placidus house system is used here.*

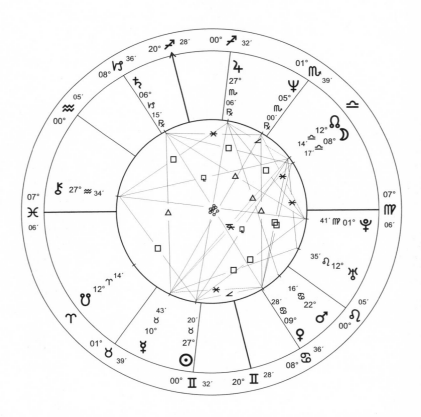

Chart 12. The horoscope of Nicole Brown Simpson, born May 19, 1959, at 2:00 A.M. CET in Frankfurt-am-Main, Germany. Information from the birth certificate, secured by Marion March. (Published in Lois Rodden's "Data News" #50 December 1994.) The Placidus house system is used here.

could produce an explosion. The Moon is domestic, and Uranus, at its un-hinged worst, can represent violence. As shown by the 911 tapes, domestic violence was the result of his lack of balance in the lunar hemisphere.

Nicole (Chart 12, page 254) has the Moon in Libra in the 7th house, depicting a lunar marriage partner. It is squared by Venus in Cancer in her 5th house, which was near O. J.'s Sun. Her Mars, at 22 Cancer, was conjunct O. J.'s Mercury, a combination that can produce many arguments. Transiting Uranus was setting off that conjunction when she was murdered on June 12, 1994, around 10:15 P.M. in Los Angeles. There is much more in both charts, and you are invited to study them. However, my focus here is on the Moon. O. J.'s lack of balance in the lunar areas of life produced a great tragedy—in the life of one of America's most-loved sports figures. And, no, it doesn't have to be that way, if men take care of their Moons rather than ignore them.[4]

"Why Can't a Woman be More Like A Man?"

That's the question Professor Higgins asked in *My Fair Lady*. It's still asked by every standup comedian and locker-room-philosopher today. It was probably the first question debated by the cavemen, as soon as they mas-tered enough language to do more than shrug their shoulders and grunt, Tim Allen style. The answer lies in our brains and our hormones.

There's a large hormonal difference between us—a lunar hormone for women and a Martian one for men. As seen earlier, women are very responsive to estrogen. It is the key to lunar functions such as water balance, mood swings, and appetite. Men have very little estrogen in their system. Androgens are male hormones, which women have only in minor amounts. Androgen seems Mar-tian, being the source of the masculine physique: the beard, the hair on the chest, the muscles, and the deeper voice. The emotional effects of androgen are not all known, but aggressiveness seems part of it. While both biology and cul-ture may pressure men to act Mars, neither can eliminate the necessity to inte-grate the feminine planets. Biology is not destiny for them either.

There are documented differences in the way male and female brains are organized. Observations from infancy onward show clear differences in

---

[4]Because Pluto was trining his Moon (the public) at the time of her murder, I did predict all along that he'd be acquitted—not in print, naturally, but you can ask the gals in my astrology group. The only exact aspect at the time of the verdict in October 1995 was Mars crossing his Jupiter, but there were several loose favorable aspects to his Moon.

the intellectual and motor skills of males and females, despite age or nationality. Thirty items had to be eliminated from the original IQ tests because they discriminated in favor of one or the other sex. Females from infancy on were more responsive to social exchanges, especially from their mothers (the Moon and Venus). Males responded more to objects and manipulating them (Mars and Uranus).

Women are apparently more developed than most men in the lunar hemisphere, and estrogen apparently has something to do with this difference. Female rats, whose ovaries were removed at birth and who therefore were estrogen deficient, wound up having brain development more like males.[5] However, men don't have a one-sided brain any more than women do. Although women are put down for being lunar, it is still "expected," whereas lunar responses are generally disapproved for men. As a result, they have even more difficulty than women do in attuning to the lunar hemisphere. It is even more important for them to participate in activities that liberate their intuitive and emotional faculties.

The Moon/Mars Aspect and Male Psychology

Men are programmed to act like Mars even when dealing with such lunar concerns as security and dependency. It struck me that most men function like they have a Moon-Mars aspect in their horoscope. An aspect combines the energy of two or more planets. When Mars programming is imposed onto lunar functions, you get a Moon-Mars result. We're not talking about an actual chart, but about the effect of sex role stereotypes. To express this problem visually, I came up with figure 4 showing the Moon forced to fit into the symbol for Mars.

Mars-ruled Aries squares Moon-ruled Cancer, and men generally have trouble facing the Cancerian qualities in themselves and others. Perhaps these qualities inhibit action. Traditionally, Mars is considered in its "fall" in Cancer (meaning, at its worst). This designation reflects how little men's lunar qualities are accepted in the Western world. Let's go through several functions of the Moon to see what happens when you try to fit them into the prism of Mars.

Men and Mothering: Mars is symbolic of independence, and the Moon-Mars merger pushes men to deny their dependency. They can go to ex-

---

[5]"Sex Differences in Brain Asymmetries," *Brain/Mind Bulletin*, v.5:14, p. 1680.

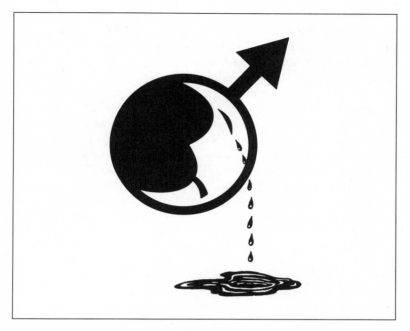

Figure 4. This is an illustration of the pain and discomfort felt when the symbol for the Moon is forced to reside within the symbol for Mars. See her tears?

treme lengths to protest their self-sufficiency, in the familiar defense of counter-dependence. The boy child is trained to be Martian: "Be a little man! Be strong. Don't cry when you're hurt." He is supposed to shun affection and turn away from his mother, other women, and girls, to seek the company of other guys. The pressure to be independent increases as he grows up. Yet, that which is suppressed becomes all the more potent under the surface.

In reality, men are extremely dependent on women in family life, sexually, and in business. Men's true reliance on women has been demonstrated by studies about what happens when that woman goes away. The divorced man has an annual death rate three times the divorced woman. Widowers died at 40 percent above the expected rate in the six months following the death of their wives. Those who have recently lost their mothers are more prone to suicide than other men. Single men of all ages have the highest suicide rates. Men who lose their female support systems experience a crisis of dependency and rage (Moon-Mars) they can find it difficult to survive. Similarly, the Moon represents the mother, and when a man marries a woman who looks like his mother, the marriage lasts twice as often as when she doesn't.[6]

Mars represents anger, and a Moon-Mars aspect can show hostility toward women. Men are angry with women, among other reasons, for the very fact of needing them. Many men hate themselves for feeling dependent on women, so they turn it around and feel hostile toward women—a defense that increases distance. A Moon-Mars aspect also shows angry frustration at not getting needs met. It's a vicious cycle—it's hard to take care of someone who is protesting, "I'm strong. I don't need you. I can handle this."

Another Moon-Mars defense is to take on the role of caretaker and protector, like the traditional male stance toward "the little woman." Men use it to avoid feeling they need anyone, or having anyone think they might be weak. The more of a caretaker you set yourself up to be, the angrier you can become, because this draining stance creates even stronger dependency underneath. The protector role is a front, because most of them find it hard to cope with taking care of others due to their own frustrated needs. Look how angry and helpless they become when the woman in their life falls ill, and they have to take care of her.

Denial of dependency is devastating when it comes to actual vulnerability, as in illness. We are all more needy when we are sick. Yet, men may deny their pain until they collapse, and avoid going to the doctor until it is too late. They may even work twice as hard while pretending nothing is wrong. Most of them have a hard time asking for help. As a result, they get more sick, stay ill longer, and die sooner than women. Men have a higher death rate in 14 out of 15 leading causes of death.

At every age, the male death rate is higher than the female. From age 20-24, it is 200 percent higher, due to Mars causes such as fights, daredevil stunts, and wars. Twice as many men as women die in accidents, and 3-1/2 times as many die of homicide or legal intervention. At all age levels, the death rate is at least twice as high as for women. During the outer planet transits, the ratio has become worse, an indication that lunar erosion is affecting men badly. In 1920, the female life expectancy was only one year higher than for men. It's now seven years higher, so the inability to ask for help has serious physical consequences.[7]

---

[6]The statistics in this paragraph are from Theodore I. Rubin and David C. Berliner, *Understanding Your Man: A Woman's Guide* (New York: Ballantine, 1977), p. 31.

[7]U.S. Bureau of the Census, *Statistical Abstract of the United States*, 114th edition. Washington, DC, 1994, pp. 88, 94.

Men and Moods: Another reason men have higher death rates is that repressed feelings are psychosomatically displaced into their bodies. Men who readily express emotions are considered weak or effeminate, so men deny them and project them onto women. As uncomfortable as men are with emotions, they are also fascinated by them. The acceptable feelings for men are the Mars ones—anger and triumph. Lunar reactions, like insecurity, are unacceptable so are forced into the mold of Mars, and are often expressed as irritability. Softer, more positive reactions have to be put down, too, because men are uneasy about "feminine" emotions. When those tender feelings are deadened, we all suffer from the loss of a kinder, more gentle quality of life. They especially hide loving and nurturing responses behind a front of toughness. Unless we read between the lines, we may never know these qualities are there.

Paradoxically, men are also not allowed to show aggressiveness. They are expected to be aggressive, but they're supposed to be cool about it. It's a fine line to walk. In particular, men are not permitted to express hostility toward women, because men who pick on women are scorned. For a man to get angry at a woman, he's supposed to have just cause, like cheating on him, insulting his masculinity, or not feeding him on time. We've already seen how unconsciously angry men can be at women. To rationalize this anger, they have to find plenty of causes in women's behavior.

And many do find serious justification, with tragic results. In the U.S. in 1992, 82 percent of those arrested for domestic violence were men. Canadian statistics show that a married woman is nine times more likely to be killed by her husband than by a stranger, with young wives at the greatest risk. The rates rise sharply when couples separate. In case you thought it was safer to just live together, the homicide rates for both parties are greater in common law marriages than in registered ones.[8] The phenomenon of stalking has only recently come to our awareness, but it is so serious and so pervasive that most states are quickly enacting laws against it. According to a recent HBO documentary on violence in the work place—another new worry—one working woman in 20 will be stalked in at least one period of her life.

What is the result of the pressures on men to deny their feelings? Besides illness, repressed emotions can burst forth in sudden, unpredictable behavior, like drinking binges, explosions of violence, reckless driving, and other "crazy" actions. A man who is explosive pushes others away, as they

---

[8]Margo Wilson, Martin Daly, and Christine Wright, "Uxorcide in Canada: Demographic Risk Patterns," *Canadian Journal of Criminology*, July 1993, v.35:3, pp. 263–281.

don't know what to expect. One minute he may be perfectly friendly and the next minute he may be ready to fight. To keep control, he has to keep his distance. He is alternately deadened or acting out wildly. We've already seen the statistics on male violence.

The growth of psychological awareness through talk shows, self-help books, and other pop phenomena create counter-pressures for men to deal with feelings more openly. That sounds hopeful, and yet it is crazy-making in this transitional era, because they're getting double messages. Our culture is still not comfortable with men who are emotional—even women who are psychologically aware can be ambivalent about it. Then, too, the demands of the business world don't disappear. Try going out on the stock market floor and bursting into tears because you've just lost a million bucks for your client. Until the public is more educated about the importance of dealing with feelings, men who try to do so will require support.

Another contribution to the problem is that men are also increasingly denied healthy channels for their Mars energy. Consider that the sign Aries, which Mars rules, has been under the same pressures that Cancer has from the outer planets. (Aries is square Cancer and Capricorn and opposite Libra.) In some parallel reality, my male counterpart is writing a book called, *Being a Mars Type in a Saturn World.* He's lamenting that there is no longer any room for the development of the warrior self—that now the side with the bigger guns invariably wins. He's scorning the gym and saying that walking a treadmill or pumping iron is hollow exercise compared to building your own barn or plowing the fields where you will grow your family's food. He's saying that "civilization" means squelching the fight response in favor of flight. He counsels, for instance, that on the job it is no longer prudent to just deck somebody who gets in your face. Now they write you up for it—if you don't get suspended or arrested for assault. Nor is one free any longer to pursue an attractive coworker, for she might just sue you for sexual harassment. He concludes that given all that bottled up Mars energy with no constructive outlet, is it any wonder that violence is on the rise? Oh, yes, Martian types are under seige, too.

Men and Security: The Moon rules security, and men crave it as much as women. Since insecurity would not be thought manly by either sex, it is not expressed openly. That beat-up old hunting cap may represent security, and that's why he gets so mad when you try to throw it out. Feelings of attachment to the home, family, and roots are unacceptable and must be put down as sentiment. "It's my old lady who's so hot on this holiday thing. I just do it for her and the kids."

A man may only feel secure if he's taking action to ward off any threat to the status quo. He's got to take charge and do battle. He becomes enraged at his own impotence if there's no action that will work, such as during a recession or the fatal illness of someone he loves. The Moon-Mars symbolism also explains why men are so willing to go to war to defend any actual or presumed threat to the HOMEland.

Meat, Potatoes, and the Moon: The Moon rules food and the stomach. The REAL MAN thrives on meat and potatoes, but that diet is damaging to the body, especially to the stomach and colon. A heavy intake of meat also increases aggressiveness, as opposed to the calming vegetarian diet. Blood-dripping, red-centered steak is the most Martian food going. With the new emphasis on health and fitness, however, many are eating differently now.

Men's dependency on women is strongly expressed in food—for instance, in the old belief that the way to a man's heart is through the stomach. A common excuse for why the wife shouldn't attend self-improvement activities, or be away any length of time, is, "What would my husband eat?" God forbid a man should know how to cook, except, of course, if he excels in gourmet cooking. Even then, the man has to watch himself very carefully, as the suspicion hovers that he might be gay.

Of course, now sophisticated urban gentlemen may cook for their dates. However, it is often more a ploy to score than a real love of cooking. The applause they receive for cooking so much as a hot dog is disproportionate to the perfunctory thanks women generally get for a great meal. (And, who ever applauded a woman for changing a sparkplug?) Still, there is more room now for men to share the cooking than there was ten or fifteen years ago.

Stomach trouble in a man is a signal that he's stuffing a load of feelings. For example, in medical astrology, ulcers are a Moon-Mars disease related to anger over unmet dependency. For most of this century, ulcers were a "guy" thing, with ten times as many men suffering from them as women. (Women are beginning to catch up, as we enter the business world.)

Men who are not Mars: Much is made of gay men's fear and dislike of women—too much, I think. In my experience of both gay and straight men, I find straight men just as angry and fearful. Straight men may not express it so openly (after all, they have to get over). It comes out in street cat-calls, locker room talk, and sexist behavior that can be extremely hostile. Male stand-up comics joke with thinly-disguised rage about the differences between women and men, while their audiences roar.

Gay men become uneasy and angry when women insist on pursuing them and trying to convert them (a common phenomenon), just as any of us would become uneasy at persistent unwelcome advances. For gay men, the fear of women may be more overt, as they are often less defended against the woman within and more afraid of being engulfed by it. They are also not immune to the cultural pressures against their so-called effeminate traits. Those who show them have been exposed to punitive measures. Nonetheless, many fine gay men I have known seem to better integrate both male and female planets, being more androgynous than men who can only act Mars. Perhaps it is because they've gone past that ultimate male deterrent to the gentler pursuits—"What are you anyway, a faggot?"

There are also many straight men who are breaking out of the Mars mold and becoming more whole and integrated. Those who move in this direction are subjected to severe counter-pressures and need support. Men are not used to supporting each other emotionally, but "Iron John" gatherings sponsored by Robert Bly, or John Bradshaw's gatherings of men, could help those who are trying to break out of the mold.

Men and Their Moon Signs

We've seen that the Moon-Mars aspect is a general signature for men. The Moon's sign, house, and aspects are important in the individual's chart, but may be hidden behind the Mars stereotype. Keep that programming in mind as you read a man's chart and interpret his Moon. For example, consider a man with a prominent Moon, or important placements in Cancer, or the 4th house. He would have strong lunar drives, and yet would feel pressure to hide them. How painful that must be, and how ulcer-making. The capsule descriptions that follow should illuminate the psychology of the individual man. We will weigh his own lunar style against the culture's pressures to deny the Moon and express it only through the prism of Mars. Remember to consult the readings based on the Moon's aspects, as illustrated in chapter 4.

Moon in Aries: The conflicts we've discussed are doubly strong in a man who actually has an Aries Moon or a Moon-Mars aspect. Dependency is threatening, and he keeps on the move to avoid sticky involvements. He looks for a take-charge female who won't expect to be babied and who might accidentally nurture him a bit while running the show. Unfortunately, Mom also wore the pants, and he's got a chip on his shoulder toward women because of it. He takes a fighting stance toward any threat to his security. Action is his remedy for any problem, even those with no immediate solution. Emotions threaten him, too, so look for a good fight if you provoke any. It's hard to get next to him with the soft, sharing aspects of relating because it's so hard for him to own up to those parts of himself. For him, sex may be a sublimation of the finer facets of intimacy.

Moon in Taurus: He accepts the cultural stereotypes of what men and women ought to be because he's old-fashioned. He basically likes women. He chooses the ones who do good Moon things in a consistent and down-to-earth way, like Mom did, in return for his protectiveness and stability. He then feels he has to make a killing in the business world. Material things are security and insurance that the lady won't leave him stranded with his dependency needs down. Food has strong associations of security, comfort, and squelching feelings that might interfere with serenity. He can, however, become the raging bull when pressured to change too quickly. Ditto when there are threats to his security, such as a loss of money, belongings, or the lady in his life! Thus, he can be possessive and rather jealous.

Moon in Gemini: Intellectually he might reject the macho stereotype because that's how he handles everything—intellectually. He knows feelings exist because he's read all about them, and he can talk about them quite articulately. Neither he nor you should get too deeply into them, however, or he might have to fight you off with that glib tongue and facile wit. Words are a screen to avoid closeness and prevent anyone from recognizing his vulnerability. Dependency simply isn't logical in a grown man, so it isn't to be tolerated. Nothing can make him insecure as long as it's analyzed and categorized. However, give him something to deal with that he can't put a label on and he gets thrown for a loop. It's nice that he's found a woman of your intellectual caliber who can appreciate his brilliance and wit. Mom always said he'd be the next Hemingway.

Moon in Cancer: These are the real lunar types, the ones who are bound to run into problems with machismo. The lunar qualities are too strong and immediate to ignore, so such a man may develop a tough shell to maintain his cool. He is also likely to marry a real earth mother who'll meet his needs automatically without him having to ask. His own mother may have been a smotherer, and he's often still tied to her symbiotically. If he has to hide his feelings, he can seek relief by eating or drinking too much, or by remaining overly dependent on his family. Stomach problems or emotional explosions can also result from repression. If he can be liberated from the stereotype, the Cancerian can be wonderfully tender, able to give and receive nurturing. He can also be warmly protective and responsive to your feelings and his own.

Moon in Leo: If you put Leo on the 1st house, the sign Cancer falls on the 12th house, showing what he keeps hidden. Thus, the Leo Moon may actually be quite dependent, but puts on a show of confidence and fearlessness. He's too proud to show his needs or confess his insecurities. He may cover up by roaring and striking out as fiercely as the lion which symbolizes his sign. Leo expects to rule, so when his dominance is questioned, he may become angry. Nonetheless he is luxury-loving and wants meals fit for a king. You, as Queen Consort, must preside at his functions as perfectly as the Queen Mother herself did when he was growing up. Leo Moons, on the positive side, are more sunny than brooding, so the general emotional tone is warm and fun-loving. I also find them (when Pluto is not conjuct the Moon) to be richly and demonstratively appreciative of the feminine. (If Pluto is near the Moon, it is far more like Scorpio.)

Moon in Virgo: He may well have had a mother who was intolerant of his dependency, who also convinced him he was incompetent to make it without her. As an adult, he continuously questions his worth and competency. He has to prove it compulsively to himself, to the women in his life, and to the world at large. He may become a workaholic, critical of himself for having any needs at all. He only allows himself to "slack off" under one circumstance. That's when he gets sick, which he can do fairly frequently as the years roll on, unless he learns to accept and meet his own needs. His dependency can come out in being demanding on the home front. He may fuss if the food isn't just right, the house spotless, and all affairs conducted according to perfectionistic standards. He is especially critical of himself for having feelings. Any upsurge of unacceptable feelings or lacks may be covered up by overworking, picking at himself, or criticizing others. Security is a long list of things to do with almost everything crossed off by the end of the day.

Moon in Libra: Many Libra Moon boys were put in the position of surrogate husband for Mother Dear and were expected to smooth over threats to domestic tranquillity. As a result, the adult tries to keep unpleasant feelings hidden—they are just too tacky, and what would people say? For him, security rests in having the love and approval of everyone always. He's extremely dependent on his love of the moment and unfulfilled with no romance on the horizon. Unable to ask for things, he shifts the focus to you and your needs so you won't know he has any. What he doesn't say is that you're expected to read his mind and balance the scale. It's only fair, and why isn't anyone considerate enough to do it? He romanticizes women and expects them to be oh so charming and lovely—don't you know that tears and ugly feelings can mar that pretty face?

Moon in Scorpio: Having had a mother who dominated either overtly or through manipulation, this man has an understandable paranoia about women. His motto is: if you let yourself be dependent, women are going to control you, so hide your needs and keep the upper hand. He believes women's Achilles heel is sex, so if you can be a fantastic lover, you've got them right under your thumb. The world is out to get you—never let yourself be weak, never lose your cool, always be on top of any situation. Emotions are dangerous. Show them and people will use them to stab you in the back. He's going to be the "Man of Steel," even if it kills him. (**Oregon Grape**, by FES, is especially helpful in letting go of this kind of mistrust of the world.)

Moon in Sagittarius: For him, security consists of knowing it all. He digests upsetting experiences, extracts every bit of wisdom, and then teaches you what he learned from it. When you talk to him about feelings, you might get a discourse like the following: "How did it feel? Well, that depends on your perspective, you see. My mother, who was a bit of an amateur philosopher, always used to say . . . and my history teacher, she was quite a sage in her own right . . . and what were we talking about? Did you say feelings? As my mom taught me, all emotions pass, so we shouldn't get attached to them, just look for the lesson to be learned and march on ahead. Attachments of all kinds are transient. Dependency? That's for the uneducated, those who don't see that real security rests in knowing the meaning of life."

Moon in Capricorn: Like the rings of Saturn, this guy surrounds himself with a protective wall, striving not to rely on anyone. Security is extremely important, but he finds it in a well-kept resume and financial portfolio rather than in people. Mother was an ambitious, perfectionistic person, dutiful rather than warm, so he experiences women as demanding rather than giving. He draws clear boundaries in dealing with them, so nobody gets too close. The safest emotion is a well-controlled depression—anger, anguish, even joy are too apt to rock the boat. In the struggle to stifle feelings and override his needs, he's likely to develop a delicate stomach, suffer from melancholy, or drink too much. You're allowed to fuss over him if he's sick. It's in your job description.

Moon in Aquarius: If he had a mother who was erratic and often cold, he has great difficulty dealing with emotions and dependency. He can get very hot under the collar about social injustices and discharge many of his feelings that way. When you show emotions or needs of your own, he dismisses them with, "Oh, everybody goes through that. It's due to the way society is set up." Women are seen as comrades in arms, and are expected to sublimate their needs to the cause or group goal. (The positive male of this type may have had a mother who was committed to social change, or she was an advanced thinker.) If he can take care of whole classes of people, he won't have to get personally involved. By staying detached, he can avoid being flooded by anything as irrational as emotions. When the flood comes, he goes. Many with this Moon sign were subjected to traumatic losses and separations in childhood. If so, he doesn't look for security in a traditional home and family setting, but in attachments to causes, ideas, or the gang. As often seen with Moon in Aquarius, repressed emotions can come out in periodic explosions.

Moon in Pisces: This placement is extremely difficult to deal with in a culture where men are expected to act Mars-like. Besides O. J., Michael Jackson and Elvis Presley share this Moon. Pisces Moons of both sexes have tremendous emotionality, sensitivity, and dependency, also great softness and other-worldliness. None of these traits are considered even remotely acceptable in macho cultures. To avoid the crushing disapproval, he may try to mask his real nature. How would a Piscean Moon do that? Well, he gets approval for "drinking like a man," and being able to hold his booze. Or, he could become a priest or the modern equivalent. Finding a wife who would be a saint/ martyr/slave just like Mom is another solution—but unfortunately women like that tend to break down or flake out. If push comes to shove, he could always become a chronic invalid—no one could blame him for that. To avoid any of these drastic solutions, a man with this Moon must work very hard on his emotions. He can use tools like therapy and meditation to forge a good connection with his unconscious, his lunar hemisphere, and his spirituality. Many also find a valid emotional outlet in music, art, or other creative expressions.

Many of these Moon signs or aspects sound quite difficult to live with. That's because they are! After years of feeling sorry for women because of their place in society, I've finally realized that men have a tough time of it, too. Forced to deny their emotions and their wish to be taken care of, they can feel alienated. They need support in getting in touch with the Moon. Men must work consciously on integrating the lunar hemisphere because that will help them find emotional balance and wholeness. Then they can live out the more positive and healthy sides of their Moon's sign, house, and aspects, avoiding some of the problems in these readings.

Men and the Cancer Rising Wheel

From working with the Cancer rising wheel, it seemed that it would contain suggestions for how a man could reintegrate his lunar side. I was startled to find that the wheel also described the most crippling aspects of Machismo! The macho man is nothing more than a closet lunar type! Let me show you what I mean.

Cancer on the 1st House: The tough outer shell keeps others from getting close and hides his vulnerability. The macho man is self-protective, touchy, and crabby.

Leo on the 2nd House: Often, the self is totally identified with his financial status, so he has to show off and spend to impress others. When he is not the main bread-winner and can't keep up with the neighbors, his self-esteem suffers.

Virgo on the 3rd House: He is highly critical of himself and others. Thinking is supposed to be down-to-earth and analytical, shunning intuition.

Libra on the 4th House: "I want a girl, just like the girl that married dear old dad." The partner is primarily a Mommy, there to feed and nurture him.

Scorpio on the 5th House: He often resents children's demands and regards conflicts with them as power struggles, challenging his authority. In love affairs, he can be possessive and jealous, with the old double standard, saying that girls you have sex with are just for fun. (When it comes to marriage, see the 7th house.)

Sagittarius on the 6th House: Excesses of food and drink can lead to health problems, but he typically will take a gamble on his health, "It can't happen to me." His greatest feeling of well-being and expansiveness happens when work is on an upswing.

Capricorn on the 7th House: "The old lady" is a burden and a responsibility rather than an equal. He wants to be considered the absolute and unquestioned authority in his marriage. He doesn't allow his mate to get through his walls. Despite what he does when he is playing around, he is very traditional in his choice of a mate.

Aquarius on the 8th House: "Love 'em and leave 'em." He enjoys the excitement and glamor of a new affair, but splits as soon as real intimacy begins to arise, or commitment rears its ugly head.

Pisces on the 9th House: He is idealistic but confused about politics and other institutions, "My country, right or wrong." He tends to get into philosophical or political discussions when he's in his cups.

Aries on the 10th House: He must display his manhood to the world and fight when it is challenged. He has to be a winner, constantly fighting for top dog position, and will strike out if his authority is challenged.

Taurus on the 11th House: His sense of whether he belongs or not depends on keeping up with the Joneses. He values the "old boy" network, where friends are people who can help you get ahead, more than friends who can share emotionally.

Gemini on the 12th House: He's too restless to dig into the unconscious or spiritual studies, or when he does, it's in an intellectualized manner. He may only talk about his real feelings when he's had too much to drink.

☽ ☽ ☽ ☽

Just as the Cancer rising wheel described machismo as a defense against lunar qualities, it also shows ways to reverse the trend. You can draw more hints from other trips around the Cancer rising wheel, but it's late in the book to do it in detail all over again.

Cancer on the 1st House: Make a concerted effort to feel and express emotions in a protective environment. Use the women in your life as a positive model to help you get attuned to what those feelings are and to nurture you as you explore them.

Leo on the 2nd House: Learn to value yourself as a being or essence, rather than feeling your worth depends on your wealth.

Virgo on the 3rd House: Analyze what your true needs and emotions are, and then work on communicating them. When psychosomatic complaints arise, try to understand what suppressed conflicts your body might be communicating.

Libra on the 4th House: Let your home be a place where you achieve a sense of balance and harmony. Keep career and home in balance so neither is shortchanged.

Scorpio on the 5th House: Learn to take pleasure in your own company and in solitude. Develop creative interests as a way of regenerating yourself. Know that your children are not possessions, and relating to them is not a power struggle, but participating in their lives can be healing. They can help you bring out the child within yourself.

Sagittarius on the 6th House: Don't gamble with your health—know that all excesses take their toll. Regard work as a place to grow and learn. Take action to keep new information flowing, as mental stagnation on the job leads to physical stagnation. Don't neglect exercise, as it can be a real boost both physically and mentally.

Capricorn on the 7th House: Delegate some authority to your partner, to take some pressure off yourself. Look seriously at your relationships to see what barriers you may have created. Take responsibility to change them so that your own emotions and needs can be recognized.

Aquarius on the 8th House: Detach from traditional sex role stereotypes and experiment with new divisions of labor. Spending time on your own away from the family can refresh and rejuvenate you.

Pisces on the 9th House: Investigate the spiritual areas of life, as they give a different perspective on the pressures in our culture. If reincarnation is a fact, for instance, we have all been both male and female in many lifetimes, so nobody is intrinsically male or female.

Aries on the 10th House: Take a fresh look at your goals. If you always wanted to pursue a certain career but were afraid to try, begin taking courses in that area. You would be less frustrated and angry if your life work were more satisfying.

Taurus on the 11th House: Good friends are more precious than gold, so invest time in friendships where you can share feelings openly and feel solidly supported. Don't let go of friendships just because you are in a relationship. If you do, the relationship becomes your only source of emotional support. This pattern causes distortion because your partner then has to meet all your needs—an impossible demand.

Gemini on the 12th House: Devote conscious effort to probing your emotions, your unconscious, and the spiritual realm. You will find this a fascinating project, a way of getting to know yourself better.

☽ ☽ ☽ ☽

Tuning into the positive attributes of the Cancer rising wheel can help men balance their lunar side. Meditation, dream work, and therapy are all ways of owning the lunar hemisphere so it can stand with the solar hemisphere in an integrated whole. Astrodrama, as illustrated in chapter 12, can be a useful tool in having a dialogue with the Moon. We've spoken about women's support groups as though men couldn't benefit, too. Men do need to learn how to be real friends to one another and to confide their feelings to other men. They have the right to freedom to care for and support each other without fearing that this is homosexual. Men's groups are still rare, but would be very helpful to those who are trying to explore their lunar side.

Flower Remedies for Men

Are there flower remedies for men? Sure, if you can get men to take them! Many men won't even take aspirin when they're in pain, so they might well balk at something so woowoo as the essences. The ones recommended in chapter 5, for integrating strong emotions, might be added to almost any mixture. Dr. Bach found a whole spectrum of remedies for anger, including **Impatiens, Vervain, Cherry Plum, Willow,** and **Holly.** Read the literature to see which one applies. **Cherry Plum** is especially important when there is a pattern of violence. In an emergency, don't forget **Rescue Remedy** as a way of remaining calm and centered. FES's **Sweet Pea** helps those prone to anti-social behavior. Pegasus' **Sunflower** and **Saguaro** help those with low self-esteem or authority problems based on difficulty with the father. For mother problems, we come back to FES' **Mariposa Lily, Golden Eardrops,** or **Evening Primrose.**

Ouapiti Robintree has found applications of **Monkshood** (Alaska, FES) for the male who has difficulty with closeness and is uncomfortable with children. Ian White, the admirably lunar co-founder of the Australian Bush Essences, recommends **Flannel Flower** for those who do not like to be touched, especially men who have suffered from abuse or assault. Cynthia Kemp of Desert Alchemy hopes to produce a men's kit to match the one for women. Her first offering, **MANifesting the Inner King,** is promising. Her **White Desert Primrose** would also help men to let go of their stereotyped macho image, in order to be more in harmony with their essential nature.

The Great Mars Massacre

It has been extremely difficult in this chapter (as in many others) to be detached and objective, as so many feelings were aroused. I learned many things. For example, many traits I found hard to deal with in the men in my life were not their fault—or worse, MY FAULT ("If I were more of a woman, he wouldn't . . .")—but part of their conditioning. Much is sacrificed to the great God Mars—lunar qualities that could make men more responsive to feelings and needs. While that sacrifice may have been required at some points in history—the frontier days or wartime—it is neither necessary nor healthy at this time. It is harmful, not only to the individual, but to all those who have to live or work with him. It contributes greatly to our culture's sickness, as in the violent crimes that increase every year.

The theme of this book is the need to minister to the lunar side of our nature. The pressures on men to deny these qualities are far more intense than any that women face. Thus, men have an even greater necessity to pay attention to their lunar hemisphere. We must be more supportive of those with the courage to meet and express their Moons, so the situation can begin to change. We have sacrificed a great deal to Mars, all of us, in accepting masculine stereotypes, but there is no reason to continue.

CHAPTER 14

THE WANING MOON—
MENOPAUSE AND BEYOND

Many women regard the so-called "change of life" with a combination of
dread, shame, and fear of losing their femininity. One key to understanding menopause is that it is a major lunar threshold, a time when the lunar
body functions and lunar roles are undergoing profound shifts. We have
considered other sharply distinct lunar thresholds—puberty, and the birth
of the first child. Because of major changes in the lunar areas of life over this
century, each threshold is a potential crisis, when much can go wrong unless
there is support for the woman undergoing it. As the traditional supports
are increasingly eroded, there is need for conscious work on developing new
and appropriate supports and coping mechanisms. This is especially true of
the menopause, because of its sometimes intense physical and emotional
changes.

Third Quarter Moon—The Menopausal Years

Because the Moon is so connected to womanhood, it strikes me that the
phases of the Moon, as delineated by Dane Rhudyar in *The Lunation Cycle*,
are a metaphor for the various phases of a woman's life.[1] He described the
First Quarter Moon as the Crisis of Action, in which people experience
conflict between the solar and lunar aspects of their being, but act it out

---

[1]Dane Rudhyar, *The Lunation Cycle* (Santa Fe: Aurora Press, 1986).

upon their environment. This is similar to the menarche, in which the young girl first experiences herself as a woman and experiments with femininity while adjusting to her new role. The Full Moon is analogous to the 30s, the fullness of womanhood, when the mature female is most fully and publicly recognized for either the traditional female roles, as a career woman, or both.

The Third Quarter would represent the menopausal years. Rhudyar called this quarter the Crisis of Consciousness. The conflicts between the solar and lunar aspects of the personality are no less keenly felt than in the First Quarter square. However, they are internalized rather than externalized, the emotions turned inward and often intensely turbulent. While the teen looks to the world outside herself for validation of her femininity, the menopausal woman must all too often draw on her inner strengths and find validation of her femininity inside. In other respects, the two phases are similar. Both the adolescent girl and the menopausal woman are plagued by mysterious physical and emotional changes over which they have little control. They often feel at the mercy of their bodies, embarrassed by external manifestations, which they imagine everyone around them must be as aware of as they are. They are at a point of questioning what it means to be a woman and to fit into the roles society has assigned.

Given the similarities, you would think they would feel a natural affinity for one another's struggles. Too often, however, they are at odds, and likely to view one another as competitors or adversaries. There are, of course, fundamental differences, particularly physiologically, in that the teen is just beginning her reproductive cycle, while the menopausal woman is finishing hers. There is also a potential difference in the economy of solar versus lunar direction of energy. In the teen to young adult years, if the more traditional roles are viewed as desirable and a priority, the solar side (self-development, self-expression) often subjugates itself to the lunar roles from here through the Third Quarter. For the menopausal woman, caretaker (lunar) roles typically are no longer so needed, and solar tasks can again come to the forefront. The adjustments to their roles are therefore opposite, just as the two lunar phases are 180 degrees apart.

The Dark of the Moon, to which Rudhyar attributes visionary and prophetic qualities, is like the Wise Woman phase past menopause, in which wisdom and experience give older women much to offer the world, if it would but listen. It has become fashionable—on the cusp of politically correct—for fifty-something feminists to refer to themselves as crones. Because the word is uncomfortable, no doubt due to ageist conditioning, I would never, ever call myself that! (Perhaps I shouldn't say never. A walk-in might take over my body and I would eat tofu and call myself a crone. That's how you would know it wasn't me anymore.)

The Invisible Rite of Passage, or, "I am NOT Menopausal—I'm Just Stressed Out!"

Consideration of the menopause was left almost entirely out of the first edition of this book. I was 35 when it was written and hadn't a clue what the so-called change of life was about. It seemed like some sort of antiquated and unliberated rite of passage, viewed with just a hint of amused superiority. It happened to one's mother, making her devilishly difficult to deal with, but it was never going to happen to oneself, was it? Certainly it wasn't going to happen to a modern woman like me who had been through years of therapy, took vitamin supplements, got regular checkups, and was fulfilled in her career.

So then it hit, and despite my prominent Pluto in Leo, I am not going to bore you with that harrowing story. However, after reading about the menopause, and getting to know the myriad signs, I began to encounter clients and friends who were in denial that it was happening. One friend, who was having hot flashes, decided she had some sort of weird illness, probably terminal, that was bringing on what she called her "fevers." Like any new body of knowledge or healing technique an astrologer acquires, the more educated I became about this phase of life, the more clients came who needed the information. Women in their late 40s to early 50s who came for readings, and who were having major transits to the Moon, typically believed they were going crazy. Although relieved to discover they were sane, they were not necessary delighted at the possibility that they were menopausal.

Especially when women are isolated from older women and extended family ties due to geographic mobility, it is all too easy to deny that menopause has begun. ("Nonsense! I still have my period every month!") We seldom recognize that years of hormonal shifts precede the actual event of menopause (literally, the end of the menses). These gradual changes can create emotional ups and downs, a dicey temperature regulator that can result in both chills and excessive heat, problems in concentration and memory, and a large variety of other odd symptoms. The last period itself is often the midpoint in as much as a decade of physiological changes—it's not over 'til it's over.

Our ignorance is changing, as there is now a rash of books about the menopause. The same feminists who led us as we burned our bras in the 60s—articulate thinkers like Erica Jong, Gloria Steinem, Kate Millet, and Germaine Greer—are now leading us into a liberated, non-establishment menopause as well. They are in their 50s, hitting that menopausal wall, and climbing over it into cronehood, writing books that let us share their wisdom and process of self-discovery for the later years.

More women are letting go of their shame and secrecy about this condition, discussing their symptoms openly. As that self-obsessed Pluto in Leo crowd, the Baby Boomers, start into theirs, we'll be hearing all about their hot flashes and their black blood clots, just as we were successively forced to sit through their psychoanalysis, their dreams, their spiritual initiation, their dysfunctional family backgrounds, and their recovery. When the Yuppies just below that enter the change, it may even become trendy, albeit high tech. There'll be menopause rooms on the Internet where we can "kvetch" to our heart's content in blessed anonymity about night sweats and even, in this tell-all age, vaginal dryness.

One reason for the heavy denial is the stereotyping of women's roles discussed previously. With the heavy emphasis on lunar roles, women who have devoted themselves to fulfilling them can feel worthless when the last child leaves home or a lunar role is changed. Women's highest rates of depression, suicide attempts, and mental breakdowns occur around the menopause, especially between 50 and 64. There are hormonal changes that contribute to emotional imbalances, yet this is not the whole answer. A study of middle-aged women in mental hospitals showed that prior intense involvement in the mother role was closely related to serious depression.[2]

Cross-cultural studies show that in traditional societies where grandmothers are highly respected, women do not have such emotional problems at menopause. As further proof that it is role pressure rather than biology, the peak of mental problems and suicide attempts for men comes at 65, when they retire, or during long periods of unemployment.[3] In an important and enlightening Chinese medicine text, *Menopause—A Second Spring*, Honora Wolfe also notes that our culture is one of the worst in terms of menopause. She says that in cultures where age brings power and status, close to 100 percent of menopausal women have no reported symptoms. However, in western societies where older women are less valued and re-

---

[2]Janet Saltzman Chafetz, *Masculine, Feminine, or Human?* (Itascan, IL: F. E. Peacock Publishing, 1978), p. 58.
[3]Ibid., p. 231.

spected than their younger sisters approximately 80 percent of women do have symptoms.[4]

Preparing Your Body for Menopause

Gretchen Lawlor, a naturopath, has a useful view of the physiology and psychology of the menopausal and immediately premenopausal years. She says that if you can prepare your body for menopause, rather than waiting for symptoms to develop, you will have an easier time. You need to be thinking of it in the 40s—sooner, if menopause is induced by surgery or chemotherapy. The liver and adrenals (which secrete adrenaline) are tremendously stressed by menopause, while estrogen levels are gradually decreasing. Although the ovaries aren't as active in this transition, fat cells produce estrone, another form of estrogen, with help from the adrenals. If your adrenals are already challenged by life style factors, such as poor nutrition, a high stress job, family problems, or caffeine abuse, you are likely to have a more difficult menopause, unless you work to mitigate these factors.

During menopause, the body's natural response is to put on an extra layer of fat cells, in an attempt to help and protect the body through these changes. Women who diet excessively for the sake of fashion or the naturally excessively thin woman may have a more difficult transition. These women need to do what they can to support the adrenals, including the right kinds of dietary fats in moderation from natural sources. Red meat does not provide the right kinds of fat. Due to the high level of artificial hormones and antibiotics introduced into the cattle's feed, red meat may cause us to store toxic byproducts in our body fat, increasing health risks.

Gretchen adds that during this transitional stage, you want to go slower, giving yourself more quiet time, so as not to stress the adrenals. Replenish your vital force through spiritual pursuits like meditation and contemplation. To continue to overwork and overproduce—as the solar world insists—creates resentment, bitterness, and frustration. Pursuing activities that stress you, or doing things you really don't want to do, builds heat and increases resentment and frustration. As you might imagine, working with the Cancer rising wheel and doing your lunar hemisphere housekeeping regularly will help you stay balanced.

---

[4]Honora Wolfe, *Menopause—A Second Spring* (Boulder: Blue Poppy Press, 1992), p. 45.

Herbal, Vitamin, and Supplement Supports

Herbs can be an excellent support for the physical changes of menopause. However, unlike over-the-counter remedies, which people take so casually, you need to know what you're doing with herbs. Something that worked like a charm for your sister or best friend might not be good for you. Even the right herb can sometimes be harmful in the wrong dose or if wrongly administered. Those with severe difficulties would do well to consult an experienced herbalist. The plants' botanical names will be listed in parentheses. Closely related species can have very different effects—e.g., one species could be an excellent healer, a close cousin may have no healing properties, or may even be toxic.

Gretchen Lawlor says that vitamin E is especially important during menopause and is helpful with hot flashes. (Those with high blood pressure may need monitoring of their E intake, starting slowly and building.) Evening primrose oil (*Onenothera hookeri*) helps the body more effectively produce its own estrogen. It also alleviates nervousness and dryness of the skin and vagina. St. John's Wort (*Hypericum perforatum*) is well regarded for this time of life, working to alleviate hot flashes, night sweats, depression, fatigue, irritability, fluid retention, and lack of concentration. The supplement magnesium may be important to take. Supporting the liver is a key to better health during menopause, including vitamins B6, C, E, and All B with C complex. Adrenal supports include vitamins B5 and C.

Matthew Wood is a very fine herbalist and homeopath who is especially gifted with female reproductive disorders. He is the author of *Seven Herbs: Plants as Teachers* (Berkeley, CA: North Atlantic Books, 1987). He was my practitioner through the acute stages of menopause and made his contributions to this chapter through an interview. He notes that the body may not absorb certain calcium supplements effectively. Calcium carbonate, described in the section on homeopathy in greater detail, helps with calcium loss or deficiency, as it is in rarefied form. It is derived from oyster shell, and the Chinese medicine pearl powder (made from pulverized pearls) is one of the few natural sources of calcium that is absorbed well. Available in Chinese pharmacies, pearl powder also lends a sense of self-value and has a strong effect on the skin, making it glow. For other natural sources of calcium, eat kale and the whole cabbage family, as well as nuts, unless fats are poorly tolerated.

Motherwort (*Leonurus cardiaca*) is an important herbal remedy at menopause. Matt says it is especially indicated where there are hot flashes, heart palpitations, spinal problems, irritability, and an anxiety or jumpiness that can come from being slightly hyperthyroid. Menopausal irritability may also respond to either the herbal tincture or homeopathic strength of camomile. Those who need it can be bitchy, with low tolerance for pain, and they complain a lot. Agrimony types may be in as much pain, but they hide it. This could be the herbal tincture of agrimony (*Agrimonia eupatoria*) or the Bach flower remedy. For excessive bleeding, Matt uses a tincture made from fresh shepherd's purse (*Capsella bursa pastoris*).

Matt recommends wild yam (*Dioscorea villosa*) for the premenopausal era, the transitional years from age 38–46. Unlike some herbalists, Matt does not find it as useful after the onset of menopause. The women who need it are overworked, with some degree of lunar burnout. Things are falling apart a bit, but not to the critical point, and they go on anyway. It is indicated with nervousness, often where you call things by the wrong name. There can be spasms or deterioration in the hip joint. It can be found herbally in a tincture, homeopathically in low potencies from 3x to 30x (under the botanical name *Dioscorea*), or even in yams from the supermarket (not sweet potatoes). A test for whether you need the remedy or not is to eat some yams and see whether you feel better.

Osteoporosis (loss of calcium and bone) is one of the sequellae of menopause that can be alleviated with herbs. One excellent herbal remedy you will not be able to try is comfrey (*Symphytum officinalis*), which had been beloved by herbalists for centuries for its strengthening effects on joints and bones. Recently, however, a study was done in which laboratory animals were forcefed massive doses of comfrey. It's not clear whether the pesticides were washed off or not, but after being on comfrey for a long time, some lab animals came down with cancer. Small herbal companies cannot command the expensive legal counsel that companies dumping toxic wastes can, so the FDA and its brothers internationally confiscated comfrey from the shelves of health food stores in short order.

Should you be so pigheaded as to insist on trying something your government is working hard to protect you from, you'd doubtless find comfrey in back corners of old gardens or deliberately cultivated by nefarious New Age ne'er-do-wells. The good news is that comfrey is available in homeopathic form as Symphytum, a form so rarified as to be free of any remotely possible toxic effects. In low potencies, like 6x, it has had excellent effects on healing osteoporosis and broken bones. Tismal, an Indian medicine man who taught Matt many remedies, recommends the herbs boneset (*Eupatorium perfoliatum*) and motherwort mixed, perhaps, with an activator like lobelia.

Chinese Medicine, Acupuncture, and the Menopause

Centuries-old Chinese medicine has much to offer, not only in treating menopausal symptoms, but also in assisting a smooth passage throughout those years. Chinese medicine includes the manipulation and flow of *chi* (life force energy) through the acupuncture meridians. The system is very different from Western medicine, and I cannot hope to convey more than a small part of it here. Review the material in chapter 10 for the Chinese view of the menstrual cycle and the role played by the liver.

The following explanation is drawn from a summary written for this chapter by acupuncturist Linda Joy Stone. Women have seven year cycles—like the phases of the progressed Moon—culminating in menopause around age 49 (seven times seven). The functions of the spleen (digestion) and kidneys are responsible for blood and energy creation. The kidney system is like the pilot light of the body, and dissipates as we age, as do the digestive functions. An early menopause is not considered healthy, nor is a too late one.

Menopause serves as a natural homeostatic mechanism. While we view it as a sign of aging, it actually slows the aging process. By losing blood in menstruation beyond age 49, one could actually lose too much essence and could experience weakness. With the cessation of menstruation, the essence lost monthly can be consolidated, and women can maintain good health for twenty or thirty more years. Continuing to bleed after age 49, as women on estrogen replacement therapy may do, could deplete the blood and chi.

You need healthy, strong chi to move the blood and sufficient, strong blood. Chi (yang) and blood (yin) are reciprocal in nature and reinforce each other's function. With chi or blood deficiency, symptoms include weakness, fatigue, dizziness, or anemia. Yin depletion (of blood, substance, or moisture) can cause yang functions to become erratic and flare up, creating headaches, hot flashes, night sweats, vaginal and skin dryness, insomnia, or irritability.

If you will recall our discussion in chapter 10, in Chinese medicine, the liver rules the psychospiritual nature and is affected by anger. It is responsible for storing and moving the blood and chi smoothly throughout the body. If there is any stagnation or constraint of the liver chi, often due to stress or emotional problems, then spasms, migraines, tendonitis, anxiety or depression can result. The liver is also responsible for the regularity, volume, and flow of the menses. Anything that disrupts the smooth flow of liver energy is likely to have a negative impact on the menopause.

Traditional Chinese medicine recognizes that life style has a significant influence on whether a woman will have a difficult menopause or not. A woman with a long-standing pattern of anxiety, depression, stress, poor diet, and overwork is more predisposed to a difficult menopause (or difficult menstrual periods) than someone who leads a more balanced and moderate lifestyle. Unfortunately we live in a hectic society that doesn't lend itself to balance and harmony. We eat on the run, experience stress and anxiety, and run on empty a lot. Chronic fatigue is one result and so is a difficult menopause. The good news is that acupuncture can be very effective at relieving the physical and emotional symptoms of menopause by soothing the liver chi, strengthening spleen and kidney functions, and calming the mind and spirit.

Chinese herbs can be an excellent adjunct to treating menopausal symptoms. However, Linda stresses that the diagnosis and prescription of these herbs has to be done on a very individual basis, according to the health pattern presented. One might take a specific formula for a time to alleviate major symptoms of excess. Then a long-term formula may be added to specifically address the root cause of deficiency. Deficiency and excess patterns can appear simultaneously. Therefore deficiencies must be strengthened and excesses sedated, which an herbal combination and acupuncture can address. Chinese herbs are based on such energetic properties as hot/warm, cool/cold, neutral, pungent, sweet, and bitter. A typical formula would usually contain a combination of these properties, some being more warming, others more cooling. If a woman presents with night sweats, or hot flashes, and mistakenly takes herbs that are too warming, such as Korean ginsing, her symptoms could be exacerbated. For that reason, it is not recommended to take a list of likely herbs on your own without having reasonable knowledge of their properties and side effects. It's best to consult a licensed practitioner.

Homeopathy as a Support to the Menopausal Woman

Homeopathy is an alternative form of healing that began developing in the late 1700s. It is still recognized throughout the world as a valid form of treatment, and is even used in hospitals, except in the United States where the AMA succeeded in virtually suppressing it by 1920. It is somewhat similar to the flower remedies, in that both work on the vibrational level through the energy body. However, homeopathic remedies are far more powerful and work more strongly on physical symptoms in addition to the emotional ones. When I entered the menopause, the homeopathic remedies were my main treatment modality and helped so profoundly that I shudder to think what that era would have been like without them. Two of the homeopaths I have worked with over the years, Matthew Wood and Brendan Feeley, contributed to the information in this section.

If your menopausal symptoms are very strong, you should see a qualified homeopath, rather than trying to do it yourself. Where there are serious physical complications, like heavy bleeding or cardiac problems, you would want to consult a physician, especially a physician/homeopath. The National Center for Homeopathy has a registry of qualified homeopaths, all of whom are certified health care practitioners—including MDs, osteopaths, naturopaths, chiropractors, nurses, and dentists. The list is included in an information packet that also contains details about membership, a list of recommended books, and an introductory newsletter.[5]

Homeopathic treatment works on very different principles from allopathic (Western) medicine, so it is important to be informed about how to work with it. Do not apply the same rules as you would with over-the-counter medications or prescription drugs. For instance, a single dose of the correct remedy, taken as infrequently as once a month, may greatly alleviate symptoms. However, in certain potencies and situations, you may need daily doses for several weeks.

Higher potencies such as 200c, 1M, or even sometimes 30c should only be taken on the recommendation of a qualified homeopath, because a wrong remedy can cause many difficulties. Lower potencies like 6x or 12c are much less likely to create difficulties. With the right remedy, even 6x can produce excellent results—correctness being more important than potency. Health food stores generally carry the 30c, which is probably too high, so you may order the lower potencies by calling Boiron (1-800-BLU-TUBE), Washington Homeopathic Products (1-800-336-1695), or Dolisos (1-800-DOLISOS). The important thing to know is not to keep taking a remedy if it isn't helping after a few doses, because it's unlikely to be correct. If you persevere in taking an incorrect one, you can wind up "proving" the remedy—i.e., developing the very symptoms the remedy is supposed to cure. You would also not want to mix remedies, for each has a distinct and generally not overlapping character portrait.

Although homeopaths disagree among themselves about this, you may want to stop using other vibrational remedies, like flower remedies and aromatherapy oils, to get a clear picture of how you are responding. You also

---

[5]To get the packet, call 703-548-7790 with your credit card, or send a check for $6.00 to the National Center for Homeopathy, 801 N. Fairfax Street, Alexandria, VA 22314.

need to know that if you cannot give up coffee (including decaffeinated) for the duration of your treatment, homeopathy may not work for you, especially in higher potencies. It's not the caffeine, but the aromatic oils, for they can antidote your remedy, so moderate quantities of tea or soft drinks are fine. Other aromatic oils that may interfere include mints—even in toothpaste or mouthwash—or anything with camphor, like nasal inhalers, Vicks, or Ben Gay. Even some of the stronger aromatherapy oils may work against your remedy. Handle the pellets minimally, never touching them with your hands but popping them under your tongue. Take the dose half an hour away from food, drink, or toothpaste.

You may be thinking that homeopathy involves many rules and considerations. You are right, and homeopathy isn't for everybody, nor is it easy to find a good homeopath in the United States. Within these qualifications and following these rules, however, homeopathic remedies can be a godsend during menopause. They result in profound systemic relief that few allopathic drugs provide, without the side effects. When you read the remedy descriptions below, you will see what I mean. Flower remedies are more self-adjusting and can more readily be self-administered, but they are not as powerful for these purposes. For everyday living, flower remedies are easier to use, but at threshold times or in crisis, you may wish to consider homeopathy.

Brendan Feeley agrees with the traditional findings that Lachesis is a major remedy for menopause. When it is taken in low potency, say 12c or 12x, use one dose a day until relieved of symptoms. If you are using 30c or 30x, then only take it once a month. It helps with menopausal flushes of heat, fluctuations in energy, heart palpitations, headaches, hemorrhoids, hypersensitivity to touch, and dark, heavy menstrual bleeding. The type who can benefit from this remedy are people who become very intense, passionate, and jealous, even suspicious. They strike out at people, and there is a desire for revenge. (This could coincide with the Pluto square to natal Pluto phase of midlife.) Usually this picture is coupled with great talkativeness, even pressured speech, and overstimulation that is seeking an outlet. There is insecurity, which often comes up strongly during the menopause.

Matthew Wood feels Lachesis works best for those who already fit that character type, who then at the menopause get aggravations, often severe ones. His own mainstay for menopause is Calcium carbonate (abbreviated to Calc carb). It's homeopathic lime, so it's like the lime in the foundations—it puts the mortar back between the rocks. Often the people who need it feel their foundation is falling apart. They also fear they themselves are falling apart—physically, mentally, and emotionally. The remedy pulls things together and makes them feel more integrated. They often feel that the world doesn't support them, including key people in their lives, and they feel undermined. They worry, lack confidence, and become anxious, especially toward night. It is generally a good remedy for the lunar type, because any undercutting of the foundations is likely to raise much insecurity. Calc carb has a strong action on the bones, hot flashes, menstrual flooding, and bladder and muscle tone. One key indicator that this is the correct remedy is that there are often sweaty palms and soles of the feet.

Matt believes Calc carb is an important transition formula. It provides stability for people crossing thresholds, like teething, the first day of kindergarten, puberty, leaving home, Saturn cycles, and menopause. (We are calling some of these thresholds lunar, but perhaps all of the ones on this list are lunar.) The remedy can be especially important with hormonal shifts. It gives structure for people going through a change—like the change of life. It relieves that insecurity of crossing a threshold. The indications for Calc carb are so clear, once you understand the threshold concept, that it is hard to misdiagnose. He finds it works well in low potencies, but 30x almost never fails. With acute situations, take it three times a day for several days, until the symptoms abate, then once a day, then once a week, and then put it on your medicine shelf and take it now and then. It does need repetition from time to time during these threshold phases.

Calc carb is also good homeopathic remedy for arthritic pain and calcifications, one of the few remedies that decalcifies. The whole person can be rather arthritic and calcified. For osteoporosis, Calc phos in the 6x cell salt is recommended by both Matt and Bredan. Matt says that the people who need it are tall, slender people with a crook neck, who tend toward decalcification. (Tall, thin people are generally more prone to osteoporosis.) Two additional remedies for this problem are Calcarea Fluorica and "Osteogenics," a product name.

Sepia is often used by homeopaths for menopause, especially with hot flashes and uterine prolapse, but with other kind of prolapses as well like the gall bladder, intestines, or hemorrhoids. The true Sepia type is the overworked housewife or career woman who is overextended and worn out. She needs to withdraw and hide to take care of herself, but can't because of her responsibilities. (Sepia is made from squid, and they lay down a cover of blackish ink in the water to hide from danger. The squid is another shellfish and is closely related to oyster, the source of Calc carb.) Sepia types love their families and may love the homemaker role, but feel so drained that they can't stand them at the same time. The remedy is not just implicated at menopause, but at other times when there is what we earlier referred to as lunar burnout. Where the symptoms are more mental and emotional and without serious prolapses, it works well at 6x, 12x, and 30x, perhaps taken three times a day for a few days, and then as needed.

Both Brendan and Matt find that another remedy for heat is Pulsatilla, which helps those who are warm blooded and feel worse in warm rooms but better in the open air. They are bothered by fatty, rich foods. The type who can benefit from this remedy are emotionally labile, weepy, moody, and changeable. They love to be consoled and crave relationships—"Do you love me? Tell me that you love me." They may feel forsaken and isolated, and are often soft, timid, and easily influenced. (This remedy is good for PMS also.) Take it in 12x or 30x potencies one to three times a day for a few days, then as needed, like before the period. (Just don't take it constantly, as you are likely to wind up reinforcing the symptoms.) Some additional remedies that are traditionally considered for menopausal symptoms are Sulphur, Caulophyllum, Sanguinaria, and Black Cohosh (*Cimicifuga racemosa*), another plant that Matt delineated brilliantly in his book.[6] To get a clear picture when you have severe or conflicting symptoms, it would be best to consult a homeopath.

Onward to the Silver Years

Arnold Lieber views the senior years as a more lunar time of life and finds that older people are more affected by the full and new Moon. Perhaps, then, rather than golden years, we should call them the silver ones, for silver is the Moon's metal, while gold belongs to the Sun. An increased life span and lowered birth rate are combining to make us more and more a nation of older people. Those outer planet transits to the U.S.'s Cancer planets reflect the fact that ours is not just an increasingly older population, but also a predominantly female one.

Many older people have made conscious preparation for retirement, not only economically, but also by developing mental interests they can pursue. Liberated from work, they can use this stage of life for intellectual growth, and exploring the talents and abilities that were neglected while work and family responsibilities took up much of their time. The older years can be a time of further growth in consciousness. Since there is no longer as

[6]Matthew Wood, *Seven Herbs: Plants as Teachers* (Berkeley, CA: North Atlantic Books, 1987).

much family assistance, the older person will also be forced to develop more independence and a network of friends to rely on. This is a final lunar threshold, a time when people have earned the right to be laid back and lunar. I have no words of wisdom for the silver years, but perhaps if I'm around for still another edition of this book, a decade past the millenium, I'll share what I've learned in the interim.

CHAPTER 15

Moonquakes—Transits to
Your Natal Moon

*WARNING! This chapter may be unsettling. It contains ADULT sit-
uations—and I'm not referring to sex!*

A powerful transit to the birth Moon is no picnic—or maybe I should say,
no moonlight stroll. It stirs up long-repressed feelings, our relationships
with Mom and other crucial women, the home life, the family history and
other critical concerns. A strong transit to the natal Moon can shake up several lunar areas at once. The past comes back to haunt us, the skeletons
come out of the closet, and we are forced to face them head on.

Here, you will learn about transits to the birth Moon by the outer
planets—Saturn, Chiron, Uranus, Neptune, and Pluto. These transits
often mark the crossing of major lunar thresholds like parenthood or
menopause. Change is difficult for most people, but lunar areas of life are
the ones where we can least accept it—they are our security blankets. We
will look at the ultimate effects of these changes and how we can cope
with them.

If you're having a difficult transit to your birth Moon, this book can be
a survival manual. The lunar hemisphere is facing an upheaval, so all the
ways of regaining balance discussed in previous chapters and the next may
be called for. Once more, we will look at flower remedies to help in these
transitions. Two of the more helpful ones in accepting change are **Walnut**,
by Bach, for transitional periods, and Pegasus' **Henbane**, for getting out of
your own way so transformation can occur.

Finding the Important Transits to Your Moon

As mentioned earlier, I use transits rather than progressions in my work. Progressions do work, and the relatively fast-moving progressed Moon is a major timing indicator among the progressions. (It moves an average of 12-1/2 degrees in 2-1/2 years, just as the transiting Moon completes a sign in approximately 2-1/2 days.) The progressed Moon sign seems to coordinate with shifts in house emphasis and in the general emotional tone or prevailing mood. However, I am a basic, no frills astrologer, ever striving to keep the chart simple so as not to interfere with the exchange with the client. Transits have been more productive for me, and so I stick with them. To add the progressed Moon's aspects, consult Nancy Hasting's book, *Secondary Progressions: Time to Remember* (published by Samuel Weiser, York Beach, ME, 1984), or Bernadette Brady's *The Eagle and the Lark: A Textbook of Predictive Astrology* (also published by Weiser in 1992).

The novice might wish to follow transits by getting a computer interpretation. These printouts cover the whole chart, but would identify transits to your Moon in the current year. If you decide to have a reading by a professional astrologer, ask for specifics about both your natal Moon and any recent or forthcoming transits to it.

The astrology student might find it helpful to make a list of degrees of all possible transiting aspects to the Moon. List them in degree order—0 to 29—rather than by sign, so it is easy to match up the numbers. The more difficult or powerful transits are the hard aspects resulting from divisions of the 90 degree angle. They include the conjunction, semisquare, square, sesquiquadrate, opposition and the often-ignored quincunx. Still, even a trine can produce a shakeup in these sensitive lunar areas. Although change may come about more smoothly with a trine than with a square, emotional adjustment to change is difficult for most of us.

Although many texts list the quincunx as a minor aspect, over the years, I have found it a powerful one. The quincunx, a.k.a. inconjunct, is 150 degrees from the natal planet, in two signs that are five signs away from the sign where the planet is placed. That is, a planet at 5 degrees Virgo has two possible quincunx points—5 degrees Aquarius and 5 degrees Aries. Natally, the quincunx is in effect for about three degrees of orb—transiting quincunxes also may be felt for about that length. The effects may be subtle and internal at first, until it is close to exact, when they may begin to manifest externally.

When a transiting planet forms a quincunx to your Moon, there is pressure to shift your functioning in the lunar areas. You must move away from the *modus operandi* of the birth Moon sign to a new way of functioning, similar to the sign of the transiting planet. Signs which are quincunx to one another are worse than incompatible—nearly irreconcilable. The resulting tension is difficult to deal with, but causes you to stretch. (The Cancer-Aquarius quincunx has been one of the themes of this book, illustrating the tensions that can arise between two such dissimilar signs.)

Over the past several years, transiting Neptune in Capricorn has been quincunx planets in Gemini and Leo. These two fun-loving, but sometimes irresponsible, signs have been forced to take life and themselves a great deal more seriously. They have wound up taking on more responsibility and stretching themselves to function more professionally. Both Neptune and Uranus transited Capricorn for nearly a decade, but both will now enter Aquarius, forming quincunxes at some point to Cancer and Virgo Moons. As Pluto shifts into Sagittarius, it will at some point be quincunx Taurus and Cancer Moons.

Table 12 shows the range covered by the outer planets each year from 1980–2000. Because they move so slowly, their forward and retrograde motions over any particular degree of the zodiac may continue for two or three years, signaling a process rather than any single event. If you aren't having any current transits to your Moon, you might find it interesting to trace past aspects and discover what was going on then. If you're facing such conditions in the future, use this interval to work on lunar issues, so they will be easier to deal with when the time comes.

Chiron and Its Link with the Moon

For the first time, I am including Chiron. I'm no expert, and have only been observing its effects. I have to confess I even thought for a long time that Chiron might be bogus, as it seemed so similar to Pluto in its functioning. Apparently my Ascendant-Pluto-Chiron-Mars conjunction keeps me from seeing Chiron at all clearly! It was only after hearing Sheila Belanger delineate the twelve sign placements of Chiron that I realized how very differently it operates in others' lives.

Thus, when it came time to write this chapter, I asked for help from my friend Joyce Mason. She's the effervescent and astonishingly productive editor of *Chronicles*, the journal devoted entirely to Chiron.[1] When you

---

[1] For information or back issues, write to *Chronicles*, Joyce Mason, Editor, Chronicles Press, P.O. Box 41127, Sacramento, CA 95841.

TABLE 12. OUTER PLANET MOVEMENTS, 1980–2000.

This table shows the range of movement for the outer planets each year from 1980–2000. As these planets move slowly and appear to go retrograde, they may take several years to finish crossing a particular zodiac degree.				

YEAR	SATURN	CHIRON	URANUS	NEPTUNE	PLUTO
1980	20 VI-9 LI	10-18 TA	21-28 SC	19-23 SG	18-24 LI
1981	3-21 LI	13-22 TA	26 SC-2 SG	22-25 SG	21-26 LI
1982	15 LI-2 SC	18-27 TA	0-6 SG	24-27 SG	24-29 LI
1983	29 LI-12 SC	23 TA-2 GE	5-10 SG	26-29 SG	26 LI-1 SC
1984	10-21 SC	28 TA-8 GE	9-13 SG	29 SG-1 CP	29 LI-3 SC
1985	21 SC-1 SG	3-14 GE	14-17 SG	0-3 CP	1-6 SC
1986	3-14 SG	9-21 GE	18-23 SG	3-5 CP	4-9 SC
1987	14-25 SG	15-28 GE	22-27 SG	5-7 CP	7-11 SC
1988	25 SG-5 CP	24 GE-7 CN	27 SG-2 CP	7-9 CP	9-14 SC
1989	5-15 CP	1-16 CN	1-5 CP	9-12 CP	12-17 SC
1990	15-25 CP	10-27 CN	5-9 CP	12-14 CP	14-19 SC
1991	25 CP-6 AQ	21 CN-9 LE	9-13 CP	13-16 CP	17-21 SC
1992	5-18 AQ	3-23 LE	13-17 CP	16-18 CP	20-23 SC
1993	16 AQ-0 PI	17 LE-9 VI	17-22 CP	18-20 CP	22-25 SC
1994	27 AQ-12 PI	2-26 VI	21-26 CP	20-23 CP	25-28 SC
1995	8-24 PI	20 VI-13 LI	25 CP-0 AQ	22-25 CP	27 SC-0 SG
1996	19 PI-7 AR	7-29 LI	29 CP-4 AQ	24-27 CP	0-3 SG
1997	1-20 AR	25 LI-15 SC	3-8 AQ	26-29 CP	2-6 SG
1998	13 AR-3 TA	12-28 SC	7-12 AQ	28 CP-0AQ	5-8 SG
1999	26 AR-16 TA	27 SC-11 SG	10-16 AQ	1-4 AQ	7-11 SG
2000	10 TA-0 GE	11-21 SG	14-20 AQ	3-6 AQ	10-13 SG

come to the Chiron segments of this chapter, Joyce wrote them and gave her permission to use them. The following paragraphs are based on Joyce's explanation of Chiron's inherent link with the Moon.

Before Chiron's discovery, astrologer and philosopher Dane Rudhyar predicted that a body would be found between Saturn and Uranus that would act like "a higher Moon." When the cometoid Chiron was discovered on November 1, 1977, it was retrograde at 3 Taurus 08, the degree traditionally assigned to the Moon's exaltation. In the discovery chart, Chiron is in the 4th house, and the Moon is in Cancer. The more we learn about Chiron's mythology and effects, the more Rhudyar's prediction has proven to be on target.

When Chiron was born half-human and half-centaur, his mother was greatly disturbed by this freakish illegitimate offspring. If you think you've suffered from your mother's rejection of parts of you, pity poor Chiron. His mother was so upset at his birth that she got the gods to turn her into a linden tree rather than raise him. He became both a kind and gentle teacher, and a wounded healer—an astrologer and herbalist who could not treat his own systemic poisoning. (He was accidentally shot by an arrow from his dearest pupil, Hercules. Mentors, beware!)

The meaning of Chiron's dual jobs as teacher and wounded healer is that *our wound is our best teacher.* Only when we have experienced enough pain do most human beings surrender to the deep inner work essential to becoming whole. To incarnate is to feel, and the body is where feelings can get stuck—the wounded healer dimension. This feeling emphasis implies a lunar facet to Chiron. Chiron the Centaur was also a nurturer—a foster parent and mentor to many young boys who became heroes, such as Jason, Achilles, and Asclepius. Chiron, himself, was taught by Apollo (the Sun) and Artemis (the Moon).

Thus, an important dimension of Chiron is a rounded, holistic approach that brings nurture into the world through the positive masculine archetype. The higher dimension of Chiron seems to merge yin and yang, where well-nurtured heroes go out into the world and presumably save the day. Those with Chiron-Moon aspects natally often suffer woundings in their relationship with their mothers, yet extend their nurturing beyond the personal to the collective. It is the epitome of the Sun-Moon merger, bringing nurture and caring out into the world at large.

In modern culture, the collective wound is the repression of feelings, instead of ritualizing and processing them in a healthy manner. Chiron's dual body—half-human, half-centaur—suggests the need to merge instincts and intellect, the split that keeps us suffering. Chiron asks us not only to reclaim the Moon, but to create an inner marriage of merged masculine/feminine and light/dark qualities—a new world where solar and lunar energies are balanced. Readers who are interested in knowing more about Chiron, the Centaur, and Chiron, the cometoid, may consult the sources from which parts of this brief explanation and the readings were drawn.[2]

---

[2]Chris Brooks, *Midpoint keys to Chiron* (Tempe, AZ: AFA, 1992); Barbara Hand Clow, *Chiron: Rainbow Bridge Between the Inner and Outer Planets* (St. Paul: Llewellyn, 1993); Erminie Lantero, *The Continuing Discovery of Chiron* (York Beach, ME: Samuel Weiser, 1983) out of print; Dale O'Brien, Audiotape *The Myth of Chiron* (Chironicles Press, 1990); Melanie Reinhardt, *Chiron and the Healing Journey* (New York: Viking Penguin, 1990); Zane Stein, *Essence and Application: A View from Chiron* (New York: CAO Times, 1988).

Why Transits to the Birth Moon are so Difficult

Let me start by saying that prediction is far from an exact science—especially given the bizarre and rapid changes of recent years. Astrologers who claim close to 100 percent accuracy probably only get feedback from the readings where they were successful. We can often infer the type of experience from the planets involved but not the specifics. For instance, my sister, Diana, manages property and was fed up with her current job and boss. Transiting Pluto and Jupiter were coming up on her 10th house Moon, so I rashly predicted she'd get a position managing some wealthy properties. She didn't get a new job when the conjunction hit her Moon, but the property sold, and she got a new boss. His name was Mr. Moon!

With that disclaimer, let's try to find some general principles. When an outer planet transits the birth Moon, it is typical to experience a crisis in several lunar functions at once, so interconnected are they. Just in the areas where we are most emotionally vulnerable, the rug is pulled out from under us. Just where we least want to feel anything, where we are the most defended and unconscious, we are flooded with emotions we may have been stuffing for years. Just where we most need safety and security, we find our foundations wobbling. Just where we are most attached to the past, where we least want change, it is thrust upon us—whether from within or without. Yet, even when it appears to come from without—Mom retires and moves away—there is also an inner stirring that says, "Yes, actually, it *was* time to leave the womb."

Just as the baby may fear leaving the womb, and yet finds its walls more and more confining, we also come to a place where we need and want to venture forth, however timidly. That's the thing we need to understand. That old devil Moon isn't causing the trouble, nor is it the fault of Pluto or Neptune. No, it's an inner evolution, an irresistible urge to grow and to experience more of life and the world than our safety nets have been providing. Crab-like, we sidestep our way into new territory. I've often felt that there is a color wheel of the emotions on a spectrum, like that of the wheel of colors artists use. On that wheel, I believe that fear is next to excitement, so some of the panic you feel may contain a wild admixture of excitement. It's like the first time you left your block on your own as a small child. Sure, it was scarey, but afterward there was no stopping you, a new world was opening up!

And yet the Moon is responsive, is reactive rather than initiating, so we seldom leave the womb until the labor contractions propel us. Let's say your natal Moon is in the 6th house—representing employment and your day-to-day work patterns. With the natal Moon placed there, the job is your home away from home—or maybe your abode is just your home away from the job. You've been at the same company for a decade or more, looking forward to that pension in the year 2020, and you'd never leave that security behind. Still, it's pretty boring, and there's no growth potential. You're tired of baking your prize-winning cookies for the office crew week after week, just because people expect it. Your ulcers are kicking up, because you're sick of mothering your boss, the customers, and everybody else on the job. But, no, you'd never leave. Not willingly.

So, guess what—you get a big transit to that 6th house Moon, there's a buyout, some foreign outfit takes over, and heads roll, including yours. You're really shook up, you eat a pint of ice cream a day, and suddenly you miss your Mom, big time! You may even fly back there for some home cooking and motherly advice. After the turmoil subsides and your nails grow out, you decide that maybe this change isn't such a tragedy after all. While you're on unemployment and still have that credit union cushion, it's time to try the home business you've dreamed about for years. You try it, and it works. Or it doesn't, but in the process you learn new skills that put you in line for a better job. Looking back on it, you decide the takeover was the best thing that ever happened to you.

Despite all the emoting, despite the unwelcome adjustments, despite your fears and insecurities, a major aspect to your Moon signals a period of great personal development. You've outgrown certain sources of dependency and security, and are leaving them behind—stepping out of the nest or being kicked out of it, it doesn't matter. The result is that you're more grown up, get to experience new territory and learn a great deal about yourself in the process. Only about a twelfth of you actually have your birth Moon in the 6th. Let's take a trip through all twelve houses to see what moonquakes in each of them may produce.

Does Your Astrologer Make House Calls?

As we learned in chapter 4, the house position of the birth Moon is an important factor. Throughout our lives, this shows the area of life where we tend to be most lunar. Successful functioning in that area of life can add to our security and sense of well-being. Difficulties or failures there can make us unhappy and insecure like almost nothing else. Generally this is an area where you have a strong emotional investment, so it is one where you periodically go ballistic. When the natal Moon receives an important transit, like the ones we will be discussing, there often are important metamorphoses in matters of the house involved. The result can be a crisis in the lunar realm, a need to transform lunar functions that have become attached to that area of life.

In working with transits to the birth Moon, then, consider the meanings of the house involved. There are likely to be profound alterations in these areas that are so crucial to your emotional well-being. Another consideration is the house position of the transiting planet, because you will often be called upon to integrate the functions of both houses. Suppose your natal Moon in the 10th house is being opposed by transiting Pluto in the 4th. There will typically be a conflict of interest between career and home life. Sometimes a shift in the home life creates stress at work, sometimes political struggles at work increase the demands on your home life, and sometimes both. Let's look at the impact of transits in all twelve houses.

Moon in the 1st House: A strong transit to a 1st house Moon requires modifying your presentation of self so that your connections with people are no longer so codependent. As your behavior changes, you are less likely to attract people who relate to you in exclusively lunar ways. Physically, this may be a time of increased sensitivity in which you must deal with shifts in diet, the menstrual cycle, and other lunar parts of your physiology. You may gain or lose weight, depending on the planet involved and on your readiness to face rather than stuff your emotions and dependency needs.

Moon in the 2nd House: When there is a transit to your 2nd house Moon, new financial developments, possibly reverses, may strike at your safe foundations. Worry and stress may well cause you to reexamine your spending patterns and establish new priorities. If you've spent unwisely or gone into debt, you may reap the consequences. If you've been an emotional spender, indulging in shopping binges when the going gets tough, you may find that you've spent your way into big trouble. If you've been codependent in money matters, either relying too much on others, or allowing others to rely too much on you, these relationships must transform. If you've sold yourself cheap all your life, you may finally have to charge what you're worth, rather than being mother to the world. The result of working consciously with these changes is to put your finances on a solid basis so that you can be safe and secure in the future. (The most positive expression of this transit is that people often buy a home. Look, however, at the section of this chapter that deals with moving, to make sure this is the right time.)

Moon in the 3rd House: During outer planet transits, ties to siblings, aunts, uncles, and cousins are likely to be shaken up. If you and a sibling have a codependent tie, the enabling must stop, so one or both of you can finally stand on your own two feet. Emotions that have been withheld in order not to rock the family boat are likely to be discussed, resulting in more authentic interaction. Reunions may occur, showing your family of origin in a much different perspective. You may ask questions you never dared to ask before about the past and family secrets. While these new pieces of information are likely to stir up feelings, there will be more clarity in your thinking and more real communication. This may not just hold true with family, but with the outside world as well.

Moon in the 4th House: Remember that the person born with this placement qualifies as a lunar type. The Moon's meanings are double strength here, just as they would be with Moon in Cancer. A Moonquake in this house may be hard to deal with, just because the home and roots are doubly important to you. A move is likely or a change in who lives with you. The nest may empty, or you may need to take care of someone—Mom, a grandchild, or a foster child. Where family relationships have been codependent, a shift to a healthier pattern of relating is likely—not that any of you will particularly relish the process! Sometimes there is reconstruction or you buy a new home or move across the country. (Again, read the section on moving.) Often there is a gathering of the clans, a trip home that makes you see the past, Mom, and your hometown in an adult perspective. Whatever the shift, you can't go home again, and you will spend the next several years establishing new and more appropriate roots. (Note: An outer planet transit to the IC— the 4th house cusp—may produce a similar effect to that described here.)

Moon in the 5th House: With the natal Moon in this house, relationships with children or romantic partners are a main source of emotional fulfillment. When they are going well, there's nothing like it for pleasure and satisfaction. When they're going poorly or changing, as they may under important transits, the resulting emotional whirlpool can temporarily take over your life. When the outer planets impact that Moon, there is a profound shift in these relationships. Sometimes a new child or romance enters the picture, sometimes children leave the nest or the romance alters in some major way.

In either case, it's so long symbiosis, hello world! All parties involved will need to function more separately and independently, because the umbilical cord is on the fritz. And, yes, it hurts. Yes, you may cry for months wishing things could go back to the way they were before. But the womb has become too confining. It's time to see more of life and to find out what more there is to either of you than mother and child. It's time to explore your creativity and talents.

Moon in the 6th House: We did your Moon in the previous section, and I've got other work to do. You understand what it's like to be busy!

Moon in the 7th House: Since you see your marriage or partnership as essential to your security, any shift in the bond between you or in the partner's circumstances is likely to be disturbing. During the transit, you must examine and modify codependent patterns that are no longer appropriate. One or both of you has changed, probably matured, and wants more from life, so the relationship has to adapt. Of all couples, however, you are least willing to separate, so the work of healing the bond is crucial. If you're having trouble, perhaps it is time for couples' counseling. Emotions run so strongly in this area that a detached third party can be helpful.

Moon in the 8th House: Many with strong 8th house placements fail to develop their own resources and strengths because family members encouraged and even manipulated them to remain dependent. An outer planet transit brings on a needed adjustment in the balance between your own and other people's resources, financial and otherwise. Work on healing, and releasing codependent ties now, can free you to put your finances on a solid foundation. You'll have little choice in the matter—Mom or other female figures can't, or won't, enable you any more, and you have to grow up. At worst, there may be a death or separation that forces you to grow up in a hurry.

The new requirement that you stand on your own two feet can be terrifying. If you've bought into the belief that you can't survive on your own, you may well feel you're not going to make it! Still, as the transit progresses and you're forced to take care of your own needs and maybe your caretaker's as well, you do become more independent. Paradoxically, you and your relationships could also become more secure. Now that you don't need to bury your feelings to keep from losing your safety net, you can risk being yourself. Your sexual expression and your connection to female sexuality may also go through profound shifts during this time.

Moon in the 9th House: Under transits to this Moon, challenges to your belief system are not uncommon. You may be disillusioned with a spiritual leader, whatever your religious orientation—be it your pastor, rabbi, guru, medicine woman, or the high priestess in your coven. This can result in a painful crisis of faith in which you no longer know what to believe. You have to search deep within for spiritual answers, because previous assumptions no longer hold true. Your very foundations can be shaken, for you took great comfort in your formerly safe and certain worldview.

For the student, a mentor or teacher may be revealed to have feet of clay. Your teachers, particularly the women, may be going through an emotional crisis, or may be moving on. Now you have to be the grownup and even the mentor for the newer students. Maybe the world is not as safe as you once thought, and maybe you're not so certain of your beliefs anymore. However, you can find unexpected gratification in nourishing the next generation of pupils. Alternately, you may leave home and move far away for the purpose of pursuing advanced studies.

Moon in the 10th House: An outer planet transit to a 10th house Moon often corresponds with a crisis or new development in the career. You may feel insecure and anxious if change is necessary, even for the better—like a promotion or a better job. Often the boss has become a parent figure—benign or nightmarish, but usually bigger than life. The workplace has become a family, so a job move may feel like being uprooted. There may be a shift either toward or away from being a professional caretaker, with lunar burnout a possibility. The notion of parental authority may also need readjusting. This may be due to a crisis with the original parent figures or to having more or fewer dependents of one's own—a new baby being born, or a son or daughter leaving the nest.

Moon in the 11th House: With this placement natally, there can be an inappropriate expectation of perpetual nurturance and emotional caretaking as a requirement of friendship. These expectations cannot always be met, and may result in occasional purging of unsympathetic pals, particularly during outer planet transits. The issue of codependency among friends, or in important groups, is likely to arise. A shift toward more adult, independent functioning will be required. A phase of isolation may occur as you reevaluate what friendship means, and as you build a more appropriate support network. Group membership is likely to prove a source of healing now, possibly a self-help or therapy group directed at family-of-origin wounding.

Moon in the 12th House: Both the Moon and the 12th house tend toward repression, so the combination makes remaining conscious of your emotions a continuing challenge. During outer planet transits, all that is unconscious or repressed comes to the surface, much to your surprise and dismay. Surely you don't really feel that way? Surely you don't still mind about what Mom did when you were 7? Do you really remember that, or are you just making it up? Can it be that you are really that dependent, that emotional, that insecure? You've always been scornful of people who go to shrinks, and now you're starting to think you need one! Well, it wouldn't be as bad as all that, now would it? Sort out your feelings and learn new ways of mastering and using them to change what is bothering you. Then you won't be hounded by that uneasy suspicion you've always had that you might be on the verge of losing it. Work consciously on fulfilling your own needs, and the conviction that the world is an unsafe place may very well leave you. Your ulcers or PMS could even clear up! In short, you could be healthier, more secure, and more on top of your life if you face and deal with longstanding lunar issues now.

$$\mathbb{D} \ \ \mathbb{D} \ \ \mathbb{D} \ \ \mathbb{D}$$

You may feel you got shortchanged in these readings—or conversely that you know more now than you ever cared to know. Some readings have been longer than others, it's true. Some house placements are more lunar than others, or more inhospitable for the Moon, and thus require more motherly advice. Don't worry, as we go through this chapter, you'll hear plenty about your own Moon transits and how to use them well.

Flower Remedies for Transits to the Moon

For starters, refer to chapter 5 for the remedies that most support emotional integration for your natal Moon and its aspects. These may be required off and on during the two years or so an outer planet transits your Moon. (Saturn transits, mercifully, are shorter and depend on where in the sign Saturn sashays back and forth.) You also may find great support in using the remedies mentioned there for integrating strong emotions. For the issues of various houses, try the monthly bouquet given in chapter 6. If your relationship with Mom or other caretakers is affected, consult the remedies in chapter 8.

There are additional remedies that help you cope with the concerns and issues raised by each outer planet. *Saturn transits to the Moon* can bring anxiety about new demands and roles, for which you might need Bach's

Aspen or **Rock Rose.** You may also experience discouragement or despair, for which Bach's **Gentian** or **Gorse,** or FES's **Scotch Broom** would be helpful. **Larch,** for the courage to try, can also be strengthening. For *Chiron transits to the Moon,* Joyce Mason recommends FES's **Evening Primrose,** which is especially useful when dealing with rejection by parents. *Uranus transits to the Moon* can bring sudden changes or upheavals. **Rescue Remedy** by Bach can be useful in any crisis. Bach's **Walnut,** for those in transition, is a steadying influence. *Neptune transits to the Moon* can coincide with a spaced out state of mind, for which Bach's **Clematis** can be grounding and FES's **Madia** can improve concentration. Try Pacific Essences' **Sand Dollar,** or Alaskan Flower Essences' **Bladderwort** for combating the illusions that Neptune transits can bring. During *Pluto transits to the Moon,* many old issues can come up for healing. Bach's **Willow** for resentments, **Holly** for self-hate and the desire for revenge, and **Pine** for guilt may be needed over time. There are many other possible remedies for each of these transits, but these are some of the most crucial.

Moonquakes in Our Relationship with Mom

As I've observed the charts of clients, students, and friends over the years, a transit to the natal Moon commonly involves a metamorphosis in the mother, herself, and in the person's relationship with her. When the aspects are hard, the mother often goes through a crisis, particularly in terms of her lunar roles. Her age, health, and marital status need to be considered, for these provide clues to what could be about to occur. It is also important to find out how she and the daughter or son are getting along, for important issues are likely to surface in the relationship.

So basic to our foundations is mother and our internalized versions of her, that any crisis in the mother's life is likely to trigger a powerful reaction in her children. This response might be termed a maturational crisis. The offspring must become less dependent, emotionally or in actuality, and more fully adult. Even those who have effectively severed their real-world connection with Mom are likely to be far more affected than they believe possible, because the inner mother never leaves us.

If your mother has passed on, or is absent from your life, consider who might be filling her house slippers, on an emotional level. A similar process to the ones described here may go on with mother surrogates, including wives, women friends or relatives, or female mentors. For simplicity, we will only refer to the mother. However, important transitions in bonds with these other important figures should also be taken into account.

Refer to the astrological exercises in chapter 8, where you considered the sign, house, and aspects to your natal Moon and how they described your own mother and your connection with her. Working with the psychological exercises, as well, can be timely and potent. Let's look now at the effects of each of the outer planets as they aspect your Moon.

When Saturn Transits the Moon, Mom or her equivalents may be setting limits on those who are excessively dependent. This may be due to keenly experiencing her own realistic limitations in energy, time, health, or other resources. She may be feeling old for the first time, more fearful, maybe anticipating a more constricted future. Whatever the cause, she's asking us to grow up and take responsibility. (The house position shows what area of life this demand is most strongly experienced.)

The effect on the daughter or son whose Moon is being transited is likely to be sobering. We don't want to grow up, nor do we welcome more responsibility, so there can be a sense of loss and some reactive depression. Because the Moon shows our security blankets, and Saturn transits are often accompanied by anxiety, we are likely to be particularly anxious and insecure. We doubt our ability to provide for ourselves or our dependents and wish for someone else to keep us safe. Everywhere we turn, there is tough love, accompanied by the demand that we grow up.

As we accept the challenge, we discover strengths that we've been developing over the past seven years—since the last major Saturn aspect to the Moon. Ultimately, there is a more solid and real sense of security. We come to know how much more capable we are than we previously thought. We become our own authorities, our own Rock of Gibraltar, and there's deep satisfaction in that.

When Chiron Transits the Moon in a challenging way, Joyce Mason says that some likely themes include the birth of a sibling, or drama around a brother or sister that may alter your relationship with Mom, leaving you to mourn the loss of a larger portion of her attention. She may change her attitude toward sexuality, becoming more or less open about it. If more open, you might have to face squarely the myth of mother's virginity (most of us can never imagine she "did it," much less does it). Her parenting style could change, perhaps triggering flashbacks of times when she wasn't there for you. She could disapprove of you blatantly, regarding something essential to who you are. At worst, she could face a life-threatening illness.

The bottom line is a sense of abandonment, generally emotionally, in the sense of her not being there for you, but sometimes more literally, as in estrangement or loss. (In mythology, Chiron was grossly rejected by his mom and abandoned by his dad. Our original birth trauma is feeling "rejected for being ejected" from the womb.) **Mariposa Lily** by FES is like mother love in a bottle for these tougher Chiron-Moon times. If you're especially close to Mom, and don't want to take in her pain (which doesn't help either of you), try **Pink Yarrow**, also by FES. At best, during stressful aspects, Chiron-Moon can coincide with a period of being almost overly involved with mother.

In a more flowing aspect, like a trine or sextile, Mom might become or seek a mentor, or dabble in alternative healing arts, such as herbs, acupuncture, or homeopathy. Chiron rules channeling, so she might become psychic or very intuitive. She could surprise you by making quantum leaps in her personal growth that, when you think about it, have actually been coming on for a long time. She might take in foster children or become a teacher. You will see her bloom into someone more integrated and versatile—a role model to you, and to perhaps others.

When Uranus Transits the Moon, my observation is that the mother typically takes sudden and surprising actions, yet often those actions have been brewing under the surface for a very long time. Under the right circumstances, she might leave Dad, quit her job, move away, go back to school, or start acting like an adolescent herself. If the 6th or 12th houses are highlighted, there can be a sudden health crisis, perhaps involving the circulatory system or an accident. These upheavals can initiate a process of seeking greater freedom from lunar responsibilities. With the softer aspects, the mother may express her individuality in wonderful new ways. She may become more active in social or political concerns and get validation for her new activities from family and friends.

The impact on the son or daughter is unsettling—the rug is pulled out from under our feet. If we can't count on Mom to stay the same forever, who can we count on? With independent Uranus forming aspects to the Moon, codependency is definitely history, so now we have to survive on our own. We are kicked out of the womb without warning! Maybe she was boring before, maybe now she's more interesting and more of an individual, but how could she do this to us? Still, our mothers remain role models throughout life, so her new freedom and expressions of her individuality give us permission to experiment with new lifestyles. Her revolution frees us as well.

When Neptune Transits the Moon, the mother may be confused and floundering emotionally or perhaps in a weakened state due to health problems. She is likely to be feeling dependent and needy—perhaps actually more physically dependent—and we may be called upon to nurture her. Roles are likely to be reversed in a most bewildering way. If she is older and frail, now may be the time when she can no longer function on her own. We may be expected to take her in or arrange for her care. If she suffers from addictions, she may be bottoming out, and we may be called on to intervene. The transit may also be a time when illusions are stripped away, especially for those with natal Moon-Neptune or Pisces Moon placements. Our idealized images of Mother, and of women in general, are shown up as sham, and we may be deeply disillusioned.

Alternately, in trines and in Neptune's more positive expressions, Mom may be going through a creative renaissance or a spiritual awakening, possibly emphasizing the feminine aspects of the divine. This state of illumination may or may not be appreciated by those around her. Some cynical Frenchmen thought Joan of Arc was nuts, and it's unlikely that her family was pleased when she started having visions.

Whether the expression is positive or negative, the impact on her offspring who are having Neptune aspects to the Moon is likely to be disturbing. The security blanket has been ripped away, and we are painfully insecure. We ourselves may feel confused, adrift and helpless. Even while having compassion for Mother, we may also feel martyred by the need to care for her, and for ourselves. Our ideas of womanhood are called up for questioning. If Mom isn't the woman we thought she was, then who, pray, are we?

The long-range effect of this less than wonderful transit is to dispel the illusion that we as adults can remain dependent. After wallowing in self-pity over this unpleasant truth for a disgustingly long time, we finally decide to leave whatever wombs we may have been clinging to and nurture ourselves from now on. We are now fully adult and in touch with reality, but doubtlessly not thrilled about it. Reality has its definite limitations.

HELPFUL HINT: This would be an excellent time to establish a connection with the Divine Mother and the angelic realm. (Useful remedies in making this connection are FES's **Angelica** or **Love-Lies-Bleeding**, and Pegasus' **Angel of Protection**.)

When Pluto Transits the Moon, a time of transformation is at hand for the woman you call Mom. Some transformations are wonderful, some more difficult, but none are easy. The house may have to be stripped to its foundations before a new and more fitting structure is built. She may be resenting the female roles and the ways she has been powerless in the past. Where codependency has gone on too long, she may end or insist on transforming such relationships. Sometimes a health crisis may propel her into establishing a new lifestyle.

You thought I was going to say she'd die, didn't you? Well, even if American astrologers didn't have this terror-striken taboo against the *D* word, this transit doesn't necessarily mean that. After all, you have some kind of Pluto aspect to your Moon at least five or six times in your life. So, yes, I've seen mothers die under major Pluto transits to the Moon or IC, but I've also seen mothers transform themselves in wonderful ways.

I've gingerly asked women clients who are having major transits from Pluto to the Moon about their mothers. Sometimes they say, "Oh, Mom is turning her life around in the most incredible ways! I've never loved or respected her so much!" Or, "Mom is finally speaking up and telling Dad she's not taking any more crap from him. And, he's having to listen!"

How do Mom's offspring take her new assertiveness? That, of course, depends on the condition of the natal Moon. (Those with natal Moon-Pluto aspects have quite a history to overcome with Mom.) It also depends on what we've done with the lunar part of our nature—how insightful, how recovered, or how evolved we have become. Even the most evolved are likely to have some less than loving reactions. After all, Mom is supposed to always be there for us—it's her job! We may manipulate Mother or her surrogates, we may try to make her feel guilty, and we may extract revenge in subtle or not so subtle ways. We may even provoke a crisis in a lunar area of life—like getting pregnant—so she will have to pitch in and help. But she doesn't enable us anymore, at least not by the time the transit is over, so we do, finally, have to grow up. Blast her!

Moonquakes in Women's Roles and Family Life

For women, especially, transits to the birth Moon are often major markers in the life cycle. These aspects can usher in anything from puberty, to leaving home, to marriage and childbirth, to menopause and children leaving the nest, to widowhood and the retirement home. (Desert Alchemy's **Celebration of Womanhood** kit has a flower remedy formula for every part of the woman's life cycle.) Each development in these roles evokes profound responses, both in the woman, herself, and in her partner and family members. Major emotional readjustments are required. As discussed previously, our relationship with the inner or outer mother is likely to be changing at the same time.

For men, these transits may primarily operate through the women in their lives. This is most true of men who have disowned their own lunar hemisphere and projected it onto women. It is least true of men who have embraced and integrated their lunar traits. At any rate, an outer planet transit may find a man going through major realignments of his relationships with key women, and the woman within. Sometimes a key woman moves out of his life, sometimes an important new woman comes in, and sometimes both. If he has been overly dependent on these women to provide him with nurturing, emotional awareness, and security, the codependency may end. He may experience vulnerability in the process that can make the lunar realms more conscious and real to him. He may find himself taking on homemaking or child care tasks, perhaps due to an addition to the family.

Again, it is important to have a grasp of the birth Moon, for it describes our stance toward these roles. It shows how we carry them out, what we feel about them, what models we had, and how we respond to changes in them. A woman with Moon in Aquarius is likely to experience far more conflict about fitting into traditional female roles than a woman with Moon in Cancer or Capricorn. A man with Moon in Taurus expects the woman in his life to be as old-fashioned as he is. Since Taurus is fixed earth, he may experience change as deeply disruptive.

When Saturn Transits the Moon, we typically take on more family responsibility, and it is one indicator of having a child, especially the first one. Saturn is a major time marker and corresponds with formal role structures. Saturn aspects to the Moon often concur with beginnings or endings in female roles and family structures. We might buy our first house or sell the old family homestead. Men may find themselves helping with homemaking or child care tasks, perhaps due to the family growing larger or the wife going to work. Or, there is both an ending and a beginning—we marry and leave home. A woman enters the menopause, but becomes a grandmother. Beginnings are accompanied by seriousness and worry about new commitments. Endings can be accompanied by sadness and anxiety about the passage of some nurturing structure. Still, we can find gratification in our new level of maturity, hard-won capabilities, and adult status.

When Chiron Transits the Moon, Joyce Mason says that you may be ready to take on or give up on being a nurturer and mentor to others. (The former is more likely in the easier aspects, the latter in the more challenging squares and oppositions.) This could include an overly dependent spouse and bring the marriage or relationship to a turning-point. During flowing aspects (trine, sextile) you will be creative in finding alternative solutions to your family dilemma, if your partner or children can come part-way. You will clarify what you need for your own growth. Especially in the more difficult aspects, no longer are you willing to let anyone get in the way of your becoming a whole person, even if it means a divorce. Your parenting style or situation could change. If you have confused motherhood with servitude and tend to let your kids get away with murder, you might become "no nonsense." Try **Centaury**, another Bach remedy (named after Chiron, the Centaur, himself) to support your new trend toward tough love.

During the easier transits, you could crave, or in fact, have, a child, adopt, or take in foster children. There could be a strong desire to teach or work with children in an alternative, integrative setting, like a performing arts camp, or a Montessori or a Waldorf school. Under stressful aspects, you could have problems with fertility, or face either an unexpected or unwanted pregnancy or gynecological problem. (Bach's **Schleranthus** can be a helpful flower remedy when feeling torn between two choices.) Conditions of the female organs or hormones, like endometriosis or menopause, may come up. Look to emotional root causes for diseases or if menopause comes early. (Endometriosis, for example, seems to come from over-mothering—pouring out too much feminine energy.)

At worst, you could lose a child in some way—a loss that is seldom literal, and more often philosophical or emotional. (He or she joins a cult, or enters a relationship with someone you can't stand). Under positive aspects, you could heal any of these issues—a prodigal son or daughter returns, you find or are found by a child given up for adoption, or you have amazing results with an alternative cure for your hormonal imbalance. In general, a change in attitude toward women, or femininity, alters the quality of your relationships, ultimately for the better, even if the short-term brings strained relations or endings. You are starting to internalize mother and nurturing, setting an example for your dependents to begin doing the same.

When Uranus Transits the Moon, I find that we typically rebel against traditional female and family roles, chafing at the constraints they bring and insisting on more freedom. Either with or without validation from family, friends, and society, we experiment with alternative ways of meeting lunar needs. (**Goldenrod**, by FES, helps you remain true to yourself despite outside pressure.) If we're unwilling to transform dependency patterns, change may be thrust upon us from outside, seemingly without warning. If we'd been paying more attention to undercurrents in these areas, however, we might have seen that change was long overdue.

In either case, a support group may be helpful, either emotionally or practically. (**Walnut** by Bach, and **Transitions Formula** by Desert Alchemy are especially helpful during Uranus transits.) With a trine the revolt is less drastic. We may get away with it, earning the covert admiration of those around us. With more difficult aspects, the pressure to conform to tradition may be more intense, and thus the moonquake when we rebel may be more disruptive. Of course, Uranus always carries the possibility of emotional detachment, an enlightened perspective, and social evolution. Don't rationalize your feelings about such modifications out of existence, however, or they may one day erupt and surprise you.

When Neptune Transits the Moon, there is disillusionment with the feminine roles. Women may feel burned out, and trapped, by lunar responsibilities and incapable of continuing to caretake or rescue others. The home feels like a prison, the children or partner's demands overwhelming. For men, there can be a period of idealizing an important woman, followed by disillusionment when her humanness is revealed. We want someone to rescue us and take us away from all this. Even if the white knight, the guru, or the mother of all mothers does appear, there is a high price for submerging yourself this way. It stops further growth and ultimately becomes suffocating. The womb becomes toxic after it outlives its usefulness. (Pacific Essence's **Barnacle**, or Desert Alchemy's **Milky Nipple Cactus** can help us relinquish inappropriate dependency.)

When Pluto Transits the Moon, an intense confrontation over women's roles can be played out. If a pregnancy occurs which the couple is ambivalent about, it may involve a power struggle or be a ploy to remain dependent. Still, a shift in role can be an intense metamorphosis in which a woman experiences the power of her femininity. When we become mothers, we transform on a deep level and become closer to mothers of all times. Puberty and menopause are other Plutonian shifts in feminine physiology and spirit. The urge to nest, or perhaps to transform our living space, may become obsessive. Pluto is deep, internal, and powerful, so the woman or man who experiences it can never again take the lunar realms so much for granted. We may grieve about leaving behind a time when we could innocently depend on Mom and her surrogates without having to repay in kind.

"Am I Gonna Move?"

Moving to a new home may be part of what happens under a transit to the natal Moon, the 4th house cusp (IC), through the 4th house, or to a planet in the 4th. As a certified Astro*Carto*Graphy interpreter over the years, I have observed such transits as primary triggers for changes in residence. Relocation goes more smoothly under a trine—with Moon-Uranus trines being the swiftest and the least hassle. A move under a Moon-Saturn trine, however, is more organized, and more likely permanent! Under a Moon-Uranus aspect of any kind, you might as well keep nonessentials packed in their boxes, as you're likely to move more than once with repeated hits by Uranus.

Buying a home, especially the first one, is a rite of passage into adulthood. Having a home of your own gives you a greater sense of security, roots, and belonging—for lunar types, especially. Moon-Saturn and Moon-Pluto aspects are the most likely to involve actual purchases of real estate, although Pluto as often accompanies major remodeling efforts. With Moon-Saturn aspects, a home of your own may be the result of well-earned success. You may be conservative in your purchase. You may settle for something smaller or less luxurious than you'd like, because you are being realistic about not taking on too hard of a financial commitment.

With some Moon-Pluto contacts, the new house may be financed by something other than your own efforts. The source could be an inheritance, a gift or bribe from your parents with strings attached, a trust fund, or a divorce settlement—or, it may be a last-ditch effort to keep the marriage together. If you've suffered lunar losses during this phase, take time to mourn the end of one chapter in your life. The grief may be exacerbated by a period of isolation in the new location.

Under Moon-Neptune transits, you're probably not thinking things through carefully enough, and may regret the decision. You're not so much moving to something as moving away from something because you've become disillusioned. Your fantasies about a wonderful new life tend to be unrealistic. If you buy property under a Neptune transit to the Moon, or other points mentioned above, you probably haven't inspected the cellar or foundation. The realtor saw you coming, and you may have a lemon on your hands for a good, long time. What to do about it? Ah, well, it would be reprehensible of me to suggest you find a buyer who is also under a Moon-Neptune aspect, wouldn't it? Maybe you could donate it to the church, your guru, or some charitable organization. Or, hang in there for whatever deep spiritual lesson it may teach you—like the time-honored one about not signing anything you haven't read and understood.

Joyce Mason says that if you are inclined to move at all under a Moon-Chiron transit you tend to be motivated by inner growth or the need to help or heal Mom, or an important woman in your life. Often, Chiron transits are when we least want to leave home and hearth where we are processing much psychological garbage, either previously unknown to us, or at minimum, not completely processed. During the most positive Chiron-Moon cycles, we are very psychically open. This might enhance tuning into the energy of a place to check for its fit with your own needs. Permanent moves can be to places where healing and new learning occur. If done under stressful aspects, however, feeling misfit, unwelcome, or isolated might be part of the experience.

The question I often ask clients to consider is that while the planet involved shows the circumstances of the move, the real issue is, why are you doing it? It is generally due to an important shift in the lunar areas of life. Often, the reason is that the womb has gotten too confining. As a young adult, you leave your parents' house to go on your own. Later, maybe you move to make a home with someone—or a home *without* someone. Sometimes, because any aspect to the IC is simultaneously an aspect to the MC, either you or your partner find a job in a new place. Maybe you have a family now and the house has gotten too small. Or, your family has grown up, and you don't need so much space. The Moon waxes and wanes, all within a life cycle. The pressure to leave the womb precedes the relocation. There is a lunar realignment before the move, followed by a long adjustment to the new home.

If you are moving more than 500 miles east or west of your birth place, incidentally, it would be important to get an Astro*Carto*Graphy map done. This is a computer-generated printout of the globe, showing the areas where each of your natal planets falls on the Ascendant, IC, Descendant, and Midheaven. Especially if you have no idea where you want to live, this map can help you find optimal locations for business, love, home life, health, and travel. It can also help you avoid really serious relocation mistakes, like moving to a place where Saturn, Neptune, or Pluto falls on an angle.[3] You would also want to read about your chosen location in *Places*

---

[3]To get your map, have your correct birth time and credit card ready and call 1-800-MAP-PING. Or, send a check for $19.50 to Astro Numeric Services, PO Box 336, Ashland, OR 97520. An accurate time of birth is important, as the locations of the lines are based on it. You will get an interpretation booklet with helpful perspectives on the various lines. However, its viewpoint on the lines for the Moon tends to be jaundiced and needs to be taken with a grain of salt. (By this time, you may be thinking the same about me!) If you find the map hard to read, ask the company for a list of certified interpreters in your area.

Rated Almanac, a reference book that belongs in any astrologer's library.[4] When considering a move based on an Astro*Carto*Graphy map, it is important to refer to the birth chart for interpretation and timing. Suppose you are thinking of moving to one of your Venus lines, considered the best places in the world to find love. However, if your natal Venus has every bad aspect imaginable, your undesirable long-standing patterns in relationships would be not only active but exacerbated there. You'd be better off picking one of the Descendant lines, like Sun or Jupiter on the Descendant, if love is a goal. Timing is also important even when moving to a positive location. Don't move when nothing is happening to your Moon, IC, or 4th house planets, or when Neptune is aspecting them. If you do, you could just sit and spin your wheels for a costly year or two.

As you can see, relocating isn't just a matter of packing boxes and calling a mover. You may find, however, that while packing, you take an intense trip down memory lane. Each object you touch has memories and feelings attached, which you may relive. The process of deciding what to keep and what to get rid of involves reevaluating your priorities and values. A move is an immense readjustment in many lunar areas of life, for what is more basic than the home? A crab goes through a period of vulnerability when it sheds its shell. We, too, may feel especially vulnerable for at least a year after a move—a complete cycle of lunations. There can even be strong somatic reactions, particularly to the stomach or menstrual cycle. Lunar types, in particular, can find moving distressing. A move is nothing to take lightly; give yourself plenty of space to feel the losses and insecurities and to lay down roots in the new home. (Bach's **Walnut,** for those in transition, may be needed for much of that first year.)

Baying at the Moon— Lunar Transits and Your Emotions

An outer planet transit to the Moon requires a shift in your emotional economy. Review the birth position and its aspects. They will help you understand your own past style of emotional management. Recall the discussions of your emotional habits and the feelings your Moon sign is most comfortable with, as well as the ones you'd prefer to deny. These old habits and de-

---

[4]By Richard Boyer and David Savageau, it is published by Prentice Hall Travel, New York, and is periodically updated.

fenses may no longer be effective under the pressure of outer planet aspects. During a siege to the Moon, people are often inundated with feelings they have held at bay for far too long. This is especially likely during the first crossover by the outer planet. Those who'd prefer to keep on repressing are reminded that even the transiting Moon can set off a tantrum or catharsis. Imagine how much more purging an outer planet transit can bring. If you work with your lunar hemisphere and embrace your true feelings all along, however, there won't be such a backlog to trigger.

Yep, given strong enough aspects, any one of these transits can provoke a lunar meltdown, and we may need help to get through them optimally. We don't have to do it alone, and it's a rare individual who would have the objectivity, anyway. Of all the times in our lives, it is one of the most effective to be in therapy. Our patterns in the lunar areas are so subjective, so habitual, and so automatic that we can barely see them. Family dysfunctions—or their results in our psyches—are likely to be stirred up. If you've never been in therapy—never exposed the dark side of the Moon to bright sunlight—this might be the time to give it a try. If you've had therapy in the past, old issues may come up for reexamination, so a brief return could be helpful.

Working with a female healer or therapist now can provide a corrective mothering experience that can bring on a deep healing. The emotional programming by our mothers is likely to come up, needing to be released. In the process, we can also deprogram any negative conditioning we got from Mom and gain a new model of womanhood. However, we might hate paying for the mothering we think we should get for free. (Male helpers would be suggested under transits to the Sun or Mars.)

What's the reward for allowing ourselves to feel and for working on integrating our emotions? We can establish a greater comfort zone for feelings our folks never approved of and wouldn't want us to be having now. We can develop healthier coping mechanisms and greater authenticity, based on attending to our lunar needs. We can experience relief from troublesome old emotional habits. You may find the flower remedies suggested for your Moon sign in chapter 5 especially important in getting through this crisis and establishing a sounder emotional balance.

Naturally, not all transits to the Moon produce the same effects. A Scorpio Moon will react more intensely than a Gemini Moon. Remember that soft aspects can be less stressful than hard ones. The Moon's natal house position, and that of the transiting planet, will show where this process is apt to be most active. However, a Moon transit is a Moon transit, and you have emotions in every area of life, not just in the matters of its natal house position. Let's look at some possible scenarios.

When Saturn Transits the Moon, we could be in a somber, even depressed state. Sometimes, if it triggers and repeats birth chart aspects, this depression can be biochemical, even genetically-based, often from the mother's side of the family. More generally, anxiety, worry, and stress plague us because we're facing reality and the passage of time. (Bach's **Aspen, White Chestnut,** and—in panic states—**Rock Rose** can help calm our fears and worries.) The worry and sadness are often related to the loss of lunar safety nets and the demand that we take on more responsibility, at certain adult rites of passage. We ultimately make those commitments—we have precious little choice— and may come to feel satisfaction at our new status and roles. (FES's **Fairy Lantern,** or **Milkweed** can help the Peter Pans among us to mature.)

When Chiron Transits the Moon, Joyce Mason says that issues of health or body awareness can arise, especially in Moon-ruled body parts. The emotional connection to illness and self-undoing through negative habits like overeating, consuming too much coffee, or alcohol may beg you to face these issues. You may also have a very strong need to have and/or give emotional support and crave acceptance of family, or family-like groups. Early wounding around family dysfunction may surface to be dealt with. Especially strong may be the feeling you do not or did not belong. The FES and Pegasus essence, **Shooting Star,** is ideal for restoring a sense of being joined with others. The need to either sever or heal family ties and salve your own soul are paramount. Rejection by mother or bonding issues may come up. **Evening Primrose** essence by FES is helpful for healing those experiences that may go back even as far as *in utero.* You may tune in to being unwanted, unexpected, or the fact that Mom just wasn't ready for parenthood.

It is an inner time, where extra solitude is essential. It is an excellent season of life for counseling and retreats, where you can sort out your feelings and seek a sense of completion. Combined with adult wisdom and experience, the outcome of the emotional reenactment and release of the past is personal empowerment.

In addition, intuition is likely to become very strong, in either sex. Unless you are well-versed in psychic phenomena, you could feel like you're going crazy because you become such a radio receiver for information all around you. At first, it can be kind of spooky. If you feel too open and overwhelmed by these experiences, try **Canyon Dudleya** flower essence by FES. **Yarrow,** made by many companies, is a near-must during these times, to clearly distinguish your own energy from that of others you are picking up on, so that you aren't stuck feeling their emotions. On the up side, during flowing aspects, you can access the subconscious mind and Higher Self better than ever. Either way, it is a time of intense emotions and sensitivity. Your perception of others' needs can become acute. If you can ground this wave of feeling through tools like meditation and flower remedies, you can make quantum leaps in your inner growth and your ability to help or heal others, as well as yourself.

When Uranus Transits the Moon, my experience is that emotions we disowned may suddenly and shockingly come to the surface. No longer the modern, rational, enlightened beings we thought, we are chastened to find out how emotional we really are. If we disowned anger, it comes at us from left field, sometimes explosively. If we disavowed grief, we are suddenly immersed in it. There is no time for reflection or processing, for our feelings are blindingly clear, impossible to deny, and demanding action. We may even think we're having a nervous breakdown, but it's really a breakthrough in which we come to act more authentically. We are revealed as human, as capable of certain "primitive" responses we prided ourselves on having evolved beyond. Get off your high horse! This transit can be truly enlightening, for it puts you back in the human race. (Desert Alchemy's **Embracing Humanness** formula can be your price of admission.)

When Neptune Transits the Moon, our emotions are all at sea and it is hard to know precisely what we feel. Then we do find out what we feel but wish to God we hadn't! Old defense mechanisms crumble, and we are flooded with emotions we felt we were too spiritual to have. In the lunar areas of life, denial may be stripped away, and we face painful realities. We want to blot out the pain, so we fog out, maybe with some help from our drug of choice. (Mine is ice cream.) We may slide into a hopeless, helpless frame of mind. "Why me?" we ask, full of self-pity. We seek spiritual answers because everyone we relied on is as confused as we are. Ultimately, we find solace in the quest, strength to face these new challenges, and a more compassionate understanding of others' suffering, including what our parents went through. We also can't fool ourselves so easily about our feelings anymore. (**Fuchsia** by FES is helpful in sorting out diffuse emotions, and **Violet Curls** by Desert Alchemy can clear out the jumble of feelings. For self-pity, try Bach's **Heather**.)

When Pluto Transits the Moon, perhaps in response to a family crisis, strong feelings may arise about the past and our earliest relationship with Mother and even grandmother. Sometimes things we forgot or repressed all these years come to the surface and we relive and ultimately release them. Lunar and family of origin issues we thought long dead come up one more time, so we can gain a new perspective on them.

You may find *Healing Pluto Problems* a survival manual for this transit. In all the lunar areas of life, the murk and mire of our shadow side confronts us and we face it squarely. (For the shadow, try **Black-Eyed Susan**, by FES, or **Rainbow Cactus** by Desert Alchemy.) With or without a plumber's helper in the form of therapy, we dredge up suppressed emotions. We feel them all, repeatedly and even obsessively, until we've drunk the last drop of bitter gall. We chew on resentments (**Willow**), and we mourn the unmourned losses in our lives (**Bleeding Heart**). We experience the betrayals and abuses of power we've been blind to up to now (**Centaury**). We ruminate obsessively on our feelings until we eventually get on our own nerves, not to mention the nerves of people so unfortunate as to be close to us. Finally, after all our work, we are lighter, clearer, and freer because we're no longer carrying around the emotional baggage of the past.

Get Out Your Quake Kit!

You know, I think this is just about the scariest chapter I ever wrote! I've written about addiction, incest, domestic violence, death, and even possession, but this is the worst! That's because transits to the Moon strike at our very foundations—the home, mother, the family, our source of security. These are the very areas where we least tolerate change, even when we're headed somewhere better. This is where we are at our most emotional. If you've found these descriptions alarming, it is only a demonstration of how crucial the Moon is in our horoscopes. Transits to the Sun can challenge us and make us stretch, but they're easier to take than transits to the Moon. If you're having one, you *will* live through it. Your life may even be better for it, but you will need to work hard on keeping your lunar hemisphere in balance. Consistant work with the tools given throughout this book can help, and so can the tools in the next chapter.

CHAPTER 16

MOON AS MANTRA—MOON AS MIRROR

Back in Brooklyn, I used to see a homeless old woman named Madge sitting on the steps of a deli in my yuppie neighborhood. Her skin was ashen with vintage dirt, she wore layers of tattered clothing, and she ranted at unseen tormenters, but she captured my imagination. She clutched a thick manuscript in her stubby hands, and it grew thicker every day. She didn't write the way you and I do, she wrote in a circle, a steadily growing circle from the center of the page to its outermost edges. Living on the streets never deterred her from her work—her powers of concentration were awesome! I always fancied that Madge was a real live crone inspired by one of the Moon goddesses—not Diana but perhaps Hecate—and that what she was writing might one day save us all.

I've been writing in circles, myself, in every single chapter. We've covered the Moon, its path through the twelve signs, and all its functions again and again. I've tried to keep this book rational and respectable by citing scientific evidence of connections between the Moon's meanings. But now it's Madge's turn. (Truthfully, you may already have caught glimpses of her here and there.) The Moon is by nature non-linear and non-rational, so not all the answers to lunar problems can be logical. What we'll be looking at in this final chapter are some looney solutions, some of them channeled and some simply off the beaten path. If woowoo is not what you do, let's part company now. Seriously. I hope you liked the book.

Genes and Genealogy—A Way back Home?

Because lunar types' family ties are strong—whether positive or negative—they are painfully affected by the death or loss of family members. Genealogy is a soothing pursuit to help them regain a sense of belonging and continuity. Its growing popularity attests to how many of us feel the need to get back in touch with our roots. Many of the people I know who pursue it seriously are either Cancerians or lunar types.

Perhaps it is not so much a hobby as a healing tool. It would be especially satisfying during a Pluto transit to the Moon, the IC, or a 4th house planet. As Pluto opposed my Moon, my mother died, and I felt drawn for the first time to track down our family tree. I was fortunate to be doing this research while a few older relatives were still around, including the family historian, 90-year-old Great-Aunt Edna. Many families are so scattered today that their records are quickly being lost. By contrast, Gretchen Lawlor tells me that Maori elders in New Zealand can—and in fact are expected to—recite up to 28 generations of ancestors before they speak out at ceremonies. Put that in your ceremonial pipe and smoke it!

The solar world—helpful at last—is rapidly computerizing major record sources, as in the Mormon database in Salt Lake City and the immigration files at Ellis Island. There are software programs for genealogy, some very inexpensive.[1] There are now CD-ROMs of databases where you can type in a name and learn where to find information about the person. The Internet has genealogy special interest groups where members share tips and sources.[2] If your own Great-Aunt Edna is history, you may have to get onto the information superhighway to find out where you came from. (Me, I'm still sitting on the on-ramp at HoJos, dunking doughnuts and wondering if I'm really up for the trip.)

An interesting Astro*Carto*Graphy application that I have found is that many people have significant MH and IC lines in the old country in the areas their forebears came from. One woman who traced her distant Native American roots found that her Moon MH line ran through the tribe's reservation. The nature of the line may tell something of the reasons for em-

---

[1] A great source of such shareware, as well as programs on astrology, numerology, and herbology, is Software Labs, 1-800-569-7900.

[2] Once you have hooked up to the Internet, you'd find six or seven of them in the news groups under *soc.genealogy*, including the extensions *.misc, .surnames, .methods,* and *.computer.* The National Genealogical Society has its own free bulletin board, which you can reach via modem by calling 703-528-2612. Their chapters in each state and major city also have their own bulletin boards, which the national organization can put you in touch with.

igrating. For instance, one descendant of Holocaust survivors had a nasty Saturn-Pluto crossing in the area of the camp. If you don't know exactly where in a country your Great-Great came from, a line running through there might give a clue. My Irish Cunningham ancestors are untraceable—they came during the upheaval of the Great Famine in the 1840s. However, my Sun MH line runs right through Galway, and I have never been more deeply stirred by a place in my life. Check your own Astro*Carto*Graphy lines to see what they reveal about the family history.

Your forerunners can be more than just boxes on a geneagram if you're at ease with talking to or dreaming about the dear departed. Death is such a taboo topic in the solar world that most Westerners are freaked out by the idea of spirit communication. Because we've become so secular and scientific, we have lost our sense of the continuity of life after death. Still, one poll showed that 60 percent of Americans felt they had communicated with a loved one who had died.

Other, more lunar cultures take for granted these contacts with deceased relatives. In their funeral rituals and other ceremonies, they regularly remember and honor the spirits of the dead. These same cultures love their elders and respect their wisdom as we no longer do, so it is natural for them to want to stay in touch. Native Americans mention their ancestors regularly in pipe ceremonies and feel they receive advice and help from them. Followers of some Eastern sects, such as the Japanese and Tibetan ones, have a special altar in their homes for the ancestors. Food and other offerings are regularly left on these altars.

I'm not suggesting that you keep serving Uncle Charlie his favorite rhubarb pie long after he's gone. I do know firsthand that consolation can come from connecting with those who've gone before. By cutting off from them, we lose our heritage and our sense of history. By reconnecting, we may also awaken inherited gifts and abilities. In some cultures, they say such practices wake up the blood, in the sense of blood ties.

This awakening of the blood, I have also experienced. Several years ago, when my parents were long since dead, I went back to my little, rural hometown. I visited and took care of a maternal aunt who was dying of cancer. When I got back to New York, I was surprised to find that my maternal grandfather had come to live with me. We weren't that close when I was small, and he had been dead 40 years, but he had apparently been tied to my aunt. He and my mother and her sisters were all brilliant with plants, although not with herbs. Living in the city, I had virtually no contact with growing things. Under his influence, I joined the Brooklyn Botanical Garden and spent hours in their various flower beds. I became fascinated with plant families, Latin names, and the history of flowers. He seemed to have a natural gift for communicating with plant spirits, and being with him opened up this possibility for me. These new endeavors greatly enhanced my understanding of the flower essences.

In the couple of years my grandfather was with me, I was conscious of building a loving tie. He was known throughout his region for improving strains of watermelon, so I kept some watermelon seeds in a special place for him. It wasn't an altar really—I'm not like that—but it was sort of an altar. It was a little one, you understand, where I kept his picture and my Mom's and maybe some flowers and, of course, the watermelon seeds.

How would you go about talking to your forerunners? Well, how did you talk to Grams when she was still around? It's not a whole lot more complex or mystifying than that. I don't trumpet it about, but I am a medium. I find that dead people are much like anyone else. If you give them love and attention, you'll hear from them. If you neglect and ignore them, you won't. (Be aware, however, that it is no more healthy to be codependent on those who have passed away than it is with the living. And there aren't any support groups for it, either.)

If you want contact with your ancestors, talk to them regularly with all your heart, letting them know you still care and want them in your life. You might make an offering or contribution in their name, especially to a cause or group they valued. Pictures or family mementos kept in a special place strengthen the contact. **Angel's Trumpet** by FES aids in the connection. You might not get answers right away, at least not answers you'd trust. Dreams are often more comfortable for such work, so you might find yourself dreaming of them or waking up with solutions to practical problems you are confronting. It's only a suggestion, but one Cancerians or lunar types might find comforting.

Lunar Hemisphere, Do You Copy?

We've spoken a great deal about the benefits of getting in touch with your lunar hemisphere. No doubt you've been wondering how to go about opening a line of communication with it. (Where, pray tell, does one address the e-mail?) We spoke about meditation, individually and in groups, full Moon meetings, rituals, and connecting with the Moon goddess. Perhaps you are unsure of how to proceed or perhaps you are uncomfortable with such unorthodox and non-Western practices. To be honest, so am I—not on any religious grounds, but simply because they are alien to one with such a corn-fed midwestern background.

To find more specific and comfortable methods, therefore, I asked for help from a very fine psychic, Andrew Ramer, who relayed the techniques that follow. Some of them sound slightly loony, but they make sense when you consider how deeply interrelated they are with all the Moon's meanings. I pass them along, and you are invited to try any that appeal to you. Because it always faces away from us, we never get to see the dark side of the Moon, but here we might just get a glimpse.

Andrew says that as a general principle, our time in the womb is the purest lunar experience, so many of the techniques are womb-like in content. The unborn baby rocks in the fluid and moves around slowly, exploring the walls of the womb and touching its own body, which is covered with a slippery substance. The womb is not dark, as we might think, but is lit with a gentle glow like moonlight. Many of the suggestions also rely on indirect light.

Water: Lie on your side in a tub of warm water in a fetal position and rock gently and effortlessly, not trying to make it happen. The use of bath oil would evoke the slipperiness of the baby's skin. This is most effective before going to sleep, and, if nothing else, is relaxing. Afterward, you might direct your subconscious to use dreams to work on lunar problems. Ask that you remember the dreams.

Massage: One reason massage is so pleasurable is that it slows the heartbeat and unifies rhythms so that perceptions are altered. Self-massage with oil and closed eyes is also evocative of the slippery coating and the self-exploration of the unborn child. It is extremely soothing, especially before going to sleep.

Rocking: Rocking yourself in a chair, or being held and rocked by someone else, evokes the lunar side. The spirits said that it would be just as therapeutic to be rocked quietly by your therapist for half an hour as to spend an hour analyzing things. (Spirits obviously don't understand the realities of conventional therapy!)

The Navel: The notion of contemplating one's navel has become slightly ridiculous to Westerners, a symbol of the impractical mystic. Nonetheless, this technique was originally for the purpose of reconnecting with the womb experience and contemplating where the life energies came from.

Food: Andrew says, "Sometimes the only thing that works is to make soup!" This makes sense—isn't chicken soup a symbol of mother-love to many of us? Andrew designated certain vegetables as lunar—root vegetables, like potatoes, turnips, rutabagas, and carrots. They should be included in the soup, but only in modest amounts, as too much of them can be toxic.

In general, we are advised to pay more attention to food and to nourishing ourselves in a loving way. Food is to the born person what the umbilical chord is to the unborn, except that for the unborn the connection is direct and effortless, while we have to work at it. Nonetheless, the right foods, lovingly prepared and eaten, can satisfy us in a deep, emotional way.

Another practice that should not be neglected is the ritual of blessing the food, as in saying grace. Charging the food with life-force energy makes it alive rather than inert. Just hold your hands over your meal for a moment, asking that spiritual energies be channeled into it. Imagine a flow of energy passing through your fingers. Junk foods that have received this charge of energy can do you as much good as health foods that haven't been charged. If you've studied reiki or some other form of energy or light, use those tools to charge your food.

Housework: Although we've come to despise housework as symbolic of feminine oppression, the acts involved in homemaking are in themselves antidotes to alienation and depression. As we all—male as well as female, children as well as adults—perform loving acts to beautify our homes and make them more comfortable, we lose our feelings of rootlessness. We line our nests with our own vibrations and make them homey and secure.

Motions associated with certain homemaking tasks can in themselves produce altered states of consciousness. The rhythmic strokes involved in sweeping or kneading dough can change you at an inner level. Dishwashing can be a water ritual, an inner cleansing, with the circular motions inducing a meditative state. It is the craft of the household arts, rather than the role of housewife, because every human being can and should be involved in making a house a home.

Artwork: Handcraft, art work, and even knitting can slow and synchronize our rhythms. Slow, short deliberate strokes, like those of a paintbrush, alter the perceptions of the artist, as they evoke the tiny movements of the infant exploring the womb. Working in clay uses those same, slow strokes and evokes the slippery feeling.

Natural Childbirth: When I shared these exercises with one of my students, Mariah Larkin, she made the additional suggestion of trying the exercises recommended for natural childbirth. The deep breathing and relaxation techniques would alter consciousness, but the further evocation of the birth experience itself could bring up emotional insights, particularly in the maternal area. (The therapy technique known as rebirthing might be quite powerful for strongly lunar individuals, especially those with family wounding.)

Candlelight: This is the most striking of the recommendations. First meditate in front of a candle for three to five minutes, concentrating on the flame. Then turn your back on the candle, so it is behind you and the light is indirect like the Moon's. What comes up is something you haven't been facing, something going on in the hidden part of yourself. Thus, this exercise may evoke unsettling feelings but will reveal parts of yourself that need working on. This last technique evokes many lunar metaphors that may help us understand the process of contacting the lunar part of ourselves. Moonlight is indirect, but we can see by it in a different way.

Remedies for the Moon—and Stars

Since we're now firmly entrenched in the woowoo side of things, we might as well go for broke. Flower essences are only the tip of the iceberg in a category called vibrational remedies. There are essences made from gems, like Pegasus Products' **Moonstone**, and there are essences made from nothing at all. That is, they are made from the energy at the height of an eclipse, or at the summer solstice, or with the light of a star focused through a telescope lens. I don't use them much because my imagination, vast as it may be, still has its comfort zone.

I have seen them work, though. I've even been knocked for a loop by a few of them, like Pegasus' **Starlight Elixir for Sirius**, the star that conjuncts my nearly 13 degree Cancer Sun. Many of these vibrational remedies seem to produce more difficult healing crises than the flower remedies do, and that is another reason I stick with flowers in my own healing work. I'm not necessarily recommending any of the essences in this category, even though I believe in them, because I don't work with them enough to be a reliable informant. I'm just letting you know what's out there.

Still, you may be interested to know about the remedies based on the planets and the fixed stars. Two companies are making them. One is Pegasus Products, listed in chapter 5. The other set is the **Star Essences**, made by Drs. Paul and Mary Nash and available through Kelley Hunter, Box 311, Montpelier, VT 05601-0311. Not only are the planets except Pluto featured but also a great variety of the fixed stars, including Regulus, Arcturus, Spica, and Algol. Pegasus even made an elixir as the biggest fragment of the Shoemaker-Levy 9 comet hit Jupiter in July 1994.

Alaskan Flower Essence Project makes **Northern Lights** essence and **Solstice Sun**. The latter was prepared at the Summer Solstice, during the midnight Sun above the Arctic Circle. Quite a few companies make gem elixirs, including Pegasus Products, Pacific Esssences, and the Alaskan Flower Essence Project. Since the jewel Moonstone has a strong historical association with the Moon and women's physiology, the gem essence would seem promising for these matters as well. Write to the companies for more information. Siskiyou Essence Company has a complete kit based on cycles of the Sun and Moon. The lunar essences include the New Moon and the other three quarters, while the solar essences include **Dawn**, **Midday**, **Twilight**, and **Eclipse**. Siskiyou Essence Company can be reached at P.O. Box 353, Ashland, OR 97520.

I'm Being Followed by a Moon Shadow

> Moon light is experienced as soothing and calming. The Moon not only reflects sunlight, but polarizes it. When light is polarized, it is channeled. The rays are concentrated in specific directions, rather than bouncing randomly around, as in sunlight.
>
> —Kathleen Rathbone[3]

Just as the light of the Moon is indirect, so must be the approach to our lunar hemisphere at times. We need not face the music to hear it, and we need not always confront the emotional or relationship issues head-on. Our nightly dreams can be healing and bring us greater clarity, if we direct them, and so will many of the techniques considered here. If you use them and nothing seems to happen, remember that things happen in the dark of the Moon even though we do not see them. The period between the darkening of the Moon and the first sliver of the new Moon is about three days. When you are stuck, you can consciously choose a three-day moratorium to do inner work on the matter. Some work will go on unconsciously and in your dreams, and by the third day, you should have your answer.

---

[3]From an editorial in *Womanspirit*, v.2:8, Summer, 1976, p. 51.

Just as the Moon is cyclical and has its own rhythms, the matters of the lunar hemisphere have their own rhythms and cycles, too. You can't rush them without losing the rhythm. We need to develop patience with internal processes and with waiting until there is readiness. The new Moon doesn't come until its proper time—you can't force it. The solar world wants to force things, to make them happen on demand. It doesn't recognize the need for womb time when we are preparing for something new or when human needs are involved.

These ideas are all metaphorical, but the language of the lunar hemisphere is more intuitive and symbolic than verbal. Similarly, art and music speak directly to our emotions without the need for words. Poetry doesn't always make sense in a linear, logical way, but it moves our hearts. It is solar to believe we must hit everything head on—verbally, rationally, and consciously. The lunar areas of our lives require gentle handling—soft, indirect light—but that doesn't mean they aren't real. Before we sent cameras to the dark side of the Moon, we didn't know what it looked like, but we trusted it was there. We have to trust our innards, our instincts and intuitions, even our own internal rhythms, and then we won't be cut off from the Moon.

We need both the Sun and the Moon to be balanced and whole, yet we live in a society which values the solar principles and devalues the lunar. We live in a solar world and we can't escape it. The solar world is not even a bad thing. It's positive that we're living in a world where women have equal opportunity to develop their solar side by experiencing the growth that education and career can bring. It's positive that we're coming to a point of choice about whether we become mothers and homemakers. It's positive that we aren't all stuck in our hometowns our whole lives but have the freedom to explore other locations and cultures. But all these choices bring stresses, losses, and insecurities that need to be allowed for.

The stresses we've been considering only become damaging when we try to be solar at the expense of shutting off lunar qualities. Instead we need to achieve some kind of balance, like the balance spelled out by the classic astrologer and philosopher Manly P. Hall:

> The Sun is of the nature of reason; the Moon of imagination. The Sun is knowledge; the Moon, hope and faith. The Sun is strength; the Moon relaxation. The life of man must have its solar aspect, which is action, and its lunar aspect, which is reflection.[4]

---

[4]Manly P. Hall, *The Medicine of the Sun and Moon* (Los Angeles: Philosophical Research Society, Inc., n.d.), p 16.

As you can see, the solar and lunar sides of ourselves are two separate processes, and neither can be neglected if we want to be complete. Yet, the only time the Sun and Moon line up exactly in the sky is at an eclipse—and then you can't see either of them!

How, then, can we survive as lunar types in a solar world? Simply by allowing ourselves to be as lunar as we need to be. The Moon rules the home, and we must make room for ourselves to be lunar in the privacy of our own homes. Not only must we develop the freedom to be lunar ourselves, but we need to foster a secure atmosphere where our loved ones feel comfortable in being lunar, too. By working together, by nurturing ourselves and others, we can all make it through these troubled times.

APPENDIX:
MOON TABLES FOR 1997–2004

1997 New Moons and the Houses they Affect.

Degree & Date: Rising Sign:	1/9 18CP	2/7 18AQ	3/9E 18PI	4/7 17AR	5/6 16TA	6/5 14GE	7/4 12CN	8/3 11LE	9/1E 9VI	10/1 8LI	10/31 8SC	11/30 7SG	12/29 8CP
Aries	10	11	12	1	2	3	4	5	6	7	8	9	10
Taurus	9	10	11	12	1	2	3	4	5	6	7	8	9
Gemini	8	9	10	11	12	1	2	3	4	5	6	7	8
Cancer	7	8	9	10	11	12	1	2	3	4	5	6	7
Leo	6	7	8	9	10	11	12	1	2	3	4	5	6
Virgo	5	6	7	8	9	10	11	12	1	2	3	4	5
Libra	4	5	6	7	8	9	10	11	12	1	2	3	4
Scorpio	3	4	5	6	7	8	9	10	11	12	1	2	3
Sagittarius	2	3	4	5	6	7	8	9	10	11	12	1	2
Capricorn	1	2	3	4	5	6	7	8	9	10	11	12	1
Aquarius	12	1	2	3	4	5	6	7	8	9	10	11	12
Pisces	11	12	1	2	3	4	5	6	7	8	9	10	11

E = Eclipse

1997 FULL MOONS AND THE HOUSES THEY AFFECT.

Degree & Date:

Rising Sign:	1/23 3LE	2/22 3VI	3/24E 3LI	4/22 2SC	5/22 1SG	6/20 29SG	7/20 27CP	8/18 25AQ	9/16E 23SG	10/15 22AR	11/14 22TA	12/14 22GE
Aries	5-11	6-12	7-1	8-2	9-3	9-3	10-4	11-5	12-6	1-7	2-8	3-9
Taurus	4-10	5-11	6-12	7-1	8-2	8-2	9-3	10-4	11-5	12-6	1-7	2-8
Gemini	3-9	4-10	5-11	6-12	7-1	7-1	8-2	9-3	10-4	11-5	12-6	1-7
Cancer	2-8	3-9	4-10	5-11	6-12	6-12	7-1	8-2	9-3	10-4	11-5	12-6
Leo	1-7	2-8	3-9	4-10	5-11	5-11	6-12	7-1	8-2	9-3	10-4	11-5
Virgo	12-6	1-7	2-8	3-9	4-10	4-10	5-11	6-12	7-1	8-2	9-3	10-4
Libra	11-5	12-6	1-7	2-8	3-9	3-9	4-10	5-11	6-12	7-1	8-2	9-3
Scorpio	10-4	11-5	12-6	1-7	2-8	2-8	3-9	4-10	5-11	6-12	7-1	8-2
Sagittarius	9-3	10-4	11-5	12-6	1-7	1-7	2-8	3-9	4-10	5-11	6-12	7-1
Capricorn	8-2	9-3	10-4	11-5	12-6	12-6	1-7	2-8	3-9	4-10	5-11	6-12
Aquarius	7-1	8-2	9-3	10-4	11-5	11-5	12-6	1-7	2-8	3-9	4-10	5-11
Pisces	6-12	7-1	8-2	9-3	10-4	10-4	11-5	12-6	1-7	2-8	3-9	4-10

E = Eclipse

1998 New Moons and the Houses they Affect.

Degree & Date:												
Rising Sign:	1/29 8AQ	2/26E 7PI	3/28 7AR	4/26 6TA	5/25 4GE	6/24 2CN	7/23 0LE	8/22E 28LE	9/20 27VI	10/20 26LI	11/19 26SC	12/18 26SG
Aries	11	12	1	2	3	4	5	5	6	7	8	9
Taurus	10	11	12	1	2	3	4	4	5	6	7	8
Gemini	9	10	11	12	1	2	3	3	4	5	6	7
Cancer	8	9	10	11	12	1	2	2	3	4	5	6
Leo	7	8	9	10	11	12	1	1	2	3	4	5
Virgo	6	7	8	9	10	11	12	12	1	2	3	4
Libra	5	6	7	8	9	10	11	11	12	1	2	3
Scorpio	4	5	6	7	8	9	10	10	11	12	1	2
Sagittarius	3	4	5	6	7	8	9	9	10	11	12	1
Capricorn	2	3	4	5	6	7	8	8	9	10	11	12
Aquarius	1	2	3	4	5	6	7	7	8	9	10	11
Pisces	12	1	2	3	4	5	6	6	7	8	9	10

E = Eclipse

1998 Full Moons and the Houses they Affect.

Degree & Date:

Rising Sign:	1/12 22CN	2/11 22LE	3/13E 22VI	4/11 21LI	5/11 20SC	6/10 19SG	7/9 17CP	8/8E 15AQ	9/6E 13PI	10/5 12AR	11/4 11TA	12/3 11GE
Aries	4-10	5-11	6-12	7-1	8-2	9-3	10-4	11-5	12-6	1-7	2-8	3-9
Taurus	3-9	4-10	5-11	6-12	7-1	8-2	9-3	10-4	11-5	12-6	1-7	2-8
Gemini	2-8	3-9	4-10	5-11	6-12	7-1	8-2	9-3	10-4	11-5	12-6	1-7
Cancer	1-7	2-8	3-9	4-10	5-11	6-12	7-1	8-2	9-3	10-4	11-5	12-6
Leo	12-6	1-7	2-8	3-9	4-10	5-11	6-12	7-1	8-2	9-3	10-4	11-5
Virgo	11-5	12-6	1-7	2-8	3-9	4-10	5-11	6-12	7-1	8-2	9-3	10-4
Libra	10-4	11-5	12-6	1-7	2-8	3-9	4-10	5-11	6-12	7-1	8-2	9-3
Scorpio	9-3	10-4	11-5	12-6	1-7	2-8	3-9	4-10	5-11	6-12	7-1	8-2
Sagittarius	8-2	9-3	10-4	11-5	12-6	1-7	2-8	3-9	4-10	5-11	6-12	7-1
Capricorn	7-1	8-2	9-3	10-4	11-5	12-6	1-7	2-8	3-9	4-10	5-11	6-12
Aquarius	6-12	7-1	8-2	9-3	10-4	11-5	12-6	1-7	2-8	3-9	4-10	5-11
Pisces	5-11	6-12	7-1	8-2	9-3	10-4	11-5	12-6	1-7	2-8	3-9	4-10

E = Eclipse

1999 New Moons and the Houses they Affect.

Degree & Date: Rising Sign:	1/17 27CP	2/16E 27AQ	3/17 26PI	4/16 25AR	5/15 24TA	6/13 22GE	7/13 20CN	8/11E 18LE	9/9 16VI	10/9 15LI	11/8 15SC	12/7 15SG
Aries	10	11	12	1	2	3	4	5	6	7	8	9
Taurus	9	10	11	12	1	2	3	4	5	6	7	8
Gemini	8	9	10	11	12	1	2	3	4	5	6	7
Cancer	7	8	9	10	11	12	1	2	3	4	5	6
Leo	6	7	8	9	10	11	12	1	2	3	4	5
Virgo	5	6	7	8	9	10	11	12	1	2	3	4
Libra	4	5	6	7	8	9	10	11	12	1	2	3
Scorpio	3	4	5	6	7	8	9	10	11	12	1	2
Sagittarius	2	3	4	5	6	7	8	9	10	11	12	1
Capricorn	1	2	3	4	5	6	7	8	9	10	11	12
Aquarius	12	1	2	3	4	5	6	7	8	9	10	11
Pisces	11	12	1	2	3	4	5	6	7	8	9	10

E = Eclipse

1999 Full Moons and the Houses they Affect.

Degree & Date:

Rising Sign:	1/2 11CN	1/31E 11LE	3/2 11VI	3/31 10LI	4/30 9SC	5/30 8SG	6/28 6CP	7/28E 4AQ	8/26 3PI	9/25 1AR	10/24 1TA	11/23 0GE	12/22 0CN
Aries	4-10	5-11	6-12	7-1	8-2	9-3	10-4	11-5	12-6	1-7	2-8	3-9	4-10
Taurus	3-9	4-10	5-11	6-12	7-1	8-2	9-3	10-4	11-5	12-6	1-7	2-8	3-9
Gemini	2-8	3-9	4-10	5-11	6-12	7-1	8-2	9-3	10-4	11-5	12-6	1-7	2-8
Cancer	1-7	2-8	3-9	4-10	5-11	6-12	7-1	8-2	9-3	10-4	11-5	12-6	1-7
Leo	12-6	1-7	2-8	3-9	4-10	5-11	6-12	7-1	8-2	9-3	10-4	11-5	12-6
Virgo	11-5	12-6	1-7	2-8	3-9	4-10	5-11	6-12	7-1	8-2	9-3	10-4	11-5
Libra	10-4	11-5	12-6	1-7	2-8	3-9	4-10	5-11	6-12	7-1	8-2	9-3	10-4
Scorpio	9-3	10-4	11-5	12-6	1-7	2-8	3-9	4-10	5-11	6-12	7-1	8-2	9-3
Sagittarius	8-2	9-3	10-4	11-5	12-6	1-7	2-8	3-9	4-10	5-11	6-12	7-1	8-2
Capricorn	7-1	8-2	9-3	10-4	11-5	12-6	1-7	2-8	3-9	4-10	5-11	6-12	7-1
Aquarius	6-12	7-1	8-2	9-3	10-4	11-5	12-6	1-7	2-8	3-9	4-10	5-11	6-12
Pisces	5-11	6-12	7-1	8-2	9-3	10-4	11-5	12-6	1-7	2-8	3-9	4-10	5-11

E = Eclipse

2000 New Moons and the Houses they Affect.

Degree & Date:	1/6	2/5E	3/6	4/4	5/4	6/2	7/1	7/31E	8/29	9/27	10/27	11/25	12/25E
Rising Sign:	15CP	16AQ	15PI	15AR	14TA	12GE	10CN	8LE	6VI	5LI	4SC	4SG	4CP
Aries	10	11	12	1	2	3	4	5	6	7	8	9	10
Taurus	9	10	11	12	1	2	3	4	5	6	7	8	9
Gemini	8	9	10	11	12	1	2	3	4	5	6	7	8
Cancer	7	8	9	10	11	12	1	2	3	4	5	6	7
Leo	6	7	8	9	10	11	12	1	2	3	4	5	6
Virgo	5	6	7	8	9	10	11	12	1	2	3	4	5
Libra	4	5	6	7	8	9	10	11	12	1	2	3	4
Scorpio	3	4	5	6	7	8	9	10	11	12	1	2	3
Sagittarius	2	3	4	5	6	7	8	9	10	11	12	1	2
Capricorn	1	2	3	4	5	6	7	8	9	10	11	12	1
Aquarius	12	1	2	3	4	5	6	7	8	9	10	11	12
Pisces	11	12	1	2	3	4	5	6	7	8	9	10	11

E = Eclipse

| Degree & Date: | 1/21E | 2/19 | 3/20 | 4/18 | 5/18 | 6/16 | 7/16E | 8/15 | 9/13 | 10/13 | 11/11 | 12/11 |
Rising Sign:	0LE	0VI	29VI	28LI	27SC	26SG	24CP	22AQ	21PI	20AR	19TA	19GE
Aries	5-11	6-12	7-1	8-2	9-3	9-3	10-4	11-5	12-6	1-7	2-8	3-9
Taurus	4-10	5-11	6-12	7-1	8-2	8-2	9-3	10-4	11-5	12-6	1-7	2-8
Gemini	3-9	4-10	5-11	6-12	7-1	7-1	8-2	9-3	10-4	11-5	12-6	1-7
Cancer	2-8	3-9	4-10	5-11	6-12	6-12	7-1	8-2	9-3	10-4	11-5	12-6
Leo	1-7	2-8	3-9	4-10	5-11	5-11	6-12	7-1	8-2	9-3	10-4	11-5
Virgo	12-6	1-7	2-8	3-9	4-10	4-10	5-11	6-12	7-1	8-2	9-3	10-4
Libra	11-5	12-6	1-7	2-8	3-9	3-9	4-10	5-11	6-12	7-1	8-2	9-3
Scorpio	10-4	11-5	12-6	1-7	2-8	2-8	3-9	4-10	5-11	6-12	7-1	8-2
Sagittarius	9-3	10-4	11-5	12-6	1-7	1-7	2-8	3-9	4-10	5-11	6-12	7-1
Capricorn	8-2	9-3	10-4	11-5	12-6	12-6	1-7	2-8	3-9	4-10	5-11	6-12
Aquarius	7-1	8-2	9-3	10-4	11-5	11-5	12-6	1-7	2-8	3-9	4-10	5-11
Pisces	6-12	7-1	8-2	9-3	10-4	10-4	11-5	12-6	1-7	2-8	3-9	4-10

E = Eclipse

2001 New Moons and the Houses they Affect.

Degree & Date: Rising Sign:	1/24 4AQ	2/23 4PI	3/25 4AR	4/23 3TA	5/23 2GE	6/21E 0CN	7/20 28CN	8/19 26LE	9/17 24VI	10/16 23LI	11/15 22SC	12/14E 22SG
Aries	11	12	1	2	3	4	4	5	6	7	8	9
Taurus	10	11	12	1	2	3	3	4	5	6	7	8
Gemini	9	10	11	12	1	2	2	3	4	5	6	7
Cancer	8	9	10	11	12	1	1	2	3	4	5	6
Leo	7	8	9	10	11	12	12	1	2	3	4	5
Virgo	6	7	8	9	10	11	11	12	1	2	3	4
Libra	5	6	7	8	9	10	10	11	12	1	2	3
Scorpio	4	5	6	7	8	9	9	10	11	12	1	2
Sagittarius	3	4	5	6	7	8	8	9	10	11	12	1
Capricorn	2	3	4	5	6	7	7	8	9	10	11	12
Aquarius	1	2	3	4	5	6	6	7	8	9	10	11
Pisces	12	1	2	3	4	5	5	6	7	8	9	10

E = Eclipse

2001 FULL MOONS AND THE HOUSES THEY AFFECT.

Degree & Date:

Rising Sign:	1/9E 19CN	2/8 19LE	3/9 19VI	4/8 18LI	5/7 17SC	6/6 15SG	7/5 13CP	8/4 12AQ	9/2 10PI	10/2 9AR	11/1 8TA	11/30 8GE	12/20E 8CN
Aries	4-10	5-11	6-12	7-1	8-2	9-3	10-4	11-5	12-6	1-7	2-8	3-9	4-10
Taurus	3-9	4-10	5-11	6-12	7-1	8-2	9-3	10-4	11-5	12-6	1-7	2-8	3-9
Gemini	2-8	3-9	4-10	5-11	6-12	7-1	8-2	9-3	10-4	11-5	12-6	1-7	2-8
Cancer	1-7	2-8	3-9	4-10	5-11	6-12	7-1	8-2	9-3	10-4	11-5	12-6	1-7
Leo	12-6	1-7	2-8	3-9	4-10	5-11	6-12	7-1	8-2	9-3	10-4	11-5	12-6
Virgo	11-5	12-6	1-7	2-8	3-9	4-10	5-11	6-12	7-1	8-2	9-3	10-4	11-5
Libra	10-4	11-5	12-6	1-7	2-8	3-9	4-10	5-11	6-12	7-1	8-2	9-3	10-4
Scorpio	9-3	10-4	11-5	12-6	1-7	2-8	3-9	4-10	5-11	6-12	7-1	8-2	9-3
Sagittarius	8-2	9-3	10-4	11-5	12-6	1-7	2-8	3-9	4-10	5-11	6-12	7-1	8-2
Capricorn	7-1	8-2	9-3	10-4	11-5	12-6	1-7	2-8	3-9	4-10	5-11	6-12	7-1
Aquarius	6-12	7-1	8-2	9-3	10-4	11-5	12-6	1-7	2-8	3-9	4-10	5-11	6-12
Pisces	5-11	6-12	7-1	8-2	9-3	10-4	11-5	12-6	1-7	2-8	3-9	4-10	5-11

E = Eclipse

2002 New Moons and the Houses they Affect.

Degree & Date: Rising Sign:	1/13 23CP	2/12 23AQ	3/14 23PI	4/12 22AR	5/12 21TA	6/10E 20GE	7/10 18CN	8/8 16LE	9/7 14VI	10/6 13LI	11/4 12SC	12/4E 11SG
Aries	10	11	12	1	2	3	4	5	6	7	8	9
Taurus	9	10	11	12	1	2	3	4	5	6	7	8
Gemini	8	9	10	11	12	1	2	3	4	5	6	7
Cancer	7	8	9	10	11	12	1	2	3	4	5	6
Leo	6	7	8	9	10	11	12	1	2	3	4	5
Virgo	5	6	7	8	9	10	11	12	1	2	3	4
Libra	4	5	6	7	8	9	10	11	12	1	2	3
Scorpio	3	4	5	6	7	8	9	10	11	12	1	2
Sagittarius	2	3	4	5	6	7	8	9	10	11	12	1
Capricorn	1	2	3	4	5	6	7	8	9	10	11	12
Aquarius	12	1	2	3	4	5	6	7	8	9	10	11
Pisces	11	12	1	2	3	4	5	6	7	8	9	10

E = Eclipse

2002 FULL MOONS AND THE HOUSES THEY AFFECT.

Degree & Date:

Rising Sign:	1/28 8LE	2/27 8VI	3/28 8LI	4/27 6SC	5/26E 5SG	6/24E 3CP	7/24 1AQ	8/22 29AQ	9/21 28PI	10/21 27AR	11/20E 27TA	12/19 27GE
Aries	5-11	6-12	7-1	8-2	9-3	9-3	11-5	11-5	12-6	1-7	2-8	3-9
Taurus	4-10	5-11	6-12	7-1	8-2	8-2	10-4	10-4	11-5	12-6	1-7	2-8
Gemini	3-9	4-10	5-11	6-12	7-1	7-1	9-3	9-3	10-4	11-5	12-6	1-7
Cancer	2-8	3-9	4-10	5-11	6-12	6-12	8-2	8-2	9-3	10-4	11-5	12-6
Leo	1-7	2-8	3-9	4-10	5-11	5-11	7-1	7-1	8-2	9-3	10-4	11-5
Virgo	12-6	1-7	2-8	3-9	4-10	4-10	6-12	6-12	7-1	8-2	9-3	10-4
Libra	11-5	12-6	1-7	2-8	3-9	3-9	5-11	5-11	6-12	7-1	8-2	9-3
Scorpio	10-4	11-5	12-6	1-7	2-8	2-8	4-10	4-10	5-11	6-12	7-1	8-2
Sagittarius	9-3	10-4	11-5	12-6	1-7	1-7	3-9	3-9	4-10	5-11	6-12	7-1
Capricorn	8-2	9-3	10-4	11-5	12-6	12-6	2-8	2-8	3-9	4-10	5-11	6-12
Aquarius	7-1	8-2	9-3	10-4	11-5	11-5	1-7	1-7	2-8	3-9	4-10	5-11
Pisces	6-12	7-1	8-2	9-3	10-4	10-4	12-6	12-6	1-7	2-8	3-9	4-10

E = Eclipse

2003 New Moons and the Houses they Affect.

Degree & Date:

Rising Sign:	1/2 12CP	2/1 12AQ	3/3 12PI	4/1 11AR	5/1 10TA	5/31E 9GE	6/29 7CN	7/29 5LE	8/27 4VI	9/26 2LI	10/25 1SC	11/23E 1SG	12/23 1CP
Aries	10	11	12	1	2	3	4	5	6	7	8	9	10
Taurus	9	10	11	12	1	2	3	4	5	6	7	8	9
Gemini	8	9	10	11	12	1	2	3	4	5	6	7	8
Cancer	7	8	9	10	11	12	1	2	3	4	5	6	7
Leo	6	7	8	9	10	11	12	1	2	3	4	5	6
Virgo	5	6	7	8	9	10	11	12	1	2	3	4	5
Libra	4	5	6	7	8	9	10	11	12	1	2	3	4
Scorpio	3	4	5	6	7	8	9	10	11	12	1	2	3
Sagittarius	2	3	4	5	6	7	8	9	10	11	12	1	2
Capricorn	1	2	3	4	5	6	7	8	9	10	11	12	1
Aquarius	12	1	2	3	4	5	6	7	8	9	10	11	12
Pisces	11	12	1	2	3	4	5	6	7	8	9	10	11

E = Eclipse

2003 FULL MOONS AND THE HOUSES THEY AFFECT.

Degree & Date:

Rising Sign:	1/18 28CN	2/16 28LE	3/18 27VI	4/16 26LI	5/16E 24SC	6/14 23SG	7/13 20CP	8/12 19AQ	9/10 17PI	10/10 16AR	11/9E 16TA	12/8 16GE
Aries	4-10	5-11	6-12	7-1	8-2	9-3	10-4	11-5	12-6	1-7	2-8	3-9
Taurus	3-9	4-10	5-11	6-12	7-1	8-2	9-3	10-4	11-5	12-6	1-7	2-8
Gemini	2-8	3-9	4-10	5-11	6-12	7-1	8-2	9-3	10-4	11-5	12-6	1-7
Cancer	1-7	2-8	3-9	4-10	5-11	6-12	7-1	8-2	9-3	10-4	11-5	12-6
Leo	12-6	1-7	2-8	3-9	4-10	5-11	6-12	7-1	8-2	9-3	10-4	11-5
Virgo	11-5	12-6	1-7	2-8	3-9	4-10	5-11	6-12	7-1	8-2	9-3	10-4
Libra	10-4	11-5	12-6	1-7	2-8	3-9	4-10	5-11	6-12	7-1	8-2	9-3
Scorpio	9-3	10-4	11-5	12-6	1-7	2-8	3-9	4-10	5-11	6-12	7-1	8-2
Sagittarius	8-2	9-3	10-4	11-5	12-6	1-7	2-8	3-9	4-10	5-11	6-12	7-1
Capricorn	7-1	8-2	9-3	10-4	11-5	12-6	1-7	2-8	3-9	4-10	5-11	6-12
Aquarius	6-12	7-1	8-2	9-3	10-4	11-5	12-6	1-7	2-8	3-9	4-10	5-11
Pisces	5-11	6-12	7-1	8-2	9-3	10-4	11-5	12-6	1-7	2-8	3-9	4-10

E = Eclipse

2004 NEW MOONS AND THE HOUSES THEY AFFECT.

Degree & Date:

Rising Sign:	1/21 1AQ	2/20 1PI	3/20 0AR	4/19E 29AR	5/19 28TA	6/17 27GE	7/17 25CN	8/16 23LE	9/14 22VI	10/14E 21LI	11/12 20SC	12/12 20SG
Aries	11	12	1	1	2	3	4	5	6	7	8	9
Taurus	10	11	12	12	1	2	3	4	5	6	7	8
Gemini	9	10	11	11	12	1	2	3	4	5	6	7
Cancer	8	9	10	10	10	12	1	2	3	4	5	6
Leo	7	8	9	9	10	11	12	1	2	3	4	5
Virgo	6	7	8	8	8	10	11	12	1	2	3	4
Libra	5	6	7	7	7	9	10	12	12	1	2	3
Scorpio	4	5	6	6	7	8	9	10	11	12	1	2
Sagittarius	3	4	5	5	6	7	8	9	10	11	12	1
Capricorn	2	3	4	4	5	6	7	8	9	10	11	12
Aquarius	1	2	3	3	4	5	6	7	8	9	10	11
Pisces	12	1	2	2	3	4	5	6	7	8	9	10

E = Eclipse

2004 Full Moons and the Houses they Affect.

Degree & Date:

Rising Sign:	1/7 16CN	2/6 17LE	3/6 16VI	4/5 16LI	5/4E 14SC	6/3 13SG	7/2 11CP	7/31 9AQ	8/30 7PI	9/28 5AR	10/28E 5TA	11/26 5GE	12/26 5CN
Aries	4-10	5-11	6-12	7-1	8-2	9-3	10-4	11-5	12-6	1-7	2-8	3-9	4-10
Taurus	3-9	4-10	5-11	6-12	7-1	8-2	9-3	10-4	11-5	12-6	1-7	2-8	3-9
Gemini	2-8	3-9	4-10	5-11	6-12	7-1	8-2	9-3	10-4	11-5	12-6	1-7	2-8
Cancer	1-7	2-8	3-9	4-10	5-11	6-12	7-1	8-2	9-3	10-4	11-5	12-6	1-7
Leo	12-6	1-7	2-8	3-9	4-10	5-11	6-12	7-1	8-2	9-3	10-4	11-5	12-6
Virgo	11-5	12-6	1-7	2-8	3-9	4-10	5-11	6-12	7-1	8-2	9-3	10-4	11-5
Libra	10-4	11-5	12-6	1-7	2-8	3-9	4-10	5-11	6-12	7-1	8-2	9-3	10-4
Scorpio	9-3	10-4	11-5	12-6	1-7	2-8	3-9	4-10	5-11	6-12	7-1	8-2	9-3
Sagittarius	8-2	9-3	10-4	11-5	12-6	1-7	2-8	3-9	4-10	5-11	6-12	7-1	8-2
Capricorn	7-1	8-2	9-3	10-4	11-5	12-6	1-7	2-8	3-9	4-10	5-11	6-12	7-1
Aquarius	6-12	7-1	8-2	9-3	10-4	11-5	12-6	1-7	2-8	3-9	4-10	5-11	6-12
Pisces	5-11	6-12	7-1	8-2	9-3	10-4	11-5	12-6	1-7	2-8	3-9	4-10	5-11

E = Eclipse

BIBLIOGRAPHY

Bailey, Alice. *Esoteric Astrology*, Vol. III. New York: Lucis Publishing Co., 1971.

"Birth, Marriages, Divorces and Deaths for 1989." *Monthly Vital Statistics Report* v.38:12 (April 4, 1990). National Center for Health Statistics.

Boyer, Richard and David Savageau. *Places Rated Almanac*. New York: Prentice Hall Travel, 1989.

Bradshaw, John. *Homecoming: Reclaiming & Championing Your Inner Child*. New York: Bantam, 1990.

"Breast Cancer Cause: Is It Too Much Fat?" *National Health* (October 1979): 1.

Brooks, Chris. *Midpoint Keys to Chiron*. Tempe, AZ: AFA, 1992.

Bylinsky, Gene. *Mood Control*. New York: Scribners, 1978.

Chafetz, Janet Saltzman. *Masculine, Feminine, or Human?* Itascan, IL: F. E. Peacock Publishing, 1978.

Chancellor, Dr. Philip M. *Handbook of the Bach Flower Remedies*. Saffron Walden, UK: The C. W. Daniel Co., Ltd., 1976.

Chesler, Phyllis, *Women and Madness*. New York: Avon Books, 1972.

Clow, Barbara Hand. *Chiron: Rainbow Bridge Between the Inner and Outer Plants*. St. Paul, MN: Llewellyn, 1993.

Cope, Oliver, M. D. *The Breast*. Boston: Houghton Mifflin, 1977.

Corea, Gina. *The Hidden Malpractice*. New York: Jove, 1978.

Cosby, Bill. *Fatherhood*. New York: Berkley Publishing, 1994.

Cunningham, Donna. *Flower Remedies Handbook*. New York: Sterling Publishing, 1992.

————. *Moon Signs*. New York: Ballantine, 1988.

DeRosis, Helen A., M.D., and Victoria Y. Pelligrino. *The Book of Hope*. New York: Macmillan, 1976.

deVore, Nicholas. *Encyclopedia of Astrology*. New York: Littlefield, Adams, & Co., 1977.

Dodson, Carolyn R. *Horoscopes of the U.S. States and Cities*. San Diego: ACS Publishing, 1975.

Flower Essence Society. *The Flower Essence Journal* v.1:1. Nevada City, CA: The Flower Essence Society, 1980.

————. *Flower Essence Repertory*. Nevada City, CA: Flower Essence Society, 1994.

Fraiberg, Selma. *Every Child's Birthright.* New York: Basic Books, 1977.

Friday, Nancy. *My Mother/My Self: The Daugther's Search for Identity.* New York: Dell, 1978.

Garn, Stanley M., Patricia Cole, and Stephen M. Bailey. "The Effect of Parental Fatness Levels on the Fatness of Biological and Adoptive Children." *Ecology of Food and Nutrition* (1977): 91–93.

Gauquelin, Michel. *Cosmis Influences on Human Behavior.* Santa Fe: Aurora Press, 1979.

Gerzon, Mark. *A Choice of Heroes.* New York: Houghton Mifflin, 1982.

"Good News for Heavyweights." *USA Today Magazine* v.120:2560 (January 1992): 6.

Gould, Jeffrey B., Becky Davey, and S. Stafford-Randall. "Socioeconomic Differences in the Rates of Cesarean Section." *New England Journal of Medicine* v.321:4 (July 27, 1993): 233–240.

Grossman. *Superman: Serial to Cereal.* New York: Popular Library, 1976.

Hall, Manly P. *The Medicine of the Sun and Moon.* Los Angeles: Philosophical Research Society, Inc., n.d.

Hammer, Signe. *Daughters and Mothers/Mothers and Daughters.* New York: Signet, 1976.

Hand, Robert. *Planets in Composite.* Alglen, PA: Whitford Press, 1975.

———. *Planets in Transit.* Alglen, PA: Whitford Press, 1975.

Hollis, Judi. *Fat is a Family Affair.* Minneapolis: Hazeldon, 1986.

Information Please Almanac, Atlas, and Yearbook, 48th edition. Boston & New York: Houghton Mifflin, 1995.

Johnson, Steve M. *Flower Essences of Alaska.* Homer, AK: Alaskan Flower Essence Project, 1992.

Kemp, Cynthia. *Catcus & Company: Patterns and Qualities of Desert Flower Essences.* Tucson, AZ: Desert Alchemy, 1993.

Kennedy, Kathy I. and Cynthia M. Visness. "Contraceptive Efficacy of Lactational Amenorrhoea." *Lancet* v.339:8787 (January 25, 1992): 227–231.

Kuczmarsk, Robert J., Katherine M. Flegal, et al. "Increasing Prevalence of Overweight Among US Adults." *The Journal of the American Medical Association* v.272:3 (July 20, 1994): 205–207.

Lantero, Erminie. *The Continuing Discovery of Chiron.* York Beach, ME: Samuel Weiser, 1983.

Laurence, Leslie and Beth Weinhouse. *Outrageous Practices: the Alarming Truth about How Medicine Mistreats Women.* New York: Fawcett Columbine, 1994.

Let's Live (April 1979): 88.

Lieber, Arnold and Jerome Agel. *The Lunar Effect.* New York: Anchor Press, 1978.

"Lipoproteins: A Delicate Balance." *Science News* v. 113 (April 22, 1978): 244–245.

Lundsted, Betty. *Transits: The Time of Your Life.* York Beach, ME: Samuel Weiser, 1980.

Marwick, Charles. "Desirable Weight Goes Up in New Guidelines." *The Journal of the American Medical Association* v.265:1 (January 2, 1991): 17.

Maternal Nutrition and the Course of Pregnancy. Washington, DC: National Academy of Sciences, 1970.

McVoy, Joseph. *Health* (October 1994): 38.

Mitchell, Ingrid. *Breastfeeding Together.* New York: Seabring Press, 1978.

Moore, Moon. *The Book of World Horoscopes.* Birmingham, MI: Seek-It Publications, 1980.

Moreines, Robert N., M.D. *Light Up Your Blues.* New York: Berkley Books, 1989.

O'Brien, Dale. Audiotape *The Myth of Chiron.* Sacramento, CA: Chironicles Press, 1990.

Orbach, Susie. *Fat Is a Feminist Issue.* New York: Berkley Books, 1978.

Ouspensky, P. D. *In Search of the Miraculous.* New York: Harcourt Brace, 1949.

Pettitt, Sabina. *Energy Medicine: Pacific Flower and Sea Essences.* Victoria, BC: Pacific Essences, 1993.

"Prevalence of Overweight for Hispanics—United States, 1982–1984." *Journal of the American Medical Association* v.263:5 (February 2, 1990): 631–633.

Price, R. Arlene, Roberta Ness, and Peter Laskarewski. "Common Major Gene Inheritance of Extreme Overweight." *Human Biology* v.62:6 (December 1990): 747–766.

Raphael, Dana, Ph.D., *The Tender Gift: Breastfeeding.* New York: Schocken Books, 1976. No longer in print.

Rathbone, Kathleen. "The Lunar Calendar as Symbol and Affirmation." *Womanspirit* v.2:8 (summer 1976): 51.

Register, Charles A. and Donald R. Williams. "Wage Effects of Obesity Among Young Workers." *Social Science Quarterly* v.71:1 (March 1991): 130–142.

Reinhardt, Melanie. *Chiron and the Healing Journey.* New York: Viking Penguin, 1990.

Rubin, Theodore Isaac. *The Angry Book.* New York: Macmillan, 1970.

————. *Forever Thin*. New York: Bernard Geis Assoc., 1970.

Rubin, Theodore Isaac and David C. Berliner. *Understanding Your Man: A Woman's Guide*. New York: Ballantine, 1977.

Rudhyar, Dane. *The Lunation Cycle*. Santa Fe: Aurora Press, 1986.

Sakoian, Frances and Lewis S. Acker. *The Astrology of Human Relationships*. New York: HarperCollins, 1989.

Scarf, Maggie. *Unfinished Business: Pressure Points in the Lives of Women*. New York: Doubleday, 1980.

Seaman, Barbara and Gideon Seaman, M. D. *Women and the Crisis in Sex Hormones*. New York: Rawson Associates, 1977.

Segal, Julius and Herbert Yahres. "Bringing Up Mother." *Psychology Today* (November 1978): 90.

Serafino-Cross, Paula and Patricia R. Donovan. "Effectiveness of Professional Breast Feeding Home-Support." *Journal of Nutrition Education* v.24:3 (May–June 1992): 117–122.

"Sex Differences in Brain Asymmetries." *Brain/Mind Bulletin* v.5:14 (n.d.): 1680.

Shapiro, David and Frank L. Mott. "Long-term Employment and Earnings of Women in Relation to Employment Behavior Surrounding the First Birth." *Journal of Human Resources*, v.29:2 (Spring 1994): 248–276.

Starck, Marcia. *Women's Medicine Ways*. Freedom, CA: Crossing Press, 1993.

Steenhuysen, Julie. "Consumers Overcome Their Food Guilt." *Advertising Age* v.65:19 (May 2, 1994): 58.

Stein, Zane. *Essence and Application: A View from Chiron*. New York: CAO Times, 1988.

Steinem, Gloria. "Politics of Food." *MS* (February 1980): 48.

Thorsten, Geraldine. *God Herself*. New York: Doubleday, 1980.

U.S. Bureau of the Census. *Statistical Abstract of the United States*, 114th edition. Washington, DC: 1994.

Van Deusen, Edmund. *Astrogenetics*. New York: Pocket Books, 1977.

Vlamis, Gregory. *Flowers to the Rescue*. Rochester, VT: Healing Arts Press, 1988.

"When Breast Feeding May Be Bad." *Women's Health Letter* (November 1994): 7.

Wilson, Margo, Martin Daly, and Christine Wright. "Uxoricide in Canada: Demographic Risk Patterns." *Canadian Journal of Criminology* v.35:3 (July 1993): 263–281.

Wolfe, Honora. *Menopause—A Second Spring*. Boulder: Blue Poppy Press, 1992.

Womanspirit v.2:8 (summer 1976): 51.

Women's Alamanac. New York: Lippincott, 1976.

Wood, Matthew. *Seven Herbs: Plants as Teachers.* Berkeley, CA: North Atlantic Books, 1987.

Wurtman, Richard, M.D. "Brain Muffins." *Psychology Today* (October 1978): 140.

Zucker, Martin. "Diabetes and Allergy: An Investigation Worth Pursuing." *Let's Live* (April 1979): 65.

Index

Flower remedies mentioned in text are listed under "flower remedies." Herbal references appear in alphabetical order.

White Chestnut, 81, 311
White Desert Primrose, 96,
  119, 271
Wild Oat, 124
Wild Rose, 238
Wild Woman, 139
Willow, 97, 156, 231, 270,
  299, 313
Wind and Storm, 95
Windflower, 95
Wolfberry, 134
Woman of Wisdom, 139
Woven Spine Pineapple, 100
Yarrow, 190, 311
Yerba Santa, 97
Ylang, 123
Yucca, 123
Zinnia, 121, 174
food, 5, 20, 64, 202, 215
  addict, 222
  binges, 222
  and depression, 83
  and fat, 214
  habits, 204
  taboos, 190
forgiveness, 155
Fraiberg, Selma, 47
freedom, 49
Freud, Sigmund, 61
Friday, Nancy, 131, 164, 165
Full Moon Tables 1996, 118

G

Judy Garland, 137
Garn, Stanley M., 205
Gauquelin, Francoise, 4
Gauquelin, Michel, 4
Gerzon, Mark, 167
ginger, 199
Gould, Jeffrey B., 164

gratification, 42
Great Mars Massacre, 271
Great Mother, 2
Gurdjieff, G., 3

H

habit-forming substances, 8
habits, 8
  changing them, 87
  depression, 83
  emotional, 79, 81, 84, 94
  guilt, 82
  negativity, 82
  self-pity, 81
  worry, 81
Hall, Manly P., 323
Hammer, Signe, 37, 64
Hastings, Nancy, 288
heads of household, female, 46
healing crisis, 90
heart palpitations, 279
Hecate, 1
Hickey, Isabel, 28
high blood pressure, 45
hip joint deterioration, 279
Hollis, Judi, 229
homeopathy, 281
hormones, 195
houses
  4th, 28
  5th, 28
  10th house, 46
hyperthyroid, 279
hysterectomy, 192

I

instinct, 205
intellectualizing, 99
intuition, 8, 14

and mothering, 256, 257, 258
and security, 260, 261
machismo and the Moon, 245
meat and potatoes, 261, 262
unmartian types, 261
menarche, 130, 192
menopause, 12, 192, 273, 275,
277, 280
  herbs, vitamins, 278
  hot flashes, 278, 284
  preparing for, 277
menses and munchies, 212
menstrual cycle, 5, 183, 184, 193
menstrual taboos, 189
menstruation, 12, 183, 193, 200
  and feminine identity, 191
  alternative means of dealing
  with, 199
messages from Mom, 141
Minnelli, Liza, 136
Mitchell, Ingrid, 169
modern science, 4
momectomy, 150
  astrological exercises, 152
  psychological exercises, 150
moods, 202
mood swings, 55
Moon, 321
  1st quarter: crisis of action,
  273
  3rd quarter: menopause, 273,
  274
  and Chiron, 289
  and feminity, 129
  and food, 206
  as Destroyer, 2
  dark: wise woman phase, 274
  full, 4, 104, 117, 274
  goddess, 1
  madness, 55

new, 104
phases, 127
plotting new, 114
strengths, 15
transits, 55, 287, 292, 303,
309
void of course, 109, 110
waning, 104
waxing, 104
worship, 3
Moon in houses
  in 1st house, 72, 294
  in 2nd house, 72, 73, 294
  in 3rd house, 73, 295
  in 4th house, 73, 295
  in 5th house, 73, 295
  in 6th house, 74, 296
  in 7th house, 74, 296
  in 8th house, 74, 296
  in 9th house, 75, 296
  in 10th house, 75, 297
  in 11th house, 75, 297
  in 12th house, 75, 76, 297
Moon in signs, 67
  Moon in Aries, 67, 94, 142,
  206
  Moon in Taurus, 67, 95, 143,
  206
  Moon in Gemini, 67, 68, 95,
  143, 206
  Moon in Cancer, 68, 95, 144,
  206
  Moon in Leo, 68, 69, 96,
  144, 206
  Moon in Virgo, 69, 96, 144,
  206
  Moon in Libra, 69, 97, 145,
  206
  Moon in Scorpio, 69, 70, 97,
  145, 206

Paul Boyer

Donna Cunningham received a Master's degree in social work from Columbia University. In 1969 she began her astrological practice and received professional certification by Professional Astrologers, Inc. and the American Federation of Astrologers. With over 30 years of counseling experience as a certified psychotherapist, she uses various healing tools—such as flower essences, guided meditation, and visualizations—in her astrological work. She has been speaking at national and international astrological conferences since 1970 and has written hundreds of articles. She is the author of *An Astrological Guide to Self-Awareness, Healing Pluto Problems,* and *The Consulting Astrologer's Guidebook.* She is also the advice columnist for *Horoscope.* Donna currently lives in Port Townsend, WA, where she has her practice.